Odyssey of a Woman in the 20th Century

QUO VADIS

Eva Maria Schrankl

Translated from the German by the author

Odyssey of a Woman in the 20th Century
Quo Vadis

Copyright © 2021 by Eva Maria Schrankl.

Paperback ISBN: 978-1-952982-81-1
Ebook ISBN: 978-1-952982-82-8

All rights reserved. No part in this book may be produced and transmitted in any form or by any means, electronic, or mechanical, including photocopying, recording, or by any information storage and retrieval system, without permission in writing from the copyright owner.

The views expressed in this work are solely those of the author and do not necessarily reflect the views of the publisher hereby disclaims any responsibility for them.

Published by Green Sage Agency   03/21/2021

Green Sage Agency
1-888-366-9989
inquiry@greensageagency.com

"Dedicated to my daughters Ariane Marie and Vivian Louise
And my grandchildren Antonia, Anton, Amelia and Sophia."

Prologue

I DECIDED TO WRITE THIS BOOK because I believe that my life has been rich and full of treasures. This wealth I want to share with others, especially with my children and grandchildren.

Today they live in a different world on the other side of this earth, and maybe one day it will be interesting to them to read about the life of their grandmother and try to understand how she viewed her own life as a European in the 20th century.

Many of the political and intellectual movements of the 20th century have had a strong influence on the course of my life. They are thus also part of my children's heritage, and my children are what they are today because life happened the way it did in the last century. In order to understand the future, one has to know about the past.

Furthermore, the writing of this book has contributed considerably to fulfilling the promises of the Sirens: It has given me great pleasure and has added to my knowledge about myself and to my understanding of the underlying interrelations between the events in my life.

The Fraueninsel in Lake Chiemsee

Chapter 1: Homeland

My Mother, Aloisia Theresia Schrankl

Again and again my mother had told me about the incident that had happened that day in front of her eyes and how it had influenced her attitude more than anything else at the time.

It was May 10, 1933.

Just a year before, my father had been appointed director of the electrical power plant in Landsberg, on the Lech River in Southern Germany. My parents had made their home on the third floor of a quaint medieval house right in the center of town on the market square.

I was seven months old. Mother had just washed and fed me and was putting me down to sleep when she became aware of what was taking place below our window. A large crowd of people had gathered on the square. Among them she could discern many young people in the brown uniforms of the SA (Hitler's bodyguard). In the center of the square, a huge pile of wood and old trash had been collected. Suddenly, burning torches were hissing through the air. The pile caught fire; soon the flames were blazing high into the dark sky.

A strange mood had seized the crowd. Young men threw heaps of manuscripts and books into the blazing fire while howling patriotic songs. This bonfire was meant to be a signal, and a signal it became: the signal for a "Neues Deutschland"—a "New Germany."

What was being destroyed here was intellectual property, spiritual values—the writings of Heinrich Mann, Arthur Schnitzler, Erich Maria Remarque, Leon Feuchtwanger, Kurt Tucholski, Erich Kaestner, and many others who were considered decadent, immoral, Jewish, and hostile to the values of the German people.

The SA had planned identical procedures, from Koenigsberg in the north to the south of the country. They had collected texts that were considered "non-patriotic, dangerous and suspicious" in libraries and bookstores and were now setting about burning them publicly in the center of town at night.

These campaigns had not been ordered by Joseph Goebbels, the minister of propaganda, as the SA later claimed. They originated in the universities and were the product of certain professors and their students who had joined the National Socialist Party. These men accompanied the SA and SS (semi-military organization directly under Hitler's personal order) throughout the country and wanted to demonstrate their zealous belief in the new national cause.

Burning books in Landsberg! My mother was aghast. All her life she had known nothing more wonderful than to read. Day and night, books were her best friends, during the long, lonely nights in boarding school and later, at the university, where she had finally been able to read those authors who nourished and inspired her rebellious and open-minded soul. And now this!

From the very beginning she had disliked these National Socialists and found their simplistic theories suspect. She especially disliked their vulgar, violent, and proletarian behavior. She could not understand how my father could tolerate this mob. How could he have associated himself with these people?

Landsberg, this ancient little baroque town situated picturesquely between Lake Ammersee and the river Lech, with an old fortress rising above it, was a peaceful place. Now it had gained a notorious fame in her eyes.

Since Hitler's seizure of power—the National Socialists had won the elections in Berlin in January 1933—the fortress of Landsberg had turned into an almost mythical place. Wasn't it here where Hitler had been "innocently" imprisoned and where he had written his famous book *Mein Kampf*? Didn't his success prove him to be right? Who could now dare to criticize these marauding brown hordes who, due to their leader's political success, had succeeded in becoming a legitimized power in the state? Inconvenient voices were now being publicly "burned at the stake." On that night of May 10, 1933, one thing was irrevocably clear to my mother: She would not have anything to do with those people in the future—and certainly her daughter would not! My mother's decision to separate herself from the common opinion of the people around her would have an enormous impact on my future education and became a guiding light for the rest of my life.

Aloisia Ilmberger, called Lulu, was born on November 3, 1899, in Munich, Bavaria. However, all her life she insisted that her birthday was on November 2, "All Souls' Day"—the day to remember the dead.

For a Bavarian girl she was small and petite—anything but the "Germanic type" en vogue in Germany during the 1930s. She had black hair, olive skin, high cheekbones, and sparkling brown eyes, and she looked more like the Slavic type.

During our daily walks through the parks and forests of my hometown, Mother used to tell me stories about her mother, her ancestors, and her own childhood in the city of Munich.

"Mama, what was Grandmother like, tell me about her!" I loved to hear her tell me the same old stories again and again.

"My mother, Theresia," she said, "your grandmother, had the maiden name Engl (angel) and had been known as a great beauty. She had long black hair, skin as white as alabaster, and melancholy dark eyes. She came from a family of master carpenters who lived in Niederbayern, north of the Danube River. This is an area where the infamous Panduren –(wild nomads on horseback) are said to have roamed the deep, impenetrable forests of the borderland between Bavaria and Bohemia."

Then Mother went on to describe her grandparents' house in the woods, where she had spent her vacations as a child; she talked about the dark fir trees whose rustle had made her shiver at night and about those dark-skinned, wild, and strange fellows who mysteriously came and went between the border of Bavaria and Bohemia. She called them Grenzler, a term that does not explain whether they had to guard the border or if they passed back and forth for some other undisclosed reasons.

My grandmother Theresia Ilmberger, 1906, Family Photo

"Grandmother must have missed her homeland very much when she married into the big city of Munich, because I often heard her sing this old, melancholy song," and then she hummed the melody of "Tief, tief im Böhmerwald, wo meine Wiege stand…" ("In the deep, deep forests of the Böhmerwald, where my cradle stood…"

Maybe we have to search here for the roots of those traits that sometimes made my mother, Lulu, incomprehensible to me but also fascinating: Her emotional—even irrational—moodiness was combined with a creative and lively sense of reality and earthiness. People call it the Slavic soul, a type of soul I would encounter again in a different form later in my life.

Yes, mother was wild and undomesticated, such a contrast to my father! He was disciplined, well adjusted, and sociable. Mother was the opposite, independent and a loner.

Mother was often very moody, straightforward, sometimes even blunt, but she was also capable of great love. She had the courage to stand up for what she believed, even in the face of opposition from others, was not afraid of anybody, and hated any kind of constraint, senseless laws, and rules of conduct. Today we might call her an emancipated woman, something that was exceptional for a woman at that time.

Clothes and luxuries never played an important part in her life. She preferred to play the piano, and she did it with passion and talent. Money was never a subject for discussion in our family, just as it had not been in the home of my grandparents.

The Ilmberger Family

The Ilmbergers were businessmen and had a well-established wine store in the center of Munich. During the Great Depression in the 1920s, the German economy had been ruined, and many people had lost all of their property. During the final years of inflation, one loaf of bread cost one million Reichsmarks. My grandparents, too, had lost all of their savings, but my mother did not remember whether they ever talked about this loss.

Keeping house and counting money never held any attraction for my mother. The life of a housewife was not her thing. But she was always open to new ideas. Even at a very old age she remained fascinated by intellectual issues, the arts, and politics.

One day—she was well into her nineties—she said to me: "You are too old-fashioned, you must think more modern."

My grandfather's family came from the little hamlet of Ilmendorf on the river Ilm in Lower Bavaria. According to church records, the family had been building carriages in their workshop since 1560.

My great-grandfather, Mathias Ilmberger, had been forced to join Napoleon's army on its march into Russia in 1812. He deserted, because he did not want to fight the Russians, who had never done him any harm; however, he was caught and given 33 lashes. So he was forced to remain in the army and walk all the way to Moscow. But soon the Russian winter caught up with them, and most of his comrades died a miserable death.

As he made his way through the snow-covered forests, suffering from typhoid, he finally fell by the wayside and was left behind for dead. A Russian girl and her grandmother found him, took him into their cabin, and nursed him back to health. He helped them battle the atrocious winter and married the girl.

Together they built up a flourishing business of building carriages, which became so successful that it aroused the envy of their neighbors. After the severe droughts in the years that followed, Mathias lost his business, his two children, and finally his wife. At the age of 42 he walked all the way back to his home village. Nobody recognized the poor beggar or wanted him back after all these years, but his old mother recognized her lost son. In later years he married again and founded the Ilmberger family.

One of my uncles, a writer of texts in the Bavarian dialect, has written a fascinating book about the adventurous life of Mathias Ilmberger, *It Began with 33 Lashes*.

Maximilian I of Bavaria had put 30,000 soldiers at the disposal of Napoleon for his Russian campaign. In return, Napoleon declared Bavaria a kingdom and appointed Maximilian I King of Bavaria. The obelisk on the Carolinenplatz in Munich reminds us of the 30,000 "Bavarian Lions," who marched to Russia with Napoleon's army. Only 3,000 of these brave men returned. One of them was my great-grandfather Mathias Ilmberger.

The Ilmberger family had three children, two sons and one daughter. The first son, Alois, died at the age of six from diphtheria. They said that during the funeral Grandmother was so distraught that she wanted to throw herself into the grave with her child.

To get over her deep despair, she began to work with her husband in the wine business. But this work did not seem to have helped her to get over her depression. Her second son, Eduard, was then only four years old. Two years later my mother, Aloisia, was born and named after her brother.

Despite being mother to two children, Grandmother continued to work in the business. She did not seem to want to take care of her children, nor did she want to admit to her feelings of closeness to them.

Grandmother was not only beautiful and intelligent but also capable and willing to take risks. Despite her depression, she was successful in her work and tried to inspire my grandfather to agree with her plans to invest in some old townhouses in the center of Munich, known as the "Old Mill" beside the Hofbräuhaus. Unfortunately, Grandfather did not appreciate such high-flung plans and the risks associated with them.

My grandparents lived for their business. It was the center of their lives. They led a bourgeois way of life with servants and a special chamber where the furniture was covered with lace coverlets and which was opened only when guests came to visit. But they were not really very sociable. One reason might have been the depression my grandmother suffered from, or maybe the fact that all day long they had to deal with strange people in their business and preferred to withdraw into their privacy after work.

My mother remembers: "I never heard my parents raise their voices. They never seemed to have had any arguments. Our parents never reprimanded us in a loud voice. If they wanted to discuss something alone, they said, with a wink of the eye, "There are shingles on the roof" and we knew that we had to leave the room."

I remember another story, which illustrates how the people in this family dealt with each other. The maid had her birthday. Grandmother wanted to show her appreciation for her faithful service and gave her an embroidered pillow for her bed for which she had paid 20 Deutschmarks (DM). At that time, this was a lot of money. When she told Grandfather the price of the present, he responded with these words: "Don't you think you are going a bit overboard?"

This seems today a very harmless expression. What he probably meant was that she seemed to be extravagant. Grandmother was so hurt by his criticism that she seemed to have suffered for weeks because of this one remark by her husband.

The Ilmberger Family: Lulu, Theresia, Alois, Eduard.

During times like this, neither her intelligence nor her success at work nor the love of her family could help her. Her depressive episodes became more frequent, and she lost all joy in life. She died at the age of only 55 years from a "broken heart" as people used to say. She never seemed to have gotten over the loss of her first child.

The life of this beautiful and melancholic woman had taken a tragic turn, and not only for herself. Her life had a great impact on the lives of her children and grandchildren.

Uncle Edi and my mother attended a boarding school early in life. Mother went to the convent of the "Poor Sisters of Mercy" in Munich and Uncle Edi to Weihenstephan, where he later graduated in the field of agricultural sciences.

Grandmother visited her children on alternate weekends, and only during vacation time were they allowed to come home. It is hard to imagine these children banished to boarding school in their own city! It is hardly surprising that uncle Edi became an eccentric and my mother a lonely rebel!

Lulu and Eduard.

Uncle Edi remained a bachelor all his life and followed his own way. He seemed to come right out of one of the paintings by Carl Spitzweg, a Munich painter (1880–1885) of humorous scenes of bourgeois society and quaint characters.

Like my mother, Uncle Edi also had a critical and rebellious character. He loved to read and write, and had really wanted to become a painter, while Mother would have preferred to study music. She played the piano very beautifully.

However, Edi's ideas were too much for Grandfather. He was of the opinion, "Two artists in one family are two too many." This invariably led to serious disagreements between Edi and his father.

"If you don't want to adjust to the life here, then go to your jungle!" Grandfather said. And Uncle Edi did indeed go to the jungle—he went to America. In Chicago he succeeded in making a small fortune working in the dairy industry.

Munich, Neuhauser Strasse 1900.

But soon afterward he had to spend all of his savings for a difficult stomach operation. He returned to Munich shortly before the outbreak of World War II, a lonely, disillusioned recluse. There he lived an isolated and thrifty life in one small room until he died. His strange way of life did not permit anyone to know much about him. After he died,

Mother found him in his room, which was filled with books, papers, and umbrellas in boxes piled up to the ceiling.

Among all these papers, she found a handwritten last will. It proved my uncle not to have been the poor man he seemed to be at all. He owned property in Switzerland and had quite a bit of cash. But this wealth, the existence of which no one in the family had suspected, he bequeathed to an orphanage in Switzerland. My mother respected his last will.

Mother probably had suffered from the sparse expression of affection by her mother. She never spoke about this, but her behavior, and later her exaggerated care for her only child, seem to point in that direction.

In the convent school, she did not like to socialize a lot. Her main joy was reading books—every free minute during the day and at night under the covers of her bed. On the weekends when her mother did not visit her, she would not play with other girls but wrapped herself in a curtain by the window, reading a book. Thus the world of books became more and more her world.

Later Mother changed from the Angerkloster to the school of the "Englische Fräulein," a Catholic order of nuns specializing in the education of girls. There she completed her secondary education.

This school also did not add much to her happiness. Strict rules and a very conservative Catholic education ran counter to her character. However, she later conceded that she had always felt secure and content in this type of environment.

The girls wore dark green uniforms and lined up in straight lines. There was law and order, obedience, and the fear of God. For her it was only a slight comfort that King Ludwig II had himself designed these Sunday uniforms with the red sash. Her father had personally met this monarch who had built the famous castles in Bavaria. The King was beloved and respected by him and the Bavarian people in general, even though he had lavished the state's money on castles rather than on the military. Because of this he was declared crazy and consequently removed from the throne. Soon afterward this unlucky King found his death in Lake Starnberg.

After Mother had passed the Abitur—the examination needed for graduation—in 1917, she was allowed to continue her education on the university level. It was her first step into freedom! This was quite unusual for girls at that time, but Grandmother had succeeded in convincing her husband that a girl also had to strive for a profession.

World War I was still going on, and people suffered. Thousands of young men had died in the trenches of France. But Mother did not choose the usual course of training as a nurse; she wanted to become a teacher. She enrolled as one of the first women in the Department of Pedagogy at the University of Munich. There she fell in love with a Communist. This first love, unfortunately, did not bring her happiness. A year later her beloved was taken to prison, where he died a short time later.

Many years later I found that she had kept all their correspondence, letters full of care and longing for love.

Again Mother found comfort in her books and with her piano. She loved music and was a member of the Munich Teachers' Chorus. Some of her fondest memories were connected with the beautiful oratory works of Bach, such as *St. Matthew's Passion* and other choral works. The new literary trends aroused her keen interest. The works of Bert Brecht especially fascinated her, and she never missed a performance of his plays on the Munich stage. Later she joined a left liberal group and spent many hours discussing the latest political trends with her new friends.

The liberal Munich artists' scene in the "wild Twenties" matched her rebellious character.

Lulu at the piano.

This was an environment where she finally found herself at home; this new world was her world. She admired the paintings by Kirchner, Marc, Muenther, and Kandinsky, all those free spirits who would be condemned as "degenerate" some years later by the National Socialists.

It was only a natural consequence that she would view with disgust the political spectres that were beginning to emerge on the horizon of her hometown, Munich. This was one of her stories:

> One day in the late Twenties, my father had come home unusually late from his favorite restaurant around the corner. He was furious. In the evening after work before going home, he used to stop in his favorite "Stammkneipe" right around the corner, the prestigious "Weisse Bräuhaus" in the center of town. There he had a fine glass of beer, something to eat and a chat with the neighbors. Every evening the same ritual since Grandmother had died.
>
> But this evening would be the last time he put his foot into that pub. During the last few weeks some suspicious men in brown uniforms had crowded the place. Among them was a certain loudmouth, with the name of Hitler, who would pour forth all kinds of impossible political theories, accompanied by the howling applause of his primitive followers.
>
> He did not like what he saw, and he would only go back to the "Weisse Bräuhaus" when that riffraff had disappeared again! He absolutely despised politics and did not want to have anything to do with it, because, as the saying goes, "The political song is an ugly song."

That was my mother's account of the situation in 1923.

Grandfather had good reason to be concerned. Bavaria found itself in a period of change, and the people felt insecure. Following the Treaty of Versailles after World War I, Germany had collapsed politically and economically. This situation had created a vacuum for many people, and consequently many antidemocratic groups had emerged that promised a "better future." Among these was the "Deutsche Arbeiterpartei," the "Party of the German Working People," which had been founded in 1919 in Munich.

Lulu with her cousin, who was her first love and was lost in a submarine in World War I.

On February 1, 1920, this party changed its name to "Nationalsozialistische Deutsche Arbeiterpartei," (NSDAP). In 1921 Adolf Hitler entered the stage and had himself called "Führer der NSDAP." His model was Mussolini, whose march on Rome would become the model for Hitler's march on Berlin.

The famous writer Leon Feuchtwanger described those days in Munich with vivid words:

> We had coffee in our empty stomachs and also beer and sausages. We were marching through the streets led by "the Führer," and as we were marching we were victorious. Today we would win in Munich, tomorrow in Bavaria, next week the whole country and after one month we would have won over the whole world.

Only the shots of the Bavarian police forces on the Munich Odeons Platz were to stop this march on November 9, 1923. For the time being! After a few years of economic and political stability the worldwide Great Depression threw Germany back into unemployment and chaos. Hitler and his NSDAP took advantage of the crisis and continued their striving for power. In November 1932, the NSDAP became the strongest party in the German Reichstag. In January of 1933, the German president, Paul von Hindenburg, appointed Hitler Chancellor of Germany.

We are still in the year 1926. Mother is young and carefree, and politics is not her main interest. She has just returned to Munich from her first teaching appointment in Ilmendorf and is enjoying life to the fullest in her hometown.

Because of her name, the government had sent her to Ilmendorf, the village of her ancestors. There she had completed her first years of service teaching. She had passed all her exams successfully. These years had been hard work, because in those days, school was taught during the morning as well as in the afternoon, six days a week, and on Sunday morning the young teachers had also to teach Sunday school. If Mother, who was really a city girl, had the chance to go home once every six weeks, she considered herself lucky. But now she was finally back in Munich, and there it was that soon after she met the man of her life, my father, Anton Rasso Schrankl.

My Father, Anton Rasso Schrankl

To the gods I am indebted for having good grandfathers and good parents…

…He was the picture of a man whom nature had made right and who needed no improvement…

In my father I observed mildness of temper, and unchangeable resolution in the things which he had determined after due deliberation; and no vainglory in those things which men call honours; and a love of labour and perseverance…

and undeviating firmness in giving to every man according to what he deserves.

He was a man who looked to what ought to be done, not to the reputation which is got by a man's acts… He showed sobriety in all things and firmness, and never any mean thoughts or action, nor love of novelty…

The things which conduce in any way to the commodity of life, and of which fortune gives an abundant supply, he used without arrogance and without excusing himself; so that when he had them, he enjoyed them without affectation, and when he had them not, he did not miss them.

Further, he was neither fond of change nor unsteady, but he loved to stay in the same places, and to employ himself about the same thing…

He was also easy in conversation, and he made himself agreeable without any offensive affectation…and he had also the art of being humorous in an agreeable way….

and to be satisfied on all occasions, and cheerful…

It might be applied to him which is recorded of Socrates, that he was able both to abstain from, and to enjoy, those things, which many are too weak to abstain from, and cannot enjoy without excess. But to be strong enough both to bear the one and to be sober in the other is the mark of a man who has a perfect and invincible soul…"

From *Meditations* by Marcus Aurelius, Roman Stoic Philosopher and Emperor. (161–80 AD) written in 167 AD during his campaign against the Danube tribes).

Anton Rasso Schrankl was a commanding figure—tall, slim, blond, and blue-eyed, with a typical Tyrolean profile. He resembled the ideal of the German man in those days, a "saubers Mannsbild" as one says in Bavarian. Father came from a large rural merchant family and was studying at the Technical University of Munich. He wanted to become an electrical engineer.

Father was the perfect gentleman already at this young age. Mother told me that he was only 23 years old when they met, so he was three years younger than she. Honor and decency were important values for him, as well as a sense of responsibility. For him, it went without saying that a man had to have good manners.

Mother felt attracted by this type of man, perhaps because she herself behaved quite differently. She interpreted good manners in her own way. When she was bored in company, she just got up and left. If she was not hungry at a dinner party, she would not eat for the sake of politeness. When she did not like someone who came to see her, she would not open the door. Rules she did not like she would simply ignore.

For my father, the rules were different. Reason, common sense, and discipline were virtues that I have always admired in my father. I never heard him complain about anything, not even about the loss of his leg during the last days of war in Berlin.

Father's word was good; you could depend on him because he was honest and could not tell a lie. Even if he sometimes had to tell a little white lie, he blushed like a small boy. His honesty and dependability were the reasons why he was respected and loved by everyone who knew him. He had no enemies, and I have never met anyone who did not admire him as a great gentleman. I personally considered him a bit too "well-adjusted," because he did not stand up against the Nazi regimentation.

When he was in the midst of his family—or his friends—he felt happiest and most content. "One has to be able to get along with other people and be considerate!" he told me.

This was his conviction, which was probably the result of his upbringing in a large family. It was important for him to know what the family and other people thought of him and how they felt, and to know what he could do for them. Consequently, it was no surprise that he loved to celebrate family reunions.

Concerning family life, he did not meet with much understanding on the part of my mother, because she disliked big family reunions. The ensuing tensions between them did not escalate, however, because of my father's mediating skills. On such occasions he considered Mother simply a "gspinnerte Urschl" and that was the end of the argument. "It is the wise person who gives in," he would say.

Father's clear and uncomplicated character has always filled me with a sense of security. With him, I always knew exactly where I stood.

Benevolent, generous, perfectly dressed, with a fine cigar in his hand, this is the way I remember him. He did not throw money out the window. He bought little, but when he did, he chose only the best because he respected good quality. "I am not rich enough to buy bad quality," he would say. When Mother could not decide between two dresses, he would say: "Why don't you take both of them?"

THE HISTORY OF VACHENDORF IN THE CHIEMGAU

Vachendorf is over 1,200 years old. During the first millennium BC the Celtic people settled in our country. During Roman times (1st—4th cent. AD) the "Chiemgau," together with Austria, was part of the Roman province of Noricum, which was bordered by the Danube in the north and by the river Inn in the west.

Some years ago an interesting archeological find, which dates back to this period, was discovered, together with some Roman coins, near my aunt's farmhouse. Archeologists call it the "Military Diploma of Geiselprechting." It consists of a small bronze tablet. Such diplomas used to be awarded to veterans after 25 years of service in the Roman army, granting them and their families Roman citizenship. They are copies of the original documents, which were kept in Rome. This one shows the date as June 15, in the year 64 AD, the name of the soldier, and that of his wife and children.

Nearby, the remains of the under-floor heating system of a luxurious Roman villa bear further witness to the presence of the Romans in our area.

When, in the year 488, the Germanic chief Odeakar ordered the Romans to leave, only some of them left the Chiemgau, which had become home to them over the centuries. Romans and Celtic people had accommodated themselves and were living peacefully together.

In the 6th century, the "Bavarians" are mentioned as a people for the first time in written documents. We assume that Germanic tribes, together with the remaining Romans and Romanized Celts, had mingled and had become one people. Scientists believe that this population consisted mostly of farmers and craftsmen, "good-natured, sensual and extravagant, stubborn and rooted to the soil, just as they are today"

After the persecution of the early Christians in the 1st century, the 4th century saw the final victory of Christianity. It is amazing how many of the old pagan symbols still exist side by side with those of the Christian culture even today.

In 788, Charlemagne stripped the Bavarian dukes, the "Agilolfinger," of their power and donated the country to the Church. Shortly thereafter, Bishop Arno of Salzburg ordered the various titles of land acquisition of his church to be registered in order to simplify the administration of tributes und duties.

This first register, the "Notitia Arnonis" of 790 AD, was followed by a second inventory, the "Breves Notitiae," which listed and specified the various donations, for example:

Weifher donates his property in "vohendorf."

Here the name of the village of "Vachendorf" is documented for the first time.

During the following centuries the Catholic Church remained the most powerful authority. Toward the end of the 13th century the Chiemgau again came under the rule of the Bavarian dukes. Religious life, however, continued to be dominated by the Archbishop of Salzburg.

During the following centuries Vachendorf, like all of southern Germany, suffered from various wars and conflicts. The Great Migrations and the invasions by the Huns in the 5th century and later by the Turks; the Thirty-Years' War; various Spanish, Austrian, and French wars of succession; Napoleon's campaign into Russia; World

Wars I and II; and the chaotic end of World War II in 1945 with all the related disasters, such as pillaging and famines—all of these have left their traces and continue to bring death, sorrow, and destruction to the families of the soldiers and the inhabitants of the village.

Only today can we say that our country has enjoyed a rare period of peace for 60 years—two generations!

The above information has been adapted from the village chronicle of Vachendorf *1,200 years of Vachendorf,* compiled in 1990.

Vachendorf in 1911. Publisher, Michael Schrankl.

The Family Schrankl

My grandfather, Michael Schrankl, came from Oed, a small village north of Lake Chiemsee in Bavaria. For generations his family had owned a large brickworks business.

He was the oldest son, but he did not want to take over the family business, because he really had always wanted to become a veterinarian. But attending university was not an alternative for the firstborn of a large rural family—the Schrankls had nine children. Grandfather stepped down in favor of his younger brother and left home to search for his own road.

The Schrankl Family. On the upper left, Anton Rasso.

In Vachendorf near Lake Chiemsee, right in the center of the village, he found a large farmhouse that was for sale. It seemed to be the right place to make a homestead for him and his wife. The estate had been built in 1589 and had been used since 1646 as a carpentry and coach-building shop. From 1870 onward it had been a bakery.

In 1898, Grandfather married Elisabeth Stuetzel, the daughter of a restaurant owner in the next village. She was the right partner to help him realize his plans for the future. Within a few years, nine children grew up in this family. Their first son, Michael, was followed by two daughters, and then my father was born. Finally, five more daughters were born.

Grandparents Michael and Elisabeth Schrankl.

Grandfather proved a very good businessman, and Elisabeth a competent and wise wife by his side. Together they remodeled the large house and turned it into a farm and business house with a bakery and a store for all kinds of goods. Behind the house they constructed a large stable and warehouses, which later became the first example for a village cooperative in Vachendorf.

Grandfather was widely respected in the village and beyond, and after only a few years he owned much of the surrounding land, while the bakery and the store developed into a lucrative business.

The Schrankl family was well known and respected as hardworking, honest, and successful. Grandfather had an impressive personality; he was a real patriarch in the Bavarian tradition.

For his community he proved to be an entrepreneur with vision. He constructed the first water reservoir and initiated the first electrical plant in the area. He had the first telephone and was the first one to drive a car. For many years he ran the first mail station in the whole area.

Besides all these activities he still found time for his hobby. He took in sick animals and nursed them until they could be returned to their owners. Soon he became well known in the whole region for his talent of healing animals.

The people in Vachendorf held Grandfather in such high esteem that they wanted him to be a member of their city council. This flattered him, but he did not think that presenting oneself in public and currying favor with the voters was an honorable thing for him. He did not really want to have anything to do with politics. To be a farmer, a businessman, and the head of a big family with eleven members plus several maids and farm hands was enough responsibility for him.

The Schrankl house in Vachendorf.

The Schrankl family was self-confident and generous. They had what was called a "noble sense." Thus, Grandfather felt a responsibility for others and taught his children to be concerned with the problems of their neighbors, even beyond the normal assistance for other members of the community. For him it was enough to set a good example.

In the Twenties, the farmers in the Chiemgau were also affected by the worldwide economic depression. Many feared the loss of their farms. Grandfather had lent many of them money or had taken up surety for them. To those who were not able to pay him back he extended the loan or allowed them to continue to live on their property.

In the Thirties some Jewish families who lived in the region asked him for help. He assisted them in raising enough money to leave the country. Sometimes he even lent them money for this purpose.

Grandfather's social commitment, his generosity, and his hospitality were an example to my father for the rest of his life.

Grandmother Schrankl was a diligent and wise woman. When I think of her I still see her slender figure, usually dressed in black, her hair pulled back into a bun, with a sweet and kind face.

Elisabeth Schrankl kept herself in the background. Her type of authority was effective without being obtrusive. Grandfather handled the business, and Grandmother saw to it that everything went smoothly. The soul of the family, she raised nine children and managed the extensive household with a strong and quiet hand. The milkmaids and farmhands felt at home in this family. Her home functioned like clockwork. Everyone had his individual assignment to do in the kitchen, the bakery, the store, or the stable. She directed her crew only by glances and flicks of the eyelash. Words were not necessary. Voices were never raised in the Schrankl house. There were no discussions.

The nine children were raised by means of nonverbal signals. The older children had to take care of the younger ones, and each one had his post in the home according to age.

Taking responsibility at an early age and respect for the elders made the large family strong.

I still can see the family gathering around the big farmers' table in the large rural dining room at lunchtime. Being an only child, I enjoyed this ritual together with aunts and uncles and the servants of the house. Twelve people were the norm. The delicious smell of freshly baked bread reminds me even today of my grandparents' house.

Before sitting down we all lined up in a big circle in front of "God's corner," which was decorated with fresh flowers. When Grandmother entered the room, everybody recited the Lord's Prayer and one Hail Mary. After that we silently sat down. "When the bird eats, he does not sing," my father used to say. In those days it was considered very impolite to talk while eating. All you could hear was the clatter of the spoons dipping into the large common bowls, filled with delicious "Schmarrn and Hollundermus."

Only when dessert was offered did people start to chat. They all liked the food they were served. No wonder, as Grandmother was an excellent cook. She made the best apple cider in the village, and I still remember its distinctive sweet-sour fragrance coming from the workroom in the back of the house.

In Bavaria it was a common custom that the oldest son inherit the farm and the second son go to a master's workshop to learn a craft or a trade. In my family, this was different.

Grandmother had recognized my father's talents early and had convinced Grandfather to let him attend the "Gymnasium" (school for higher education) in the nearby town of Traunstein.

At that time it was quite unusual in the countryside for someone to continue his schooling on a higher level. He was considered a do-nothing (lazybones), who just did not like to work.

This was no easy life for Father. For years he had to get up at four o'clock in the morning during summertime as well as in the winter.

First he had to help in the bakery, where he worked until six-thirty, and then he sat down for breakfast. At seven, he took his bicycle to go to his school in Traunstein, which was some four miles away. In the winter he had to push his bike up the hill in the deep snow. In the summertime he had chores to attend to in the fields in the afternoon. Especially during harvest time, bringing in the hay for the animals took precedence at any time when the weather permitted it.

Early in life Father realized that it would take strict discipline to reach his goal—admittance to the university. It would be necessary to combine his dreams with his daily duties at home. Father had chosen this road and would succeed in reaching his goal. This insight molded his character, and it made him well adjusted and at the same time strong.

Only after the Abitur (high school diploma) did his life became somewhat easier. In 1920 he went to Regensburg to prepare for university and then was admitted to the Technical University in Munich to study electrical engineering.

Coming from the Bavarian countryside to live in the big city was a bold step in Father's life.

Munich, the seat of the Bavarian King, had experienced a new period of growth after the first years of the 20th century. The city had developed into a center for the fine arts, a development that was initiated and supported by the liberal and art-loving royal family, the "Wittelsbacher," who had ruled Bavaria through the chaotic times in European history with a wise and strong hand.

Travel was a privilege only for a very small educated elite element of society, known for their love of culture and the arts. Munich became known for its international art exhibitions and attracted artists from all over Europe. These exhibitions brought money to the city, and the city flourished.

In the "Künstlerhaus" the masters of contemporary art celebrated themselves. The "Jungen Wilden"(young savages) began to protest against the old masters and founded the famous art school called "Der Blaue Reiter." Their members, Wassily Kandinsky, Gabriel Muenther, Alexej Jawlensky, Franz Mark, August Macke, Paul Klee, and others were destined to become famous as the founders of modern art in the 20th century.

In those years, the spirit of *Simplizissimus* dominated the life of the students in Munich's artists' quarters. This first journal for political satire delighted the Munich bohemia and challenged the establishment. Its profound sense of humor did not hesitate to satirize the king and his entourage, and its illustrators, like Olaf Gulbranson and T. T. Heine became famous beyond the borders of Germany. The artists' scene of Schwabing survived the horrors of World War I as well as the fall of the monarchy in Bavaria, and it was revived in the "Roaring Twenties."

This world of the Munich Boheme, the home of Aloisia Ilmberger, now became the new home for a fine young man: Anton Rasso Schrankl.

In the big city Father missed his large family, and he was looking for company.

His student room in the "Türkenstrasse" was located exactly between the Technical University, the Ludwig-Maximilian–University, and the "Simpl," the intellectual center of the student scene. In Vachendorf, everybody knew him and even in Traunstein he had a lot of pals, but in Munich he did not know anybody, since none of his friends went to university here. So he welcomed the opportunity to join one of the many fraternities and decided to become a member of the "Corps Suevia." He would remain their treasurer until shortly before his death.

The "Corps Suevia" was founded in 1803 at the University of Landshut and had a seat at the University of Munich since 1926. Only during the time of the Nazi regime was it closed down for almost 10 years, because it had refused to dissociate itself from its Jewish members as demanded by the new racial laws of the Nazis.

The roots for the intellectual background of the Corps' ideals are to be found in the classical German idealism of the late 18th century. Lifelong friendship and cooperation between its members, personality education, and character training have been the objectives of the "Muenchner Schwaben" and are to this day. The Corps has always been, and still is today, independent of the influences of current politics and of any religious affiliations. This principle of tolerance, as valid today as it has been in former times—to be free from indoctrination of any kind and to take individual responsibility for one's actions and views of the world—must remain untouched.

The "Corps Suevia" was a "Schlagende Verbindung"—a dueling fraternity. Matching one's strength and ability by means of fencing with the classical saber, the so-called "Mensuren," was a hard test for its young men. Another reason for these exercises was to teach how to endure pain in a manly way without complaining.

Another goal of this education was to train young men to "hold their liquor." They should be able to maintain their countenance in any situation and always behave like a gentleman, especially toward women.

Anton Rasso Schrankl as a student at the University of Munich and member of the Corps "Suevia."

By his character Father exemplified these values; they matched his upbringing and were in line with his personality.

Chinese Girl Meets Bear "Fasching" with Consequences

Discipline and manners, honor and courage, that is all very nice, but Munich was no city for boredom. Thus, you had to learn to hold your liquor and not behave rudely or dishonorably toward women.

There is much to celebrate in Munich: the "Auer Dult" in spring and the "Oktoberfest" in the fall. There is fine beer all year round, and a lot of it, too! But things really become hazardous in the fifth season: during the time of "Fasching," called "carnival" in other parts of the country.

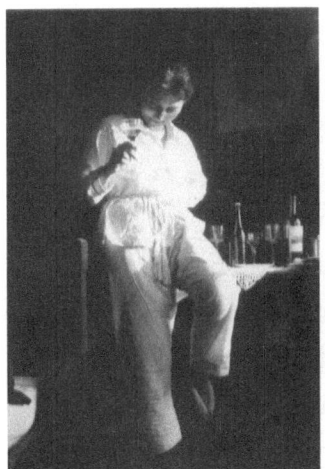 

Lulu and Anton: ... "and they were singing sweet love songs!"

Notices for missing persons were common in those days, and the police comforted the worrying families by saying, "Just wait a few days and he/she will show up again. He/she will be home at the latest on Ash Wednesday." This is the day when carnival ends, six weeks before Easter. You put ashes on your head to show repentance for your sins, publicly wash out your billfold, and begin the fasting season.

It was February 1927. The season of Fasching was coming to its zenith. In the evening, there would be a fantastic costume party at the

"Löwenbräukeller," one of Munich's many famous beer halls. My father and his friends had been planning for weeks which costume they should choose. After a lot of pros and cons he decided to dress up as a bear. The previous year he had been successful with it. Maybe it was a bit hot, but he could always take off the head later.

While the boys got ready in the house of the Corps Suevia (they had one more beer for the road—just to be sure), my mother was attaching the long braid onto her black hair. She was already wearing a richly embroidered Chinese style silk jacket and pants. "It looks great on you, Lulu," her girlfriend said. "But you need to put on some more makeup, let me help you." This was something my mother had little experience with.

The Chinese costume had been good advice; it seemed to suit my mother perfectly.

The two girls were excited. The Faschings party in the "Löwenbräukeller" was always the highlight of this crazy season. "Hurry up, we must not be late!" Mother said.

As the bear and his friends entered the enormous halls of the Keller, the party had already come to a peak. Gleaming colored streamers and balloons fluttered from the walls and covered the paintings on the high ceilings; dancers in fantastic disguises moved like specters in the dim shadows of the cavernous halls. The walls reverberated with the band's dizzying rhythms, as Father and his friends joined in with the rollicking crowd. The Chinese girl and her friend were right in the center. They were dancing ecstatically amid the whirling crowd of merrymakers. What a party!

In the meantime, the bear had positioned himself at the balustrade above the large staircase. From this point he could best survey the whole scene.

Worn out by the deafening tumult, the Chinese girl and her friend escaped to the top of the staircase. As they reached the last steps before the railing, Lulu caught sight of the bear.

"This one I would like," she muttered breathlessly in a barely audible voice, as she whizzed by him.

The bear showed no sign of having heard her remark. He did not want to embarrass her.

He had been watching her all evening and waiting for the right moment. And now, what a happy coincidence, she had run straight into his arms. He turned toward her and held her tight. Then they danced, the Chinese girl and the bear, all night long. After that it was clear to them this was love at first sight!

Father was happy. Mother, who was considered an exotic type in that period, fascinated him, and had actually bewitched him. Her wild, nonconformist character—so contrary to his own—her intelligence, and her Bohemian way of life—he just adored it all.

The fraternity brothers were also impressed by this emancipated little woman. Mother herself had fallen head over heels in love. She tolerated his brothers, although the spirit of the "Corps Suevia" was not exactly her thing. Self-control, strict discipline, and perfect manners, and on top of it, the patriotic convictions of the Corps—all that she had experienced to the utmost during her time in boarding school! For herself she had chosen a different world.

My father's parents, the Schrankl family, treated the "young teacher" with an air of polite distance. They might have wished a quite different type of wife for their son. The fact that Mother was a "city girl" was questionable enough, but on top of that, it was clear that Mother did not conform to the current model of a good housewife. She did not seem to be the kind of woman who would patiently subordinate herself to the wishes of her husband.

Probably Mother had been aware of these reservations from the beginning. She later told me that she could never feel at home in this family. And, as usual, she found it difficult to hide her feelings.

But it was springtime in the mountains and they were young and in love!

On July 3, 1931, my parents were married in Munich. They celebrated a small wedding with only their closest friends in Vachendorf.

The Young Family

With the day of my birth on October 31, 1932, things changed in the Schrankl house.

The cat was banned from the apartment and my father from the bedroom. I called the shots, supposedly.

But actually, it was my mother who commanded. With my first cry she had taken possession of me, completely and irrevocably. I was what one would call nowadays "overprotected." And I resisted from the very beginning.

I was barely six weeks old when I refused any kind of nutrition. Mother did not know what to do and took me to the hospital. The doctors could find nothing wrong with the baby. They kept me for observation and sent Mother home.

Lulu and Anton.

And surprise! As soon as she was gone, I drank my milk and everything was all right again.

Market Square of Landsberg/ Lech - Grandmother Schrankl.

This was my first act of protest, and many more should follow.

Mother became my truest confidante and best friend. During all of my life she was my most trusted helper in any kind of situation, despite the fact that I continually had to oppose her possessive love and care.

During the first three years of my life we made our home in Landsberg on the river Lech. As was common in those days in bourgeois families, my parents employed a cook and a nurse. The cook took care of the household, and the nurse and my mother concentrated their care on the baby. I was the center of the family, and relatives and friends of the family came to admire the baby.

When she married, Mother had to give up her beloved profession as a teacher. It was unacceptable that a married woman with a child would hold down a teaching job. (Only years later would the government recall all women into their working positions.) Mother was no housewife and did not intend to become one, so now the baby became the center of her attention.

It seems that from the day of my birth my father no longer commanded the attention of my mother. She did not even permit him to take me on walks without her. The reason was probably her exaggerated concern for her child. Another reason might have been the fact that their marriage had become complicated. Father was a real Bavarian male and expected a down-to-earth country girl with a healthy attitude toward all things of life. Mother, however, had a more complicated attitude toward these things, probably because of her puritan Catholic education or maybe also by disposition. I guess that this may have been the reason why I remained a single child. Another reason could be found in the fact that that my father had a realistic type of character, which did not meet Mother's emotional and romantic expectations. But somehow Mother succeeded in making up for her feminine deficits during the long years of a difficult marriage by means of her strong and earnest character. Apparently life was often a burden to her and she was aware of the fact that she was her own worst enemy. I often heard her say, "The only thing I have to reproach my mother with, is the fact that she has put me into this world!"

Chapter 2: Early Childhood Memories

Munich 1935

My first childhood memory is connected with another act of liberation. At that time we were living in Munich, Bavaria. Father was working for the Siemens Company.

We lived in the center of Munich at St. Anna Platz. St. Anna Square is an especially romantic corner of the city. A large church in the Romanesque style, surrounded by old chestnut trees, dominates the square. I can hear the bell of the church clock, which still strikes every hour and the sound makes me feel at home.

I must have been about three years old. I remember one day when Mother was pushing me in a stroller across the ancient stone bridge, the Maximilian Brücke. We were already on our way home from the park along the Isar River.

It was a sunny day, but there was still that chilly breeze in the warm spring air, which carried the musky odor of rotten leaves from the waters below the bridge. I was wrapped up in a warm coat, a woolen hat, gloves, and a shawl.

In the middle of the bridge, in front of the Bavarian Parliament Building, towers a statue of the Greek goddess of wisdom, Pallas Athena. There she guards the river, sternly looking South toward the snow-covered mountain chain of the Alps and beyond into the direction of Italy.

Just as we were passing the "Isar-Athena," a small boy, clutching his mother's hand, passed us. Suddenly he pointed his finger at me. "Look, Mama, this girl still has a pacifier!" I stared at him, and then I reached for my pacifier, pulled it out of my mouth and hurled it into the river below. Then I grabbed my woolen hat and flung it into the river too. Athena seemed to look down at me with a smile. I distinctly remember that I felt like a hero.

Isar-Athena, Maximilians Bridge, Munich.

Eva and Mother.
Eva (1935) At the Odeonsplatz in Munich.

There was this exhilarating sensation of freeing myself from some kind of inner or outer compulsion or constraint. Later in life I would experience this feeling many times again. It was always associated with allowing myself to escape from the constraints of everyday life. It was like jumping into the cold water of the river—into the unknown—while at the same time being sure that everything would go well.

It was at this same place, at the feet of Pallas Athena, that fifteen years later I would make a most important decision that would change my whole life—the decision to "Go West," to go to America.

Only few pictures of my life in Munich are left in my memory. There was the neighbor's boy Fritzi (eight years old), who secretly climbed down from the apartment above. He would come over the balcony and steal through the window into our bedroom where I was taking my afternoon nap. Sometimes he would cuddle up in my baby crib. It was much too small for him, and he had to pull up his knees all the way to his chin. On other days we would play with my dolls. This went on until one day when my mother found out and told his parents not to allow him to come down any more.

My mother used to take me on long walks through the Hofgarten (the garden of the royal residence). Now it was winter, and the flower beds were covered with snow. I remember strolling under the arcades, my mother explaining to me the paintings on the wall that showed scenes from the ancient history of Bavaria. I looked at the fierce battles with proud kings and knights, rearing horses, and dying heroes. These pictures intrigued me. Was the real life outside of my sheltered world really concerned with such battles and violence?

I was also impressed by the proud and tall buildings at the Koenigsplatz. There, way up in the architrave of the Glyptothek, I found a statue of my friend Pallas Athena from the bridge over the Isar. She seemed to be smiling down at me. I loved these characters from classical mythology and the thrilling stories my mother told about them. And I loved the stately columns and high-gabled buildings that the city of Munich was full of. They aroused my curiosity for the world of classical Greece at quite an early age.

But most of all, I remember the hand of my mother, which never let go of me. I was never allowed to play with other children. Not even Father could take me out after one day we returned home with my new white furry coat all dirty with mud.

Berlin 1936—The Olympic Games

When I was four years old, we moved to Berlin. Father had been called for military duty in the "Heereswaffenamt" (Army Headquarters) with its seat Unter den Linden. As an electrical engineer he had to inspect technical installations of the Army, at first only in Germany, and during the war in all of Europe.

My first memories of these years are connected with the Olympic Games. The year 1936 was an important year for Germany. The whole world came to Berlin and paid homage to the "Führer." His success during the previous three years, the gradual annulment of the Treaty of Versailles, the continual reduction of the number of unemployed, the reconstruction of the economy, and the recovery of Germany's prestige abroad had silenced the critics of his leadership and had made Hitler very popular among the German people.

The Party and the government knew how to set the stage and to present themselves to the world. These Olympic games became the most exciting international event, brilliantly presented by the famous movie director Leni Riefenstahl. This extraordinary photographer had to pay for her artistic success after the war by a life of ostracism by society and politics.

I was not allowed to accompany my parents to the games, but the beautiful ball with the colorful rings that my parents brought me when they returned from the games became my favorite toy for years.

The general mood in political and social life in those days is still very clear in my mind. Every afternoon I went to the park with Mother. One day a sign had been placed above my favorite sandbox: "For Jewish children only!"

"What does this mean?" I asked Mother. "It means that you are not supposed to play here any more," she said with a frown on her face.

"But I will play here, just because of it," I exclaimed defiantly.

Mother did not object but tried to interest me in some other activity. We never came back to that place. This time it had not been the opposition against my mother that had caused me to disregard the rules. I remember that I felt a keen sense of injustice regarding my Jewish playmates.

In those days I always used to eat very little. The doctor had told my mother that I was a very delicate child and she should see to it that I ate enough, since I was "a candle that was burning on both ends." I think I only looked so thin because I had very large, blue eyes with deep circles underneath. Once some people even gave me a piece of bread on the street: "Come on and eat, little girl, you look so hungry."

But this was not the case at all. My mother had always tried to stuff me with food. Even before dinner. As a consequence I lost my appetite and could not eat anything at all and then I had to remain seated in front of my warming plate for long periods of time until I had finished my plate. I could not have been that delicate, judging from the way I usually managed to get my own way.

Another incident comes to my mind. This time it had again something to do with my mother. I must have been about five years old, because I was not yet in school. This day I was allowed to go with her to the zoo. I loved watching the monkeys in their cage and the lion pacing majestically up and down behind his bars. Suddenly I had disappeared. I had simply run off without a word. Mother was worried sick. She looked everywhere for me, checked the lion's cage, the monkey house, inquired with the caretaker of the ice bears. Nothing—little Eva was gone. Finally she called the police and they sent some men who started a general search. After two hours, during which my poor mother must have gone through hell, they found me.

I was sitting amid a group of soldiers, happily spooning a huge bowl of bean soup from the soldiers' kettle. I still remember how much I had enjoyed the feeling of breaking away from my mother's controlling hand. It had been a big adventure.

I grew up like a typical single child. There were advantages as well as disadvantages in being an only child. On the one hand, I never learned to defend myself against other children or to accept a fight as a normal part of life. Later in school I also tried to avoid conflict as long as possible. I am still this way today. I am always very surprised if some person does not like me, is envious of me, or just wants to pick a fight.

On the other hand, I have never known a feeling of envy toward anybody, a feeling that seems to be very common among brothers and sisters. I have never envied anyone for his or her talent, beauty, or possessions.

I was at home in my own little world. There I was my own boss, sheltered from the world outside. I also liked to play by myself, and thus I learned to be happy in my own company. To me, being alone is the normal situation. I enjoy other people's company, but only for a limited time. Then I long to return into my own world, my books, to continue my work or my projects. I have always loved the beauty of nature, especially my Bavarian mountains, and I don't mind enjoying them alone.

I don't need other people in order to experience the feeling of happiness.

Despite this disposition, I never experienced any trouble in getting along with other children in school, at university, or later in my professional life as a teacher. On the contrary, when working in a group, people would usually accept my opinion or would even ask my advice. Sometimes, however, I sensed that there was a feeling of envy behind some friendly faces, but I decided that there was nothing I could do about it and did not worry, or I simply ignored the fact.

Another incident comes to my mind, when I think about my first year of school.

There was a girl in my class who enjoyed teasing me. She either pulled my braids, or put them into the inkbottle on her desk behind me. I seemed unable to defend myself. One day she followed me up the stairs and pulled my hair again. I kicked her with my foot and hit her right on the mouth. Blood was dripping from her lips. I was stunned. The teachers came running and I was taken to the headmaster's office. I could not find a word to defend myself but I heard how my classroom teacher said: "Eva is always such a quiet and well-behaved girl. She would never hurt anybody. This must have been an accident!"

This story shows quite well that I am quite hot-tempered and sometimes overreact if someone provokes me long enough. This character trait would show up again and again in my later life and cause me some trouble.

VACHENDORF

Vachendorf is my childhood, the Chiemgau is my homeland!

Home means the fragrance of the freshly cut grass on the meadows and of the hay on the haystacks, where we used to play hide and seek until darkness crept in from the nearby forests. It means the snowy mountains and the haunted forests, and it means skiing down the snow-covered hill all the way to the first house of the village.

Vachendorf today.

Every time I come to visit, I climb to the top of the "Türlberg," the small hill right behind the village.

Looking down from here, the small village, surrounded by soft hills, dark forests, and green meadows, seems to rest in God's own lap. The baroque "onion" dome of the church towers high above the gabled roofs of the farmhouses.

In the south, the twin peaks of the "Hochgern" und "Hochfelln" are silhouetted against the mountain chain of the Alps—the sight is so beautiful that it almost seems it's not real. In the foreground, fertile green fields surround the village.

In the east, in the direction of Salzburg, rises the little chapel of St. Georg on top of the highest point of the chain of hills. Legend tells us that it had been built in medieval times on the ruins of an ancient place of worship of the pre-Christian Celtic people. Here they venerated a white horse and offered sacrifices to their gods, asking them for the protection of their horses.

To the west I can barely discern the shining surface of Lake Chiemsee, with its two islands. The larger one holds King Ludwig's majestic castle and the small one has a fishing village and the enchanting 1,200-year-old convent, Frauenchiemsee, where pilgrims still venerate the grave of St. Irmingard, the granddaughter of Charles the Great.

"Homeland" also means my memories of the "Schrankl House," the cradle of our family. I loved our old house with all its hustle and bustle. But most of all I loved Grandfather.

Grandmother Schrankl I only met for a short while. She died in 1937 at the age of 65 from a stroke. I was only five years old then.

My favorite childhood memories are connected with the visits to my grandfather. I really felt at home with him, and not only because I was allowed to do everything. With him I was finally liberated from my mother's constant presence—at least sometimes.

There was so much to discover! Grandfather showed me the little store where one could buy everything. It had a peculiar bittersweet smell about it—a mixture of paper, liquorices, and sauerkraut. There was the bakery, where the loaves of dark bread were pushed into the oven and the pretzels were formed with art—the smell of freshly baked bread penetrated the whole house. Even today this wonderful smell takes me back to Grandfather's house. Behind the house there were the stables, where some twelve cows had to be milked twice a day, the chickens and the pigs, the barn with the sweet smelling hay, and the stable for the horses. And I was allowed to ride Grandfather's most gentle horse.

Together with Grandfather Schrankl.

Riding horses was my most favorite activity.

Once in a while he would ask me: "Want a pretzel or a Semmel?" or he gave me a glass of fresh milk directly from the cow and still warm.

I also liked my aunts and uncles. Uncle Michael and his wife Christine were running the farm and the store. At that time they had two children, Michl and Peter, later three more joined the family.

Aunt Marie was at work in the store—without a rest from morning to night. She never had time to get married and remained at home until she died. She was already sick when one day at the age of 67 she finally got on an airplane to visit our distant relatives in America. It did not seem to bother her that she neither spoke nor understood one word of English.

Aunt Adelheid started her work in the bakery at midnight. She and her husband, Uncle Florian, had four children, and the couple built a house and ran a inn, "Beim Floriwirt," in the next village.

Aunt Irma wanted to emigrate to America, but the beginning of the war thwarted her plans. In 1940 she became department head of a large food store in Munich that still exists today.

Aunt Nandl (Anna) married into a large farm in Irlach, not far from Vachendorf.

Aunt Lisl had become a nun in the convent of the Sisters of Mercy, where she took care of old and sick people for the rest of her life.

I never met Aunt Rosl—she had died of pneumonia at the age of 14.

Aunt Berta was the youngest. She and her husband Joseph, a tailor, built a small house at the edge of the village. After only three years of marriage he was killed in World War II in Russia and left her a young widow with two small children. She never remarried.

Eva and two friends in Vachendorf, 1936

All of them have mastered their lives despite tragic strokes of fate. The feeling of solidarity and loyalty to the family were the most important values for them. The question of individual happiness was a secondary one.

Every summer Mother and I spent our vacation in Vachendorf. Father, who had to stay in Berlin, would join us for a short visit. During these years he used to wear a gray uniform with a saber, which made a strong impression on me. Only many years later, when I was 16, did I ask him about his political attitude during the time of the Third Reich. I will say more about that later.

CHAPTER 3: CHILDHOOD DURING THE WAR

BERLIN

THE NAZI REGIME CONTINUED TO extend its powers, and politics began to affect the private lives of the people. Even though I was still a child, I could feel the change in the general atmosphere that surrounded me.

There was, for instance, a woman called "Blockwartsfrau" (block-leader) whom the Party had assigned to spy on the people. She took her job very seriously. She showed up regularly at our front door without announcing her visit and went through our apartment to check which radio station we were listening to. Nobody was allowed to be engaged in any "subversive activities," such as listening to foreign radio stations.

"Pull yourself together and be more polite. You cannot say everything that's on your mind. Be careful!" Father warned Mother again and again.

I have already described Mother's attitude toward the Nazis. Her sense of individualism and her stubbornness were beginning to be a threat to all of us.

When the war started in 1939, I was seven years old and was attending the second grade in the elementary school in Charlottenburg.

I remember well when one day when Hitler's blaring voice came from the radio shouting his historic sentence: "Since five o'clock this morning the German army is returning the fire...."

With my parents in Berlin.

The war had begun with a lie; but this we should learn only many years later.

Hitler's armies had invaded Poland—without any declaration of war. Nobody envisioned at that time the catastrophe which would befall Germany.

Father was constantly on the road now. His orders were to inspect the technical installations of the army, at first in Poland and later in France and Denmark.

At home in Charlottenburg (a neighborhood in Berlin) we were not yet affected very much by the war. There were, however, those loud, unpleasant, aggressive voices from the radio. I was aware of a mounting aggression around me, and this sometimes scared me.

But everything was more or less the same, school in the morning and in the afternoon we went to the park.

I became aware, however, that the peace in the family was beginning to be affected by what was happening outside. One afternoon my uncle Edi, Mother's brother, came for a visit. He was a soldier now and was stationed in Crete. He was on home leave and knew a lot about what was going on in the world, things that my parents never discussed in my presence. He had a worried expression on his face, and Father and he closed themselves up in the "Herrenzimmer" (study) for several hours. Dense clouds of smoke from Father's cigar and Uncle Edi's pipe drifted through the cracks of the door, accompanied by an increasing level of loud voices.

When they finally joined Mother and me in the living room, the expression on Uncle Edi's face had turned from worried to furious and the veins on my father's neck were swollen. Shortly afterward Uncle Edi hastily left our apartment. He did not even stay for dinner this time. It seemed that the two gentlemen had very different opinions about the political situation.

Christmas 1938 with our maid Maria.

Soon after this incident the air attacks on Berlin started. First the Allied Forces bombed the city only once in a while and only at night. Later they bombed the city also during the day. At night we had to keep the windows covered with black shades so that no light could escape to the outside and attract enemy planes.

After 1942 the raids became more and more frequent,

It was always the same: First the shrill, unnerving howl of the Sirens, then my parents burst into my room, wrapped me in a blanket, and carried me four floors down into the air-raid shelter. Most of the time I only woke up after the first explosions when we had reached the shelter. I remember an uncontrollable trembling that would sometimes overcome my body, which was, however, not a feeling of fear.

Many times we had to seek shelter up to three times a night. Sometimes I was afraid that we would be buried alive under the rubble, or drown due to a burst water pipe. For my parents, the daily struggle for survival became more and more unbearable. I, myself, was not really that scared. On the contrary, everything still seemed like a big adventure to me.

After the Siren had signaled to leave the shelter and to return to our apartment, the whole city often seemed like one sea of flames.

If the planes dropped their bombs after 2 a.m., we had no school the next day. We children enjoyed this free day.

1942, Father in the rank of a Colonel of the Army.

Then we went out on the street to kick the remains of the incendiary bombs with the heels of our shoes and made them hiss into the air like fireworks.

Only once I recall being scared to death. It had been the third alarm that night. This time the bombs seemed to explode right above our heads. The roaring of the anti-aircraft artillery rocked us from our seats. I imagined the most terrible scenes. What would happen if the whole house came down on us or if the shelter filled up with water to the ceiling?

The wailing and the prayers of the adults around me added to my horror fantasies, and I hid my head underneath the blankets. Finally, the all-clear signal sounded. It seemed a miracle that our house was still there.

When I was back in bed, the city around me looked like one big fireball. This must be hell! Only in the morning, I dared to look out of the window. The smoke had cleared. Most houses around us were no longer there. Only their façades were left and the neighboring houses resembled skulls with empty eyes above the streets full of rubble.

We used the basement door to keep track of the bombing. Every attack was marked by a cross. When in January 1942 we marked the 300th cross, Father said in desperation: "I have had enough. You are not safe here any more. You have to get out!"

He sent Mother and me down south to his family in Bavaria. He had to remain in Berlin, where he was being cared for by our maid, Maria.

At this point I want to write about our maid Maria.

Maria, our loyal soul, joined our family at the age of 21 in 1936. I was just four years old. From the first day onward she took care of our household and remained dedicated to our family until the death of my mother, on April 1, 1998, when she was 99 years old—a period of 62 years! Maria was a typical Berliner, with common sense, dry humor, and a lively mind. She was a hardworking and responsible girl, loved children, and was very religious. I loved her dry humor, which she has retained until today. Her father had owned a roofing business, and after the early death of her mother—Maria was only 12 years old—it was now up to her to run the household for her father and her six brothers. since she was the oldest and only daughter. There was no way she could have continued going to school. Taking care of such a large family was a lot of work, and she was devoted to her family. She never married. This early burden of responsibility gave her the feeling of having sacrificed a lot. On the other hand, it gave her a lot of self-confidence. Sometimes she even seemed to scorn those who did not have to work as hard as she did in the course of their life. Her favorite saying still is: "Oh dear, these people are simply not mature. They don't know what it's like, they never have been through a lot!"

Maria revered my Father, but Mother and Maria were not of the same world. Maria used to bear Mother's moods with stoic calmness. Most of all, Maria loved children, and when she talked to them a seldom-heard soft note would enter her voice.

As a child I used to hide in her kitchen where she would comfort me, when Mother had "a bad day" or one of her migraine headaches. She was always on my side and she often taught me, even if it meant scolding me a bit, and I listened to her, because she had a strong sense of justice.

As the war continued to move into the country, Maria stayed behind in Berlin with Father. She was not afraid, and she took care of him after his injury in 1945.

Later she followed us to Bavaria.

Today she is 90 years old and still helps needy people. Looking back, I ask myself, "What would we have done without Maria?"

Vachendorf 1942

We are back in the year 1942.

In the morning after the 300th air raid, we packed our suitcases and went to the central train station of Berlin.

There was utter chaos on that day. People, loaded with bag and baggage with all of their belongings, were storming the trains to leave the city. The crowd consisted mostly of women with their children and some old people. People were hysterically screaming in order to not get separated from their family members. Mothers were fighting to get the last train tickets and pushed their way through the crowd, shoving those before them aside to get breathing room for their children.

They were pressing so hard that I was actually lifted up into the air. An old lady beside me stumbled and fell. As my mother pushed me on, I did not see what happened to the old woman. Mother and I were practically squeezed to pieces. I don't know how she managed to get a seat on the train.

It was a slow, endlessly long trip south through the night with many long stops at bleak and devastated train stations.

For the first time I saw the endless trains going to the front in the east, full of soldiers who crowded every bit of standing room in the train. Even the toilets were packed full with kit bags and pieces of luggage.

Thank God we were going south to Bavaria—to Vachendorf.

When we arrived, everything looked like always. But this was an illusion.

Since our last visit in the summer of 1941 many things had changed. The big house of Grandfather was filled with people, so we moved in with Aunt Berta in her little house at the edge of the village. There in the "Zaunerhausl" we found a new home in a nice room with a balcony that had a view of the mountains.

Aunt Berta had to take in women and children that had been evacuated from the big cities in the North because of the increasing bombing raids of the Allied Forces.

Grandfather Michael Schankl and grandchildren Bernhard, Elisabeth and Eva, 1942, Family photo

The southern part of the country was still relatively safe at that time. She was allowed to keep two rooms for herself and her children.

Her children, Elisabeth, five, and Bernhard, two, now became my first playmates.

Life changed radically for me as an overprotected city girl. My nicely ironed dresses remained in the closet and I wore Dirndl and apron. The village children went, of course, with bare feet as soon as the snow had melted off the mountains. So off with the woolen pantyhose and the Lackschuhe as soon as I had disappeared from Mother's sight. In the beginning my feet hurt terribly, but soon I got used to it.

Mother did not believe her eyes when she scrutinized me coming back in the evening dirty, with clothes all wrinkled, and with bruised and cut knees.

Aunt Berta knew what to do. A pail of water, soap and a brush. After that, some ointment to heal the cuts and bruises.

At first I was astounded how fast Aunt Berta's children Lisbeth and Berni emptied their plates. Only after Mother had taken off the skin from the sausages did I begin to eat. I was still very picky, but after a while the fresh air and the merry crowd around the table made me hungry.

Aunt Berta was a wonderful cook. There were always fruit and vegetables freshly picked in the garden. We went to Grandfather's or Aunt Nandl's to get fresh milk and butter, and the chickens provided eggs. When we helped to bring the hay in during harvest time, Grandfather paid us with bread and flour.

At the end of August it was great fun to go into the forests to pick berries, from which Aunt Berta made the most delicious jam and jelly. In the basement the canned fruits and vegetables from the fall all stood in rows ready for the winter. Glasses full of delicious pears and cherries, apples, and boysenberries. Everything biologically healthy!

Vachendorf in summer and winter. 1943, Family photo

In the fall, the house began to be crowded. Tante Berta had to take in some more "Bombenfrauen"—women who had lost their homes due to the bombing raids—with their children. There was only a small kitchen and no bathroom. I did not mind, but for Mother this was sheer horror. It was extremely difficult for her to adjust to cooking in a small kitchen, which had to be shared by other women she did not know. Every mother wanted to take care of her own children first.

Tante Berta tried to establish some kind of order. She wrote a schedule for the week.

Saturday was the day to take a bath. Early in the morning Tante Berta fired a large kettle in the basement with wood and began to heat the water. Around noon it was finally hot enough to be emptied into the old cast iron bathtub. One child after the other—the youngest first—was lathered thoroughly and dipped into the tub.

After everyone was dried off, the hair combed and put up in braids, we had Wiener Wurstl and sauerkraut with potato salad. Thus, the day of the bath became a day of fun.

I enjoyed life in the house of Tante Berta very much. I finally had playmates, which I had to do without in Berlin.

Even though most people began to starve in Germany by that time, we were never hungry in Tante Berta's house. She had everything that grows in a big orchard and vegetable garden. For milk and bread we went to Grandfather's house, and in the summer we went into the woods to collect berries. When we worked in the fields to help bring the harvest in, we bartered for the things we needed.

At that time we did not suffer from hunger in Vachendorf, but things would change soon.

I enjoyed life in Vachendorf. I finally had other children to play with. Therefore, I quickly got over the disappointment of not being allowed to go to school with the other children.

Mother had applied for permission to home school me, claiming that my health was too delicate. She obtained a certificate from our pediatrician. The truth was that she did not want me to be indoctrinated by Nazi propaganda, which had infiltrated the schools and their teaching.

Since she herself was a teacher, she actually got permission to teach me at home. I learned very quickly, and two to three hours in the morning were enough to teach me the reading, writing, grammar, and arithmetic that the other children at my level got in the village school.

Elisabeth and I became like sisters. We strolled through the fields, especially when the wheat had grown tall and the blue cornflowers, the red poppies, and the white daisies lined the fields along the pathways. There, so I had promised her, I would show her the mouse holes and the cricket holes that were really an entrance to the underworld. Elisabeth believed in my fairy tales and listened to me with her eyes wide in amazement, even though we never did get to see the elves and dwarfs that I had told her were living there.

One special place, which had fed my imagination like no other, was a small, haunted moorland lake, called "Tuettensee."

It was hidden amid a wild forest of fir trees and blackberry bushes. Its gloomy, dark water seemed indeed to be the entrance to the underworld. To reach it we had to take the path through the "Hexenwald"—the witches' forest—where trees grew tall into the sky and below their crowns the voices of the birds resounded like in a dark and mysterious cathedral. I walked very softly and quietly, because I did not want to disturb them, the gnomes and elves or maybe even Hansel and Gretel. At the edge of the lake I imagined the nymphs and water sprites dancing together with the Frogman on the moss in the afternoon twilight.

Mother wondered why I would always follow her, lost in silence. I did not tell her anything about my secret thoughts, because I was sure that adults would only scare the elves away. So I saved my fantastic stories for Elisabeth; she would gratefully listen to me.

As much as I liked life in the Zauner household, Mother could not stand the cramped conditions any longer. Our small refuge now housed five adults and eight children. What a crowd in the kitchen, in the bathroom without a bathtub, and on Saturdays in the basement! Mother, the absolute individualist and recluse, moved with me to a small rented room in Siegsdorf, a village nearby.

My life changed radically. The room was tiny, it could not be heated, we had almost nothing to eat, and I no longer had friends to play with. On top of it all, in 1943 we had a terrible winter. The temperature dropped to 42 degrees C, below freezing, and we were snowed in up to the roof. We had no more water. Everything was frozen up. Even the toilets. On one side of the house we emptied the night pots into the snow and on the other side we took the snow to melt it down to have water for drinking and washing.

Eating became a problem again. Mother really was not the greatest cook, but there really was very little to cook. The only two dishes I remember were "Mehlmus" (boiled flour and water) and "Blutwurstgroestl" (fried potatoes and blood sausage). I often thought of the large bowls of sweet apple fries and elderberry sauce we had in my grandfather's house.

In late summer of 1943 we went to Berlin to visit Father. It was a time when I should have entered "Gymnasium" for higher education. Our short stay in the inferno of Berlin was a nightmare. In Vachendorf we had been spared most of the commotion of the war.

The war had only threatened us from a distance, at night when the city of Munich was being bombed. The night sky in the Northwest showed a weird and at the same time beautiful spectacle: a glow of fiery flickering colors and lights. It was exciting and threatening but very far away!

In the German capital the bombing raids had left deep craters everywhere and the beautiful city was ravaged. Many people had lost their homes and all their belongings. Thousands had died under the ruins. Those who remained fought an everyday fight for their daily bread. Mother and I wanted to go back home to Bavaria as soon as possible.

TRAUNSTEIN 1943/44

In the fall of 1943 we moved to Traunstein, a small town with an ancient history, an old city wall, a castle, and a baroque church. This was where my father had gone to school.

Mother had rented a small room in the center of town. She had been called back into public service as a teacher and was to start teaching at the elementary school in the fall. I also had to enter public school, because I had reached the age for the qualification examination for higher education.

My first year in high school was dominated by National Socialistic education. Mother had done everything in her power to keep me away from Nazi propaganda, but now, since I was in high school, she could no longer prevent my exposure to the propaganda.

At the beginning of the school year I was obliged to join the BDM (Bund Deutscher Mädchen), the youth organization of the Nazi party. The admission ceremony followed a certain ritual. We had to pledge our allegiance to the German flag, the fatherland, and especially to the Führer. There we were, all girls lined up, straight and proper, wearing our uniforms, a navy blue skirt and a white blouse with a little scarf around the neck. From the loudspeaker came a stern, military voice telling us to repeat a solemn oath. We would from now on dedicate our life to our country and to the Führer. As I repeated the words of the oath, I crossed the fingers of my left hand behind my back. Thus I had done my duty, I thought, but I had really not sworn anything. How could I swear unconditional allegiance to a person unto death? Who knew what he would order me to do in the future? It seemed wrong to me to give up my freedom to decide things for myself.

I really did not dislike the BDM itself. On the contrary, the girls were nice, and I would have liked to spend the weekends with them, as the rules of the school stipulated.

Again, I was not allowed to join the others. Mother would not give her permission.

Of course I was punished on the following Monday. "Schrankl, get up! Why were you absent on the weekend? Get into the corner and stay there! And think about your misbehavior!"

How unjust! I thought. Here I was being punished twice. First by my mother, who would not allow me to meet with my friends in the BDM and again by my teacher who publicly criticized me and made me stand in the corner. On top of it all, I was punished by my classmates, who regarded me an outsider with whom they would not have anything to do.

In the meantime, the war had reached Traunstein. The city was filling up with soldiers, most of whom were wounded. During the night we heard the trains roll by that brought more wounded and sick men from the Eastern front.

Every morning on our way to school we came face to face with new suffering. The hospitals were overcrowded and they began to house the wounded and the refugees in large public buildings, like schools, office buildings, and sports facilities.

Finally, also my school was converted into a military hospital. I had just attended school for a few months when we had to clear out and teaching was reduced to a few hours a day in some former café or restaurant.

The winter of 1944 was again incredibly cold, and we painfully felt the freeze. Wood and coal were needed for the hospitals, and the schoolrooms remained unheated. We sat there in our coats, hats, and gloves. I remember not being able to write well with my gloves on, but if I took them off, my fingers would freeze. At home in our little room, it was by no means any better. During the day we put sweater over sweater and at night we stuck warming bottles into our beds. But we never really got warm.

It was no wonder that my mother and I often got into an argument. It was mostly about cleaning up my things. The room was always in disorder, and we were constantly looking for something. Having to live in such a small room, filled up to the ceiling with boxes and bundles, together with a girl who was nearly a teenager, was hard for my Mother—as it was for me to live with her. For the first time in my life I was really hungry, and Mother could do nothing. She even gave away my dolls to the farmers in exchange for bread and milk.

In the winter of 1944, the temperature dropped below 40 degrees C and we could no longer stay in our room during the day. We received coupons from the government for coal and wood, which we gave to so called "Waermestuben"—warm-up places. Every afternoon I did my homework there and Mother corrected her papers. In this way we managed to get through the cold season.

Once we received a coupon for wood, but we were told to pick up the tree in the forest ourselves. Neither Mother nor I knew how to handle a saw. But luckily a young soldier who was home on sick leave helped us.

Food was, of course, rationed. We received coupons for bread, milk, meat (100 grams per week), and butter. We took these coupons usually to some restaurant to eat. It was more fun there, and the food tasted much better than what my mother could have cooked us on her little gas stove in our room. It is no wonder that I did not learn how to cook at that age; there simply was nothing to cook.

In the fall of 1944 the situation in Traunstein became frightening. Trains and trucks brought wounded men into the city day and night. Many of them were still boys—hungry, worn out, apathetic, with dirty bandages and blood clots all over their tattered uniforms, and without sufficient medical care.

Then the refugees arrived—thousands of desperate people, women and children and old people in rags, starved and frightened.

They came in horse-drawn wagons or on foot, the remains of their belongings in a rucksack or in a baby carriage. Many had lost everything they owned, except the clothes they were wearing.

War was now showing its most cruel face also in Traunstein.

Our house was overflowing with newcomers from the Eastern provinces. The staircase was filled with boxes and bags, the corridors no longer passable.

One day I was standing at the head of the stairs in front of our door when I heard a dull droning sound above me. The whole house began to vibrate. I heard a hissing sound and the thunder of an explosion above my head. The shock wave threw me down the stairs. This terror had just lasted a few minutes, and then everything was quiet.

I found myself at the bottom of the stairs. The house was still standing but there was broken glass everywhere around me. I had only a few bruises on my back.

The area around the nearby train station had been almost completely destroyed. There were many dead and wounded. Most of the victims were refugees who had just dragged themselves into the city with their last strength.

During this bombing raid, an American plane had been shot down. I can still see the men dangling in the trees from their parachutes and remember my thoughts: "What would happen to them if they were taken prisoner?" Some people were so full of hate that they might kill them. I myself had no angry thoughts concerning them. Probably those poor guys were just doing their duty!

After this bombing attack in 1944 the schools were closed. Nobody knew when they would open again. Mother wanted us to return to Vachendorf. Even Vachendorf had not been spared. When we came to Tante Berta's house on November 12, 1944, we could not believe our eyes. Five huge bomb craters surrounded her house. The roof and the windows were shattered. There was neither water nor electricity.

But the house itself was still standing. However, a nearby building hut, where the children used to go to play, was completely destroyed.

On November 11, Tante Berta suddenly said: "Today you are not going out to play; today we are taking a nap." Despite the children's protests, she had insisted. Shortly after lunch, one hour later, the bomb had hit.

Had this been a premonition? A sixth sense? Be that as it may, Tante Berta had saved the lives of nine children.

Later we heard that only a few miles away where the railroad track passes from Munich to Salzburg, Hitler had passed by in his sealed train on his way to his Eagle's Nest in the Obersalzberg. The train and Hitler had remained unharmed, as was the case so often, but in Vachendorf 13 people had lost their lives.

This had been only one of the 14 unsuccessful attempts to kill Hitler, the first one taking place as early as 1933. People often wondered how he had survived so many attempts, ending with the tragic conspiracy of some of the most trusted officers of his army chief of staff on July 20, 1944, which was led by Graf von Stauffenberg. Again the attempt failed due to a chain of unforeseeable circumstances, and the high-ranking officers were hanged for treason.

The war had spared us in Vachendorf until shortly before the end.

THE END OF THE WAR 1945

We were back in Vachendorf, in Tante Berta's little house. I had my old playmates, and there was enough to eat.

Now everyone was tuned in to the radio all day long.

There were two stations; one was run by the remaining German army, the other one by the Americans, "Radio Free Europe," as it was later called.

The German station called on the population to under no circumstances surrender but to keep up the resistance. Every house whose inhabitants disobeyed this order would be punished severely. This was not an empty threat, and many courageous people lost their lives shortly before the end of the war.

The other station called on us to put out white flags as a sign of surrender on the church tower and on every balcony if we did not want to risk our lives. What should we do?

Soon we could see the white flag waving from the church tower. Probably our priest had advised the sexton to do so.

Despite threats by some nationalistic neighbors, Tante Berta decided to hang a white sheet from the balcony, like some of the neighbors were doing.

The next morning I heard a distant rumbling of heavy engines.

I ran out on the balcony. From there I could see the bridge of the Autobahn Munich–Salzburg. There I could see them, like a huge black snake rolling over the bridge—American tanks and trucks.

The day before we had buried our silver tableware and other valuables under the big apple tree in the garden of Aunt Berta. My ancestors had done so for centuries whenever marauding hordes had invaded the country. Around 2,000 years ago the Germanic tribes had chased the Romans out. The Romans were followed by Celtic tribes; then came the Goths and later the Huns, who, coming out of the distant steppes of the East, looted and devastated the countryside as did the Swedes during the Thirty-Years' War. The French had been there, and so had the Austrians and many others during the innumerable wars and conflicts throughout the ages.

It was April 1945.

"We are out of milk, go and get us some more from Grandfather's!" With this order my mother sent me off. I took the old-fashioned metal pitcher and strolled in the direction of my grandfather's farmhouse. The village street was deserted that day. Not a soul was to be seen. They must all be hiding behind the white curtains of their little windows!

Then I heard them come. At first there was only a faint, indistinct rumble in the distance coming from the direction of the Autobahn. Then a threatening roar was moving up the hill until the tanks, their chains grating, turned the corner at the village entrance, right by the old Gasthof "Zur Post."

A little girl with long blonde braids and a suspicious-looking metal container in her hand was walking slowly down the empty road as though she did not hear the tanks behind her.

The soldiers had been warned of the "werewolves," young kids who threw themselves headlong against the enemy tanks to destroy them with a bazooka in their bare fists. This group consisted of old men and very young boys. It had been recruited as a final show of resistance against the Allied Forces during the last days of the war. Many of them paid with their lives for a wrongly understood allegiance to the flag and their loyalty to the "Führer" and the fatherland.

The tanks grated to a halt behind me. Soldiers in helmets and battle gear, guns in hand, jumped off the tank and motioned to me to show my milk can. With a deliberate look of nonchalance I lifted the container so they could see the milk inside it. They examined everything carefully. Then, laughing cheerfully, they climbed back unto their vehicles, waving in a friendly manner as they left the village in the direction of the nearest town.

At Tante Berta's house we had different problems.

We had hidden a young German officer in the attic of the house, behind a wall.

What would happen to him if he were discovered by the Americans? Or was the danger to be caught by the SS of the Nazis still greater?

This young man had been an officer in the "Waffen SS," Hitler's elite guard.

He had been stationed in Sweden. There he met a Swedish girl and fell in love with her. Against the wishes of her family, she had married during the last days of the war. Then he was called back to his unit. He then was stationed in Bavaria in order to stop the Americans and defend Hitler's Eagle's Nest, close to Salzburg.

His young wife had followed him through all of Europe and had found him again in Traunstein. When she told him that he was going to be a father, he looked for a hideout for his wife and defected. Tante Berta had to find one more floor mattress. She convinced him to remain in the house. It seemed so senseless that he should risk his life again in a war that had been lost already.

In the meantime, Tante Adelheid had also taken her wounded husband, Florian, out of the military hospital in Bad Reichenhall and brought him home to Tante Berta to nurse him.

It was forbidden by penalty of death to hide foreigners or soldiers. In all wars, deserters had been threatened with a dishonorable death.

Now we had a Swedish woman in the house, a wounded soldier in bed, and an SS major in the attic. We were leading a dangerous life in April 1945.

Two days later the Americans returned to Vachendorf.

This time they stayed, occupied the largest farmhouse in the village, and installed their headquarters there.

I had been studying English at the high school for two years. Aside from the Swedish girl, I was the only one who could communicate with the Americans and act as an interpreter. What a task!

I had been a bookworm during recent years. I had read especially the books by Karl May. I would climb up into my favorite tree and devour his adventurous stories about the American prairie. America, that meant to me the noble Indian Winnetou and Old Shatterhand, the trapper, and his white friend.

Americans, that was, to me, the Indians. And now they were in Vachendorf.

They had guns, went hunting in the forest, and rode horses. This was the final proof for me: All Americans were Indians!

It so happened that among these American soldiers there really was an authentic Indian. He had straight black hair, rather dark skin, and melancholy black eyes. Exactly like Winnetou.

I had to translate something for him, and his friendly manner had encouraged me to ask him whether he was an Indian. He said, "Yes, I am," and so we started a conversation. He told me some stories about his home, and finally he asked me whether I wanted to ride his horse.

I could not believe my good luck. I was riding with a real Indian on the back of a horse through the Chiemgau prairie!

Mother, of course, must not know about this adventure—she would have died from fear.

Every now and then American soldiers came to our house and exchanged chocolate and oranges for fresh eggs and the crunchy German dark bread.

We children had never seen oranges before. We tried to bite into the peel, which turned out to taste very bitter. Soon we discovered the wonderful taste and learned to cut the skin up in little pieces. We children got the sweet fruit and Tante Berta collected the peels. She covered them with sugar and made the most wonderful marmalade, which we enjoyed with a big piece of bread and fresh butter.

Among the soldiers were also black men. They were especially nice to us children. They always had some sweets for us, or a piece of some strange gummy substance one could chew and that would keep forever in one's mouth. They always seemed to smile and be happy. Their good-natured ways were very reassuring, and we were never afraid of them.

In contrast to some of the stories we heard about the occupational forces in other parts of Germany, the arrival of the Americans in Vachendorf is connected with happy memories for me. This is hard to believe if one knows that thousands of German soldiers, who were taken prisoner of war at the same time, starved to death in the Rhineland or had to go through terrible suffering.

The End of the War in Berlin

My father was stationed in Berlin during the war and had worked in the Ministry of Defense up to the day of his injury.

Our maid, Maria, held out with him bravely. She spent nights in the shelter because of the bombing. During the day she queued up in front of the few stores left in order to find something to eat.

Then the first waves of refugees from the Eastern front arrived in the devastated city.

Every day they brought new stories of the horrors of war, of killings and rapes by the Russian troops who were moving in across the borders of Germany.

On April 24. the terrible final battle for the capital began. The cruel fighting lasted for nine days—man against man, house by house.

On May 2, the city finally capitulated, destroyed and starved, a victim of a crazed delusion.

Father had been seriously wounded in the last three days of the battle.

Only years later was he able to tell me the whole terrible story. Together with his comrades he had sought refuge in a bunker during the heavy shelling of the city. He suddenly saw a Russian soldier running along the street with a hand grenade.

After a few minutes of silence there was a deafening explosion—and then again a deathlike silence. Father looked around. Everyone in the bunker was dead. He was stunned. He felt no pain. As he looked down at his legs, blood was dripping from his left boot.

A piece of shrapnel had cut through his left leg below the knee. He knew that he had been hit badly. Instinctively, he pulled off his belt and tied it tightly around his upper leg. Then he loses consciousness.

When he regained consciousness, he was on a truck. Many wounded men are around him. It was a Russian truck. Some of the truckloads of men were quickly deposited in a cemetery; others were dumped in front of some hospital door.

My father was among the lucky ones to be taken to the hospital. His leg was amputated below the knee on the same day in order to avoid an infection and to save his life.

Somehow Maria had found him. During the daytime she would hide in a chest in the attic. When night fell, she stole through the rubble to the hospital to bring him some food. In the hospital there were no longer any cooks in the kitchen nor nurses to take care of the wounded. All the women had fled before the Russians to the Western part of the city in fear of the Russian soldiers.

Mother had heard about the terrible days in Berlin. She told me only later. The daily struggle for life was more than she could handle. Her foremost goal was to protect me, and she probably thought I was too young to share the worries of the grown ups.

75% of the city was destroyed, Munich 1945, Old postcard

Chapter 4: Higher Education in Traunstein

In the fall of 1945 the schools had reopened. Mother also had to continue to teach, so we moved again to Traunstein. In October I turned thirteen. I was now a teenager, which is what my Indian called me. English, the language of the occupation forces, began its victorious campaign to become the world's international language and was successful, as we know today.

I still enjoyed climbing up into trees, but I also began to be very interested in my American Karl May characters in a very childlike, but somehow romantic, way.

During that summer I spent a lot of my time in the garden of our neighbors in a tall beech tree. Nobody knew where I was, and I could read in peace and quiet. I had read all the available books by Karl May. I also read the stories about the Knights of the Round Table. I had made a bow and arrow for myself and also a sword, covered with tin foil.

After some time I was beginning to get tired of those stories. What could I read next?

One day I happened to come across some stories about saints, which belonged to our village priest. I was fascinated. Finally, I had found the right thing for me. A girl as a knight was probably very hard to find. But now, I was sure, I would become a saint.

However, this plan did not materialize, because very soon it had become very clear to me that this calling would somehow have a lot to do with obedience.

The word "obedience" was really a bad word for me at that time.

This theme of insubordination has played an important role in my life and has remained important up to this day.

So I had to come down to earth again and face reality.

In Traunstein I had made a new friend, the young priest from an American Protestant church, Norman. He was an especially kind man and has added a lot to my good memories about the American occupation forces.

It was his job to contribute to the reeducation of the German youth. Small groups of interested young people talked to him about religion, and he told us stories about America. Our ideas about democracy and politics began to assume an American face—it was a pleasant face. All this was very much in violation of the strict laws of the occupation forces, such as, "No fraternization" and "off limits."

The American Protestant Church in Traunstein, 1945, Family photo

During the last year of the war, and especially after the collapse of the Third Reich, food had become extremely scarce. The black market blossomed. For a box of cigarettes one could get almost anything. So one had to get this new type of currency somehow, but how?

Food from the farmers against cigarettes! But what could you do if you could not get anything more from the family?

Note: I don't think the above paragraph makes sense.

Somehow Mother was able to get food from someplace, I don't know where.

Of course, new clothes were no issue. There were none. So we looked for old clothes, took them apart, turned them inside out and made something new from the pieces. Or we took old curtains or unraveled old sweaters, which had become too small. I see my mother forever mending old socks and stockings with a "mending egg" in the evenings.

Once Mother took an old military coat, cut it up and sewed it together in a new way. I finally had a new coat for the winter. I don't know how she did it.

The only new merchandise we sometimes could buy were "Clip Claps," wooden shoes that made this clicking sound when we walked down the street. When I hear this sound today, my mind is taken back to the bright summer days after the war in the Chiemgau.

I and my classmates were young girls then. Life lay before us, and except for some of the usual troubles in school, we had no other worries.

At that time I kept a diary. Unfortunately, it was lost in the course of some 25 moves to different places during my life. I remember one entry dated summer 1945: "The war is over, but when will we have the next one? The only thing we can do to prevent that, is for the countries of Europe to unite and become one country."

There were some people who believed in a United Europe at that time. I met with them and they gave me a button that said "VEREINTES EUROPA," which I proudly pinned to the collar of my coat.

There were two instances during that time that have made a permanent impression on me.

First, It was during those days when there was practically nothing to buy in the stores. Only the Americans had everything they needed and more. People went to the exit of the military mess halls to wait for the doors to open. Then the cook would come out and throw a lot of food into the garbage cans.

I was curious and joined the line. When it was my turn, the black cook threw a bag with coffee grounds toward me (coffee was a most treasured item at that time).

Note: "Are you imply that coffee grounds were used a second time to brew coffee?"

Suddenly I felt a wave of shame and anger rise up into my face. I threw the coffee bag back to the cook and left.

I felt sorry for the cook, who stared at me in disbelief, but I promised myself that never again would I get myself into such a degrading situation!

Traunstein, 1945, Family photo

The second occurrence would hold an even more important lesson for me. I was standing on top of a railroad bridge looking down. I noticed a well-dressed and good-looking man who was poking a stick with a nail at the end between the train tracks.

As soon as a train was slowing down to enter the train station, he would go after the cigarette butts that had been thrown out of the windows to pick them up with his stick and suck on them greedily.

This event sticks forever in my mind and is responsible for the fact that I never started smoking. I swore to myself that I would never allow myself to become so dependent on anything—or anybody—that I would have to degrade myself in order to get it.

The Joys and Woes of a Teenager

I was now a full-fledged teenager and went to a mixed school with boys and girls. I enjoyed learning new things. If only there had not have been this school principal! Her lips were pressed together tightly, and her hair was combed back into a bun. She wore a long black skirt and enormous boots.

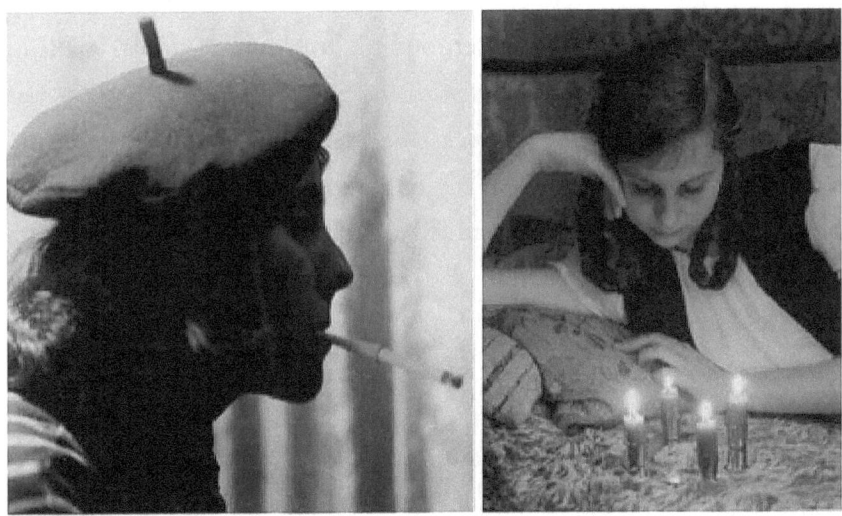

Eva and Maria, highschool years, Bad Reichenhall, 1947 Family photo

This was our principal, Frau Bach. She was also my math teacher. She not only looked like a witch; she really was one.

We just called her "die Hexe."

Hexe Bach had been a principal already under the Nazi regime and seemed the prototype of a mean, narrow-minded old spinster. She was a frightening creature and above all, a relic from the time of Nazi prominence.

Girls who were pretty and joyful, and who dressed better than others, were the special objects of her persecution.

My best girlfriend, Lilo (we had been friends since the age of 10), and I had to suffer a lot under her. Even the smallest mistake on our part was punished severely or we were made to appear ridiculous before the rest of the class.

We now were 15 and started to be interested in our looks.

The shops had been empty up until the conversion of currency in 1948. There were no clothes, no material for sewing, no wool, and no shoes. But there were the care packages sent by kind Americans. In one of these packages mother found a dress for me. It was made of black nylon and had a pattern with happy green flowers. Nylon was something special in those days.

It fit me perfectly and was my only pretty dress for years to come. Since I was growing, Mother added a band of green material every so often. There were three bands in all, and then I stopped growing.

This dress is connected with the following incident involving the witch Bach.

The theaters had reopened. Our school had been invited to see a performance of Schiller's *Die Rauber*. We were standing in the school court, the girls on the right side, and the boys on the left side. For this event I had put on my favorite dress and had borrowed a fine chiffon shawl with beautiful flowers from my mother, which I had slung elegantly around my head a la Grace Kelly.

Suddenly Hexe Bach snapped her fingers in my direction: "Schrankl, come here!" Surprised and not aware of any wrongdoing, I stepped out into the center of the court.

Then she shouted at me: "Take that shawl off your head immediately, you look like an "Amiflittchen!" (These were girls who sold their love for cigarettes and nylon stockings to the American soldiers in houses of ill repute). This was about the worst thing one could call a girl in those days.

I thought I would sink into the ground. And this in front of all the boys!

This was only one of the many mean acts against me by the Hexe Bach. Luckily I had good grades, so she could not do too much for the moment.

The other teachers were much nicer toward me, and they seemed to have more sympathy for our problems connected with puberty.

While growing up I probably needed a lot more explanation about the facts of life from my mother. But she was not very willing to talk about such things. Even though she was very emancipated, her relationship to men had suffered from the prudish teachings at the convent school in her childhood.

She considered me to be a nymphomaniac, only because she had found out that a boy had kissed me good night at the doorsteps after bringing me home from ballroom dance class.

To find out about these mysterious secrets between boys and girls began to become a very important topic among the girls. Our mothers had what they thought was a very good way to solve these problems: They gave us the well-known book by Van der Velde, *The Perfect Marriage*, to read. There we could find everything a young woman had to know to prepare her for marriage, expressed in inoffensive and romantic language.

For me it was the right book at the right time. Boys were beginning to become interested in me, and their interest in me aroused my interest in them.

I would say I fell in love with being in love.

My first love was Wolfgang from the boys' eighth grade. We had met in the ballroom dance class. He wrote love letters to me in the old "Runenschrift," an alphabet that the old Germanic Norsemen had used and which was still taught during the Nazi years.

I really liked Wolfgang.

But Hans Hass, the famous underwater archaeologist, who had given a speech at our school, fascinated me much more.

After his presentation I had asked him a few questions, and he told me that he would be glad to answer my questions if I would join him for dinner.

Afterward I showed him the old city wall in Traunstein.

The sightseeing tour lasted for hours. When I asked him whether women could also join his underwater expeditions, he just gave me a kiss and took me home without delay. Maybe this was the time when I started to dream of a world full of extraordinary men.

The year 1948 was the year of the Conversion of Currency. Every single person got 48 DM and no more. All the previously used coins and paper money became worthless overnight.

Suddenly the shops started to fill up with goods. But now we did not have any money to buy things. This situation did not last long, however, because with this Conversion the so-called German "Wirtschaftswunder" (economic miracle of Germany) started, at first slowly, and then it gathered momentum.

The year 1948 was a very important one for me.

I was turning 16, and we would have a big celebration. A celebration with consequences!

Mother had given me permission to invite my girlfriends to a small restaurant on the outskirts of Traunstein. We knew that the school had forbidden us to stay in public places after 10 o'clock p.m. But I thought that it was my 16th birthday, and my Mom knows where I am.

Mother actually did come at around 9:30 p.m. to see to it that everything was okay. We had drunk a few glasses of wine and were in a joyful mood. Long before midnight we happily went home.

The next day I was called to the principal's office. So was my friend Lilo.

Hexe Bach really gave me a dressing down. She said that it had come to her attention that my friends and I had been loitering about in public places during the night hours after 10 p.m. There was no way to explain to her that it was my 16th birthday, that I had received the permission of my mother, and that she herself had been present.

Eva and her best friend Lilo Nonweiler, 1974, Family photo

She just did not even want to listen to my explanations.

The next day I got an official notice from the principal's office. This was serious!

In my opinion, this was the height of injustice. I have had enough of this, I thought.

I went to my mother. Under no circumstances would I ever put my foot inside this school again. This was November 15 and in January, I would go to another school.

There was no discussion about it.

Many years later it turned out that the whole incident had really been a blessing in disguise.

My poor mother was shocked. She tried to insist that I should continue at the Gymnasium in Traunstein. But I remained adamant. I would go to any other school she wanted me to go to, but not to this one.

I decided to ask my father for help.

By this time my father had found a new job in the Bundeswehrbeschaffungsamt (Army Acquisition Office) in Koblenz on the Rhine River. Friends who had known him during the war had helped him, so that his application for denazification had been processed quickly and he had been allowed to work again.

I was sure Father would help me. He had always stood by me, even when he was at a distance and could only help me through his letters.

I waited until Mother had gone to sleep—I had already packed my little suitcase—and climbed outside through the bathroom window. I had to hurry to the train station and take the train to Koblenz.

Somehow my mother must have caught on to this. She intercepted me while I was waiting for the train and took me back home.

It had become clear to her that she would not be able to force me to go to this school any longer. She accepted my position and promised to find another school for me.

My friend Lilo and her mother had accepted the reprimand and had apologized for Lilo's breach of the rules. Many years later she told me that she now considered this as a mistake.

The Karl's-Highschool in Bad Reinchenhall

THE CONVENT OF ST. ZENO

In January 1949 my mother and I took the train to Bad Reichenhall. She had found what she considered the right school for me. It was the convent school of St. Zeno. This was the first time I was separated from my mother. I felt very good about it. A new chapter in my life had begun.

St. Zeno was a boarding school for girls run by the Englische Fraulein, nuns who specialized in the education of girls. My mother had herself had attended such a boarding school in her childhood and believed me to be safe there. I attended the convent school for one year. After that, I continued to live in the convent, but went out to the nearby school, the Karls Gymnasium for boys and girls.

The convent of St. Zeno in Bad Reinchenhall, 1949, Family photo

The first nights in the convent were oppressive. I felt doubly closed in by the convent walls and by the high towering mountains, which surround the valley where Bad Reichenhall is located.

But soon I had adjusted and began to love the convent. I especially loved the little romantic monastery gardens and the cloisters with the cross vaults, where I spent hours.

In St. Zeno time seemed to stand still. These walls had protected its inhabitants for more than a thousand years. In the year 1136 the convent had been mentioned in the archives for the first time. For me there were many things to investigate.

For example the life story of St. Zeno the patron of the convent, who looked down on me every day with the same kind smile. He came from Africa, Mauritania. From there he came to Verona in northern Italy, where he became bishop in the year 362 AD, the time of early Christianity.

The Cloister of St. Zeno, 1949, Old Postcard

I admired the wonderful stone relief on the side of the garden. It shows the protector of the convent, the famous Kaiser Friedrich Barbarossa, and in his hand the imperial insignia. He is represented there in the clothes of Charles the Great, whom he had admired very much. According to legend, he is still sleeping in the Unterberg.

Right beside it another stone relief depicts a fable by the ancient Greek poet Aesop, the *Wolf and the Crane*, which I had known since childhood.

On my way home from school I always passed a cross vault. Sometimes I entered this room of silence and left the busy world outside, and I would feel quietness and peace in my soul.

This architecture of the cloisters, an area, though closed off from the outside, did not seem to enclose me. On the contrary, it opened up an unexpected eternal universe to me, the exploration of which should become a theme of my life in later years.

I realized somehow that the individual Self had to turn away from the world outside toward an inner space in order to find God—the "Brahman." In the beginning I did have difficulties in school.

I had entered the school in midyear. I was far behind in math, French, and Latin, so I lost one year and repeated a grade. I did not mind that, because I really liked going to school. I loved books, and studying had never been hard for me. I enjoyed the feeling of suddenly seeing and understanding some new thought. What was harder for me was learning things by heart, like formulas in chemistry or vocabulary in Latin. In the first months I was under strict observation.

During our daily outings in the beautiful surroundings of Bad Reichenhall we were never allowed to walk alone.

The landscape around Bad Reichenhall is beautiful and impressive. This Bavarian health spa is situated in a valley that is surrounded by the high mountains of the Salzburg area. The little city has wonderful public parks for the people who come here for the cure of illnesses of the respiratory tract in the clear air of the mountains, and to take the healing waters of the saline fountains.

I somehow enjoyed the freedom of being on my own, away from mother's constant surveillance. For the first time I felt free in my young life, but this pleasure turned out to be of short duration.

I had never been able to keep my mouth shut about things I did not like.

I talked with my new friends openly about everything that came to my mind, about the strict sisters, the beautiful Mother Superior who had a clubfoot, about interesting books, and of course, about boys.

One day I was called to the Mother Superior's office. I was questioned inquisitively about what we had talked about during our walks. At first I answered somewhat evasively because I did not want to get my friends into trouble. Finally, I was being confronted with my own words about one of the sisters, word for word, because everything had been noted down on paper.

It turned out that among the girls who accompanied me during our walks there had been one whose job it had been to write down in shorthand everything I had said. I was the new girl and had to be carefully spied out. I was flabbergasted. God knows, I had imagined my new freedom to be different!

If my mother had overprotected me until then and had limited my personal space to move about, I experienced now for the first time that my mental freedom was being restricted.

This situation could not go on for very long—I was aware of this.

I had always been a rebellious girl, from early childhood on. Especially when something seemed unjust, I was not willing to keep quiet about it.

Events took the course they had to take.

I spent only one year in the convent school; then they wrote my mother that they did not think that I was the kind of girl that fit well into this type of school. They were probably right, but the reasons they picked were another example of injustice, I thought.

Of course some things had happened that did not meet with the approval of the sisters, but in my opinion these were not sufficient grounds to ask me to leave.

I tried to reconstruct the list of my transgressions!

Already as a child I had loved dance, and especially classical ballet. This was not well received by the sisters in the convent. Despite this, I went to ballet lessons secretly after school hours. I had hoped nobody would ever find out about it. This was my mistake! At this point I have to go back to my time in Traunstein.

My friend Lilo and I—we were still attending the Gymnasium— had a crush on the main actor in the famous play by Schiller, *Die Raeuber*. We brought him a cake for his birthday and asked whether we could possibly join the cast and work as extras on the stage. We were lucky. We were allowed to join the chorus in *Der Vogelhaendler* a popular musical, and to dance with the group in the cast.

I have always liked dancing and being on the stage very much.

In Traunstein I usually was asked to play the Mother of Jesus, St. Mary, in the children's Christmas plays—I must have had a very mild appearance.

When I was 17, our class in Bad Reichenhall performed the medieval French play *Columbine et le Chevalier* in French. I was given the role of the wife of the chevalier, who is lost to the devil by her gambling husband but later saved by St. Mary. We even performed this play on the stage of the Felsenreitschule, one of the most famous theaters in Salzburg.

Lets return to St. Zeno.

The sisters there were very strict and skeptical about anything that had to do with the body. Even normal body hygiene seemed suspicious to them.

In the summer of 1949 the weather had been hot, and in those days I felt the urge to take a shower at least once a week, especially in the evenings before going to bed. I felt sweaty and uncomfortable. We did not have permission to go to the basement where the showers were located more often than once a week. I thought these to be very silly rules and therefore not worthy to be obeyed. I remember my mother telling me that when she had been in the boarding school as a child she was allowed to take a bath only with her undershirt on.

I snuck downstairs after all had gone to sleep and the lights had been turned off.

At the beginning of the summer vacation my mother received a letter in which the Mother Superior informed her that I was in breach of the school's rules and would occupy myself in an undue way with my own body, and would not fit into this school. She suggested that I should leave the school at the end of the school year.

My mother was completely on my side. She considered the arguments by the Mother Superior just as ridiculous as I did. She never scolded me once.

I was very surprised when she told me that she had found a room in a small pension of good repute for me and I was allowed to stay in Karls Gymnasium in Bad Reichenhall and live by myself.

In the last year of school both of my parents moved to Bad Reichenhall and I lived together with them in a new home.

Celebrating the Abitur the class of 1952

The class og 1952. Foto Zenker, Bacd Reinchenhall

For the first time, I was responsible for myself. My mother's trust in me was probably very helpful to me. There would have been many opportunities to fool around and neglect my studies. I had girlfriends and many admirers, and I loved to flirt and have a good time. But that was all.

My attention was mostly centered on my work in school. I wanted to get good grades and pass the examinations for my high school diploma.

THE SONG OF THE SIRENS—CANTO I

It was the first day of the New Year of 1950, a day from a winter fairy tale. There was a crisp, cold breeze in the air and the snow crackled under our shoes. My girlfriend Marita and I were watching the New Year's ski jumping competition in Bad Reichenhall. The sunlight glistened on the snow-covered fir trees. We were admiring the courageous young men who threw themselves fearlessly off the ski jump into the valley below them.

Suddenly and seemingly out of nowhere the idea hit me: "This year I will go to Italy!"

Was my old childhood friend Athena talking to me again?

Never before had I thought about traveling, let alone going as far as Italy. And now, on this frosty day in the snow, I made a quick decision: "This Easter I will spend in Rome!"

Mother burst out laughing when I told her of my plan. "If you have the money for such a long trip you can go!"

This meant I needed money. The little allowance I received had been used up every month by my ballet lessons, and the in-service training I had done in the local hospital had been on a voluntary basis.

As I said before, I loved books. There was a little bookstore on a street close to my school. I had been there often. The owner was a nice old man, and one day we started a conversation. One week after New Year's I told him of my plans and that I did not have the necessary money. He asked me what I was able to do. He could always use a helper in the store. I was a student at the Gymnasium, and I could type a little bit, I said.

From then on I worked almost every afternoon in his store. My homework had to wait until after the store was closed. I packed books and took them to the post office, checked the mail, and dusted the shelves.

I thought that I could not go alone to Italy, so I looked around for a group to join. Soon I found out that the ASTA , the student organization at the University of Munich, was organizing a pilgrimage to Rome during the Easter holidays.

The trip would cost 150 DM, but I had only earned 70 DM so far. I decided to ask Grandfather Schrankl for help. I went to see him in Vachendorf. A trip to see the Holy Father? Grandfather thought that this was an idea that merited support. He gave me the missing 80 DM and his blessing.

Now I only had one more problem to solve, my age. I was only 17 years old and not yet enrolled at the university. My only chance was to convince the travel guide to let me come along. I wrote him a letter. We discovered that we both were born on October 31.

He was interested in meeting me, and when we met, he gave me (and my friend Marita) his permission to join the group and we became friends for life.

I was really lucky, because even the mother of my girlfriend Marita from Traunstein consented to let her daughter travel together with me to see the Holy Father in Rome. On April 10, 1950, I embarked on a fateful journey. Marita and I met our group at Munich's central train station and boarded the night train to Rome.

The first surprise awaited us upon our arrival at the Stazione Termini in Rome. When Marita and I got off the train, our group was nowhere to be seen. They had simply, inexplicably, left without us. We later learned what a scatterbrained fellow our guide really was! There we were, two 17-year-old girls amid the hustle and bustle of the huge Italian train station, without passports and without money, both of which our travel guide had with him. We did not even know the address of our hotel, and did not understand one word of Italian.

Thank God we suddenly thought of the address of a monastery of the Cistercian brothers in the outskirts of Rome, where a relative of Marita's mother lived. We took a taxi there, hoping the Good Lord would see to it that the taxi driver would get his money upon arrival.

After we had tried to make ourselves understood by means of hands and feet at the gate of the monastery, the young padre stood before us. He was the first human being after three hours that understood our language. What an adventure!

After listening to our story he said, "Only the Holy Father can help us now! Every day at noon he receives groups of pilgrims in front of St. Peter's Cathedral in the center of Rome. We have to hurry!"

We arrived at St. Peter's Square. I was overwhelmed at its expanse and beauty. I would not mind spending the night here. This was truly "the navel of the world!" All our worries had suddenly left us.

At 12 o'clock noon the different pilgrim groups that were in town were called up and welcomed. "We welcome a group of students from the University of Munich in Germany to an audience with the Holy Father!" we heard over the loudspeaker.

There they were, our people. I could hardly believe that we had found each other again in this enormous, international city.

Shortly thereafter I made a deep curtsy and grasped the outstretched hand of Pius XII. He asked me where I was from and I answered "from Traunstein—do you know it?" "Yes, I know it," he answered with a nod, to my great surprise.

From then on it seemed to me that I was moving about in a dream, seeing the holy city of Rome with the ancient remains of the Roman world, the Forum Romanum, the Pantheon, the Colosseum, and the thousands of churches built in medieval times up to the Renaissance. It was as if I were in a trance, and somehow it seemed that I had come home into a world much larger, more profound, and more ancient than the world I had known until then in my beloved Bavaria.

On the last day of our trip we took a bus south to Napoli, which would have an important impact on the rest of my life.

When I was standing on the railing of the ship that took us to the Island of Capri, a soft wind blew from the islands. This was the Mediterranean, the famous Gulf of Naples with its lovely islands Capri and Ischia and the volcano Vesuvio, all in the middle of the "wine-dark sea."

At this moment I seemed to hear the song of the Sirens, as they had chanted to the passing Ulysses:

> Come here, renowned Ulysses, honor to the Achaean name, steer your ship on land and listen to our voices.
>
> No one ever sailed past us without staying to hear the enchanting sweetness of our song,
>
> And then he went on his way not only enjoyed, but also the wiser,
>
> For we know all the ills that the gods laid upon the Argives and Trojans before Troy and we can tell you everything that is going to happen in the whole world.
>
> (Homer, *The Odyssey*, Chapter XII, (lines 184-190))

I would come back and listen to their song when the right moment had come!

This I promised, because I knew then that I would always return to that enchanted place.

Odysseus and the Sirens (Black figured Amphora, 4th cent. B.C.E.)

Chapter 5: A Year of Studies in America

A Fulbright Scholarship at Evansville College

It is July 20, 1952. I am sitting in an airplane in a window seat. The four turbine engines are making a hellish noise. The city of Munich below me is becoming smaller and smaller. The landscape is turning into a mosaic of small green and brown fields.

Then I am up in the sky, amid the clouds, and this is the way I feel: "I am going to America! Unbelievable!"

What had happened?

Three weeks before the Abitur (final school-leaving examinations), I was sitting together with my classmates in a large hall of the Maximilianeum (the Bavarian State government) in Munich. The minister of cultural affairs had planned to extend the number of school years from eight to nine years for our school. We hired a bus to drive to Munich so that we could protest against this new ruling. Our argument was that it was unfair to our age group to do this only three weeks before the final examination, since we all had made plans for the coming year already.

I had to do the talking and the representatives of the different parties actually listened to us, and we actually succeeded in convincing the minister. He decided to start the new ruling one year later for the next age group.

My classmates and I were just strolling happily on Maximilian's Bridge across the Isar river in front of the parliament building to celebrate our victory when I heard the hurried footsteps of a woman coming up behind me. She reached me exactly below the large statue of Pallas Athena in the middle of the bridge. She was a member of the SPD Party and had been listening to my speech.

"You there," she called out, "would you like to go to study in America? I know a lady from the American Consulate, Mrs. Hoerburger, who could arrange for that, if you are interested."

She went on to tell me that the American Consulate was looking for applicants for a Fulbright Scholarship to an American college. She thought I seemed to be a suitable candidate when she had heard me speak in the assembly.

It seemed that Athena, my old friend, was speaking behind me. "Just do it! Go West!" And without reflecting very long I answered her, "Yes, I would like to go to America."

I distinctly remember my feeling as I spoke. It was a this exhilarating feeling of freeing myself, and it reminded me of the feeling I had experienced as a small child, 15 years ago in exactly the same place, when I threw my hat into the river below.

One week later I received a registered letter with the invitation of the American Consulate to come to Munich to meet the committee that interviewed the candidates. My English was quite good, due to the contacts with Americans at the end of the war, and I was not worried. We sat down at an oval table, and then the 12 members of the committee asked me to tell them why I was interested in going to America and about my interests, part-time activities other than school, and my future plans—in English, of course. The board members seemed to like what they heard.

One week before the Abitur I received the exciting news that I had been chosen as the only girl among 50 boys to receive a Fulbright Scholarship to Evansville College (now the University of Evansville) in Indiana. It was one of the most sought-after scholarships and was named after Senator J. William Fulbright, who originated the idea of the scholarship. His idea was to bring young, intellectual Germans and others from around the world to the United States and teach them about democracy. Fantastic!

I was sure that I would pass my examinations, but I was doubtful whether my parents would agree to my going to America. They were both living in Bad Reichenhall at the time.

I did not tell my parents about this incident when I got home. And I still had a lot to do. I had to say good-bye to my friends, and to my fiancé, pack my suitcases, and spend time with my parents.

The subjects German, English, and French were no problem for me, but physics and the terribly long equations in chemistry were hard to remember. Mathematics gave me a chill of fear, because I knew that when I was nervous, I could no longer calculate correctly.

But I was lucky. My grades were good enough to convince my parents not to stand in the way of my happiness and with a heavy heart they agreed to let me go.

A week later I asked my favorite teacher—Mr. Schelenz, the teacher for German—for an interview. I put one question to him as we walked through the park at the school: "I would like to really achieve something great in life. How do I go about this?"

He thought for a little while, and then he said: "Whatever you are doing at the moment, even the most unimportant task, do it well and with a sense for excellence."

I will never forget this advice. It has helped me later in life, even if I did not always succeed in doing perfect work.

So there I was on the airplane on my way to America!

I thought of Helmut, my fiancé. He was a good-looking, nice, and decent young man. He was studying jurisprudence at the faculty of law in Munich and was two years my senior. His father had a well-known law office in Bad Reichenhall. He was a "good catch," as one says.

The course of his life was already predestined. He would take over his father's office. A life bourgeois and well protected. This was *not* the kind of life I was looking for.

I must add that he actually had not yet officially proposed to me, but he had been to see my father one day after my departure and had asked him for my hand. An engagement ring was in the mail to my new address in America.

During the coming year I would have time to think.

I was curious about how Americans would receive me as a German. Only now did we learn bit by bit all of the terrible things that had happened in the name of the Germans. I remember a discussion with my father that took place one year before my Abitur.

What role had he played during the Third Reich and the war? I admired my father very much and knew him to be a tolerant and kind man. But I needed to clear up this point in his past. This concerned the question that the young people of my generation keep asking, and later spawned the famous "generation 68: " "How could all this have happened in a country so aware of culture and philosophy—in the country of the "Dichter und Denker"—the poets and thinkers?"

This became the only serious confrontation that my father and I ever had. The occasion was banal. I think I had told him that on that day in school, the wife of a famous German writer, Gerhard Hauptman, had given a speech about America. During the discussion that followed about the Third Reich, she had said to me: "You should go to America; they like people like you over there."

Suddenly father and I were involved in a hot discussion about the time of Hitler's Reich. We especially discussed the crimes against the Jewish people. I had talked myself into a rage and screamed at him: "As a Colonel in the German army, you can't tell me that you knew nothing about what the Nazis did with the Jews. Why didn't you do anything against it?" We were standing in the living room, both of us with dark red faces, and for the first time I was in open opposition to my father.

"Do you really know what love of one's country and loyalty to one's people really mean?" he responded in a loud voice, obviously angry. "At that time Germany was in a desperate situation. At such a time you do not stab someone in the back. And by the way, you too will learn to knuckle under in your life."

"No!" I shouted. "I will learn a lot of things in my life but I will never learn THAT!"

Shortly after this confrontation I felt sorry for him, because he had snarled at me like an animal in a trap with his back against the wall. I have never found him to be as stirred up as on that day.

We landed at our first stop to refuel at the airport in Iceland's city of Reykjavik. What a gloomy place it seemed to me! No trees or green bushes anywhere, only rocks, dark-gray gravel, ice, and snow. I had always imagined the legendary island of Thule, to look like this, mystifying and inhospitable. No wonder it took a special hero like Sigfried to win and abduct the beautiful sleeping valkyrie Brunhilde from there!

But then we resumed our journey to New York, the next leg of our trip.

I could not take it all in. What a city! Breathtaking, the skyline in the light of the setting sun and the Statue of Liberty! I was overwhelmed. I wanted to come back to this town and stay there if only for a short time!

I was still dreaming of the future when we again took off, this time to the northwest to Lake Michigan, to Detroit. The flight took another couple of hours. What dimensions there were in this country! My home in Bavaria receded into my memory like a childhood toy village.

New York, NY, Arival view 1952, Old Postcard, Source unknown

College would start only a month from now. Until then, the American Field Service had found a place for me to live with an American family and get adjusted to the language and the American way of life.

The Woodhouse family was a typical American family. They were very extraverted, easygoing, very friendly, and hospitable.

The father was an architect, the mother a housewife, and the three daughters were in high school and college. The main topics of conversation were parties and friends, clothes, and some kind of entertainment, and of course "going shopping."

I was a bit disappointed. Nobody was really interested in Europe or Germany, or even asked me any questions about the life on the other side of the Atlantic Ocean.

After four weeks in Birmingham, Michigan, with the Woodhouse family, I went to Evansville, Indiana, where I was enrolled in Evansville College. My worries about having to study a lot to make up for any deficiencies quickly proved unfounded.

Every course I took was easy to understand. I had no problem with the language. I especially enjoyed the fact that I could choose any course I wanted. I took English Literature, Public Speaking, and Introduction to the Arts. I would have liked to take more, because I felt like a child in a candy store and did not know what to try first. The only course that I had trouble with and had to drop was Economics. I simply could not understand what the professor was talking about. It made no sense to me.

All the other courses were lots of fun and the examinations were easy when compared to what I had had to study in Gymnasium and taking into account that you never had to formulate your own answers but that the answers were already presented to you and all you had to do, was check one of them.

There is really an enormous difference in the quality of colleges across the country.

A good education is a very expensive investment for parents to make.

This may suggest that education is not very democratic in the United States. Achievement is being honored, however. Every good university offers scholarships to very able students and in this way an intelligent and determined student coming from a lower-income family can also get a degree from a prestigious university.

It is difficult to compare the American and the German school systems, because they are based on very different philosophies. While

European students who are able to go to university are being filtered out at a relatively early age (10 years), American pupils of all levels of intelligence stay together as long as possible. Only after high school do they separate into various tracks, higher education in colleges or different, more practically oriented, schools.

My Fulbright Scholarship also included a certain sum for basic expenses for a room and for food. My parents did not send me any money, and since I was planning to see more of the United States after school was over, I got myself a job with a Jewish family as a babysitter.

I had room and board free, so I was able to save some money for the trip after school was finished.

My American classmates were a disappointment to me. Most of the girls, especially those who were members of a sorority, were mostly interested in their looks and in boys. Interesting lectures or new ideas never seemed to be discussed outside of class.

With foreign students in Evansville College, Evansville, IN, 1952, Family photo

The foreign students were quite different. They were interested in everything, in America, the country, the history, the people and their problems, and politics. They were the only ones who asked me about my own country, Germany.

I had thought that I would be some kind of representative of my country and believed that I would have to explain the happenings in Germany during World War II, how Hitler had come to power, and what life was like during the war.

But I soon found out that nobody was really interested in these things.

One person who did show a lot of interest was a student from Bali who came from the royal family. He probably was more interested in me personally than in my country. But I enjoyed very much being courted by him since he was a very handsome and elegant young man. When he proposed to me, however, I did not consider Indonesia a place where I could be happy because of the extreme differences in culture and the distance from my homeland.

Lieutenant Philip Diehl Cox

The year passed quickly, and the center of everybody's interest was the final graduation ball. Every year Evansville College stages a formal dance, which was the high point of the season.

Our Foreign Student Advisor had arranged for me to accompany a young American Lieutenant to the dance. His mother had called her and asked whether she knew a nice young girl he could take to the ball.

I was pleased and curious. Now I would have my first "blind date."

I was excited and got ready much too early. I put on my black evening dress and draped a yellow hand-crocheted shawl over my shoulders. With a rose behind my ear, I felt like Carmen in my favorite opera and thus I was waiting for my unknown beau.

Exactly at seven o'clock there was a knock on the door. My heart was beating in my throat, I opened the door. There he stood before me. Tall and slim, dense black hair, and clear blue eyes in a finely chiseled face. He looked like my favorite movie hero, Gregory Peck, and I found him very likable from the first moment.

Lieutenant Philip D. Cox took my hand and he did not let go of it.

Eva Waiting for her blind date, Evansville, IN, 1953, Family photo

We danced all night and did not talk much. It did not seem necessary. It was love at first sight!

Finally, on the way home, we found time to ask and answer some questions. He told me that he was just out of ROTC and on his way to fly airplanes in Korea. When I asked him what his plans would be in the next six weeks, he said "I will marry you!"

Everything seemed so right and I said yes.

The next day Lt. Philip D. Cox wanted to take me to meet his family.

I really wanted to take a good look at Philip's parents before taking such an important step in my life, because as the German proverb says: "The apple does not fall far from the tree!"

Phil picked me up in his dark green Pontiac, and we drove to his home.

The family lived outside of the city. We drove up to a red brick house in the English style that was situated in a beautiful and large garden. There was even a small lake on the property.

Here the family lived with their four sons and two adopted sons.

As I walked up the stairs to the house, everything seemed like a perfect dream.

My fiancé was truly an officer and gentleman, and I was sure Father would like him.

He did strike me as very quiet, but I thought that he was probably very shy and that "still waters run deep," as another saying goes. I was sure that I would be able to "lure" him out of his silence in the end.

The family was not only well-to-do but was also socially minded. I liked all of his family members right from the start.

Phil's father, Dr. Warren M. Cox, Jr., impressed me by his open mindedness, intelligence, and education. He adored Ting, his wife, and her wishes were his command. Ting was the perfect lady, very quiet and always poised. She felt loved and admired not only by her husband but also by her six sons, her friends, and her neighbors. Everyone was always trying to prove his respect for her. Thus she reigned like a queen over her little empire.

Philip and Eva in Evansville, IN 1953, Family photo

One important member of her court was Henry, the black gardener. He took care of house and garden in a perfect "southern" way and seemed very proud of "his" family.

Phil's father was vice president of Mead & Johnson, the well-known baby food company.

As a young Ph.D. in chemistry he had been teaching at the university in Peking, China, when he met Ruby, his wife, who worked there as a nurse. From then on she was called Ting.

When I met him, his hobby was to give lectures about philosophy and the Old Testament at the university in Evansville. I guess he inherited this interest and his love for discussions from his mother, Eva Cox, who came from a Jewish family.

I have always maintained an affectionate relationship with him. It was he who, many years later, made me a present of a book that served as the impetus for me to continue my education: *The Second Sex* by Sartre's friend, Simone de Beauvoir.

Back to the wedding!

First of all, my parents had to be convinced to give their consent to the marriage because I was at that time not yet legally of age. Phil's father took it upon himself to write a letter to my parents in which he asked for the hand of their daughter in his son's name.

The preparations for the wedding occupied me so completely that I had no more time for any thoughts of doubt. There was also another problem. The Cox family was Presbyterian, and the Catholic Church in America did not favor mixed marriages. We could not get married in the Catholic Church.

I was still waiting anxiously for an answer from my parents.

Finally, one week before the wedding date, their telegram arrived. They did not want to stand in the way of our happiness, but they could not come to our wedding.

One day before the wedding, together with a fine bouquet of flowers, a little package arrived. Mother had sent me a beautiful white lace shawl. Now I knew I had her blessing and was relieved.

We were married on June 9, 1953, by a Presbyterian minister in the garden of Phil's house in Evansville.

Everything was like a German teenager would imagine the happy end of a Hollywood movie: The good-looking young Air Force lieutenant in his smart uniform, pleased in-laws, happy five brothers, smiling friends, and relatives.

I remember that shortly before the ceremony I suddenly turned to Phil's brother, David, our best man and said, "I really need a whiskey now!"

We were young and in love. It was springtime, and Philip had to go off to the war in Korea.

As soon as we had exchanged our vows, cut the wedding cake, and accepted the congratulations, we jumped into the green Pontiac and took off toward the west among the cheers and the rattling noise of something attached to our car.

Lt. Philip D. Cox and Eva Evansville, IN, June 1953, Family photo

It is the custom that friends of the newlywed couple tie a string of empty food cans to their car before letting them go on their honeymoon trip.

Mrs. Philip D. Cox

It was spring, I was in love with a nice American boy, and together we went on a discovery trip through the "Wild West." This was more than I would have dreamed of. And I was full of the joy of life. The future stretched out before us like the endless expanse of this wide land.

That night we made it to St. Louis, in the state of Missouri, where we crossed the "Old Man River," the Mississippi. There we checked into a little motel for the first time as Lt. and Mrs. Philip D. Cox, "JUST MARRIED!"

The next day we did not get a very early start, but we did want to reach Kansas City and begin to cross the great plains of Kansas. Until now the country seemed well populated and we met little traffic. But after Kansas City I began to feel that this was the end of the world.

The countryside stretched endlessly beyond the horizon. After half a day of driving, we had not seen any houses.

The highway pointed in a straight line to the west and we hardly met any more cars.

The radio became our companion. It announced to us in which area of this wide land we were at the moment.

The sun hovered over the landscape like a fiendish planet and shot its relentless rays against us like hot arrows. I felt I was in a furnace. This sun, which had always been such a kind friend in Germany, had now turned into a hostile enemy, which seemed to want to chase us away from this country.

In order to keep my temperature down, I had to wrap wet towels around me.

Once we passed what I thought to be a lake in the glistening heat. We stopped and I ran toward it, hoping to take a dip in its cool waters. I did not get very far when I found myself stuck in the mud up to my knees. Dead fish covered the edge of the lake that had receded to become a small, muddy waterhole. Cattle had completely trampled the shore of the lake.

In the evening the sunset of the Far West, a wonderful spectacle of nature, repaid us for the day's tortures. The distant mountains of Colorado were golden red on the horizon!

We had reached our first goal. Tired, overwhelmed, and happy, we checked into a small motel near a lonely gas station in the middle of nowhere. There was no air-conditioning. We were the only guests.

We left the flat countryside the next day and turned north, toward the red-golden mountains of Yellowstone Park. It was cattle and horse country here also.

After three days of driving we reached Yellowstone in the evening.

In the morning we drove slowly through the park. Philip warned me not to leave the car. We saw our first bear and then, not far away, we saw the masters of the prairie, a herd of wild buffaloes. The signs on the side of the road said that getting out of the car would be very dangerous. I was mesmerized, and despite this warning I could not resist getting out of the car and running into a field to take some photos of these imposing animals that were slowly and menacingly moving toward us.

At that time I also "shot" my first bear, as he came to our car looking for something to scrounge.

Philip stayed in the car, shaking his head about my stubbornness. He kept the motor running so that I could quickly hop into the car if the situation would become too dangerous. After using up all the film in the camera, I got back into the car, unhurt, and we went on our way.

Our next goal was the Grand Canyon. We passed Salt Lake City and the waters of the Great Salt Lake.

On arrival on the upper rim of this gigantic rift in the National Park, we rented two mules that patiently carried us down the narrow path to the bottom of this grand valley of the Colorado River. When the path became so narrow that one could no longer see the rocky slide leading down the cliff, I closed my eyes and thought, "I never heard of a mule slipping, so I will be okay, too." I marveled at this glorious spectacle nature had created there over millions of years!

From there we took the road over the Rocky Mountains toward Las Vegas.

I thought with awe and admiration of the early settlers who had braved heat, cold, and wild Indians on their hard journey to the West where they hoped to pursue their search for freedom, riches, and happiness.

We passed Death Valley with its summer temperatures of up to 104 degrees Fahrenheit, and feeling dizzy with the flurrying heat, went on our way to Las Vegas. That city seemed somehow bizarre. Like a Fata Morgana in the middle of the untouched and inhospitable desert, a world of such perfect artificiality! Night is turned into day and day into night, because even gamblers have to sleep sometime.

In the evening we strolled through the streets. We ventured into a small piano bar. Later that evening the piano player, who had recognized me immediately as a foreigner, asked me to sing a song from my country.

I was so surprised that I could not think of any other song than "Lili Marlene," which I thought people here might know. I stepped near the piano player, had a little tryout with him, and then sang into the microphone for the first time in my life. People seemed to like this song because they stopped talking and applauded loudly. A few minutes later, a gentleman sat down at our table, introduced himself as some producer from Hollywood, and asked me whether I would consider signing up with him. I looked so typically like a German Fraulein, just like he had always thought Lili Marlene must have looked, and he would make me a star.

Philip and I looked at each other and laughed. "No, thank you," I said. "We have just gotten married and have other plans."

Two days later we were on our way to San Francisco. From here Phil was to report for duty and start his assignment in Korea, but we did not want to think of his imminent departure yet.

We took a drive through this romantic city and enjoyed the view from the top of the hill over the Bay toward the Golden Gate Bridge and Sausalito in the background. In the evening we had dinner in a quaint old restaurant in Fisherman's Wharf, which at that time was still a run-down area full of crumbling buildings, before it had been turned into an elegant tourist attraction in the 1970s.

The next morning when we wanted to leave our motel—big surprise! Our car had been broken into and all our belongings were gone. Luckily we had taken our passports and some money with us, but besides that, we only had the clothes left that we were wearing.

We reported the theft to the police and decided not to let this ruin our good mood. We phoned Philip's father and asked him to please send us $500.—which he did the next day. Then we started driving south on Highway 1, along the coastline toward Monterey.

The expanse of the Pacific Ocean and the wildness of the rugged coastline were of overwhelming beauty. Those days in California seemed like a dream to me, a dream from which I would suddenly be roughly awakened.

On the day before Philip's departure we had taken a trip to the cliffs south of San Francisco to watch the seals on the rocks. Dressed in short pants and just a little top, we chased each other through the underbrush. We enjoyed the strong sunlight, the salty smell of the sea, and the eucalyptus trees and other exotic plants. I loved California and the lifestyle of the people.

But nature is not your friend on this coast, a fact that I was soon to learn.

Honeymoon trip to the California coast, 1953, Family photo

Because Philip would have to report for duty and leave for Korea early the next morning, we spent a wonderful day strolling hand in hand through the underbrush that covers the cliffs of the coastline. Our parting loomed on the horizon, and we tried not to think of it. We decided to have one last candlelight dinner together.

A splendid sun was slowly setting behind the Golden Gate Bridge, golden rays touched the waters of the bay, and even the infamous prison island of Alcatraz seemed a romantic place. With a heavy heart, we said good-bye to each other. We would not see each other for a whole year!

In the evening, Philip checked into his duty station and I returned to my hotel. I would also leave this city with its almost Mediterranean flair, the only city where I had felt close to home since my departure from Europe.

When I woke up the next morning I could no longer move. With my last strength I reached for the telephone and told the concierge: "Please help me, I am very sick!" Then I lost consciousness.

When I awoke I found myself in a hospital bed. My whole body was covered with blisters and itched painfully. I remember a doctor telling me with a serious face that I had been subject to a severe allergic reaction due to poison ivy. I was treated with cortisone and had to stay in the hospital for six days.

My plane back to Germany had left without me.

I hardly remember the days in the hospital; I seemed to have been in a state of stupor. I do not remember who paid for the hospital and doctor bills, probably the Air Force, since I was now Mrs. Philip D. Cox!

Philip had already arrived in Korea when I finally boarded my plane to Europe.

It had been a year full of adventures. I had attended an American college, had married an Air Force Lieutenant, had found a new family, and traversed a whole continent, the "country of unlimited possibilities."

How differently people thought in America! How small and unimportant seemed Europe to them! And how far away! No one wanted to learn more about the history of the continent where 100,000 young Americans had lost their lives. The liberation of Europe seemed "snow from yesterday."

High above the Atlantic Ocean the world looked so different.

But how did it really look in that summer of 1953?

America and Russia had won the war and divided the world among each other, and the Allies, France and Great Britain, played from now on in the second row.

Europe was divided. The Iron Curtain ran from Finland via Kongsberg on the Eastern Sea Coast straight through Germany and in the South through Austria. Then it went across the Balkans toward the Black Sea.

When the North Koreans attacked South Korea on June 25, 1950, a bloody encounter for predominance in Asia had begun and America's young men were again sent into a war. The Allies of Potsdam had become adversaries.

The war had already been going on for three years when Philip had started his tour of duty.

At home in Germany the reconstruction had begun. My parents still lived in Bad Reichenhall. Only in 1954 did they move to Munich when father started his new job as a high civilian official in the German Army in Munich.

I was truly anxious to see Mother and Father again despite the fact that I had decided to soon leave again. I wanted to spend the next year in Spain to learn the language. During my trip through the United States I had learned that many people in the South spoke Spanish. Young and carefree as I was, I did not ask myself if I wanted to spend my whole life in America. I just planned my own near future, full of curiosity and optimism.

Philip on his way to Korea, 1953, Family phoo

The Abduction of Europe by Zeus, Greek vase, 4th century B.C.E.

Chapter 6: "Wanderjahre"("Wandering Years") in the U.S. Air Force

A Meeting in Hawaii

One year later, I was again sitting in a very different type of airplane, in a carefree and curious mood, just as during my previous journeys.

Dressed in military overalls and flyer boots, my hair tucked under a cap, I climbed into the cockpit of a small Air Force fighter plane. Phil's friend and copilot wanted to show me the volcanoes of Hawaii from above.

Of course it was strictly forbidden to take civilians into a military plane, and a woman at that!

But nobody noticed me hopping up into the plane—with some help—that afternoon.

Our first assignment in America was in Sacramento, California. After a few months, Philip called me up from somewhere one day and asked me to meet him in Hawaii. I had taken the next plane out of San Francisco and had met with him for a short vacation in Honolulu.

A few days later he invited me to a trip of a very special nature. I found myself at the military airport in Honolulu.

I wondered why they would not put a parachute on my back. The pilot mumbled something, which I understood to mean, "If we have to go down, you better disappear!"

I was quite excited when the pilot, Phil, and I took off with a deafening roar of the engine. The pilot was trying to make an impression on me. He performed some rolls and loops above the island and then passed over the group of islands of Hawaii and its neighboring islands at a hellish speed.

We rose in circles up into the clear, limitless sky, and seconds later plunged down toward the dark blue waters of the ocean.

Hawaii from above! My nervousness was gone and I took out my camera. I was overwhelmed by the natural beauty and untouched wildness of the mountains below me, especially of the waterfalls. It was the world of the jungle as I had imagined it.

The mysterious green of the forests and then the sparks of the fires from the craters of the volcanoes, the white sand beaches with coconut palm trees, all that filled me with an extreme sense of adventure.

We circled one more time above the airbase and then came down in a sharp descent and to a quick stop. With a bit of shakiness in my knees, I quickly climbed out of the cockpit, glad to feel solid ground under my feet. With a proud smile Philip helped me down and took his "Sweetie" into his arms.

Eva outside of Honolulu, Hawaii, 1954, Family photo

There he was, my hero, my "Marlborough" man, and I could understand that Philip liked his work, and how this spectacle of speed and sense of control over the elements would compensate him for the tedious and dangerous aspects of his profession.

It was now the year 1954.

Philip had returned unharmed from his tour of duty to Korea.

He did not tell me much about his stay in that country. I imagined that it was part of his job not to talk a lot about his missions. Only later did I realize that it was probably part of his nature to communicate little about himself and his thoughts.

My year in Spain had been an adventurous intermezzo.

With the 500 DM that Philip sent me every month I had been able to make ends meet. I had found a room with a Spanish family. They cooked internal organs six days a week, but on Sunday there was some other food on the table.

I signed up for a class, "Spanish for Beginners," and later attended "Spanish for Advanced Students" at the university. I taught myself reading and writing by translating articles from the daily newspaper into German and then translating them back into Spanish, thereby checking my mistakes.

I signed up for a flamenco dance class.

I enjoyed nothing more than learning more about this graceful and passionate dance style, practicing the twirling of my skirt, the rhythmic clatter of my heels on the wooden floor, and expressing my moods by the sensuous rattle of the castanets.

Of course I took trips through the country, followed the procession through the dark streets of Granada on midnight of Good Friday in the Semana Santa, marveled at the Alhambra castle, a relic of the occupation of Spain by the Moors. I joined a flamenco dance group and visited the famous feria in beautiful Sevilla with them.

I saw one bullfight and was almost thrown out of the arena by the excited crowd when I cheered for the bull as he attacked the matador.

By the end of the year I spoke Spanish quite well and had a strong impression of Spanish culture.

I had not met Athena there. Even though Spain had been a Roman province 2,000 years ago, it had not belonged to the Magna Graecia of the Greek.

Back to Hawaii!

Philip had shown me one aspect of his military life. So this was what it was all about! My husband was one of the heroes of his country.

Only a few months ago we had met again in New York. I came from Europe and Philip from Asia. From there we had proceeded to Sacramento, California, our first assignment.

My odyssey had started.

For Americans, Hawaii is a dream island and at the same time a place of national trauma.

The 50th state consists of eight large and several smaller islands. On the main island, Oahu, is the capital, Honolulu. It had been known under the name "Sandwich Islands" and was known for its volcanic landscape, spectacular tropical vegetation, and most of all for its perfect climate. All year round about 60 degrees C or F?, mild winds, and a few friendly, short showers every now and then during the day.

Hand-in-hand Philip and I wandered through the lush countryside. I got to know the island and I got to know my husband. We stopped at a pineapple plantation and burned our lips from biting into the spiky outside of the fruit, and we found a ripe coconut on the beach, just at lunchtime when we were beginning to get hungry.

At the local markets we admired the lush and exotic fruits. I had never seen such a variety of shapes and colors. We wound "leis" made of the most beautiful flowers around our shoulders and felt like King and Queen of the island.

Philip showed me Pearl Harbor, the largest naval base of the United States in the Pacific.

On December 7, 1941, the Japanese Air Force had attacked Pearl Harbor and thus forced America to enter into World War II.

Traces of the attack had been removed, but the shock of the defeat still lingered in the memory of the whole nation and has assumed new meaning in the wake of the attack on the United States on September 11, 2001.

The islands hold 49 volcanoes. The most important ones are situated in the west of the main island, Hawaii, and they are still active.

We were just having dinner on the porch of one of the main restaurants on the beach of Waikiki when we heard a deafening noise in the distance. The night sky was painted in red and orange. One of the main craters had erupted, and we were witnessing one of the most impressive and awe-inspiring spectacles nature has to offer. Somehow the images of the fires in the night sky of the burning Munich came to my mind. Was this the work of Kali, the Hindu goddess of destruction and rebirth?

The holidays in Hawaii came to an end too quickly, but I had learned a bit more about my husband's world and a beautiful part of the United States.

SACRAMENTO, CALIFORNIA

I met with another side of the American way of life in Sacramento.

Philip's first tour of duty in the United States was at a U.S. military airbase in Sacramento. We had rented a small apartment in the center of the city. Philip had to return to San Francisco and from there to Korea, and I remained alone at home and had to tackle the problems of everyday life in a new and unknown culture. Since this assignment was probably only for a few months, I wondered whether it was worthwhile to get to know people and make friends. I did not know anybody in Sacramento, so I decided to join the Officers' Wives Club that met at the airbase.

There I got to know the other side of the "American way of life." The women there all shared the same fate; their husbands were always out of town, and they tried to find consolation in the Club. The major topics of discussion were the children, the food, or some entertainment like Bingo, Bridge, or a "crazy hat contest."

Serious subjects were not discussed, but there was quite a bit of drinking.

I did not find anyone with whom I could share my interests, and I was bored. At first I spent my time reading all the books I had not had time to read. But locking oneself up in a small apartment all day with a book quickly leads to depression.

I tried to go out to enjoy nature, but this was also not possible, because hiking along the highways alone or going through the dense forests without trails to follow was dangerous. In fear of "poison ivy," I finally decided to stay home.

Then I decided to look for a job. I discovered Arthur Murray's dance studio, where they were looking for instructors for ballroom dancing. I had always loved to dance; maybe I could even earn some money this way and have fun at the same time.

At first I had to take classes myself, Foxtrot, Cha Cha Cha, Viennese Waltz, Rumba, and Tango. I loved the training lessons and was looking forward to soon having my own pupils.

I passed the training period with flying colors and was offered a job—but only under one condition. The prospective teachers had to pledge beforehand how many dance lessons they would "sell" in the next few months. The quality of the instruction was unimportant. I had not imagined my future job to be a sales job.

This business model of committing yourself for something your students would have to decide for themselves in the future seemed really absurd and unethical to me.

I immediately quit my work.

Maybe I should have made an effort to understand what they had taught in college in economics class rather than dropping the course and taking Introduction to Philosophy instead.

My next project was the decorating of our apartment. I took a course in woodworking, learned to carve and work with wood, and built a bookcase for our books. Then I bought a sewing machine and taught myself to sew by buying patterns and materials. I made my own curtains. They were very beautiful but unfortunately never matched the windows again in the homes of our later assignments.

After I finished decorating our home, I joined a tennis club and began taking lessons. There I met two nice girls, and just when we were beginning to become friends, we had to leave because Philip's next assignment was near Houston, Texas.

Homemaking in Sacramento with our beagle Sinbad, 1954, Family photo

This was the kind of life we led for the next eight years. A life amid moving crates and suitcases, in the car with our pets—a beagle dog, named "Sinbad the Sailor," a parakeet in a cage, and tropical fish from an aquarium. (The latter usually did not survive the long trips in the car).

I felt like Ulysses being blown by Poseidon's storms from one island to another and back again, never knowing where he would land next.

It meant never putting down roots anywhere, meeting so many people and making acquaintances, and leaving them before they could become friends. We moved ten times in the next eight years—this was pure mobility—this was the life of my American husband in the Air Force.

A German proverb says three times moving is like burning down once. This would mean that we burned down three times.

Texas

From Sacramento, California, we went for a short period to Houston, Texas.

There the climate was unbearably hot and the air was very bad. There was no air-conditioning in those days. The smallest chore, like going shopping or cleaning the house, seemed like a major effort. To sleep at night was difficult because of the incessant humming of the fan and the fact that there was no cool breeze.

From there we moved to another airbase in Laredo, Texas, on the Mexican border near the Rio Grande.

Laredo was one of those faceless towns that one can often find in America. No real center of town, a gas station and a supermarket and the land surrounding it, flat, gray, and endless plains. And then there was this unbearable heat in the summer, up to 100 degrees Fahrenheit.

This was an ideal training area for pilots.

But for me it was pure torture.

I dreamed about my beloved Chiemgau, with its lovely green hills and the dark green forests, where you could hike for hours through the countryside and were inspired by the beauty of the mountains.

Here the landscape was boring and monotonous. So was the town. The officers' wives had no other pleasure than to drive cars across the border to Mexico to go "shopping" and smuggle cheap whiskey in the bottom of their cars back into the United States. I guess this was the only "kick" they could find to interrupt their boring lives. I must admit I also joined in on those "fun runs" because the Mexican side of Laredo across the Rio Grande offered a type of adventurous ambience and a new and colorful culture.

Philip and I agreed that it was time for us to have a child. We had been married for three years, and were becoming impatient. Since Philip had been home so seldom, this was not surprising. I went to a gynecologist to ask him about the "calendar method" and he informed me about all the details. From then on I kept a close watch with calendar and thermometer. After only a few months I was pregnant.

I was very happy when I heard that I would become a mother. If it would be a boy or a girl, that would not make any difference to me. From then on, my interests centered on the baby and my new role as a mother. I almost forgot where we were stationed.

But as soon as we were sure to become parents, we already were on the road again with dog, bird, and most of our things in the back of the car.

This time we remained in the South: Philip's new place of duty was in Greenville, Mississippi, in the "Deep South" of America.

The Rio Grande in Texas, 1955, Family photo

Small ranch in Texas, 1955, Family photo

GREENVILLE, MISSISSIPPI

The little wooden house we moved into was built on posts and had a large shady porch. It looked very romantic hidden amid the lush tropical vegetation, beautiful magnolia trees, and bushes with magnificent colorful hibiscus flowers. Curtains of long, delicate Irish moss hung from the branches and gave the whole garden a dreamlike, melancholy atmosphere.

The climate became a problem for me. We usually had 95 degrees F and 95% humidity.

The heat and the high degree of humidity lay like a cloud of drugs over the town. You just did not want to move very much and if you had to, you moved very slowly.

It was there that I was for the first time confronted with the great differences in the living conditions between the white and the black population. We were advised to avoid driving through the slum areas of the black population. But I was curious to see these people from "the other side of the tracks," black and poor white families, crowded together in run-down huts, surrounded by garbage and junk, living in intolerably poor conditions. The misery was just barely hidden behind a veil of green vegetation.

I was shocked. I seemed to be in a poor, undeveloped country. The "American dream," the right to the pursuit of happiness for all citizens, did not seem to be in the reach of the inhabitants of these areas.

What could I do about these injustices? For the moment, nothing, because I had my own family to worry about. But in later years I was able to make some contribution.

Barely moved in, I began to make a nice nest for my family and started to redecorate the house with great zest. Because of the humidity, the house had a damp and moldy odor that I could not get rid of, even after the most thorough cleaning with Clorox and Tide, the most common cleaning products of that time. I felt that I constantly had to clean everything, and I still did not succeed in chasing away the putrid smells and the ever-present roaches.

Soon I began to suffer from a very vicious type of allergy. Little blisters filled with a liquid began to cover first my hands and then my arms. They itched like hell and I could not touch anything with any acid substance. Even holding a tomato or a potato would immediately produce a violent reaction of my skin.

Whether this allergy was due to the strong antiseptic cleaning liquids of that time or whether they had psychological causes, the doctors could not tell.

This acute case of neurodermatitis caused my hands to look like red meat, and I had to wrap them up with bandages to keep from scratching. Finally, I could not do any more work in the house and I had to go to the hospital where I was treated with high doses of cortisone.

The acute attacks abated slowly, but as long as I lived in the United States I suffered from this allergy when subjected to humid heat and housework.

Since the hot and humid climate kept me from going outside, I tried to occupy myself with activities inside the house. I did not feel that I needed a television set at that time, and I decided to sew everything for my family and me by myself. Later I began to embroider nice wall hangings and tablecloths, and even a rug,

I spent many hours of the day reading. With every book I read, my homesickness and the strong desire to return to my home in Europe, my "Ithaca," grew.

I identified myself with the strong longing of Ulysses for his homeland, as it is so beautifully described in Homer's *The Odyssey*:

> Nothing is as sweet as our homeland and parents, even
> if you call a house full of riches and feasts your own
> among strange people and separated from your own
> family it mean naught.

Today one would say that I was a victim of what is called by psychologists "culture shock." The more independent I became, the more I was aware of the world around me, and the more I knew that this world was not my world. Added to this was the constant moving from one place to another, which made it impossible for me to become really acquainted with the way of life and to develop a feeling of friendship for the people around me. We knew many people, but there was no personal friend worthy of the name. As a consequence, I had only myself to turn to for the solution to any problem.

It was 1956. I had bought a small transistor radio to hear news about Europe via short wave radio. One morning I made out among the screeching sounds of the radio the desperate voice of a reporter: "SOS,

SOS, Save Our Souls! The Soviet tanks are shooting at our town!" In Budapest martial law had been declared; the population of the city was calling the Western countries for help. I was beside myself.

I ran to our neighbor's home. My American neighbors knew of nothing. I seemed to them as though I had come from another planet. Europe was endlessly far away for them. Who should be interested in a small country in Europe? Where actually was it located? Hungary, was that in Germany?

There it was again, the culture shock, my culture shock.

With whom, pray tell me, should I talk about the happenings in Europe?

Philip, my only point of reference, was usually out flying training missions. At the same time, when he was home I could not talk to him about my communication problems. He would not have understood what I meant. Didn't I speak English very well? What's the problem?

My problems would have put added strain on him, or might even have offended him, so I kept my problems to myself.

ARIANE IS BORN IN PHOENIX, ARIZONA

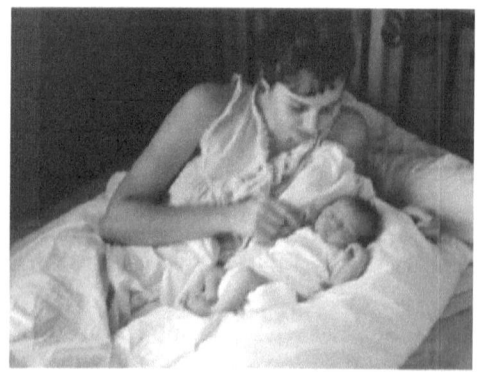

Baby Ariane in Phoenix, AZ, August 18, 1957, Family photo

Here we were on the road again, the car packed up with our belongings, with Sinbad in the back and the bird in the cage.

This time we were heading west again, toward Phoenix, Arizona.

I was sad to leave our romantic house in Mississippi, but now I had to think about something more enjoyable, our baby.

Arizona was a surprise for me. What a country with its singular play of light! The air is clean, crisp, and dry. The sun-baked primeval rock formations change colors from ochre to orange to dark brown with the light of the day.

The desert does not welcome an intrusion by humans.

Yet there seems to be a lure about the desert, challenging and honest, because it confronts man with the uncompromising demands of the forces of nature.

The beauty of the countryside made me feel close to nature as I had not found elsewhere in America. The vegetation with its wonderfully survival-wise cacti and palm trees fascinated me. It seemed to point back into a past that cannot be measured by historical terms.

Arizona has not only captivated me; it also had attracted many artists who lived and worked here. Max Ernst did some of his paintings here, and Frank Lloyd Wright built his house in the desert, Taliesin West. It is still today a home and inspiration to a school for young architects, artists, and craftsmen. Wright had been inspired by the nature around him as well as by the indigenous tradition of pueblo architecture. The original Indians had built their settlements by piling their adobe houses on top of each other on terraces that followed the natural rock formations. Thus they succeeded in integrating human habitat into the landscape in a pleasing and harmonious way.

By this time I was in my ninth month of pregnancy. Soon after we had occupied our little house in the adobe style in Mesa, a small town near Phoenix, my labor pains started. We were in the month of August and had no air-conditioning.

Suddenly the forces of nature came upon me. Philip took me to the nearest hospital and left me in the care of the local doctor. I felt lost and abandoned. At that time it was still common practice to send the father home and let the woman have her baby without any support by her husband, practical or psychological.

I would have welcomed my mother's assistance at the time, and was quite shocked when I heard the loud moaning and screaming of women in the rooms next to me who were also giving birth. This forebode nothing good for the coming hours. So I asked the doctor to give me a shot for the pain.

However, everything took a natural turn, and in due course, after six or seven hours—a short time for a first birth, I was told—a healthy, tiny baby girl was born and I fell into an exhausted sleep. When I awoke, the nurse put a little bundle into my arms, my daughter, Ariane.

She was a healthy, perfect, beautiful, and very sweet baby, and she looked at me in a curious way, as though she wanted to say: "Aha, you must be my mother!"

The happy father was notified of the birth and soon after came to visit us. He might have expected a son, but when he held his little daughter in his arms he seemed very happy and content.

I was a happy mother, but I had a lot to learn.

In those days no courses were offered to teach young parents child-rearing skills. We learned by trial and error. When the baby would wake up and cry because she seemed hungry, but then, after a few sips of milk, would fall asleep again, and this procedure would be repeated every half hour during the night, we were tired, perplexed, and helpless. Child-rearing practices have changed very much since then. Nowadays the closeness between mother and child is stressed much more than was the custom in those days.

My life changed completely. Sleeping, eating, and time for a bath—everything was determined by the rhythm of the baby.

It was a most fascinating experience to watch this little human being unfold and develop. Every day she made some new discovery and learned a new skill.

I must admit, however, that after a few months I became a bit impatient with my role as a mother. Feeding, bathing, changing, washing and drying 24 diapers all day long, and being completely controlled day and night by the needs of a small child was a way of life that began to frustrate me. It seemed that I was no longer in control of my life.

After several months I began to look for some activities outside the home. The local art school was looking for models for a portraiture class and I signed up. There I could take the baby with me.

I also started to play tennis again. My neighbors disapproved of these activities. One just did not take a young baby to the tennis court! I can't say that I completely ignored the criticism of my neighbors, but I did not like being reduced to just the role of a mother.

My life had changed drastically, and it did not seem very exciting at the time.

I wanted to use my time constructively with activities that produced some results or achieved certain objectives. I did not like wasting my time on the household and the decoration of houses, and chores that had to be done over and over again in an endless cycle.

So I learned hand-weaving and produced some nice cloth. I had already learned a few basic crafts like woodworking and sewing. So it seemed only logical that I turned my attention to architecture. The New York School of Interior Design offered a correspondence course in Interior Design, for which I signed up. Soon the material and the books arrived, and I immediately explored them anytime the baby was asleep.

During day-trips in the surroundings of Phoenix, I made some interesting discoveries. I became aware of the interplay of human habitat and nature, as demonstrated by the building methods of the Indian pueblos, with their terraced adobe structures. This organic way of building shows how shape and material can unite harmoniously to create a wonderful formal beauty.

Indian Pueblo village in Arizona, 1957, Family photo

I had heard that the famous architect Frank Lloyd Wright lived very close by. He had made his home in Arizona in the 1930s and had built his well-known house, Taliesin West, in the desert hills near Phoenix. There he lived until his death in 1959.

When Phil asked me what I wanted for Mother's Day, I asked him to plan a trip there.

We drove with Ariane in her bassinette and Sinbad in the back of the car to the famous site.

During the guided tour of Taliesin, Philip, who was not that interested in architecture, stayed with the baby in the garden and I went through the house, with Sinbad following me.

Taliesin became a formative experience for me.

As I entered the house, I knew at once: This is it! This is the kind of house I would want to live in! I did not know then that this wish would be fulfilled two years later.

The structure of the house resulted organically from the conditions of the surrounding landscape and the requirements of the purpose, and used the natural building materials that were available in the area. The architect had joined together the interior building with the nature that surrounded it in such a way that the transitions from inside to outside and vice versa were gradual and hardly noticeable.

Just how well he had succeeded in implementing his idea was vividly demonstrated by our dog Sinbad. As we entered Wright's living and working area and were gathered in reverence around the oaken desk of the "master," Sinbad actually raised his leg and urinated at the base of this desk.

Sinbad had always been a perfectly well-trained dog and had never had any accidents inside a house. This time he obviously thought he was in the garden.

Las Vegas—A Fata Morgana in the Desert

Our next assignment sent us to Las Vegas, Nevada. That city was an artificial oasis for night owls, gamblers and sharks, alcoholics and drug addicts, movie stars and starlets, lonely people, winners and losers, and Mafia bosses and criminals.

This city of megalomania is really the exact opposite of Wright's idea of harmony between man and nature.

The town seems a gigantic artificial structure in the middle of the desert of Nevada. Artificial living space has been created by means of technology, and vast amounts of money as if in defiance to the inhospitable surroundings of the desert.

Endles Highway in the West, Old postcard

A life in accordance with nature was at that time only possible for the farmers. But they also considered nature as their source of income and not as a place for contemplation or as a counterbalance for a well-balanced life.

One can say that generally, throughout the whole country, nature shows itself as rather hostile toward man—blazing sun in the desert areas, impenetrable forests in vast areas, filled with poisonous plants or endless swamps accessible only by motorboat. In addition, there are the vast distances that can be overcome only by motorized means of transport, and these distances add to the feeling of being lost once one moves away from urban centers.

The idea of the pedestrian was not a general concept in the United States at that time.

There were no paths for what we call in German "Spaziergaenger." Sidewalks were found only in larger cities. The car was the only mean of transportation. I remember one incident when I had been in college in Evansville. I had taken a walk on a bridge across the Ohio River and was standing against the railing looking down into the river. Suddenly a police car pulled up behind me. The Sheriff got out, took my arm and said, " For a nice girl like you, life should not be so bad!"

People from passing cars had called to inform him that there was a girl on the bridge who obviously wanted to commit suicide.

Las Vegas was to me a fiendish place. During the day it was a dead city and at night a hell. Gambling saloons and gambling machines—"one-armed bandits"—wherever one went. Even in the post office and the public restrooms, wherever people had to wait, one could not escape them.

In the last 50 years, however, the American attitude toward nature has changed a lot. Today most people regard nature as "Mother Earth," worthy of love and protection for the well-being of mankind in the future.

During the day in many houses the windows are darkened and on the door a sign appears saying: "Don't disturb! Day sleeper!'

One day Philip discovered his interest in gambling. He went out several times a week. Sometimes he brought back some winnings, but most of the time these were lost again.

Soon money became scarce, so we gave up our apartment and shared a larger apartment with another young couple. They were nice, and we became friends. Only for the baby there was too little room, and Ariane's baby crib had to be put into the closet in the hallway. Thus the bedroom door had to be kept open to hear her cry during the night.

Two days before Christmas Day, I realized that our money would not suffice for a really nice celebration. I took the remaining household money and went to the gambling casino. There I witnessed how a completely drunk and stupid customer—they served you free drinks as long as you remained at the gambling table—had won enormous amounts of money all evening long.

I was sure I would be able to do the same and bring home a lot of money to increase our holiday funds.

But I had badly miscalculated my abilities. In a short time I had lost even the last remains of our food funds and sneaked back home with a terribly bad conscience.

This was another valuable lesson for me, and I never was tempted to gamble again.

Philip listened to my story with a laid-back sort of reaction, while the other couple looked disapproving for a little while—and then everyone started laughing.

There was now a new challenge: How could we celebrate Christmas without any money?

On the next day we drove to the nearby mountains, and cut a little tree.

With the last few cents in our pockets we bought some boxes of popcorn. Then we set about stringing the popcorn on thread and decorating our Christmas tree. My mother had sent me real candles and candleholders from Germany. It was the prettiest tree anyone had ever seen.

We found a few cans of oyster stew and some corned beef in the kitchen cabinet.

As unholy as the stay in this town had been, the Christmas of the year 1957 still lingers in my memory as one of the most enjoyable holidays in my life—a Christmas completely without money or presents!

But then everyday chores took over again.

Life in this town became more unpleasant every day. Philip had asked to be transferred to another duty station. In the meantime, he sent the baby and me to his parents in Evansville. I was happy to have escaped unharmed from this hell of artificiality and vice.

Never would I have dreamed of what would happen when I had to come back to Las Vegas again six years later.

I have always had a very good relationship with Philip's parents from the beginning.

Ting Cox was a soft-spoken and kind woman, a good mother, and she lived the typical American life of a housewife—children, kitchen, and neighborhood.

With Dad (my father-in-law, Warren, Jr.), I could discuss everything. He was very well educated and interested in everything. After dinner we would talk for hours in front of the fireplace. He drank his usual martini, and I felt safe and secure.

Dad liked to compose short sermons on certain parts of the Old Testament, which were later replaced by weekly family letters about interesting subjects and were sent to all family members who were absent.

I was the only one of his daughters-in-law with whom he could really have vigorous arguments, which we both enjoyed. One bone of contention, on which we liked to disagree, was the term "culture." In line with my critical character, I had provoked him by making the simple statement that America had no culture.

Only after many discussions did I realize that the disagreement resulted from a different definition of the term "culture." This term has a different meaning in English than in German. In English, "culture" has an objective connotation meaning "way of life." For instance, one can say the "culture of the aborigines in Australia," or the "culture of early cave man." In German, we would call this "Zivilisation," whereas in German "Kultur" implies the fine arts, music and theater, and intellectual activities.

We also discussed the relationship that Americans had to the space around them in this seemingly limitless country, which shaped their attitude toward nature. In Europe, every square meter of ground has been worked by people over generations, and so it had to be taken care of for the next generation. In America, people felt that they could simply move on when one plot of land had been exploited.

Another topic of discussion was the military life. The United States has a professional army. This means that the army is a job like any other job. The military profession is well respected in America, because a soldier serves his country and Americans are proud of their country.

Ariane with Henry at 'Turmoil', Evansville, IN, 1957, Family photo

Consequently, the attitude of the population toward the military is very different from that found in Germany, a country that lost two wars and survived the horrors of the Third Reich. Most people disliked the idea that Germany should again have an army. Those who supported the idea were easily suspected of dreaming national socialist dreams again.

When I met Philip in his good-looking officer's uniform, I had been quite impressed; maybe that because he reminded me of my father, whom I had seen as a child mostly in uniform. Phil was a responsible, reliable, well-mannered, and very quiet young man.

He was always laid back and introspective. Also, in these respects he seemed to resemble my father. However, he seldom communicated his thoughts and kept his emotions to himself. I would have wished for a more active interchange of our inner worlds. Then, maybe, I would have understood him better.

Ulysses and the Sirens, red-figure stamos, (5th century B.C.E.) See Source Index

Chapter 7: Return to Europe

The Ferme de Bel Air

There I was again in my "air ship" sailing across the big ocean, this time with Philip beside me and Ariane on my lap. We were on a flight from New York to Paris.

During the preceding few years, I had entreated Philip to apply for an assignment in Europe. Then one day, while in Phil's home in Evansville, we got good news! Philip's next tour of duty was in Nancy, at an American NATO airbase in France. I was overjoyed, and Philip was also looking forward to his new assignment.

The American unit was stationed in Pont-a-Mousson, between Nancy and Metz. The families were housed in mobile homes. Such housing was not at all acceptable to me. So we decided to live outside the military zone and went in search of a suitable home.

We found a charming old farmhouse on top of a hill overlooking the Mosel River, with the name "Ferme de Bel Air," in Pont-a–Mousson, near Nancy. This farm was situated in the midst of extended orchards full of mirabel fruit trees (yellow plum trees) and was surrounded by green pastures where some fifty head of cattle were peacefully grazing.

The animals were taken care of by a farmer who came twice a day. We had the huge farmhouse all to ourselves.

The location was delightful, but the house was in a very poor condition.

But I did not mind that at all. On the contrary, I had had a lot of practice in renovating and decorating homes in the recent past, and this situation gave me an opportunity to apply my skills. We were willing to invest a lot to make this blessed place into an enchanting home.

Philip had to leave again for flight training in North Africa soon after we settled into the house, and I went to visit my parents in Munich to show them their little granddaughter. They had moved from Bad Reichenhall to Munich and now lived in the Sckellstrasse, near the park behind the Bavarian Parliament.

We spent wonderful days in Munich, and Ariane was the joy and pride of the new grandparents. Of course my parents and Maria spoiled her all day long.

I told them about my plans for the renovation of the farmhouse. Mother immediately put an ad in the newspaper for a suitable maid and Father looked for a craftsman who would help with the building. A few days later I returned to Pont-a-Mousson with a nice young girl and a competent plumber.

My first project was to install a bathroom with a bathtub and a toilet.

Then I proceeded to paint and decorate the walls. I had found some lovely wallpaper in Munich and with the help of the girl and the plumber I covered the walls of the bedroom, the living room, and Ariane's room. I sewed new curtains and tried not to worry about whether they would fit our next home after that.

During our next trip to Munich I introduced Philip to my parents. They liked their new son-in-law very much, even though communication was somewhat reduced by the fact that my parents did not speak English very well. So Mother tried to show her care by constantly offering him all kinds of Bavarian specialties to eat, which Philip did not appreciate after a while and misinterpreted her attention in a negative way. (Cultural differences!)

Philip bought me a young German shepherd dog named Arco that protected us from then on in our isolated house. He turned into a very handsome dog that was very serious about protecting us. After some three months, the old farmhouse had been turned into a really beautiful home and had all the modern conveniences.

Ariane was now already one year old and a pretty, lively, and inquisitive little girl.

Ariane and Arco at the entrance to "Ferme de Bel Air," France, 1958

It was time for a little brother or sister for her. I did not want her to grow up alone. I still remembered the negative sides of growing up as an only child.

Bel Air was a wonderful home, my parents were not far away, and we hoped to be able to stay for at least three years. So this was a good time to have a second child.

Vivian Is Born in France

On a beautiful day in spring, on May 18, 1959, Vivian Louise was born.

My labor pains had started, and Philip rushed me to the military hospital in Pont-a-Mousson. But then Vivian decided that she was not quite ready to enter this big, dangerous world and the doctor sent me back home. Eight hours later we came back to the hospital and the doctor gave me a shot to speed up the birth process.

It seems that Vivian had been right about waiting to make her appearance, because during her birth a terrible thunderstorm started and the whole hospital was flooded. The nurses paid no more attention to me when I told them that the baby was about to come.

If I could have walked out at this moment I would have done so, but then everything went very quickly, without any need for medication.

Now we had another little girl, and it was hard to tell which one was sweeter. I was happy to know that my girls had each other and made sure to teach them to be responsible for each other in the future, because I would not always be around. We were a complete family now, and Philip and I were very proud parents.

We enjoyed our beautiful home, the lovely garden, and especially the two little girls who presented us with a new adventure every day.

I had time to occupy myself primarily with my children.

Philip was frequently gone for flight training, and when he returned I did not want to drag him through the country for sightseeing. He wanted to be left in peace and play with the children, read, or play golf or chess. Consequently, we did not participate in "the French way of life," which is meeting with one's neighbors and having a good time drinking wine, eating delicious food, and chatting.

I did not want to waste my time with a lot of social life. There were not any close neighbors. The French people were not interested in establishing friendly relationships with Americans who would not stay long anyway. The military people were living in their "covered wagons," completely shut off from the local life around them, since they did not speak French. Whatever was going on in the officers' wives' club was of no interest to me.

The family under the Christmas tree, France, 1958, Family photo

Christmas 1959 and 1960, France, Family photo

But I had my two lovely little girls, our beautiful dog Arco, our good maid from Bavaria, and "my home was my castle."

I missed my husband, who was gone most of the time, but I did not feel lonely. There was always an option to see my parents or old school friends in Munich. Sometimes they came to visit us on the farm, or I would pack up everybody in the car and drive to Munich. There Grandpa invited everyone to the Oktoberfest, and my mother and my parents' maid Maria spoiled us all with Schweinebraten and Knoedel, Plaumenmus and rote Gruetze. Then I would catch up on the newest theater plays or movies, music, or books. Once I even found time to take an exciting trip to Paris together with my cousin Elisabeth from Vachendorf.

Our life consisted of the pleasant daily routine of a country home, surrounded by nature and the farm animals. Everything revolved around the two little ones, and there was no television.

Often we took a picnic lunch out into the garden and enjoyed our meal under the flowering fruit trees, took walks in the nearby forests with Arco making sure nobody came too close, or we just looked over the hills to the valley of the Mosel River.

Every day I discovered new adventures together with the children. They were developing very well, were healthy, and were usually well behaved. Of course they seemed to be very intelligent to their proud mother.

Ariane was talking quite well already. During the day we spoke German, and when Daddy came home in the evening, we spoke English.

I was already dreaming of the day when I would travel through Europe with them, to show them all the things that seemed interesting and were so dear to me.

Life in this idyllic Arcadia proceeded in an undramatic way; it was governed by the course of the seasons, the cycle of the sun.

The most exciting adventure that could happen was when Arco again chased and killed a chicken of the neighboring farm and proudly placed it at our feet.

I was never afraid to be alone, but one day a strange incident happened that did indeed strike me as very eerie.

Life in Europe, 1960, Family photo

One evening I heard a strange noise. It sounded like someone snoring or snorting. It was coming from the high tower beside the barn on the other side of the courtyard. At first I thought I was imagining things.

On the next evening I again heard the weird noises. I called the maid, and she confirmed that she too could hear some unidentifiable noises. We did not dare to climb up into the tower at nighttime; who knows whom we would find there? Maybe some roaming tramp had made a bed for himself there.

A few days later Philip came home and I told him the story. He listened but could not hear anything. As soon as Philip had left, I again heard the spooky noises. Now, I wanted to investigate this mysterious situation. I took a tape recorder and taped the sounds coming from the tower to play them to Phil when he came back next time.

But when the noises continued every evening late at night, I lost my patience. I wanted to find out for myself from where they came. The maid brought a long ladder, and armed with a flashlight, I climbed up into the tower.

Suddenly I found myself in a ghostly white cloud. Everywhere hoarse shrieks and a fluttering of feathers surrounded me. I was startled. The flashlight fell out of my hand and it became pitch black. After a while I saw in the dim light the "ghost" that had haunted us every night: In the tower there was a nest filled with young white owls. I had scared them up with my flashlight. The downy little birds were just as startled as I was. But soon they settled down again, six in a row, on the top rafter under the roof and looked at me with big reproachful eyes.

Their mother had flown out to hunt and they were crying for her.

We laughed in relief, and I was pleased to know that Athena had not forgotten me and had sent her owls to keep me company.

Ariane and Vivian "Schwesterchen, komm tanz mit mir..."
German nursery rhyme, 1961, Family photo

But our life in Arcadia was to end abruptly.

It was a bright afternoon in June 1959.

Arco was running through the garden to scare the chickens, and the cows were peacefully grazing, accompanied by the rhythmic ringing of their bells. It had been a pleasant warm spring day. The sun was about to set behind the hills in the west and painted a mild Monet-like light over the landscape. I was reading a little fairy tale to the children.

At that moment, Philip came home. "De Gaulle had a falling out with the Americans within the alliance of the NATO forces. France will be leaving NATO. The American airbases will be closed."

And then the thunderstorms of politics swept over us and brought our life in this Garden of Eden to a sudden end.

We had to pack up and leave again!

For just barely one year we had enjoyed the pleasures of this beautiful place. It had been the longest period in one place since Philip and I were married.

I just had begun to practice my French and made a few friends in the city of Nancy.

In two months we were to move to Germany, to Bernkastl near the Mosel River. This would be, I think, my sixteenth move. I had lost count.

Bernkastl was somewhat closer to Munich, but this was only a small comfort for the loss of my newly found Arcadian life in Bel Air in Pont-a-Mousson.

After a three-month stay in Bernkastl we were stationed in Ulm.

Philip had agreed to spend our vacation in Italy, while my mother took care of the children in Munich. My parents loved the children and for them it was a rare pleasure to see them more than a few days, especially since Maria did all the cooking and cleaning.

I was thrilled to return to the happy place of my teenage years.

We drove to Florence, then to Rome, and finally to the Gulf of Naples.

Quo Vadis—The Song of the Sirens—Canto II

At least once a year I come to this place. For me it is not only the most beautiful place in the world, but it also is almost a sacred place to which I own the fulfillment of my favorite dream.

The gardens at Villa San Michele are situated high above Anacapri. On certain days the sky, the sun, and the sea unite to become a mythical meeting place for the gods. Together with the marble Sphinx, I love to dream about the presence and the past of the Gulf of Naples. My hand touches the warm marble of her back, just like on that day, many years ago, when Philip and I stood here together in Axel Munthe's sumptuous villa on the rock above Capri, way below us the sea, and in the distance the Sorrentine Peninsula veiled by floating clouds.

The marble Sphinx that Axel Munthe had brought from the mainland to the island rests on the farthest corner of the garden wall, just at the spot where the garden seems to break off abruptly into the sea below. She turns her back toward the villa, and her face, looking toward the distant peninsula, is invisible to any visitor.

The sphinx in the villa of Axel Munthe on Capri, Italy 1959, Family photo

View from the sphinx in the villa of Axel Mun the on Capri, summer 1959, Family photo

Every time I place my hand on her back I make a wish. I know that wishes will be fulfilled if one desires something with all one's heart while one's hand is placed on the back of the mystic creature. The living proof of this phenomenon is our house, *Quo Vadis*.

"*Quo Vadis?*" *Where are you going?* I had to ask myself this question so many times during my marriage to Philip. We always had to start anew. We always were being moved to some new, unknown place.

In August 1959 we were on the way from Naples to Capri. Philip had fulfilled a wish of mine and had taken me on a trip to Italy as consolation for the loss of our dear home in France.

I was overjoyed to be able to finally show him "my Italy." I took him through the city of Naples and showed him all the places of interest that I still remembered from my trip nine years before at Easter in 1950. He seemed to like the area very much.

We continued to Sorrento, and from there by boat to Capri. The sea was dark blue and the silvery rays of the morning sun touched the steep rocks of Capri. Hand in hand we followed the ancient trails of Tiberius. I told Philip about the lonely Roman emperor who had lived on this island for the last ten years of his life. He left many remains of the twelve villas he had built, stone witnesses to the splendor of the Roman Empire in the Gulf of Naples. The island has never lost its original magic. It has survived all the storms of history, Greek and Roman, the dark Middle Ages, and the tumultuous following centuries.

Amid the encounters of worlds and cultures it has remained a place of refuge for the rich and powerful, the artists and literates of their age. Even today the sensitive visitor can feel this magic when exploring the hidden paths of the island, away from the modern tourist track. In moments of "lucid stillness" in the gardens of San Michele, on the rock of Tiberius, one can still hear these voices from the past, the enchanting voices of the Sirens that bewitched Ulysses when he sailed past these shores.

Philip had already entered the little chapel of San Michele, which lies in the northernmost corner of the garden, directly under the mountain slope. San Michele overlooks the whole Gulf of Naples from here.

I was standing directly behind the Egyptian marble Sphinx that Axel Munthe had brought from the mainland to the island. I was awake, but at the same time I was in a dream. Far below me I heard the pulsating sounds of the waves beating against the rocks, and I saw, across the sea, the coastline of the Sorrentine Peninsula in the mist of the morning sun.

There they were again, the voices of the Sirens, this time more perceptive:

...

And he who listens will go on his way not only charmed, but wiser,

For we know all the ills that the gods laid upon the Argives and Trojans before Troy

And we can tell you everything that is going to happen in the whole world.

I put my hand on the Sphinx's back: "Let me find a secure anchoring place for the rest of my life here in these lovely grounds!"

The Sphinx seemed to answer me.

I should turn to Athena, who had had her temple there at the southernmost end of the peninsula more than two thousand years ago. The Romans had called it "the temple of Minerva," the Roman name for Athena, and which, some legend tells us, was said to have been founded by Ulysses himself when he had passed the rocks of the Sirens. It had given its name to the whole peninsula, the "Promontorium Minervae" of ancient times.

Suddenly Philip stood beside me. "Are you dreaming?" he laughed. "Let's go on!"

"Just give me another five minutes " I pleaded.

The next morning we started from Sorrento to follow the coastline to the end of the peninsula across from Capri. We took the highway called "Nastro d'oro," the "golden ribbon." Sorrento is an enchanting little town, situated on a steep plateau above the sea, south of Mount Vesuvius, and is of Greek origin, owing its name to a temple of the Sirens said to have been located in the ancient city. Sorrento comes from "Sirenussai," land of the Sirens. A legend says that the city was founded by a son of Ulysses and Circe.

Athena seemed to guide us, and at the end of the day, to lead us to Santa Maria Annunciata, a fortified citadel above the harbor of Massa Lubrense. According to another legend, the church of Maria della Lobra was built on the remains of the temple of the Sirens. But historians still disagree about the precise location of this temple, the existence of which has been mentioned in various historic sources.

The view from Santa Maria Annunciata was overwhelming. The blue waters of the Gulf gushed into the little inlets of the rocky coastline in big waves. On the hillsides small settlements clustered like bird nests on the steep precipices. In the distance to the north, Naples glimmered in the blue mist, while in the center of the Gulf the volcano Vesuvio pointed into the sky like an enormous exclamation mark, calling attention to the enormous powers only sleeping beneath it, always ready to awake and reinvent the life around it. Below us spread the terraced land with the fabulous lemon groves of Massa Lubrense.

"This is the place where you have to search," Athena seemed to whisper.

We took the curving road back to Sorrento. Suddenly a sign on the side of the road caught my eye: "Si vende," "For sale," it read.

We turned the car and followed a steep side street, descending toward the coast amid olive and lemon groves. "Where defiant rocks surrounded the shore and the roar of the breakers resounded from the cliffs." (Homer, *The Odyssey*)

The street came to an end in front of a large house surrounded by a walled garden. The door opened, and a small, vivacious man with sparkling eyes greeted us.

He was the architect and spoke only French. Somehow he reminded me of a faun with his mischievous eyes and vivid gestures, and he seemed to have been waiting for us.

"We saw the sign on the road and are looking for a piece of land," I said.

He scrutinized us intently and then motioned to us to follow him.

He led us to his most beautiful piece of property, a terrace, high above the sea on the hill, amid olive and lemon gardens. The intoxicating, sweet fragrance of the lemon blossoms lay in the air. The bright chirping of the birds came from the olive groves, where silvery leaves glistened in the gentle breeze from the sea.

The sea below reflected the golden rays of the setting sun and painted the waves in hues of myriad colors. To our left the island of Capri cast its shadows, across the sea Ischia marked its dark silhouette against the sky, and to our right the lights of Naples began to sparkle in the growing darkness.

"Even an immortal god, if he passed by, would halt his step and would enjoy gladly this view." (Homer, *The Odyssey*)

Two hours later the contract for sale was signed and the property was ours.

Again, this was a fast decision. I knew that in life it is the present moment that counts. Yesterday has passed and has become part of today, and tomorrow does not exist yet but will be decided by today. The only reality that exists is the present moment.

The moving finger writes and having writ, moves on. Nor all your piety nor wit will lure it back again to cancel half a line, Nor all your tears wash out a word of it.

(*The Rubiyat of Omar Khayam*)

Marina Lobra the harbor of Massa Lubrense, Italy, 1998, Family photo

From across the sea the Sphinx was looking at me. I felt her gaze, and from the sea I seemed to hear the voices of the Sirens as they sang, this time more distinctly:

> Come here, renowned Ulysses, honor to the Achaean name, steer your ship on land and listen to our voices! No one ever sailed past us without staying to hear the enchanting sweetness of our song, And then he went on his way not only enjoyed, but also the wiser. for we know all the ills that the gods laid upon the Argives and

Trojans before Troy and we can tell you everything that is going to happen in the whole world.

(Homer, *The Odyssey*, Chapter XII, (lines 184-190))

Our next duty station was Bernkastl on the Mosel River. There we stayed for almost another year.

As often as I could, I traveled from there south to Italy while my mother helped me with the children. I could not have otherwise managed the chores that waited for me.

There was a lot to do in Massa Lubrense.

Philip and Eva on the newly acquired property, Villa "Quo Vadis," Massa Lubrense, Italy 1960, Family photo

The plan of our architect was meager and unimaginative. I did not like it at all: small rooms in a small house hermetically closed off from the outside. This was not what I had in mind. I wanted a roofed resting place between heaven and the sea.

The house should become a home in the Roman tradition of the "villa sul mare" (house overlooking the sea). In his guide to Italy, C. Hoecker describes the Roman villa as the architectural expression of a lifestyle. He wrote:

> In ancient times the coast of Southern Latium, Sorrento and Capri were covered with so called "Villas of Leisure" of their Greek and Roman owners, and reached the pinnacle of their development in the 1st and 2nd century A.D. The "Villa" served its owner as a place of retreat and hide-away and thus defined in its function of "otium" (leisure) stands in contrast to the "domus," the city home, where the aristocratic citizen of these times pursued his political and commercial interests.
>
> This contrast between "Otium" (leisure') and Negotium (busy absence of leisure), which manifests itself for the first time in architecture determines the structural plan of the villa.
>
> This plan combines an opulently furnished living space with a large atrium and side rooms, bath facilities and various dining and sleeping quarters as well as a library, with an extended tract for utility facilities, such as, a kitchen, heating plant, cisterns and servant quarters. Additional features of the villa included external complexes, like a garden, a subterranean cryptoporticus, extended colonnades, porticos, and sometimes belvederes (observatory) on the sides.

One of the most outstanding features of the Villa is the concept of combining architecture and landscape. At the same time the surrounding landscape was being integrated on various levels into the concept of the villa. Thus nature became an integral part of culture.

This meant that within our own financial limits I had to put into practice these ideas that had been in my subconscious mind ever since I had been confronted with the architecture of Frank Lloyd Wright. So I proceeded to draw up my own building plan.

Our house was to have an enclosed space, comparable to an atrium, but at the same time, a wide terrace that opens up to the sea and the landscape of the Gulf.

And I wanted a house built on various levels, with gradual transitions from the inside to the outside.

"A covered resting place between heaven and the sea!"

In addition, the house should be oriented toward the daily and seasonal rhythms of the sun. This meant that time and place for taking the meals of the day was determined by the present location of the sun.

The house should also be a home to accommodate individualists. It should allow every guest to come and go at will, enjoy the landscape, the view, and the sun whenever he or she wanted to. He or she should be able to retire to his own space or socialize with the others depending on his or her personal needs at the moment.

In my opinion, I succeeded quite well in realizing my dreams. In the last 45 years I have never felt that I wanted to make any substantial changes in the ground plan of the house.

Those necessary additions that the ancient Romans had already incorporated into their villas, such as a thermal area, swimming pool, sauna (calidarium), observatory veranda on the roof, and ceiling heating, were all added in an extensive renovation project only twenty years later.

The result was the villa *Quo Vadis*, my own personal hymn to the Mediterranean way of life that was open to the sea and the surrounding gardens.

Even on the hottest summer day, the breeze sweeps through the house from the sea up the hill and brings refreshing coolness to the terrace.

Also, the shady atrium offers a cool place to meet and enjoy the hours of leisure during siesta time or in the evening.

Like its Roman predecessors, the house is built on several levels, to be exact, on five levels.

As you enter the iron gate on the ground floor, a steep stairway leads up to the next level where the first floor of the house is located. You pass through a lodge, from which you enter the guest apartment, another guest room, and the basement storage room. On both sides of this lodge stairs lead up to the main living area. You pass a semi-enclosed patio with trees and flower beds and pass through the living room into a large terrace.

From there you have a spectacular view of the whole Gulf of Naples. To your left in the South you see the Isle of Capri.

From the patio a small staircase leads to the fourth level of the house.

You pass the wall towards the neighbor's lemon grove. A wall of cypress trees surrounds the area of the swimming pool.

When we turn around to look up the hill, we see olive groves and the lemon grove of a large neighboring estate.

Also adjacent to the living room is the open kitchen with the best view in the house. Its setup is a concession to the American way of life. Since we nowadays no longer believe in the institution of slavery, and no one else but the woman of the house herself has to slave in the kitchen, I insisted that my kitchen window face the view of the Gulf and facilitate conversation with family and guests during preparation of the meals.

On one side of the atrium is the bedroom, and on the other side is a library.

From the atrium, a small stairway leads up to the fourth level of the house, passing the wall of cypress trees. There, we find the swimming pool, romantically carved into the hillside, and a little sauna that has a window overlooking Capri and is, so far as we know, unique in the world.

Then we pass to the upper terrace with its breathtaking view of the Gulf and the surrounding hills.

The entrance to villa "Quo Vadis" 1961, Family photo

"Quo Vadis" today, a modern "villa sul mare." Family photo

View of the roof of "Quo Vadis" today, Family photo

The young family on vacation.

Ariane and Vivian in "Quo Vadis" 1962, Family photo

Ariane, the young painter and Vivian, Angela and Ariane in"Quo Vadis," 1964, Family photo

*Eva on the rock where she saved a young man's life,
San Montano, Italy, 1962, Family photo*

At the back of the terrace, a glassed-in gazebo protects us from any cold winds and offers another resting place for the hours of leisure. It can also be a hideaway for adventurous guests to put their bed and count the stars during the hours of the night.

The terrace seems to float above the Gulf of Naples. The eye passes from there to the islands of Capri to Ischia, Procida, and further to the coastline of Pozzuoli and Naples.

The time of construction was a difficult one for me. Philip had made a little model based on my plans, and I tried to explain to the Italian workers the best I could what I wanted. I admit to naïvely thinking that giving orders without checking up on them would automatically lead to the desired results. Not knowing much about construction, I sometimes overlooked some mistakes they made.

But the result is the villa, nestled into the hillside, with its olive and lemon groves. The friendly chirping of the birds is mixed with the murmur of the sea far below; the house is closed in and open at the same time.

It is truly "a covered resting place between the sky and the sea"!

Quo Vadis, a place that provides security, gives me strength and offers freedom!

When Philip and I had built the house, we were still "on the road."

Bernkastl was to be another short assignment, and we knew that eventually we would have to return to the United States. *Quo Vadis?* again!

But anyway, we now had our little house in the Gulf of Naples, a wonderful place for the family. At least once a year we all met there. My parents came from Munich, and Philip's parents joined us from Evansville. To them I had to promise that wherever we would go, I would retain the house for the grandchildren, regardless of where we would ultimately land.

During my later travels we returned there every year, from the United States or from Beirut, from Manila or Addis Ababa. Here was our haven, our home, and here we are happy to the present day. Here my daughters, their families, and I come back every year in the springtime and find it a wonderful place to relax, meditate, and get a new perspective on life.

Ship to America, the "Leonardo da Vinci," 1960, Old postcard

"The Battle of the Giants," Pergammon altar-frieze, marble, (2N° entury B.C.E.) See Source Index

Chapter 8: Studies at Columbia University in New York

The City that Never Sleeps

I AWOKE EARLY IN MY LITTLE room on the twelfth floor of International House at 300 Riverside Drive beside Columbia University in the center of Manhattan.

It was November 22, 1963, and we were expecting important guests. President Eisenhower and John Jay McCloy wanted to meet with us international students for lunch. As representative of the Student Council of the International House, I was responsible for the common lunch with these sponsors of this institution, Eisenhower and McCloy.

It was very exciting for me to meet these two gentlemen personally. After all, it was a meeting with General Dwight D. Eisenhower, who had ventured the invasion with the Allied Forces on the coast of Normandy and then had defeated Nazi Germany, and with John Jay McCoy, who was the former High Commissioner of Germany.

McCloy was a highly educated man who had a typical example of the "American Dream" career. His mother, a nurse, had worked day and night to be able to send her son to law school at the university. Her son thanked her by means of his career. He became head of the Pentagon and later president of the World Bank before he was sent to Germany with the mission to build up a democratic postwar system of government and to take part in the drafting of the new German Constitution.

I had been studying in New York for two months. I had sent the children together with our German au pair, Hermine, to their grandparents in Evansville, Indiana, where they would be in the best hands. I had embarked on a new career and felt like a new person.

I was politically engaged, interested in everything, and I loved meeting young people from many countries throughout the world and encounters with so many different interests, political inclinations, and cultural characters.

During the day we studied hard because we had to show a good grade average if we did not want to lose our scholarships. At night we talked into the wee hours—Arabs, Jews, South Africans, Indians, and Japanese. All of them seemed instilled with a new, common political awareness and a belief in the possibility of overcoming all problems if we worked together. We wanted to create a new "world order." It was the intellectual power and the charisma of one man that inspired us. John F. Kennedy, the young, beaming president in the rocking chair was our idol.

In the summer of 1962 I had come to a decision. I knew that Philip would have to return to the United States after three years abroad. We had been stationed in Neu-Ulm, Germany, when I asked myself the question of how my future life should look. We had finally arrived in my "Ithaka" and become reacquainted with life in Europe, and now I should go back again to America?

Marriage to an Air Force captain would mean many more years moving from one place to another. It meant the monotonous daily life amid ever-the-same "officers' wives clubs," always only children, kitchen, and parties—I shuddered at the thought. I had to talk to Phil.

I wanted to wait for a good occasion. It finally seemed the right moment when we were in *Quo Vadis*.

The children and I were playing on the roof terrace, when we heard the jet. Phil did two ailerons above our house and then went on to land at the NATO airbase in Possible near Naples. This was SOP (standard operating procedure) when he came home from some mission abroad. We waved to him before he disappeared into the afternoon sun. I jumped in the car to go pick him up.

Today I would talk to him. On our way back to Massa Lubrense I plucked up my courage and said: "I will only return to America if you agree that I can finish my studies there." I had expected a strong reaction from him, even an argument, but there was no such thing. Phil was in agreement.

After that, everything happened very quickly. By means of an ad in the *Sueddeutsche Zeitung* we found an aupair who would come with us to the United States to learn English. Hermine was a young girl of eighteen who came from the countryside in Kempten in the Allgaeu. She loved children and was efficient, practically oriented, dependable, friendly, and patient. The children loved her. Together with her, we boarded the ship *Leonardo da Vinci* in Naples harbor in August 1962 to leave Europe.

The trip took some five days to New York and from there we went on to our next home, Phil's new assignment in Hampton, Virginia. The Air Force had promised him that he would be stationed there for at least three years. This meant that it would be worthwhile to buy a small house. We soon found something suitable for $19,000. It was a bungalow made of brick painted white. It had a nice living room with a fireplace, three bedrooms and two bathrooms, and in the back a small garden. There I built up a portico with white columns and a trellis for the rose garden I wanted to start. I also planted bougainvilleas to climb up the columns like in *Quo Vadis*.

On our first Christmas back in the States, Christmas 1962, my father-in-law gave me the book *The Second Sex* by Simone de Beauvoir. That event was a milestone in my life.

Jean Paul Sartre and his companion Simone de Beauvoir had been among the forerunners of the first student movements that had started from Berkeley in the Fifties and had spread from there to light up Europe in the "wild Sixties." *The Second Sex*, this well-meant Christmas present, gave me the final push to free myself from the usual life of an American housewife and to pursue my professional education in earnest.

Back in Hampton, I immediately looked for the next college. I found it in Williamsburg, Virginia, not far from our home in Hampton. The College of William and Mary had been founded in 1693 by the English King William III and his wife Mary during the time when the country was still a British colony. It is the second-oldest college in the United States (the oldest being Harvard) and had a reputation for excellence. I was in high spirits.

Vivian, Ariane, Hermine in front of the entrance to the College of William & Mary

But first of all, I had to earn my tuition money, because I did not want to ask Phil to finance my "crazy ideas." The year's tuition would cost $5,000, and that was a lot of money for us. I looked for a job and quickly found one in a furniture store that sold mattresses. There I worked on commission only in the evening until the day I had my $5,000.

In the meantime I also knew what I would study. We had visited Phil's brother Warren in New York who was a psychoanalyst. During this visit I took the opportunity to ask him what profession he thought I should go into. "Why don't you ask the Oracle?" he laughed. He told me to keep my question in mind and throw three coins. Then we read in a Chinese book what meaning this constellation of the coins could have. The name of the book was *I Ching*, and it was an ancient Chinese book of oracles that describes 64 combinations.

I actually was more interested in archaeology or anthropology but I Ching gave me a clear answer. Three times I threw the coins and three times the same answer seemed to be clear: I should become a teacher.

I thought about it, and my reason agreed with this choice. As a teacher, I would have more time for my children during their vacation. Also, since my mother had been teacher, I was already familiar with the teaching profession.

The decision had been made. I made an appointment with the Dean of the Faculty of Education at William and Mary College in Williamsburg.

A heavy rain was pouring down on the campus on that day. Soaking wet and my hair mashed to my head while the water was running out of my shoes, I stood before Prof. Howard Kingsbury Holland, dean of the faculty, and immediately stated my case: "I am from Germany, I have my Abitur, my University Admission Examination, and I had a Fulbright Scholarship to Evansville College. I have two children and an au pair who will go back to Germany in a year. I want to become a teacher. What do I have to do to finish my bachelor's degree in one year?"

"You would have to take twice as many courses as normal," Dr. Holland answered in a quiet voice. Only then did I realize who sat on the other side of the desk. I saw an elegantly dressed gentleman with a soft but firm voice, with beginning gray hair, clear blue, very awake but kind, eyes, a man who was open but reserved at the same time.

"What an unusually likeable man," I thought to myself. I immediately trusted him, not only because he took an interest in my case and encouraged me in my endeavor but also because he had a very special charisma about him.

Suddenly he stood up quickly, as if somebody had pulled him from his chair, and he scrutinized me exactly. I had no idea what fate had planned for the two of us.

I was overjoyed and studied my courses in education, psychology and philosophy with great enthusiasm. The first year was an extremely hard one for me. I had taken an overload of classes. When the second semester was finished I took the rest of my classes in summer school. I was so thirsty for knowledge and could not get enough of all these interesting facts and scientific theories. Unlike my fellow students, for whom all these things seemed to be uninteresting, I finally found an explanation for many experiences that I was confronted with every day in real life.

After nine month of classes and a full summer semester, I received my bachelor's degree in teaching. This degree, however, was not sufficient to find a job in an institute of higher education. Dr. Holland advised me to go to the Teachers' College at Columbia University in New York to get my master's degree in the Teaching of English as a Foreign Language (TOEFL). There I would be able to get my degree within one year. Beside that, my grades were good enough to apply for a scholarship.

November 22, 1963

On November 22, 1963, I was finally sitting beside John Jay McCloy, having lunch at the International House at Columbia University. We talked about Germany. He was telling me about the time during the end of the war when he was stationed with his army near Rothenburg ob der Tauber. The American commander suspected that there were SS military personnel there and wanted to bomb the city. But he remembered his mother talking about Germany. She had told him that Rothenburg, this little town in Oberfranken, was a real jewel of an old medieval city. He stopped the assault on the city at the last moment, thereby saving the city. I was very impressed by this intelligent but unassuming man. Only later did I learn about his extraordinary career. Some years later he became president of the Chase Manhattan Bank and was an advisor to Ronald Reagan before he became president.

After lunch, President Eisenhower and McCloy said good-bye to us students and I accompanied the two gentlemen to their limousine. They disappeared slowly into the dense traffic on Riverside Drive. The sun lit up the west side of the city. It was an unusually warm afternoon.

When I passed through the front door and reentered the big hall, an ear-piercing outcry of horror went through the crowd. Students of every country cried out, and tears were flowing down their faces as they embraced to console each other. Many had pulled out their transistor radios, and there was a clamor of voices in different languages. It took a while until I finally could make out what had happened: "John F. Kennedy is dead! The President of the United States was shot this afternoon in his car in Dallas!" It seemed as if life had come to a standstill for a moment.

With former President Dwight D. Eisenhower and John Jay McCloy International House, New York, NY, Nov. 22, 1963, Family photo

John F. Kennedy had been our idol, the hope of the younger generation. Lyndon B. Johnson became his successor—what a weak substitute!

But New York did not mourn for long. Life had to go on, and especially my life. I fully enjoyed the city, and I tried to make up for what I had missed in the previous ten years. I went to the theater, went to the Metropolitan Opera, combed through every museum, and did not miss any musical or interesting film as long as the money lasted. I had to save. In International House, my room only cost $50. It was the smallest one they had, but it had a large window and a magnificent view over Washington Bridge. I did get a scholarship, and in the Chinese restaurant on the corner, one could get lunch for $1.20 with soup, vegetables, and rice, tea, and a fortune cookie for dessert.

I flirted and went dancing as often as I could. I organized a folk dance group, and we performed Mexican, Russian, Greek, and Israeli dances on stage at the end-of-the-school-year dance. A group of Israeli film students studying at the New York Film Academy made a short movie about me.

And then I was on the Student Council of International House.

I made friends with a Japanese professor, Yoshi Satow. He really became a longtime friend of mine and later even visited me in Germany for several years with groups of his students.

I also became acquainted with a Russian professor. He seemed to be watched by the KGB, however, and was worried about being seen with me, a fact that limited our friendly relations considerably.

I preferred to be involved with my black student friends in the black parts of town. There we found the best jazz, and I even met the famous black boxer, Muhammad Ali, personally.

Sharing International House with students from 60 different countries, I became very interested in international politics. We discussed until late hours of the night all the problems of those days, the Cuba crisis, the Vietnam War, Che Guevara, and Castro, apartheid in South Africa, and the problems of the emerging countries in Africa.

Practice Teaching in the Bronx

I did my practice teaching in the Bronx in the spring of 1964. In the high school in which I taught, there were only black students and Puerto Ricans taking my English course. When I arrived, the woman in the office smiled and said, "You don't need to be afraid, the students haven't locked their teacher into the closet for a week!" There had been no shootings at this school, because the kids were searched for weapons every morning at the door. I really was not afraid anyway; I was much too curious about my new assignment. I even made friends with some of the boys and took them along to International House. I visited one of them at home and got to know his brave mother. This single mother took care of her five children in a one-room apartment as best as she could. I could understand why this boy never came to school with his homework done.

The reaction of the white population of New York toward blacks and Puerto Ricans was astonishing to me, and slowly I began to understand reality.

My young friends from the Bronx had never left their part of town until then. They began to trust me enough to talk to me about their everyday problems. The problems of a youth without chances in the middle of New York. They also seemed to have lost their hope for equal opportunities with the death of John F. Kennedy. The atmosphere on the streets of the Bronx seemed to become more tense. The racial unrest in the South of the country provoked the institutions of the state. One could notice this very clearly in the Bronx.

Martin Luther King became the Mahatma Gandhi of the black population. "I have a dream" was the dream of peace and justice, equal rights for all races, and equal opportunity for everyone. Many dreamed with him, and so did I.

I began to visit the dark jazz halls of the Bronx with my black student friends, and I began to love their music, especially the erotic sound of the saxophone of Louis Armstrong. I also loved the "cool" rhythms of the Modern Jazz Quartet, John Coltrane, Stan Getz, and Grover Washington. I lost myself in the indescribable world of "soul" music, a world whose codes cannot be deciphered with one's brain.

At that time my interest was mainly in the question of whether there was a common language that connected all of mankind.

But I also became interested in the problems of the so-called "disadvantaged children." My generation of teachers was convinced that we would be able to help these children, who already had been dealt worse cards than their white classmates from middle-class families before they entered school. All educational measures indicated that the latter would have a better future. Their major problem was the language. Later, I taught a college course in Remedial English," that is, pronunciation, sentence structure, grammar, and vocabulary. Oral Communication and Public Speaking would become my most important teaching subjects.

Language was not only a problem for children of Puerto Rican immigrants, South Americans, and black families. Children from families that had broken up because of the unemployment of the father and head of the family also had language problems. These children usually had already missed the boat by their second year in elementary school, and from then on disliked going to school. Every year the gap between them and their white classmates became wider. The teachers' ability to convince the students to stay in school was greatly reduced. In particular, boys began to miss school more often, dropped out completely before the end of the year, and ended up in the army of "unemployables." Many of them joined neighborhood gangs, where they tried to gain respect and recognition by committing especially "cool" deeds. The Broadway musical *West Side Story* gives insight into the lives of these teenagers and their ideas of the "American Dream," the idea that everyone can make it from the dishwasher to the millionaire if he only wants to.

The big topic of discussion for my generation was the question of whether genetics or education played a more dominant role in the development of a young person. We teachers believed, of course, that we could solve all the problems of these children if we only found the correct methods to teach them. However, the idea of equal chances for everybody met with only limited success.

I did not think that we should give up, because "it is always better to light one candle than to curse the darkness."

An important lesson I learned while I was the representative of the Student Council in International House was that whatever you do, you are going to make some people unhappy with your actions. One of my responsibilities was to be on a mediation committee. The committee's job was to mediate between groups in the case of conflicts between ethnic or national groups. I had good friends in the Israeli and in the Arabic groups. But as soon as I tried to establish some kind of understanding between the groups when a conflict arose, my friends in one of the groups suspected me of taking the side of the other group, and I lost my friends in both groups.

All my efforts had been unsuccessful. One day a well-known Palestinian politician planned to give a lecture about the situation in the Middle East in the International House Auditorium. On the morning of that day I noticed that our Israeli students had mobilized the whole Jewish community of New York; all tickets for this event had been bought up. I could just imagine how this evening would end under these conditions, so I hurried to my Arabic friends to tell them what had happened. They were just getting up and asked me with a yawn what they were supposed to do now. Of course nothing happened.

In the evening things took the turn they had to take. The speaker did not even have a chance to make his case, because he was immediately booed off the stage as soon as he opened his mouth. Any discussion about this topic was and remained completely impossible. I asked myself whether it was at all possible for an objectively thinking person to influence other people when they were so emotionally involved. I learned then that obviously reason was much less successful in educating people than emotion.

The "Master of Arts"

In the summer of 1964 I took my final examinations. I was awarded the Master of Arts in the Teaching of English as a Foreign language, M.A. TOEFL. I had reached my goal, and my grades were very good, also.

Master's degree from Columbia University, New York, NY, 1964, Family photo

The family on the campus of Columbia University
New York, NY, 1964 Family photo

Everything went right that summer. During the dinner party in the evening before the graduation celebration I had met the president of a college for black students. I told him about my experiences in the Bronx and my sympathy for the black students in New York. He asked me whether I would consider taking a position in his college.

"Yes, but …."

"My college is in the southern part of the United States, in Virginia, in Hampton," he said.

For a minute I thought I had not heard correctly; it was not possible to have so much good luck! Was it Fortuna or Athena that had interceded for me?

There I stood on the campus of Columbia University, with my fine family, my diploma in my hand, and a good job in my pocket, exactly in a college in Hampton, Virginia, where Phil was stationed.

I really felt blessed by fortune.

Chapter 9: Teaching at Hampton Institute in the Deep South

The Civil Rights Movement in the South

I found myself in the fall of 1964 in front of my students for the first time. I had signed a contract with the college to teach the following courses: German, Written English, Public Speaking, and Introduction to World Literature. I was free to create my own course outlines, and I had my own agenda: I did not want to confront my black students as a "white teacher" and did not want to aggravate the two-class system as a representative of the white middle class and a sympathizer of the "superior" adult generation. I tried to overcome these traditional dividing lines and drew them in a new way.

I was the only white teacher in the college and was very much aware of my role in that situation. Until then, I had seen myself as an outsider, and thus it was easy for me to meet my students on a different level. I confronted them with this approach: Here am I, a European, and there are you, Americans.

Martin Luther King, the theologian who was born in 1929 in Atlanta, Georgia, had been awarded the Nobel price for peace for his nonviolent resistance against inequalities and racism, a method that he had used successfully during the American Peace Movement.

I was a great admirer of his, which helped me to gain the trust and respect of my students—I was just as involved and committed as they were.

I had not realized how difficult and even dangerous it would be to stand up for civil rights in the South during those days. My students and my black colleagues had a much keener sense of the prevalent moods in the white population. After a few unpleasant incidents, I was duly warned. One of the less violent ones happened in a coffee shop, where the waiter just "happened " to pour hot coffee down the back of my black colleague.

I often had young blacks in my car and it could happen that we were not served at the filling station or that we were received with snide remarks. I decided to keep a pistol in my glove compartment like many others did.

I got along so well with my students that I wanted to continue the dialogue started in class in my home. In order to avoid trouble with my neighbors, for whom I already was a suspicious person, my students told me that it would be better for me if they came after dark.

I did not see the difficulties with doing that, or rather, I did not want to see them.

I loved my work, and I disregarded the fact that it was difficult to combine them with my family life. I had worked too hard for it.

When I started teaching at Hampton Institute, a very hard period of my life began. Hermine had returned to Germany. She had already agreed to give me one more year of her time when I had gone to New York. But this time I really had to let her go home.

We all really missed her very much.

*Martin Luther King at the march on Washington,
August 1963, from www.archives.gov*

The children, the household—but most of all my new profession—took everything out of me. I was exhausted all the time.

Never before had I found myself in front of a class of young adults between 18 and 22 years of age. The young blacks that had were able to go to college in those days were very intelligent and eager to obtain the college degree that would mean a ticket to a job in the white middle-class society—as well as its lifestyle.

This was a time shortly before the slogan, "Black is beautiful" became popular. There still existed an organization for "light-colored girls" among the black population. But this "Uncle Tom" mentality was beginning to be criticized and was hotly argued among young activists such as the "Black Panthers."

There were no lesson plans, and I was only given the title of the course that I had to teach. I had to work out the course outline and obtain most of the reading material myself. Whatever I could find in books written for white colleges presupposed students' knowledge either of facts or ideas, most of which were unknown or uninteresting to my students. Thus it was up to me to find and establish the connections to their background.

For example, one of the topics of the final examination in the course "Introduction to World Literature" was: "Compare and contrast the nature of the devil in Goethe's play *Dr. Faust* and Dostoevsky's novel *The Grand Inquisitor*."

I had to prepare myself for four different lectures per week and wrote many of my exercises myself. I was busy preparing texts late into the night as well as correcting exercises and examinations.

In the years that followed, my work became easier because I could reuse some earlier materials and had developed a certain routine. But in my first year I was sometimes desperate and tired out. But my interest in this fascinating challenge kept me from giving up.

I was surprised myself at how much energy I was able to derive from my enthusiasm for my work, an energy I never knew I had.

When an article about me appeared in the local newspaper, it concluded with this sentence:

When asked whether it was very difficult to combine the career of a teacher at a black college with the role of a wife and mother, the blonde answered: "If you want your omelet, you have to crack your eggs!" And continued correcting her papers."

Yes, that was my attitude.

As I found out many years later, my children considered me quite intolerable at that time. They remembered me as always working or being tired in the evening. This quite possible, because I was so involved with my profession and my own development that I did not have much energy left for anything else—or anyone else.

One thing I did notice, however, was that Philip and I had drifted apart. This process had already started while I was in New York, but actually the roots were to be found long before.

From the beginning, Philip had never been very communicative. I had become aware of this during our "wanderjahre" and during the time when the children were small, but I did not really see it as a problem.

Since New York, however, our relationship had deteriorated. Maybe my getting my master's degree had made him more aware of the fact that he had interrupted his own education when he joined the Air Force.

What the real nature of our alienation was I have not been able to fully understand. But judging from some bits of information and remarks I have picked up over the years, the real reasons might have had their origin in the time before we had even met.

We really had no common ground for communication, but we both did want to save our marriage for the sake of the children. So we bought books about how to cope with marriage problems, but they were not very helpful.

The End of a Marriage a la Hollywood

It was late one night when someone rang the doorbell violently.

It could not be Phil, because he had his key.

When I opened the door, there was Phil's officer friend. At the top of his voice and with shaky legs he gave vent to his anger. Was he in the wrong house? No, he was talking about Phil. He claimed that my husband Phil had made improper advances toward his wife. This was scandalous, and he would find a way of getting even with him, for example, by suggesting that I and he do likewise.

I was shocked and did not know how to respond, so I simply slammed the door in his face.

It suddenly became very quiet, and I tried to regain my senses.

I could not believe that I had heard correctly. My quiet, well-mannered Phil, with whom I was working so hard to mend our marriage, made advances to a married woman? This was not like him at all! This was unthinkable!

I tried to imagine what I would say to Phil when he came home. He certainly would tell me that this was a lot of nonsense. Or he would admit what he had done, and take me in his arms and say that he was sorry. And I would forgive him if he told me he loved me.

Vivian and Ariane with Sindbad, Hampton, VA, 1963, Family photo

Ariane and Vivian on Ward Drive, Hampton, VA, 1963 Family photo

Learning to ride a bike on Ward Drive, Hampton, VA 1963, Family photo

Vivian$ 4th birthday, on Ward Drive, Hampton, VA May 1963

But things took a very different turn.

Suddenly the door opened, and my accused husband came in. I noticed that he seemed a bit uneasy on his legs. Instead of asking him quietly what this visit had been about, I confronted him with reproaches. "What do you think you are doing by proposing to other women while we are trying to fix our marriage?"

There was no explanation and no excuse from his side. He simply did not answer me.

I was infuriated and kept reproaching him. This was the first really aggressive fight we had ever had and unfortunately it ended in violence.

I was horrified and panicked.

Ariane and Vivian in Hampton, VA 1963, Family photo

Wearing only a nightgown and robe, I ran out of the house and drove to the local police station, where the officer looked at me very amused and mumbled that things like this happened in every family. I declined to make a report because of Phil's career as an officer. Confused and ashamed, I got back into the car and went home.

There everything was quiet. The house was dark.

I unlocked the door and did not suspect anything to be wrong. I called for Phil but there was no answer. I became worried and ran into the children's room. Everywhere I saw pieces of clothing lying about, pulled out of open drawers and closets. Phil was not there, and the children were gone.

I had not noticed that his car was gone. Phil was gone and had taken the children with him. It hit me like lightning.

What could I do? Should I call my in-laws? I tried to calm myself. The children were with Phil, and nothing would happen to them. He would come back after his anger had passed.

But there was no news for three days. Finally Phil called, only to tell me this: "We are okay. The kids are with me, but you will not see your kids ever again!"

Now my fighting spirit was awakened.

It was too late for any kind of reproaches. I had to act if I wanted to get my children back.

First of all, I had to find out where Phil had gone. As a member of the military service, it should not be difficult for me as his wife to find out where he had himself transferred.

I still had to teach for another four weeks, and then spring break would start and I would be able to leave Hampton.

Four weeks later I found myself in an airplane to Las Vegas, with $300 and a small pistol in my bag.

Phil had requested transfer to Las Vegas, but I did not know his address. I needed help.

I entered the small, shabby office of a detective an hour after landing in Las Vegas.

It felt like a scene with Philip Marlowe in one of Raymond Chandler's films.

In the dimly lit office I made out a platinum blonde secretary and two bulky bodyguards near the door. The boss himself, behind a messy desk filled with heaps of papers, was sitting in a huge armchair covered with a leopard's skin and was smoking his pipe.

Despite the scary atmosphere, the detective seemed like a pleasant type of guy.

He listened to my story, as it seemed to me, with some sympathy. "My husband has abducted my children. He must be here in Las Vegas but I don't know where," I said.

"That happens here all the time. I can help you, but it will cost you $300."

"At the moment I don't have that much money," I replied.

"Never mind, give me what you've got, and the rest you can pay later."

The next day I really felt as if I was in a murder mystery story.

Wearing a headscarf and large sunglasses, I was sitting in the car of my Philip Marlowe on the way to Phil's new house. It had taken the detective only a few minutes of telephone calls to find out Phil's address.

In the yard I saw Ariane playing, but I could not see Vivian anywhere. The detective asked me whether I wanted to take Ariane with me immediately. I declined, because I wanted to have both children and I didn't want Philip to become aware of my presence in Las Vegas.

"Then you will have to wait until tomorrow when both kids are in school," he said.

The next morning, with headscarf and sunglasses in place, we drove to the school.

The detective had found out the address of the school and also the time when the doors of the schoolyard would be closed. He was obviously a very experienced professional.

We drove up to the gate at exactly five minutes to 8:00 a.m.

"You have to get the children yourself. I am not allowed to even touch them. I could be accused of kidnapping and lose my license" he explained.

I was on my own. The schoolyard resounded with the happy voices of hundreds of children, like a flock of birds. How would I possibly find my two little ones?

Suddenly the sound of a little well-known voice reached my ear: "Mommy, Mommy!"

Ariane ran into my arms. "Hi, my dear, where is your sister?"

"Over there in the kindergarten!"

I took Ariane by the hand and ran to the open door of the kindergarten on the other side of the courtyard. I entered the room and immediately saw Vivian and picked her up.

"Excuse me, I am her mother and I have to change her shoes," I shouted at the teacher who was staring at me in surprise. Then I walked out the door and across the schoolyard toward the gate, trying to act as cool as possible.

At that moment the school bell rang. The children began to rush to their classrooms and the gate was beginning to close automatically.

With both Ariane by the hand and Vivian in my arms, I lunged toward the gate and squeezed through the closing doors at the last moment. I jumped into the car, which had been parked on the sidewalk with its motor running and off we sped in the direction of the airport.

Our Philip Marlowe did not lose time by going through the gates. He drove directly onto the airfield and to the airplane. If the school had informed Phil immediately of the departure of the children, I had to expect a rough encounter at the airport.

The stewardess let down the ladder, which had already been pulled up for departure.

We climbed up, entered the plane, and a few minutes later were high up in the sky.

I heaved a sigh of relief. The two children were, of course, very excited. They looked out the window, and every time they saw another airplane they called out, "Daddy is coming after us!"

It seemed like a fantastic adventure that the three of us had experienced together.

I was looking with mixed feelings into the future. On the one hand, I was extremely happy to have my children back, but on the other hand, it meant the end of my marriage to Phil and an uncertain future as a single mother.

When we were back in Hampton, I took the children with me to the college, where I could watch them. The college was well guarded in those days because of the racial disturbances. I had to expect that their father would come and take them back. There was an experimental school and kindergarten at the college, and thus they became the only white kids among a group of black children.

My fear of Philip only disappeared very slowly. But a sense of responsibility began to weigh on me. During the day I was full of energy to tackle the daily problems—my lectures and the children let me forget—but at night a hitherto unknown fear of failure and loneliness began to take hold of me.

An Angel

In my second semester, I had five classes. In two of them, "Introduction into World Literature," and "Advanced German," there was only one white boy. His name was Anton Schueszler, and as one could guess, he was from a family with German background.

Anton seemed a living copy of the Greek god Dionysus with his blond hair and clear blue eyes. His skin was as white as alabaster, his youthful cheeks rounded and his lips full. He listened to me quietly and attentively, completely unaware of himself and his gracefulness. He was a highly intelligent young man with an aura of complete innocence. I immediately liked his soft voice and modest manners, and I was mesmerized by this beautiful youth who attentively took in every word I spoke and never missed a single class. He remembered every word I said and always had the right answers to my questions. The perfect student!

Anton had been sent from heaven, a guardian angel in human form.

At that time I really needed a guardian angel for my girls when they came home from school and I was still busy at the college. I asked Antonio, as I called him, if he would help me and he immediately agreed. I hired him to be there and watch the girls after school.

I was thus able to concentrate better on my work, while Anton could practice his German with the children. Since Anton was also studying music, I rented a piano for him. I hoped to raise the girls' interest in music this way, and they loved to have him practice his etudes. I was delighted to hear the music of Chopin and Mozart when I came home, tired and worn out.

This gracious young man, the heavenly music, my loneliness—I did not know what caused this bittersweet sensation I felt in his presence.

Antonio, poetic and dreamy, idealistic and intellectual, he was so different from the other men around me. I had not remained unaware of the fact that Antonio had wildly fallen in love with me, but that I would also succumb to his charm was a confusing surprise to me. Anton was fifteen years younger than I, and I was fully aware that this enchanting affair would have no future.

Nevertheless, it became the most positive love relationship in my life. Maybe this was so because it seemed like one of those roses that when in their prime are put into a plastic shell to protect them from the process of decay and decomposition by the forces of our daily life. "Deep frozen" so to speak.

I was happy, and at the same time bewildered. Nobody was to know about our relationship. This had to remain our secret; I would have risked my teaching position. The more I became involved in my emotions, the more I also felt a responsibility toward Anton. This sensitive and idealistic boy had actually set his mind on wanting to marry me, despite our difference in age and my two children.

I was really in a dilemma and had to urgently speak with someone.

There was only one person whom I could trust. That was Dr. Howard Holland, dean of the Faculty of Education and Philosophy in my old school, the College of William and Mary in Williamsburg, Virginia. William and Mary was not far from Hampton. Dr. Holland had advised me well in 1962. After my return from New York, we had met again. He wanted to know everything about me, how I had fared at Columbia University and how my studies had been completed. We had developed a warm and trustful friendship. I needed his friendly advice again, and the result was amazing.

Howard was a wonderful human being, fifteen years older than I, well educated, kind, and sensitive; he was also very religious, a person who had a heavy cross to bear and who did not complain. He had four children, the youngest of whom was seriously handicapped, and his wife was an alcoholic. He came from a German family.

On the evening I sought his advice he declared his love for me. He had already fallen in love when I had stood before him the first time, dripping wet and raring to go. He asked me to become his wife.

At first I was speechless. As I looked at him, my heart said, "Yes." He was the only right man for me. As with Phil, I said, "Yes!" But this time I did so with a bit more consideration. My answer was given not in a state of being carried away by emotions, but in the conviction to have found the right partner, after all the ups and downs of my life.

Howard and I understood each other from the beginning. From the first moment on, we spoke the same language. He loved his profession as much as I loved mine. Our interests were the same. Both of us loved Greek philosophy. We had the same view of the world and of our common European roots.

The next evening Howard had a long man-to-man conversation with Anton.

Then he applied for his divorce. I did the same.

Portrait of Eva, Munich, Germany, 1966 by Photo Sahm

"Phoenix and Briseis," Athenean red-figure vase,
(480-475 B.C.E.) See Source Index

Chapter 10: From Island to Island—My Marriage to Professor Howard K. Holland

Wedding in Munich

It was on one of these enchanting days, when the sky shone over the Bavarian country in the colors of its famous flag, white and blue, that we said: "I do."

Munich's most romantic registry office is in the Mandelstrasse, a cozy, small street near the English Garden. The office is housed in an elegant old mansion that opens its colonnade and terrace with a large staircase toward the Seestrasse. Many generations have officially sealed the "happiest day of their life" in this house; whether it was for the rest of their lives, the proud building remains silent.

On July 26, 1966, we stepped onto the large staircase, accompanied by my parents, my two little daughters, my cousin Elisabeth, and a group of old friends.

My name was changed to Mrs. Howard K. Holland.

Howard was an intellectual person with great kindness. A rare combination of heart and intellect in equal balance, he was basically of a cheerful and optimistic nature. But most of all, Howard was a deeply religious person. He had told me that during recent years he had attended the Catholic Mass every morning to pray for strength to master the deep sorrows in his private life.

Then he had met me and had begun to remember the cheerful side of life. The following quotation of an anonymous poet best describes our feelings in those days:

> I think love has to do with finding someone who opens you up to yourself as you help him to do the same. And the way you satisfy him the most is by being yourself. Love is a difficult time too.
>
> You are always aware of time lurking in the doorway and laughing when you kiss.

Our wedding in the Mandelstrasse, München 1966.

Where else could our honeymoon trip have taken us if not to Athens?

Full of joy, we strolled through the ancient city, which had been the cradle of European civilization. It had always been Howard's dream to see Athens, which was the godfather of American democracy. He loved Plato and Socrates as much as I did.

During our long walks we discussed Plato's ideas about the perfect state, whose kings were philosophers, and joked about Aristophanes's story about man's two halves eternally searching for each other, which had been recounted in the *Symposium*.

Howard in the Alps.
On our honeymoon trip in Athens below the Acropolis.

The Symposium was a kind of standing meeting in antiquity, where Socrates's philosopher friends met at a specific time interval, such as once a month, for a banquet to discuss certain philosophical questions. More than anything, they cherished this entertainment: winning an argument by the intellectual weapons of logical argument and brilliant rhetoric.

Our favorite topic of discussion in Athens was, of course, "love." We wanted to find out how the ancient Greek defined this term and had encountered Aristophanes's famous story:

> At the time of their creation, human beings had been one single person who possessed male and female qualities and attributes. This made them so strong that they considered themselves undefeatable and threatened to storm Olympus, the seat of the gods.

> The father of all gods, Zeus, had to react. Should he send a flood to annihilate this annoying race in order to find peace? But then he decided to send them a warning that would remind them for the rest of their days that they were not infallible: he simply cut them in half to break their hybris. Ever since, human beings go through life searching for their lost other half. The desire to become one again is so strong that only the fulfillment of this desire can heal man's state of agony. It is this desire that we call "Love."

On the way to Beirut, Lebanon.

After our trip to Athens, Howard, the girls, and I spent three joyful days in *Quo Vadis*. Howard became a loving friend and father for the girls. They loved, respected, and accepted him. He had a good way with children and was kind and patient. It was his sense of calm and his level-headedness that let us find our inner peace. With Howard we felt safe and at home, wherever we were. This was our good luck, because our travels continued.

BEIRUT, THE PEARL OF THE ORIENT

In September 1966 we were again on our way to a new country; this time it was Howard who determined the destination of our voyage. We boarded a Turkish ship that would take us across the Mediterranean Sea, from Naples to Alexandria to Beirut. We carried only the most necessary things with us; the rest was to arrive by a container ship at a later date.

After his divorce, Howard had to look for a new job. As a divorced man, he was no longer acceptable as dean of a school in the conservative College of William and Mary. He applied for a sabbatical year and looked for work somewhere closer to Europe.

Happy days in Beirut, 1966, Family photos and Howard and Eva in Beirut, 1966 Family photo

The start of our new family life seemed to be blessed with good fortune. Howard found an interesting position as professor of education and philosophy at the American University in Beirut, and I accepted a teaching position as English teacher at the Beirut College for Women.

To arrive in Beirut by boat was breathtaking.

We had crossed the southeastern part of the Mediterranean Sea and were approaching the Levantine coast. The shore presented itself with a breathtaking view: Out of the shimmering blue of the sea rose a line of snow-covered mountains like a string of white pearls—the Lebanon Mountain Range, and at its feet, the vibrant city of Beirut amid cypresses and cedars.

The city welcomed us with the familiar sounds and smells of a Mediterranean seaport. I immediately felt at home. This sea that bathed the Levantine coast was the "mare nostrum" as the Italians call it, "our sea," and its waves were the same that had only a short time ago washed up on the coast of the Gulf of Naples. Everything seemed familiar, yet different and strange.

The traveler coming from the West finds himself in the Orient; the traveler from the East feels that he has arrived in Europe. In any case, he puts his foot down on ancient ground, and every step leads him back to the origins of Europe. Even the word "bible," meaning "that which is written" in Arabic, originated in the 7,000-year-old Byblos, where scribes had invented a written alphabet for the first time in history.

The Levant is called the "cradle of Europe." From here, the Phoenicians had started to conquer the world. Long before the Greeks, they had founded trading centers along the African coast, in the eastern Mediterranean, and in the Gulf of Naples.

It is believed that it was the Phoenicians who brought the cult of the Sirens, these mysterious mixed creatures, half-bird, half-woman, to the Sorrentine coast via Crete.

Another legend tells us that Zeus himself, in the shape of a bull, had abducted the princess Europa from her parents' palace in the Levant to the Island of Crete. There she gave birth to King Minos, the first king of the island. Their daughter, Ariadne, is said to have assisted the Greek hero, Theseus. With the help of her thread he succeeded in escaping from the labyrinth of the ferocious Minotaur.

On the Levantine coast, the influences of the most ancient cultures mix. Mesopotamia, the land between the Euphrates and Tigris, today the country of Iraq, was home to the oldest known culture of mankind. Influences from there mingled with ancient Egyptian culture as well as that from the world of the Old Testament.

In the course of history, Hebrew heritage, Greek thought, and Christianity as it had developed during Roman times became the spiritual basis of our modern Western world.

When we stepped ashore in Beirut in 1966, we entered a wealthy, joyous, and very cultured metropolis, which was called "the Paris of the East." The capital of Lebanon still showed the strong influence of the lifestyle of the French, whose administration had shaped the country from 1920 to 1943. During World War II the country had declared its independence. In the following years, Lebanon had seen strong economic development that allowed it to become the commercial center of the Middle East. The population, which consisted in more or less equal parts of Christians and Moslems, still lived in apparent harmony. The official languages were Arabic and French.

In the streets of Aleppo, Syria 1966 Family photo

The inner tensions, however, remained. A constant stream of refugees from Palestine caused the proportion of the Moslem population to increase sharply. In 1958 intense conflicts between the pro-Western and pro-Arabic supporters occurred. They came to an end only after American intervention. By 1966 the situation seemed to have calmed down, but this peace was deceptive. The Middle East remained a powder keg.

We found an apartment in one of the modern apartment houses at the Corniche, the main boulevard that follows the coastline. From our balcony we could observe the colorful hustle and bustle in front of the splendid hotels.

Across the street lived a sheik with his whole entourage, several wives, children, and various servants. On certain holidays a sheep was slaughtered according to Moslem rites on the balcony and blood was seeping down the wall. But nobody cared. That was the Oriental side of Beirut.

In the streets of Beirut, Lebanon, 1966, Family photo

While strolling on the streets, we could observe the most elegant girls, either veiled or dressed according to the newest Paris fashion, always adorned with gold jewelry and with carefully made up, mysterious, large eyes.

The street was populated mostly with men, either in Western suit and tie or in long white or black gowns and artistically draped headscarves. One could tell that their appearance was carefully designed and a source of pride.

We noticed that they often strolled the boulevard hand in hand. We were surprised, until we learned that holding hands among men was no more than a sign of good friendship.

In the "souk" of Beirut, Lebanon, 1966, Family photo

Luxury reigned in Beirut. Young Arabs drove their expensive cars up and down the Corniche. Luxurious restaurants competed with each other, and the hotels equaled their models from the Cote d'Azur. The famous Casino du Liban outdid the gambling halls of Monaco with incredibly sumptuous presentations of their shows. Saudis, Kuwaitis, and even Beduins came here to have a good time, with suitcases full of money, well guarded by friends and bodyguards.

We had no problem adjusting to our new home, and the Orient offered its own particular magic.

Early in the morning, the chant of the muezzin from the nearby mosque called us from our sleep into the new reality. Every six hours his voice called Moslem believers to their prayer and provided a clear rhythm for my day.

After some time, I had gotten used to this monotone melody, and I even began to like this pleasant interruption of the hectic activities of the day in order to be reminded of God's presence.

Mixed with the muezzin's call to prayer one could often hear the bells from the Christian churches.

We had found a servant, a young Arabic girl. She was almost still a child, but she was very dependable in her work in the kitchen and the house and liked the children. Communication was no problem, because, besides French, she also spoke a bit of English. She loved to cook and she cooked well. Soon we felt that she was part of the family and treated her accordingly. Despite this, she refused to eat at the table together with us and preferred to retreat to the kitchen.

Our greatest pleasure was a visit to the market. We were often accompanied by our little Arab girl. She was a great help as I tried to understand the local life better, at least as far as the things of the household were concerned. As in all

A courtyard in Beirut, Lebanon, 1966 Family photo

Oriental towns, a large part of daily life took place in the bazaar. In Beirut it was called "suq," meaning "covered shopping streets." There you could find everything in abundance. Despite the apparently chaotic hustle and bustle, the suq functioned according to clear rules. Every part had its particular function.

It was pure sensuous pleasure to stroll through the vegetable and fruit market, to taste all the many tempting fruits, and admire the variety of their colors. In particular, the thousand and one smells of the spice market told us that we were in a different world.

The meat and fish market, on the other hand, was less inviting. The blood of the slaughtered animals covered the ground in front of everyone's eyes and attracted swarms of flies. Hygiene did not seem to be any criterion for quality in the eyes of the shoppers.

Much more attractive was the rug market. The eye was enticed by real miracles of the art of weaving from all countries of the Middle East and even the Far East.

The jewelry market was the most popular. Here the ladies of Beirut met

A courtyard in Beirut, Lebanon, 1966, Family photo

to show their favorite jewelry and to look for new acquisitions. Men liked to display their wealth and generosity by presenting prestigious pieces of jewelry to their wives, and for the women this was their bank account.

It took me some weeks to learn to barter correctly. This is not an activity I like. But bartering is part of the life at the market. He who does not participate in this game deprives his opponent not only of a feeling of success, but also of his pleasure.

Life in Beirut happened on a high noise level. The unfamiliar sounds of language and music from the radio emerged from every door and window. I soon got accustomed to it, and even in my home the radio was constantly accompanying my daily activities. Soon I had learned to enjoy Arabic music, especially the mournfully warbling voices of the female singers, like Fairuz or the legendary Umm Kalthoum, who sent not only the Egyptians but the whole the Arab world into a trance with her "Taarab" songs. These songs always deal with love and yearning, jealousy and treachery. They usually lament the loss of the man who had left them, either because he loved another woman or because the world was more important to him than life at the side of the beloved. Women do not understand this. It seems that love and pain are the dominant themes for women everywhere in the world.

I also trained my ear to enjoy the Arabic language. Its strange combinations of consonants and guttural sounds were exotic and pleasant to my ear. For the Arab, the beauty of the formulation of the message is as important as the content itself. The artful construction of the language often vouches for the truth of the text. Reciting a sura of the Koran aloud is in itself a prayer to God.

The Arabic language offers an enormous spectrum of flowery and elegant phrases to express feelings of gratefulness, respect, and admiration.

The formulation as well as the abundance of expressions can be only partially translated into English or German. Furthermore, the structure of the language is very different from our Western languages and makes it difficult to learn Arabic. I tried to take classes, but my limited attempts were not really successful.

Even more fascinating is the Arabic script. Calligraphy is a highly developed art in the Orient. It may have something to do with the fact that it is forbidden to depict God and even his creatures in a realistic way. Mohammed had conceived his new religion as a conscious counterpole to the polytheistic religions of his time. He believed that man should not confuse the images of God with the reality of God and pray to mere idols. Thus artistic expression was concentrated on a more refined ornamental art. Artful calligraphy became the proper way to represent the word of God as it appeared in the holy book, the Koran.

The American University of Beirut

Howard now taught as Professor of Pedagogy and Philosophy at the American University of Beirut. I had been offered a teaching position at the Beirut College for Women, which was housed on another campus, as Lecturer of English and English Literature.

There existed two famous American universities in the Middle East: one in Beirut and the other in Cairo. They were both supported with sufficient funds by the American government and could afford excellent teaching personnel from all over the world. Their students came from the richest families in the Middle Eastern countries, who could pay the high tuition fees.

The students were strictly divided into classes for men and for women, and this division applied to the teaching staff as well. Men did not teach women students and female professors did not teach male students. On campus, however, students could meet freely. The language of instruction was English, but most students conversed among themselves in French or Arabic.

The campus of Beirut College for Women was in an idyllic location on a small hill above the city, amid a park with cypresses, palm trees, and cedars. From there one had a breathtaking view of the city and the sea. On hot days I enjoyed teaching my girls under a large cedar tree in the park. There I was really inspired and could feel the breath of history. This was not true for my students, however. History and politics could not hold their interest for very long; their thoughts were mostly occupied by romantic feelings and love.

Illustration from "The Arabian Nights Entertainment." This is the way my girls imagined their future life to be.

I was surrounded by the most charming girls of the Orient. At the beginning of the semester they arrived at the college escorted by their family clan. Deeply veiled, and with many tears and sighs, they said good-bye to their parents, aunts, uncles, and cousins. The next morning they appeared in my lecture hall dressed in short miniskirts and valuable jewelry, their beautiful dark eyes carefully made up. I was surprised by such a show of Western elegance and poise.

In Beirut one could immediately recognize the social status of a person by his or her appearance. In the upper classes, one met primarily beautiful and elegant women.

Beauty was an existential question for a woman in the Orient. Physical beauty was definitely a status symbol. Besides descent, it certainly was a major criterion by which the families of the bridegroom selected the future wife for their son. Education, personality, and character seemed to be of rather secondary importance; at least it was considered less important than in our culture.

Women in the Islamic world had to obey and subjugate their own will to husband and family. This is why the art of pretension was a question of survival. The relationship to men was in the beginning one of romantic infatuation; later it was the care for the common children that determined their relationship. A deep friendship, as we understand it, and the sharing of common interests was rarely found, and almost impossible.

There were, however, sincere and close friendships among men, and the young girls also had a way to interact with each other that at first sight appeared strange to us. They openly expressed loving and tender emotions in bodily contact for each other. Romantic feelings and fantasies seemed to dominate their thoughts.

As a teacher, one is often the object of intense admiration. I had experienced that in the United States. But I was not prepared to deal with such tender adulation as I received from some of these girls. I received love letters, music cassettes, and lovely poems addressed to me.

The main interest of my girls was, however, concentrated on men. Many times I became their confidante and listened to their problems. Men certainly were unknown creatures for them. Meetings were only allowed in the presence of another, older woman. Thus, they did not have much chance to really get to know each other. This fact did not seem to play a major part in their preferences. Major criteria were the man's outward appearance, what kind of car he drove, and of course, from which family he came. Their ideas about love seemed to be determined more by the stories told in *One Thousand and One Nights*.

LEBANON

…Thou art all fair, my love; there is no spot in thee.

Come with me from Lebanon, my spouse, with me from Lebanon: look from the top of Amana, from the top of Shenir and Hermon, from the lions' dens, from the mountains of the leopards!

Thou hast ravished my heart, my sister, my spouse; thou hast ravished my heart with one of thine eyes, with one chain of thy neck.

How fair is thy love, my sister, my spouse! how much better is thy love than wine! and the smell of thine ointments than all spices!

From thy lips, O my spouse, drop as the honeycomb: honey and milk are under thy tongue; and the smell of thy garments is like the smell of Lebanon.

A garden enclosed is my sister, my spouse; a spring shut up, a fountain sealed.

Thy plants are an orchard of pomegranates, with pleasant fruits; camphire, with spikenard,

Spikenard and saffron; calamus and cinnamon, with all trees of frankincense; myrrh and aloes, with all the chief spices:

Thou art the fountain of the garden, a well of living waters, like the streams from Lebanon.....

(Song of Solomon 4)

There are many passages in the Old Testament that mention the beauties of Lebanon, but none does justice to the mountain range that has given its name to the country at its feet as impressively as the *Song of Solomon*. It shows this wild range of mountains full of dangers and ancient mysteries, but also a life full of abundance—a country of milk and honey.

The prophet Jeremiah calls it a "place of depot for many countries." So many cultures have left their traces and way of life in Lebanon. I was fascinated by these traces and was following them during this first semester break.

It was a clear spring day in 1967 when we left the city early in the morning. We took a "domus"—a taxi for general transport—to the central square in the main suq. We wanted to travel to Damascus. Unfortunately, Howard could not join us, so I decided to take the trip alone, together with the girls.

When we arrived at the suq, it took me a while to make out the station from which the bus was supposed to leave amid the milling mass of the market. Finally, I heard the shrill calls of a young Arab, which hovered like those of a hawk above the buzzing hum of the crowd. A beard, piercing black eyes, and a hooked nose, as well as the skillfully wrapped turban and a dark caftan, revealed him to be a Syrian. At the top of his lungs he called out the departure of his bus to Damascus.

The bus had already arrived, and he was waiting for passengers. When we climbed on, it was filled with colorful characters, farmers with baskets filled with chickens, women with veils and those without, many children, and a lot of bundles.

I asked the Syrian driver when the bus would leave and received a short answer: "When the bus is full!" And when would we arrive in Damascus? "In the evening, Inshallah!" We waited.

People in the Orient have a different sense of time. Also the use of gestures is something one has to learn to interpret. For instance, if someone nods his head upwards, he means "No" and not "Yes" as is customary in the West.

We were the only foreigners on the bus: two blond, blue-eyed little girls and their mother, without a veil and with only one small traveling bag. Curious glances followed every one of our movements. The driver cleared his best seats for us in the first row, right behind him. It seemed to take an eternity until the bus was finally filled up to the last seat. Some people even squatted on the floor between their bundles. The women gabbed in Arabic, the chickens cackled in their baskets, the engine roared—we were finally on our way.

After about one hour we had left the crowded streets of Beirut behind us and were ascending the winding road toward the snow-capped summits of the Lebanese mountain chain. The view was breathtaking. Way down below us lay the buzzing city and the blue Mediterranean, and above us the famous cedars of Lebanon. The "holy wood of the gods," as these trees were called in antiquity, were known for the hardness and durability of their wood. Therefore, it was highly treasured as building material for ships and palaces by the Babylonians, the Egyptian pharaohs, and the seafaring Phoenicians as well as, of course, the Romans, who almost completely denuded the holy forests.

Today only few of these majestic trees have survived the age-long overexploitation. Some of these stately trees have been resisting the weather and man for a thousand years. Today they are under protection by the state.

The people on the bus were very friendly. We tried to keep up a conversation in French, English, and the few words of Arabic I had learned.

On both sides of the road there remained heaps of snow, and somehow I was reminded of Switzerland. The landscape with wild cliffs, dark valleys, ruins of old castles, ancient monasteries, and mosques built like nests into the hillside passed by our window and stimulated our imagination. Many old myths are connected with these snow-covered mountain peaks and the clouds that often hide them like ghosts from the view of man.

In ancient times this was the world of mysterious *djinns* who struck terror into peoples' hearts. My girls loved these ghost stories, and we kept spying out the window to maybe catch a view of one of these mixed creatures, half-man, half-animal.

I was reminded of the hero of my favorite epic poem: *The Epic of Gilgamesh*. This oldest-known work of literature was carved in cuneiform script onto hundreds of clay tablets that were found in the palace of the Syrian king Assurbanipal. The Sumerian legend tells the story of the mythological hero-king of Uruk, a city at the shores of the Euphrates in Mesopotamia—now Iraq—who ruled in the third millennium B.C.

This is the way I told the story to the girls:

> The proud Gilgamesh, who had become disheartened with his rule in Uruk, together with his beloved friend Enkidu, slays the guardian of the Cedar Forest, a djinn named Humbaba, and transports the stolen cedar trunks to Uruk. There he wants to build an impregnable wall and an imposing city gate.

When Enkidu is doomed by the gods to die, Gilgamesh realizes that man is able to conquer everything except death. He starts on a journey to the end of the world to find immortality. When he finally reaches the abode of Ushnapischtin, the biblical Noah, he implores him to disclose the mystery of eternal life. But here too, near the waters of death, his search is futile.

The barmaid Siduri reminds him:

"Gilgamesh, where are you going?

The eternal life you seek you will not find!

Men come and go. When the gods created man,

They kept eternal life for themselves

But decreed that death be the fate of man.

Someday you will depart. But till that distant day sing and dance!

Eat your fill of warm cooked food and drink cool jugs of beer!

Cherish the children your love gave life!

Bathe away life's dirt in warm drawn waters!

Pass the time in joy with your chosen wife!

On the Tablets of Destiny it is decreed for you

To enjoy short pleasures in your short days."

Now we started our descent to the Bekaa Valley, which opens up to the north of the mountain range. In the north, toward the Syrian border, rises the mountain range of the Anti-Lebanon, toward the south, Mount Hermon, in front of it, the Schuf. In this soft, hilly countryside nestle the villages of the Druze, one of the many Moslem groups in Lebanon.

Then the endless valley of the Bekaa Valley surrounded us. Its abundance is based on the fertility of the red earth and on a system of irrigation invented in antiquity. In Roman days, the Bekaa Valley was the granary of the Roman province of Syria.

Spring had painted the whole valley with tender green. Trees and bushes were covered with blossoms. There was a breath of paradise in the air.

"Yes," I thought, "this is paradise the way the Koran describes it so beautifully:

> The true followers of Allah shall receive certain favors in paradise:
>
> They will be offered luscious fruit, and they will be honored in the Garden of Eden.
>
> They shall recline with each other on sumptuous pillows.
>
> A jug, filled from the cool spring, will make the round,
>
> A clear drink, a refreshment for the thirsty.
>
> They will not receive anything that may bewilder their soul.
>
> And chaste virgins will keep them company, with large, black eyes,
>
> Beautiful like the hidden egg…

The Roman ruins in Baalbek

Suddenly the ruins of the proud Roman temples of Baalbeck rose in the distance. The contrast between the slender arcades and columns and the wide expanse of the fertile valley and the austere rocks of the Anti-Lebanon gave the scenery a magic touch.

Were we in Italy? Had a time machine transported us back to antiquity? Again, we felt strangely at home. What a haunting place of mysticism and solemnity!

Our trip continued to the north of the country, and then we crossed the border into Syria. We passed the old Islamic city of Anjar, and soon we could see the first Syrian villages. Their houses surprised us with their strange architecture: round houses made from mud bricks with dome shaped roofs, built like beehives joined to each other. In Southern Italy I had already seen this extraordinary domestic architecture, called "Trulli."

The women who worked in the fields wore handsome, hand-embroidered dresses. Those who deemed themselves "more modern" had changed to the garish colored prints that were sold at the markets.

As we passed through small towns, the women were completely veiled in black.

We stopped in a city called Hama, famous for its ancient water wheels, and I left the bus to take a few photos. I rushed through the street, dressed in a long-sleeved blouse and semi-long skirt. Suddenly I felt like I was running the gauntlet: The men on the street stared at me as though I were naked. In their eyes, I saw not only surprise, but also a strange mixture of desire and threatening hatred. I remembered that many Moslems considered women to be the hideout of the devil. This thought scared me, and in that moment I wished I had a long, non-transparent veil in which I could wrap myself. Quickly, I crawled back onto the bus.

On the ancient Roman road in the Bekaa Valley.

Late in the evening we finally reached Damascus. This city was already 5,000 years old when it was conquered by the Romans, and it is the oldest continually inhabited city in the world. Legend tells that a grandson of Noah founded it. This was centuries of Oriental history carved in stone and set in gold and silver.

In the center of town we found a Western-style hotel and spent the night there.

The next morning we started on a discovery trip through history. We began with a visit to the National Museum. The building itself was already an optical pleasure: The entrance consisted of the original stucco façade of the desert palace, Quasr-al-Hayr Gharbi, which the Caliph of the Ommiads, Hisham, had built in 730 A.D. Inside we found treasures from 9,000 years of Syrian culture, among others, the famous scriptures with the Old Testament from the time of 250 A.D. I was completely frustrated not to have studied archaeology, or at least to have prepared myself better for what I was about to see, so that I could have better understood the treasures before me. I could have spent the whole day there, but the girls were anxious to move on and visit the market.

Taking a rest in the Bekaa Valley

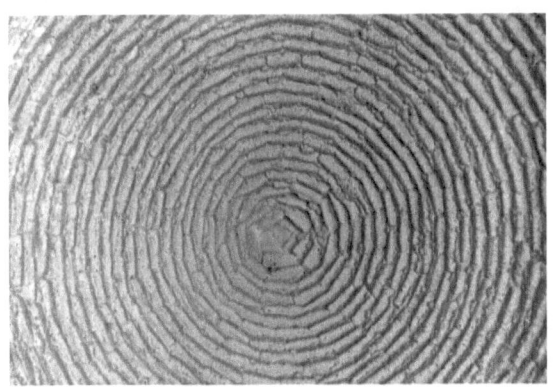

Beehive villages in Syria.

Looking up into the domed roof. Syrian women in their colorful dresses

The walls of Damascus.

In the afternoon we submerged ourselves in the bustling life of the suq of Damascus, probably the largest market in the Middle East. In contrast to the wide-open atmosphere in the suq of Beirut, foreigners were strangers here. I felt like an immaterial ghost walking through the crowd. No one would openly look into my face, but I felt the curious glances on my back.

Suddenly the girls had disappeared. I panicked, but a few minutes later I made them out near the ancient gate amid a group of teenage boys. Most of them were blond and were eagerly talking in English to them. They seemed excited but were talking with friendly smiles on their faces and with gentle gestures. They were young Russian students who had just left their school. Their parents worked as advisors to the Syrian government. I suddenly realized that Syria was under the influence of the Soviet Union, which had even opened a Russian school for these children. This fact might have been the reason for the undefined suspicion I had felt everywhere. We were not only easily identifiable as non-believers but we were foreigners from the Western countries, perhaps even from the "great devil," the United States. Here we were confronted with the East–West conflict firsthand.

Syria, the castle of Aleppo. Taking a rest on top of a heap of ancient cannon balls. Veiled female soldiers in Syria.

In the North of Beirut

Howard and I had an invitation from UNRA, the United Nations Relief and Rehabilitation Administration to visit, together with a group of educators, a school in a camp for Palestinian refugees in the north of Beirut. Up to this point I had not been very familiar with the political problems of these people. I was familiar with the history of Israel, of course, and had read about the fierce battle of the Israelis for the survival of their young nation in 1948. Since that time, bitter conflicts had flared up again and again in this region. I knew that, but the true extent of this continuously smoldering conflict, its background, and especially the toll it had taken on the people, came to my awareness only during my visit to this camp.

For the first time in my life I was confronted with dire destitution. Hundreds of dilapidated huts were crowded into a minimum of space. They housed families of ten or more persons in their small, rundown rooms—mostly women, children, and old people. The men were absent. They tried to earn a few pennies outside of the camp while their families vegetated amid dust and trash.

Why were these people prohibited from integrating themselves into the country?

Whom would they disturb? Or were they simply incapable of integrating into a society? All these questions raced through my mind as we entered the school of the camp. We had arrived just as the children were lining up for the morning roll call.

Hundreds of children crowded around a flagpole with the Palestinian flag in the schoolyard. With their faces excited and bright red, and at the top of their voice, they repeated the words a prayer leader was spelling out for them in Arabic. The words ran something like this: "We promise to sacrifice our blood and our lives for our beloved country, Palestine. We will not rest until our enemies are defeated and the land of our ancestors is ours again! I swear to give the last drop of my blood to destroy the enemies! We will drive them into hell! The final victory will be ours!"

I could feel a cold shiver run down my back. I could not believe what I saw and heard. Every day these poor children were fanaticized in such an irresponsible manner. That tone of voice and those slogans! I had heard something similar in my own childhood. But never had I met with such an aggressive feeling of hate.

Palestinian refugee camp.

This was a commitment to eternal revenge. Revenge, for what was felt as the gravest insult. Revenge for the miserable life in the camp. Revenge for the loss of one's homeland. It was pure hatred, which was being infused into the hearts of these children. I was deeply disturbed and followed Howard and the rest of the group who had already entered the school building.

After our tour I had the opportunity to start a conversation with one of the young teachers who had impressed me with his intense concern for his students. I asked him about the subjects he taught. His somewhat shy response was, "Reading, some writing, simple arithmetic, and of course the holy texts of the Koran."

I wanted to know whether he also taught some practical know-how, which would enable his students to make a living and support their families? For instance, how to repair cars or build houses? Wasn't this the only chance for these children to become integrated into society and lead a normal life outside of the camp?

He hesitated, and then told me that indeed he had tried to teach these skills, but then he was called to order and was accused of betrayal of the "Palestinian cause." He had almost lost his job. Now he was resigned and had given up.

With a feeling of helplessness, irritation, and depression we left the camp and returned to our still "safe and secure world"!

Howard's Crisis

From that day on, things were not the same. Not that I would have become politically active, but somehow I had been awakened to reality. I began to become aware of a certain nervousness in Beirut, an irritation between the different religious groups as well as toward foreigners in general. There were no concrete incidents, but below the surface a feeling of insecurity began to make itself felt.

In this highly sensitive atmosphere, Howard had met an Irish monk. Howard, who had always been very religious, wanted to receive Holy Communion during the Easter celebration. He was looking for a father confessor. This confession had disastrous consequences. It was a confession that meant the end of our family life and the beginning of the most serious crisis in Howard's life.

This fanatical servant of God succeeded in convincing Howard that he was "living in sin" with me. His reproaches hit Howard right in the heart. His feelings of guilt about having left his family were deeply felt. Howard was thrown into a deep emotional conflict.

On the one hand, he loved me more than life itself, but on the other hand, it seemed impossible to make peace with his Catholic faith. This he could only achieve if he obeyed the orders of the priest.

A troubled time began for us. I noticed that there was something wrong with Howard. He was very irritable and reacted with impatience to the children, which was not his nature. He repeatedly criticized the lack of order in their room. I myself lost my patience, and one day I explained to them that they had to keep order in their room as long as they lived in the same house with us. If they did not like this rule, they would have to move out.

They actually took us at our word. Ariane and Vivian began to pack their clothes and toys into a suitcase, and declared that they would prefer to move out.

I feigned agreement, but kept a close eye on them. They spent a whole day in one of the locker rooms on the beach, right across the street.

In the evening they were back home.

After the children had gone to bed, Howard and I talked about the situation. Very quietly and in a loving way, Howard spoke about his father confessor and about his inner torture.

I could see how much he had tried to fight these inner conflicts. I understood his plight, but what I had to listen to then was impossible for me to comprehend: It was me, Eva, whom Satan was using in order to get hold of Howard's soul to lead him straight to hell. In order to save his soul and receive the holy sacraments again, he would have to immediately leave me and sue for divorce. Such was the order of the Irish monk. I thought we had returned to the Middle Ages. Howard had not been able to come to any decision so far, he said. The idea of leaving me had been insupportable for him.

Now I began to observe our life together more closely. It seemed to me that Howard was suffering under this strange new culture. Added to this was the feeling of insecurity about his job. Up to now, the university had not renewed his contract. Howard was completely uncertain about himself and our future life, and obviously suffered from a severe case of culture shock.

The Irish monk had advised Howard to have his teenage son join him in Beirut. Chris arrived soon after. He was a quiet and pleasant boy, and the girls were happy to have an older brother. On the outside, everything seemed to be in order again, but Howard and I were very insecure with each other.

One day, when Chris had been a few weeks in Beirut, Howard moved to a separate apartment together with his son. I had not expected this turn of events. I was immensely sad and insecure at the same time. On the one hand, Howard could not separate himself from me, and on the other hand, he felt that he had to obey this monk. He was in a serious conflict of conscience, but for me it was impossible to help him, other than by accepting his decision without dramatic scenes, which would have made everything even harder for Howard. The fatal influence of the monk became so strong that soon afterward we actually found ourselves in front of a lawyer to arrange for a divorce, despite the fact that we both loved each other dearly.

We did not see each other for the next three months, and Howard avoided any contact. Only once, on a soft and pleasant afternoon, did we meet by chance on the campus of the university. I was sitting under a tree on a small hill with my girl students. We were discussing a romantic novel from the 19th century. At the same time, Howard was giving his lecture in philosophy on the lawn not far from me.

Again and again our glances met and it seemed as though the air between us was loaded with electricity. But both of us kept control over our feelings, and we did not exchange one word. Was this pride, reason, or simply stupidity? I do not know.

Howard had been gone from our apartment for over a month when I suddenly began to suffer from unbearable pains in the abdomen. I was desperate. Alone with the children in this strange city and now in a bad physical condition! I would even lose my job. What could I do?

In the emergency ward of the hospital of the American University, they gave me a pain pill and sent me home. It was Sunday. The pains went and came back in intervals.

Three weeks later I decided to fight my depressive mood. I wanted to take a short trip to Jerusalem before my contract with the university would end. I still suffered from the pains in the abdomen at irregular intervals. Therefore, I decided to ask the doctor at University Hospital to check me, just in case.

He took one look and did not allow me to go back home that day. His diagnosis was ectopic pregnancy in an acute stage. I had to be operated on immediately.

I was lucky, however, because there was the little Arab girl and my mother, whom I had called and begged to take the next plane to Beirut in order to take care of the girls and the household.

In this situation, I appreciated those qualities of hers under which I had suffered as a child: her energy, her willpower, and her practical strength.

Never in my life had I needed Mother as much as now. After the operation and the associated change of hormones, I fell into a deep depression. When I left the hospital I was still very weak and was suffering from great pain. I was so weak that I could not even stand the noise of the traffic on the street. The constant pain tortured me. I spent all day in bed, could not eat anything, and thought of death, which I had escaped at the last moment only by chance.

The queerest ideas began to cross my mind. For instance, I tried to imagine what it would be like to throw myself out of the window, or I thought of the vegetable grocer from the store at the next street. That good-looking Lebanese man had always been very friendly and had cast an eye on me whenever I did my shopping at his store. Should I go to see him and ask whether he would accept me into his harem?

At that time, a life in the security of a harem seemed much more pleasant than the fate of a single mother with an uncertain job all alone in this strange city. In a harem, women are protected from the rough battle for survival in the outside world. They divided the tasks of household and family in a harmonious way and could support each other when they felt bad, physically or psychologically. Now this lifestyle did not seem so bad to me.

Mother's energy and comfort and my improving health chased these crazy thoughts from my mind after a while, and the rest of my melancholy mood disappeared when I reentered the campus after six weeks. As far as my teaching activity was concerned, I had been lucky, because most of the time of my illness had chanced to fall during the spring semester break.

Back among my colleagues, I sensed a certain pervasive feeling of nervousness. The political situation in the Middle East had escalated at that time and was giving grounds for serious concern. The news coming from Syria, Egypt, and Israel did not point in the direction of peace. On television one could always see the same pictures, outraged Moslems, who aggressively screamed their slogans at the top of their lungs: "Death to Israel! We will drive the infidels into the sea!"

In the city, everyday life seemed to continue as always. People went to the suq, the traffic was dense, and the muezzin chanted his prayers. Nevertheless, there was some undefined threat in the air. I could not worry too much about all this, because I had problems enough with school, children, and household. Besides all this, I had dropped a marble table on my toe and had to walk around with a cast.

I was alone with Mother and the girls and did not yet have a new work contract for the next academic year. Howard was out of reach. We now had a date for the divorce. What would happen? However, I could not stop to think, because the final examinations for the school year were close.

The Six-Day War

On the morning of July 5, 1967, I entered the campus; under my arm I was carrying the examination papers for my classes. I found the whole building in an uproar. I could not believe what I saw. Were these my sweet, demure, gentle girls? They were dancing wildly on top of the desks and tables, which they had pushed together and their shrill voices were echoing throughout the campus: "Long live Palestine! Americans out! Long live Palestine! Americans out!"

Only now did I find out what had happened: During the night Israel had launched a blitz attack and had destroyed the complete Egyptian air force on the ground of its own country.

This meant war in the Middle East!

There was no longer any thought about lectures or examinations. I left the university and immediately went to the German Embassy. There I found the doors closed. Only a small door to a side entrance was open. Yes, of course the German citizens would be airlifted out of the city. With my German passport I could join them, but only without my children. After all, they were American citizens and not the responsibility of the German government. Of course, this was no option for me, so I hurried to the American Embassy.

There I explained my situation and received my instructions: The security of American citizens in Lebanon could no longer be guaranteed, and all U.S. citizens would be evacuated tonight. As the mother of American children, I could leave the country together with them. We were to assemble within the next three hours on the campus of the American University. We should bring food for one day and blankets, because nobody knew where we would go and how long the journey would take.

Now everything happened very quickly. I raced home, collected the children, and discussed the situation with Mother. She wanted to remain in Beirut until all our belongings were stowed away in containers by the American embassy and then return to Munich as fast as possible, either by plane or by ship.

It was hard for all of us to say good-bye to our little Arab girl; we had become really good friends. But there was no time for a long good-bye. We had to get out of there! Mother packed food into some bags, as well as sweaters and blankets and gently pushed us out the door. "We will meet in Munich!"

Shortly after that, we were sitting on our blankets on the lawn of the American University. For the first time I looked at my watch. Not more than three hours had passed since I had left the campus this morning. It seemed so far away.

The vast campus was now filled with people. Nobody seemed nervous or even aggressive. People were conversing quietly and in a friendly manner. If someone needed any help it was given immediately. For the first time I noticed how quiet and disciplined Americans are in situations of crisis. They showed their best side: helpful, disciplined, and very professional.

By evening the campus was overcrowded. Everywhere there were families with children, sitting on chests and suitcases, wrapped in blankets, talking quietly.

Despite all the havoc, I had tried to reach Howard at home, but there was no getting through to him because all the lines were busy.

When darkness had set in, suddenly, there he stood before me. Without a word we fell into each other's arms.

At this moment we both knew that we belonged together. Nothing should ever separate us again. The forced atonement and the tortures of conscience were forgotten. The date for our divorce had been cancelled by decree of a higher power thanks to the Six-Day War!

We left around midnight. Some groups ended in Ankara, Turkey, and we landed in Athens, Greece. There we found ourselves in another situation of turmoil. The military junta had come to power by means of a coup d'etat just a few weeks before and they were nervous. The streets were full of tanks. The war in the Middle East seemed very close.

Amid the crowd at the airport we had to make a quick decision: Both of us had lost our jobs, what now? We agreed that Howard would fly back to the United States to look for a new job abroad there. The girls and I would go to Munich and wait for him there.

After such a short interval of time, our lifelines were again turning in different directions.

But this time our hearts were relieved. We had found each other again and would not let go any more. This was all that mattered.

Athena and Nausikaa. Red-figured vase, (470 B.C.).

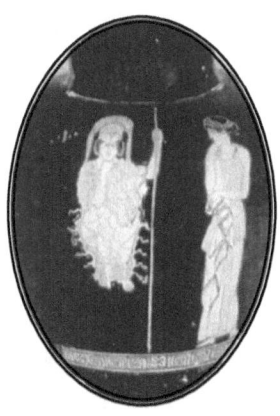

Chapter 11: Intermezzo in Munich

Teaching at the Goethe Institute

It was well after midnight when we finally arrived in our apartment at Gruetznerstrasse 6 in Munich. Ariane and Vivian had been overwhelmed by fatigue and had fallen asleep. The last 24 hours had been extremely exciting and tiresome for all of us. As usual, the girls had been very brave. I myself was completely hyped up, wide awake, and at the limit of my psychological endurance. Too much had happened that had again put my life on a completely new track.

I had managed somehow to reach Father at the last minute before our departure from Athens to inform him about our sudden arrival in Munich. I burst into in tears when I saw him waiting for us at the gate in Munich. These were tears of relief to have arrived home. Father, dependable as always, gave me back my feeling of security in his manner of calm and serene cheerfulness.

We had not yet heard from Mother, but we were not very worried. We knew of her down-to-earth strength and assertiveness and were sure she would make her way against anyone. Soon we would have her with us again. Father helped me to carry the sleeping girls upstairs. It was only then that the tension left me and I fell into a deep, dreamless sleep.

It was one o'clock in the afternoon when the familiar screeching of the streetcar curving around the Maximilianeum behind our house woke me up. Our apartment, which is situated snugly in the park between the Wiener Platz and the Maximilianeum (Seat of the Bavarian Government) was a haven of peace on that day, June 6, 1967.

I could look into the lush green of the tall beech trees on both sides of the apartment. No roaring traffic and constant hooting like yesterday on the Corniche in Beirut. The only noise came from the south side of the house, where the homely sounds of tinkling beer mugs in the beer garden below, mixed with the joyous twitter of the birds who inhabit the old chestnut trees, combined into a joyous melody of well-being and happiness.

In 1966, while I still lived in Hampton, Virginia, Mother had heard that there was an apartment for sale on this cozy little street, the Gruetznerstrasse, not far from her own house. Howard and I had set our hearts on buying this apartment, despite or perhaps because of the fact that we knew that we would go to Beirut.

The Gruetznerstrasse apartment was just perfect for us. It was the right size, was situated near the bank of the river Isar, right in the center of town, and was close to my parents' home. My parents and we bought the apartment in the 100-year-old house immediately. This turned out to have been an excellent decision, which influenced my life several times later. Today this enchanted house has become my home; here, after years of my odyssey, I have found my peace.

In 1967 the Gruetznerstrasse apartment became our place of refuge. I suspect that Athena had had her hand in the endeavor. Her statue, which I recalled from the days of my childhood, stood on the bridge over the Isar River and was now only a few yards from our new home.

When we picked up Mother from the airport five days later, the Israelis had decided the war in the Middle East in their favor. Israeli soldiers had occupied the Gaza Strip and the Sinai Peninsula; they were in West Jordan and vast parts of Syria. On June 10, 1967, the United Nations ordered an armistice. However, all international attempts to find a way to permanent peace ended in failure.

In Munich, the young people took to the streets. It was the time of the student peace movement. Since the middle of the Sixties they had protested against "the Establishment," against "the Emergency Laws," against the Shah of Iran and his police escort in Berlin in 1967, against the power of capitalism, and against the shadows of the German past.

I had different problems. I was again a single mother, and I needed a job. I was running out of time and money. What chances did I have?

I was a trained teacher with a university degree in "Teaching of English" and had teaching experience at the college level in the United States and in foreign countries. Maybe I had a chance to teach adults at the Goethe Institute (a worldwide, government-supported institution for the teaching of the German language and culture). I took the bull by the horns and applied, even though I knew that they would only accept teachers with a degree in German studies.

To my surprise, I was accepted as one of many applicants, and thus I would at least have a chance to introduce myself. The head of the institute's language section, Dora Schulz, an impressive grand dame who had helped to reestablish the Goethe Institute after the war, examined each applicant herself and made her choices. That day about 15 applicants were sitting in a circle. We had to introduce ourselves in short and concise sentences, describe our curriculum vitae, and explain why we wanted to teach in the Goethe Institute.

All the other applicants were German studies students. They introduced themselves in polished German. As far as my language capabilities were concerned, I was at a disadvantage. I had spoken only

English during the last 14 years, and my German was anything but perfect. The longer I listened to my colleagues, the less I believed in my chances.

Then it was my turn. I took a deep breath, thought of my girls, and just started to tell my story. I noticed that everyone listened with great interest, but I was in doubt whether I would be able to convince them with my formulations and my professional knowledge.

A few days later I received a letter telling me that I had been accepted as a teacher at the Goethe Institute. I was overjoyed. I would have to pass an in-service training period of six weeks. At first I was to audit the classes of experienced teachers, and then I was allowed to teach my own classes while under the supervision of the teacher. The training at the Goethe Institute was thorough and demanding as far as theory and practice were concerned.

After completing my training, I was offered a permanent job in the schools in Ebersberg and then in Kochel. For me, this was a great success, but it also had its consequences. Now I had a "full-time job" and this meant that I would not be home during the week and could take care of the children only during the weekends. It seemed like an insoluble problem. Mother again came to our rescue. Again she was our savior in our need. She and our maid Maria took care of the girls during the week, and I could concentrate on my work without worry.

With the girls in Kochel and on Lake Chiemsee, the Fraueninsel in the background.

For my girls, difficult days lay ahead. Up to now they had attended international or American schools. They only knew a school system that was very oriented to the needs of the students. In Germany, the teaching plan had priority, and the teacher was a person of absolute authority.

The adjustment to these different expectations alone would have been enough. But, in order to relieve Mother, I had decided to place the girls into the boarding school run by the Catholic sisters of St. Anna, not far from home. It turned out to be a catastrophe. The girls pleaded tearfully to be allowed to get out as soon as possible. In the convent they felt like they were locked up in a dungeon. When Vivian told me that one night when she had to throw up she had been severely scolded because she had left her bed, instead of finding comfort and help from the sisters, I took them out immediately. The girls returned to their grandmother's apartment and came to visit me in Kochel or Ebersberg on the weekends. There we took wonderful trips into the countryside, which we enjoyed very much. I was convinced that it would be better for our relationship to live as one family together, than to put them into another boarding school.

The girls loved their grandparents and slowly they began to feel at home in Munich.

Teaching at the Goethe Institute was a great challenge for me. Students from many different foreign countries were in my class. Most of them were adults with successful professional careers, who had set high goals for themselves. They could neither communicate with me nor with each other in one common language. We were not allowed to speak English (although this would not have been entirely helpful, as many of them did not know English).

Teaching German at the Goethe Institute.

I had to start at a point where communication did not seem possible at all. Thanks to the well-developed teaching methods of the Goethe Institute, it was not long before I had established a basis for future instruction in the German language. After six weeks, my students were able to go shopping in town and make themselves understood on their own. This is why I enjoyed beginners' classes most. The students were wise enough to know that they knew nothing, and the success was very tangible. I was always surprised with the results. Never in my career as language teacher did I have such verifiable results as during my time at the Goethe Institute.

It was interesting to see how certain national characteristics and behaviors could be identified and confirmed over and over again. When the class consisted of many students from the northern countries, progress proved somewhat slow. Only in response to some pressure and with many incentives were they willing to speak.

Many Latin Americans in class meant a certain amount of chaos, but the atmosphere was more entertaining and relaxed. These students not only enjoyed talking and laughing with each other during class but they also got up and joked around. They disliked learning grammar rules and did not always do their homework, but after a short time they were able to talk, even if without much attention to correctness.

Japanese students were hardworking and disciplined. They listened intently to what the teacher said and always had their homework done correctly, but they had great difficulty speaking. The highly educated and older Japanese students had the most problems. The better they were educated, the higher was the demand they placed on themselves and their performance. Often they avoided speaking altogether out of fear of making mistakes. They did not want to lose face.

My work was very satisfying to me, and a year and a half had gone by in a flash. This was fortunate for me, because it took that long for Howard to find a new job and for us to be together again.

The long separation had been painful for us both, despite the fact that Howard showed his devotion to me in a very special and romantic way: Every week for a year and a half he sent me a dozen red roses. They were of some comfort to me, but I still felt lonely.

*Heracles in battle with the River God Acheloos
red-figure stamnos, (525-500 B.C.E.)*

Chapter 12: An Adventure in Southeast Asia

Rendezvous in Hong Kong

The four-motored Boeing of Pan American Airlines slowly rose into the sky.

Below us the city of Munich became smaller and smaller. On our left, the peaks of the Alps gleamed in the morning sun and on our right were the snow-covered fields of the Dachauer Moos.

The first of January was a winter day out of a fairy-tale story. During the night it had snowed heavily, and in the morning the sun painted sparkling lights on trees, and roofs, and the church towers of the city. Munich seemed under a spell, and our house near the park had turned into a winter wonderland.

We had to get up early on that beautiful winter morning. We were embarking on a new adventure—an adventure that should take us to Southeast Asia, to Manila in the Philippines, far away on the other side of the globe.

It was hard for me, Ariane, and Vivian to say good-bye to our home in the Gruetznerstrasse.

We quickly forgot the pain of departing from our home when we took off and the stewardess began to explain the safety regulations in pure American English. Our curiosity was awakened, and most of all we were looking forward to seeing Howard, whom we finally were to meet again in Hong Kong. A year and a half had been a long time.

Howard had accepted a position with the U.S. State Department, with USAID, the American agency for foreign aid and development. His task would be to advise the South Vietnamese government in matters of higher education, teacher training, and university education. As a member of the State Department, he now held a political position. This was new for him and quite a challenge even for a man with his experience.

He had been trying for a year and a half to find a position at a university in or near Europe. Now he was assigned to Southeast Asia. Since in Vietnam the war between the capitalistic South and the communist North had been escalating, it was really an adventure we were embarking on. But our yearning to be together was stronger than all our apprehensions.

Our flight was routed via Istanbul, Beirut, Karachi, Calcutta, Rangoon, and Bangkok to Hong Kong. Shortly before Beirut we were informed that the astronauts had safely landed in Hawaii. Up here between the earth and the sea, we felt very close to them.

After a short stop in Beirut we read in a French newspaper that a Palestinian terror group had executed a bombing attack on the airport of Athens. The commando had blown up a jumbo jet of the Israeli airline El Al. There had been many dead and wounded.

As we came closer to our destination, the faces of the passengers began to change.

There were more and more Asian faces. I could not guess from which country in Asia they came. I only recognized the Japanese, since I had seen many Japanese students in the Goethe-Institut.

We passed the hours by telling stories. For hours we had been flying through the night.

As we looked down to the dark countryside we began to think up fantastic stories. Stories about Arab caravans that were passing through the desert, their camels loaded with beautiful oriental rugs. I told about secret oases, resting places for the caravans where the travelers were sleeping in luxurious tents, and of the oil that issued forth from secret wells right out of the ground and which had provided the Arab countries with unheard of wealth but had failed to give them the peace they hoped for. Just the opposite had been the result.

In the meantime, we had reached Karachi. We saw a bay with thousands of lights below us, similar to the Bay of Naples or the coast of Beirut.

Karachi was our first step into an unfamiliar world. When I realized this, I planned to meet the new situation with as little prejudice as possible. I intended to just simply take in these new impressions without filtering them first with a prejudging and scrutinizing mind.

In Karachi we had a short stop. The children were fast asleep. I also was dead tired and did not feel like getting out to look at the airport. The stewardess woke us with a cheerful "good morning;" it was half past three a.m. At home in Munich it was eleven o'clock in the evening. A thought briefly crossed my mind about how relative our feeling for time was and our idea of time itself. Then I went back to sleep. Once in a while I heard the soft voices of the Pakistanis who had gotten on the plane. They spoke a strange kind of English.

I thought about the fact that as a mother with two children, one was perfectly safe anywhere. Wherever I had been, people were helpful and had treated me with respect. People took notice of us, a young mother and two blond little girls, but no one ever bothered us.

In Rangoon we left the plane for a short period. The tropical heat, with a humidity of 95%, hit us like hot steam. It was the first taste of what lay ahead for us in Manila. I was glad to have packed summer clothing into our hand luggage so that we could get rid of our warm sweaters.

Then we were back in the air. Burma seen from above was a beautiful sight in the morning sun. Extensive rice fields changed to intermittent stretches of lush tropical vegetation that surrounded clusters of temples with pagodas and their gold-covered cupolas.

When we landed in Bangkok, the picture changed. We flew over a rich and well organized countryside—squares and rectangles as if drawn by a ruler and bisected by canals and rivers like the veins of a vast body. As far as one could see there were rice fields that painted the countryside in a rich, light-green color.

Bangkok International Airport was very well kept and looked more like a garden with exotic lush plants.

We could make out Jumbos (airplanes) from every part of the world, one beside the other, even in 1969.

On another part of the airport was the military section. I saw a long row of military jets; they seemed brand new and polished. They were a beautiful but somehow threatening sight.

Our departure was delayed because gasoline had been detected on one of the wings.

The leak could not be fixed as quickly as expected, so we had some time to enjoy the pretty airport.

Among the slim and delicate Thai people we felt as if we were in the country of the Lilliputians. For the children it was an interesting experience. The women were of a size between Ariane and Vivian. All of a sudden the two girls felt grown up, and I myself felt like an elephant.

The rooms were furnished to suit this petite and graceful people. The toilet seats were very low and the mirrors in the bathroom were hung so low that I had to bend my knees to comb my hair.

The Thai women speak with a soft and singing voice in a very charming and sweet manner, and most of them were elegantly dressed and very pretty. Their olive skin and faces did not betray their age.

Ariane remarked that she felt like a pancake that had not been fried long enough. My girls suddenly seemed somehow coarse and big boned to me in comparison to these graceful and delicate girls.

We were delayed for three hours. Everybody waited patiently. Nobody seemed nervous. Time did not matter. Most of the problems seemed to solve themselves somehow on their own. Here I met a very different mentality from that in Europe or the United States—different also from Beirut. I liked this experience. But I myself would have to change my personal concept of time radically. Up to now I had been so used to getting things done quickly and efficiently, from now on I would have to practice patience, which was not one of my strongest virtues.

After a delay that eventually turned into five hours, we finally landed in Hong Kong. I worried that we had missed Howard. He had come from the United States to meet us here, and he could hardly wait to see us. But as we left the plane the stewardess met us with this happy message, "Mrs. Holland, your husband is waiting for you in the reception hall." When we finally held each other in our arms it seemed that the time we had missed each other and the place around us faded into the distance and there was only the two of us on this planet.

Hong Kong

The whole town seemed as if it were exploding in one enormous fireworks display.

Only a little while earlier we had felt dead tired, but suddenly the tiredness had completely disappeared. We were overwhelmed by the bustling life in the streets, and the exotic beauty of the city intrigued us immediately.

Eva and the girls with a rickshaw in Hong Kong, 1968, Family photo

Howard, the girls, and I were sitting on the terrace of one of the elegant hotels in Kowloon, admiring the spectacular skyline of the city, the junks and houseboats of the bay, and in the distance the mountainous peninsula where the skyscrapers rose up like ant hills. The sea surrounds the city like a blue ring and dresses it with a blue mist during the day. At night the city blazes in the innumerable colors of its flashing billboards, which are reflected a thousand times in the waters of the bay.

If one looked closely, however, it was clear to see that Hong Kong suffered from a chronic lack of living space. Millions of people were crowded together in a small peninsula between the sea and the mountains. Beside each other and on top of each other we saw modern high-rises next to areas covered with flimsy huts with dark backyards where people, chickens, ducks, pigs, dogs, and cats were cramped together in a tiny space. If there was one thing that was scarce in Hong Kong, it was affordable space. The price of living space was astronomically high in Hong Kong.

We had three days to visit this fascinating city. Howard and I hand in hand, together with the children, explored the city. We rented a rickshaw and submerged ourselves in this cosmos of Chinese tradition and modern Western life. On every corner we met with a new culture. It seemed like a melting pot of all of Asia, which had gone into symbiosis with the achievements of the Western world.

After three days we were sad to leave this fascinating world full of life without being able to study it any further.

A happy reunion, Eva and Howard in Hong Kong, 1968, Family photo

IN A GOLDEN CAGE IN THE PHILIPPINES

When we left the airplane in Manila, it took my breath away. I felt like I was entering the rooms of a steam bath. The humid, hot air lay oppressively on my chest. I hoped to be able to get used to it soon. As we walked away from the airplane, the heat of the tarred field actually melted the plastic soles of my sandals.

Vivian, Eva and Tuilan, our cat in Manila, Philippines 1968, Family photo

The girls did not seem to suffer very much, and Howard also did not mind the high humidity.

Our jeepney (were old Jeeps that had been reconstructed as taxis and painted with surrealistic designs) wound its way through the dense traffic of this huge city of one million inhabitants. The heat, the noise, and the exhaust fumes became physical torture until we finally passed through a big gate and found ourselves in a place of peace and calmness. I took a deep breath.

We had arrived in one of those luxurious oases in one of the many housing areas where foreigners or rich Filipinos live. They are virtually fortified

Siesta in the patio, Manila, Philippines, 1968, Family photo

villages, surrounded by high walls and protected by armed security guards at their entrances.

Howard was now an employee of the U.S. State Department; this meant that the U.S. government was responsible for everything, for moving the family, for housing, and for the security of its personnel and their families.

For us this meant a luxurious life that we had never known up until then.

We lived in a beautiful house with a garden full of palm trees and other exotic plants.

In the beginning we had one maid who was responsible for the kitchen and another one who cleaned and did the laundry.

This seemed a bit extravagant to me, but the climate conditions soon convinced me otherwise. As soon as I had dressed in the morning, my clothes were already wet with sweat and had to be changed. Consequently, we had masses of laundry to do every day.

Vivian and our cook, Leyti and our maid, Rami, 1968, Family photo

Eva and Leyti planning the meals for the week, Manila, 1968, Family photo

The world around me seemed to move at a snail's pace. At first it had made me nervous that the two servant girls seemed to move only in slow motion, but I noticed soon that I, myself, began to dislike moving at high speed in this unbearable heat.

Howard could only stay for a short time with us.

The month of January had passed so quickly. We just barely had had time to take care of the most important chores in order to set up our new household when he had to proceed to his duty station in Saigon to begin his new work.

I was somewhat worried to know he would be in Vietnam. The news from that country, which had been a war zone since 1965, was not at all reassuring.

The war had escalated.

By the end of 1968, the Americans had stationed 543,000 soldiers in Vietnam.

Vietnam had been a divided country since 1945. The Communists under their leader Ho Chi Minh ruled the northern part. The southern part was still under French administration until France had to accept defeat by the Vietminh at Dien Bien Phu in 1954 and had to leave the southern part of the country.

The Vietminh had started as a National Liberation Army at the time of the Japanese occupation of Vietnam. Under the French occupation they had developed into a Communist-oriented liberation movement whose purpose was armed resistance against the corrupt, capitalist government of South Vietnam after the departure of the French.

In the early Sixties, the South Vietnamese sought the support of the Americans, who only sent military advisors at first.

In the meantime, Ho Chi Minh had built up a dense system of supply routes through the jungle of Laos, Cambodia, and South Vietnam, the so-called "Ho Chi Minh Trail." By means of this path the Communists transported armaments and later soldiers into the South. The country did not feel threatened only by the Vietminh; it feared infiltration by the Vietcong, a partisan group that was supported by the Communist People's Republic of North Vietnam, which controlled their activities from North Vietnam.

Ho Chi Minh, the president of North Vietnam since 1954, became something like a hero of the resistance against Western capitalism for the worldwide student movement in Europe and the United States. Only Che Guevara could rival his aura and charisma in the eyes of the rebellious young people whose student protests had started to spread from Berkeley in the Fifties. From San Francisco to Berlin, young people took to the streets to fight against economic exploitation and the power of the state. In the Sixties, their major issue was the war in Vietnam. With the slogan "make love not war," they tried to wake up the general population and the politicians to put an end to the senseless carnage in East Asia. But their voices did not seem to have reached the Philippines. Neither the media nor the occupants of the clubs of foreigners discussed these issues very much. Our reality was a different one.

When Howard started his job in Saigon, the war had already been going on for five years. With the exception of a few terrorist attacks, Saigon had been relatively spared until then. Life was going on more or less "normally" in that charming and lively city, if one could call the presence of so may American soldiers and tanks "normal."

Howard and I took turns visiting each other every two weeks. Howard came to see us in Manila, and I flew to Saigon several times to see him there. This marriage at a distance turned out more difficult than we had expected.

We comforted each other by talking to each other every day. Calling long-distance was too difficult and too expensive. So we communicated by talking to each other on the tape recorder about our feelings, our problems, and everyday occurrences. We sent the tapes by courier every week. There was always some member of the embassy that went back and forth between Manila and Saigon. Thus, at least our voices reached each other, and we could share our moods and feelings. It worked pretty well; there was no other choice.

I embarked with all my energies on my role as mother and lady of the house. The children went to the International School, and I helped them with their daily homework.

They had to do a lot of adjusting to the American school system. A year and a half in German schools had been a long interruption, even though I had sent them to the American school in Munich for the last six months to polish up their English.

I was eager and curious to discover my new environment. But soon the heat almost disabled me and prevented me from doing anything. Only very slowly did my body become used to the new conditions. I had been used to moving around, walking, cycling and hiking a lot in the fresh air of Bavaria. Those activities were absolutely impossible here. The sun burned down so aggressively that one would get a dangerous sunburn after a very short time. If I went downtown to the older center of Manila, there was more shade, but it was hard to fight one's way through the narrow, crowded streets. Especially as a foreigner and a woman, it was better to stay away from those parts of town, so we were told.

In the modern parts of town, the distances were quite far and you needed a car. The embassy had warned us not to drive with one's own car, unless you had your own Philippine driver. That was because many accidents had been intentionally caused in order to cash in on a foreigner's ability to pay.

The different parts of the city were connected by dusty traffic lanes on which the colorful jeepneys raced back and forth at breakneck speed. The traffic was hellish. Everyone drove as he wanted to. It was a free-for-all on the streets. Whoever had the bigger or faster car passed the others without regard for the proper method of passing another car. Nobody cared. Only a few cars had air-conditioning, and so one had to drive with open windows to avoid heatstroke. Did it matter if you were covered with dust from head to toe after only a few minutes? The speeding cars actually disappeared in a dense, dusty cloud.

There was nothing else to do but to stay inside the house from the late morning onward until the late afternoon, when the temperature fell.

But as soon as the sun went down you had to watch out for mosquitoes.

We had been looking forward to our first dinner in our new garden. The girls and I had invited some neighbors and we were just about to start dinner when a giant cloud of mosquitoes attacked us. No, they were not shy little insects, but huge, hissing, bloodthirsty monsters. We left everything on the table and ran into the house, forgetting to close the door immediately behind us. The swarm of mosquitoes followed us into the house, where they actually darkened the whole room. I remembered the "Hospitality Kit" the embassy had given us, and there I found some spray with which we finally got rid of the nasty attackers.

In my opinion our life in Manila was seriously restricted.

On the other hand, the Philippines offered opportunities that I had never known in Europe or the United States. At the market I could shop for every kind of beautiful handicraft, like woodcarvings and woven fabrics, for very low prices. Almost everything could be made to order—clothes, furniture, curtains, and even rugs.

It was easy and a lot of fun to furnish our home, and we did not have to spend a lot of money. This was a nice comfort for the pains that the sun inflicted on me every day.

Our first home had only one air-conditioned room. The other rooms, which had south and west exposure, were uninhabitable during the day. I began to really hate the sun.

Every day I told myself that the next day it would be easier and then I would go out and do something or explore the city. But the next day dawned and the heat was just as unbearable as the day before.

The girls went to the International School. They were picked up by bus in the morning and brought back in the afternoon. It was quite a chore to organize transportation. Some foreign families had organized a bus. We found a trustworthy driver, but the bus unfortunately did not have air-conditioning.

We got up at five to be ready in time. It took almost an hour for all the children to be picked up. Inside the bus it was stifling, dusty, and hot. So I gave the girls some wet towels they could hold up to their faces to protect themselves from the dust. This was a very exhausting time, especially for the girls, but they did not complain.

After three months we had adjusted somewhat, the children in school and I to my everyday life as a housewife. Despite the heat, I was anxious to explore the life outside of our little safe refuge.

The inlaid chest, Manila, 1968, Family photo

Manila was an international city, and it reminded me of Beirut. There did not seem to be any one predominant ethnic group. The major part of the population was Malayan, a very friendly and joyful people, whom I liked to call "the Italians of Southeast Asia." Even though they made up the largest part of the poor population, they were very likable, gentle, good-natured, and open, with an even-tempered disposition and many talents in the arts and especially in music.

The second largest group was the Chinese, who were very business-oriented and hardworking. Many of them had achieved great economic success, and it was only natural that they played an important role in the economic life of the country. These people seemed much more closed up and much less joyful than the Filipinos. Maybe this was the price they paid for their wealth.

The third group was the Moslems. Their religion seemed to have changed the character of these Filipinos. They were not apparent in the capital of Manila. The followers of Islam lived mostly on the islands of Mindanao and other small islands in the south of the Philippines.

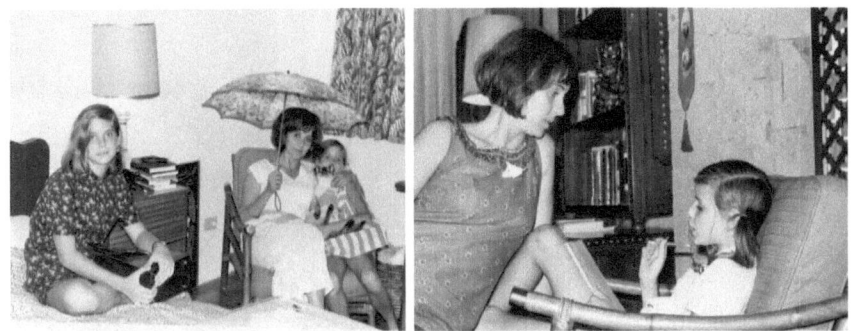

Manila, Philippines, 1968, Family photo

Even in the early Sixties, their religion had been used for political purposes, and they had become more radical over the years. It was from these islands that the first terrorists were sent out to fight against President Marcos. We had been warned by the embassy not to go sightseeing in these parts of the country.

The Spanish made up some kind of local elite. They were descendents of the old families who had colonized the islands originally under their king, Philip II, who had Christianized the country and given it his name. The Philippines are still predominantly Catholic. Spanish is the second official language. English is the first official language.

The Spanish conquerors had not only influenced the arts but they also influenced the architecture of the country, especially that of the churches.

In Manila we find churches everywhere. They show the South American style and are overloaded with statues of saints who evoke a deep, if not to say, fanatic veneration.

To attend Holy Mass in Manila is an exhilarating experience. It is very touching to see how the people celebrate the Mass. The church is filled with the sound of guitars accompanying old pre-Christian native songs mixed with Christian gospel music and modern rhythms in a very appealing way.

It is a musical ode to the Lord full of joy and happiness. Their joy of life surely originates in the natural wealth of the Malayan islands.

The landscape in the Philippines is full of exotic treasures.

Rich and luxuriant vegetation covers the soft hills and reaches down to the endless white beaches. However, this natural beauty cannot be enjoyed without paying strict attention to the lurking dangers. The forests hold many poisonous plants unknown to the foreigner, and the clear blue enticing waters of the reefs are home to sharks, stingrays, prickly plants, and sharp coral reefs that do not welcome intruders.

We find tropical rain forests in the east. In the west, the landscape shifts to sugar plantations, rice terraces, and extensive marshes in which herds of water buffaloes graze peacefully.

Now and then we passed small, picturesque villages with huts built on stilts. The huts are covered by straw roofs and do not have windows. They have sliding doors that allow a soft light to enter the interior by means of window frames made of wood and wafer-thin capiz shells.

Domestic animals are kept under the house, dogs and small pigs as well as the roosters for the popular cockfights. These villages do look very romantic, but a second glance reveals the extreme poverty of the population. Despite this, the people meet foreigners in a friendly manner and seem to be good-natured and happy.

The social differences between rich and poor were very stark and manifested themselves even more in the large city of Manila, where large parts of the city were covered by shantytowns. These were occupied by squatters whose huts were regularly swept away when the rains of the monsoon came and rebuilt to live in until the next monsoon hit.

Whether the situation has improved since Marcos, I do not know. One can certainly understand the terrorist attacks as an cry for help by the poor part of the population.

We Europeans often commit the error of judging other societies by our own standards.

We assume that our ideas of democracy and economic progress would surely help other peoples to lead a happy life. The history of the colonization of Africa shows to what catastrophic consequences the exportation of our social and political concepts and rules can lead. The Western companies exploited the continent with the high-sounding excuses of bringing progress to the people. The same thing happened in India and Indochina. In these countries, a smart elite cooperated with the colonial powers in order to take control themselves after the colonists' departure.

The results of this so-called progress have been civil war and chaos everywhere, which finally led to the destruction of the cultural identity of these countries.

The Americans succeeded the Europeans, and today we call this economic and political process globalization, meaning progress for everybody.

The result is that we, Europe and the United States, are involved in wars as far away as Afghanistan or Iraq because we feel that our security is threatened. Fundamentalism and terrorism are one response. Note: This last sentence still is a problem. We don't just "feel" threatened. America was attacked. Islam is a totalitarian political system that wishes to destroy all who refuse to believe in their "god." Fundamentalism and terrorism are one response *to what*? Fundamentalism and terrorism are part and parcel of the system of Islam, which is total subjugation of populations or annihilation of those populations. The sentence is missing it's last half.

At that time in Manila I was still very much convinced that establishing the democratic model would be the only chance for achieving social progress. But my stay in Southeast Asia made me see things in a less biased way. Today I believe that these countries must find their own system by which they can find a just distribution of wealth.

In 1969 there were elections in the Philippines. General Marcos had set himself up for reelection. He had ruled the country since 1966 like a despot. Corruption and nepotism had marked his government, and Marcos had filled his own pockets.

International newspapers had reported the corruption, and in the country itself all this was no secret.

One day, as I took a taxi downtown, as we were stuck in the usual traffic jam, I started up a conversation with the driver. We talked about Marcos and his corrupt regime, and I asked him whether he would vote for the other candidate, presuming that he was aware of the political reality in the country.

In the countryside, Philippines, 1968, Family photo

Philippines, 1968, Family photo

In the countryside, Philippines, 1968, Family photo

To my great surprise, he answered, "What do you mean? Of course we will reelect Marcos. Maybe you don't understand this, but Marcos has already plundered the state and taken what he needs for himself and his family. If we elected the new candidate, the whole story would start from the beginning again. He would also have to take care of his family and friends first, and the state would again lose a lot of money. So it is much better to reelect Marcos."

The political situation interested me very much. The newspapers reported on scandals of corruption as I had never experienced in any country before. The ruling class in Manila must have been corrupt to an extent that bordered on lawlessness.

On the other side, there were the so called Hooks, Communist-infiltrated gangs that tried to portray a kind of Robin Hood image but operated like criminal gangs and were not really a political counterweight that could be taken seriously.

These so-called revolutionary powers limited their activities to robbing the rich and even killing them. Thus, they acted in ways that made it impossible for the mass of the people to follow them in order to change the situation by political means.

A few days after my interesting discussion with the taxi driver, I met with an acquaintance who was a Philippine lawyer, a typical member of one of the families of the sugar barons that still could be found to rule their own little kingdoms on one of the many islands.

He usually carried a gun, and this time he again had his revolver in his holster under the full, white Philippine shirt that men wear there. He was on his way to elections on his island where his family had a sugar plantation. I asked him why he wore a gun and what was going on in the country.

He explained that he was making sure that his party, that is, the party of Marcos, would win the elections. And this was the way to do it: Before the election, the rumor was spread that it would be a "bloody election" and that there would be a lot of shooting.

Consequently, the people were scared and did not vote at all.

To make sure that the people who had been frightened by the Communists and the Moslems would really remain home, this man and others would organize some shooting in the morning in front of the polling place. Then his friends could comfortably go to the election and make sure that the "right" candidate would be voted for.

Democracy in a Philippine version! A change of government could only take place by means of violence.

Another incident demonstrates the social situation in Manila very vividly.

Learning to dance the Hula, Manila, Christmas 1968, Family photo

I had been shopping downtown and took a taxi home with my new purchases, a radio and some other expensive household items.

The taxi stopped in front of my house, and exactly in the moment when I had opened the back door to take my things out, the taxi driver hit the gas pedal and took off, never to be seen again. Everything was gone, the radio, the other purchases, and my handbag with all my money. I was furious and immediately went to the closest police station to report the theft.

The policemen listened to me politely, but instead of following up the case, they advised me to forget the incident. I would only get myself into trouble, and the whole thing could become quite dangerous.

Now I was really mad—a typically European response—where were law and order?

I had remembered the number of the taxi and began to investigate on my own.

I actually succeeded in finding out the address of the taxi driver. I took a taxi and went to the man's house to confront him. Naïve as I was at that time, I really expected him to present some excuse and give me back my purchases.

The man denied ever having seen me, in front of witnesses. I had taken the other taxi driver with me. I saw the area he lived in and became aware that his family was coming out and moving in on me. Completely frustrated, I left the scene and vowed that this would not be the end of the story.

Two days later, in the evening, there was a knock at my front door. The president of the police of Makati, the district in which I lived, personally gave me the honor of his visit. He presented me with a bottle of champagne. During a pleasant chat he told me how he wanted to make sure that no harm would come to me, but at the same time he could do nothing for me. Of course, he could lock up the taxi driver, but then I would really be in danger by all the members of the man's family, and he did not want to take this responsibility.

He suggested that instead of dwelling on this issue any longer, we should open the bottle of champagne and make ourselves a nice evening. Luckily, I succeeded in telling him good-bye in a friendly manner and showed him the door.

In the meantime, we had moved to a new house. We now lived in a so-called village, ironically also called Bel Air. There were very attractive homes on both sides of the streets, and the streets were guarded by armed guards. Beautiful, majestic King palms and blooming hibiscus bushes shaded the street. The houses were barely visible among the luxuriant tropical gardens.

Our house was on a relatively small lot, but it was built in a very appealing bungalow style. It seemed hidden amid an enchanted garden. Its basic plan was like the letter "T." The center had a large living room with a terrace on either side. To the right were the bedrooms, with separate dressing rooms and walk-in closets.

The family at the Pagsanjan Falls, Philippines 1969, Family photo

The house was almost hidden by lush, tropical plants, such as hibiscus, palm trees, and bamboo. Our bamboo furniture, the Indian rugs, and the soft light of the lamps made of capiz shells made it very "gemuetlich." (cozy and homelike). The architecture, the layout, and the structure, as well as the furnishings, fit well with the local South Sea building style.

Soon we employed a second housemaid, Leyte. She came from the same region as Remi, from the north of the country, who was provided by the American Embassy and had worked for Americans before. Both girls had worked for American families before. Remi and Leyte worked perfectly together. They seemed to manage the piles of laundry easily, despite the fact that they had to wash everything by hand. Leyte had reorganized the furniture within a short time, and I had to admit that it was placed more conveniently than before. She had also brought her aunt's old sewing machine, and after I had shown her how to sew, she made the most darling outfits for the girls. Remi was very dependable and managed the household money accurately and responsibly when she went to the market. She was really very competent and a good cook.

She did her work while taking care of her own small child on the side. Remi received about $50 and Leyte $40 per month, besides room and board. Both of them did not like our food and cooked their own dishes for themselves, like fish heads and crabs with rice.

The two girls helped each other and preferred sleeping together in one room despite the fact that I had given them each their own room.

What a luxury for me to have two such friendly and efficient servants in the house!

Everything was always sparkling clean, the beds were made, the laundry washed and ironed daily, and breakfast, lunch, and dinner were punctually served in the nicely decorated dining room.

Thus I had time for my children. I helped Ariane with her homework; it was hard enough for her to have to adjust to yet another school.

We had our happiest days when Howard came to visit us. Once he surprised me with a weekend trip to Baguio, a fashionable vacation resort in the mountains in the north. We flew over a hillside covered with extensive pine forests. As the airplane descended, we could recognize a small village on the hilltop among dark green fir forests that spread over the entire mountain range. When the door of the airplane opened, I took a deep breath, what a wonderful smell, what pleasant coolness!

The embassy had invited us to stay at its guesthouse. We had the whole house just for the two of us. The house had a two-story living room with a huge fireplace. There were four bedrooms, and from the terraces one had a gorgeous view overlooking the house's large garden and the mountaintops in the distance. And the best thing of all was that in the kitchen we had our own cook and a maid. But the greatest luxury for me was the fresh air and the cool breeze. Why should we want to go out if just the two of us could cuddle in front of the fire while wine and dinner were served to us whenever we wished?

Now I felt safe and secure, with Howard beside me. He took me as I was and thought as I did. I only needed to start a sentence and Howard would end it. We were on the same wavelength.

Here, far away from the strangling heat of Manila, I could finally talk about everything that had perturbed me during recent months. During our short weekend visits I never found the opportunity to talk about everything openly nor did I want to give Howard any reason to feel worried about the two of us. Furthermore, our tape-recorded messages had no room for the thoughts that weighed upon my heart.

Howard was an attentive listener, and I started to talk. There was the worry about how to educate two teenage girls correctly in this different culture. Another problem had to do with living in Manila as a woman alone, because I had to go to every event by myself. This was no fun, even though I was protected within the diplomat's compound by Howard's colleagues in the foreign Service and their families. I also told him about the Philippine lawyer who went out of his way to assist me in all situations and who acted as my escort when I wanted to go to events. His behavior irritated me and I had difficulty evaluating him correctly.

Howard had a wise answer for each of my questions. He never tried to teach me. With much intuition and empathy, he put questions to me that resolved themselves as I answered them. He was, after all, a pro when it came to the Socratic teaching method.

We enjoyed our perfect togetherness in those days, but the time was always too short.

Howard also confessed that this forced separation was also a serious problem for him. He simply did not want to be separated from me any longer. Life was too short to be always waiting for the future. During one of our walks through the woods we decided that Howard would apply for a position in the Foreign Service in a place that would enable us to lead a somewhat normal family life. The girls and I, we needed him and he needed us. When we returned into the damp kettle of Manila, we took this promise back with us: We would plan to leave Southeast Asia as soon as possible.

Howard had to return to Saigon, and I had another one of those days when things simply cannot get done. This time I was stuck in traffic with what turned out to be, thanks be to God, a friendly taxi driver in the jungle of the crowded streets of the old part of town. He was a good-looking, intelligent young man and we started a conversation. At first he wanted to know everything about America and Germany. Then he described to me how he came from a simple background, had gone to school, and now wanted to succeed in life. He lamented the fact that he could not afford a good school in this country. All schools cost a lot of money. Even in elementary school there were costs that some families could not afford. Most families had five to ten children, so how could poor families be able to send their children to school?

He had decided to become a policeman. But in order to pay for the school, he had to drive a taxi for a while. I asked him why he wanted to become a policeman and he answered me: "In order to become rich. There are so many people here in Manila who want to enter or leave the country. There is a good chance to really cash in as a policeman." When I told him that policemen in Germany did not have a very high income, he thought I was making fun of him.

Life in Manila could be quite pleasant if one was member of some club. There one could refresh oneself in the cool water of a swimming pool and relax in a well-kept green garden. The clubs were situated in the higher parts of town where one could feel a breeze coming from the sea once in a while. Membership in these clubs was exclusive. I was a member of both the Embassy's Women's Club and the American Women's Club. One played polo or golf and enjoyed all the comforts of a well-kept and protected spa. Such a life seemed almost provocatively unjust in the face of the general poverty, but after a while I had to admit that, as a light skinned foreigner, one could survive in this climate only under such advantaged conditions.

As my daily life in the "golden cage" proved to become more and more intolerable, I decided to look around for a meaningful activity. I offered to teach German at the International School. My classes were in the morning from seven to nine o'clock.

This was just right for me, because after ten o'clock temperatures would rise.

When the summer vacation began, my classes came to an end. This fit into my plans, because I had an idea which, if successful, would give me the opportunity to get to know the people of this country better.

"Paligsahan," a Folk Music Festival

Even during the first days of our stay in Manila I had noticed that one could hear exclusively American music on the radio. But when we traveled throughout the country, I realized that in the villages there did exist a long tradition of wonderful old folk songs that were not heard anymore because the young people said they were "old-fashioned." What could be done about that?

I strongly felt that this treasure of musical heritage should be protected. But how? My own experience with my teenage girls showed me that something had to be "cool" in order to be held in high esteem by the young people.

So I discussed this question with the ladies in the American Women's Club. My idea was to organize a folk-song contest, a "paligsahan," among the schools in Manila. The Filipinos are very musical people, and I was sure that young talent would be found. The idea was to get the media interested and focus public interest on the country's own musical heritage. There would also be nice prizes for the winners. This should be "cool."

The ladies in the club were immediately enthusiastic about the idea and promised to support me as best as they could.

'AWITING PILIPINO' TILT

The local YWCA World Fellowship Committee is launching this month its "Paligsahan ng mga Awiting Pilipino." Open to all high schools and Y-Teen clubs all over the country, the contest aims to focus the Filipino public's interest to its own musical heritage. Committee members seated from left are Prof. Eliseo Pajaro, Mrs. George Grande, Prof. Felipe Padilla de Leon, Mrs. Eva Marie Holland, Mercedes Santiago and Mrs. Lucy White. Standing same order are George Grande, Angie de Jesus, Mrs. Marita G. Bumatay, Mrs. Rosalinda Guerrero, Mrs. Eva Ventura, Mrs. Catherine Heraldson and Mrs. Lily Isaac.

The American Women's Club in Manila, 1969, newspaper clipping

My first action was to write to all the schools in the school district of Manila to explain my project. The concert should include only genuine Philippine songs in the local dialects, and the performers should wear their beautiful traditional clothes. The event would be on television.

The reaction was a surprise. Seventeen schools responded and promised their participation. That was more than I had anticipated. The music teachers of the schools were, of course, enthusiastic. I was overjoyed. Here I was, able to do something for the protection of traditional music! At the same time, it was nice to be accepted as a woman and organizer of such an important event, and to move about freely in Philippine society and among conservative American colleagues without being looked upon askance.

I worked together with three different committees, the "American Women's Club," the local YMCA, and a group of representatives of the Philippine School Board. This way I became acquainted with Manila's social structures and met with people from all social backgrounds. I met with the music teacher of each school personally, and they thanked me profusely for siding with them about what they had been preaching all the time.

I also learned a lot about organizing events, leading meetings, and tricks to bring together people with different interests. The work was demanding, but I really felt like a fish in the water and was happy to be doing something meaningful. We also appointed a board of judges, people with an interest in and knowledge of music. All the participants shared my feelings about the necessity of saving the musical heritage of the country.

The "paligsahan" was planned for December 12, 1969, in Lunetta Park, the largest park in Manila. It had taken almost nine months to prepare for this event. Radio and television stations had promised to come. No wonder I was nervous. Would all these people be dependable and work together in an orderly way? And then, there would be so many kids!

On the morning of our great day it was raining cats and dogs.

> **Rizal Park 'paligsahan' set Dec. 12**
>
> Catherine H a r a ldson heads the world fellowship committee of the YWCA of Greater Manila in charge of a choral singing competition in Pilipino. The 'paligsahan' starts at 6:30 p.m., Dec. 12 at the Rizal Park open auditorium. Judges will be Candida Bautista, Dr. Rodolfo Cornejo, Prof. Felipe Padilla de Leon, Dr. Eliseo Pajaro, Mercedes Santiago and Lucy White.
>
> Participants will come from 17 member-schools of the Y-Teens Committee. Eva Marie Holland of the world fellowship committee will collaborate with Lily V. Isaac and Mrs. Ildefonso J. Hermoso of the Y-Teens. The sponsoring committees calculates the contest to enhance the Filipino youth's interest in their own music, to focus the interest of the Filipino public to their cultural heritage, to discover and encourage talents among amateurs and to develop a critical sense of quality.

The folksong festival in Manila, 1970,

All night long the monsoon had been pouring rain into Manila's streets, and they were covered with mud. When it rains in Manila, the water pours down as though the heaven had opened its floodgates, and the streets turn into flooded rivers. Parts of the town were even inaccessible.

The telephone began to ring at 7:3 in the morning and did not stop until noon.

Everyone wanted to know what would happen to our open-air event in the evening. Nobody would come to our performance, particularly the VIPs, if one would sink into mud up to the ankles. I did not know what to answer. In my desperation, seeing the result of our nine months of work at risk, I sent a prayer to heaven and told everyone that I was sure that the rain would stop in the afternoon and that we could proceed as planned.

And really, in the early afternoon of December 12, the sun suddenly appeared from behind the clouds, the water started to flow off the streets, and the streets were free again. Everybody had arrived to admire the many beautiful young people, particularly the girls in their charming dresses. They sang their melodious songs in the different dialects, accompanied by traditional instruments, and performed a dance with bamboo sticks. There were several prizes for different criteria: best solo, best chorus, best costumes, and so on.

The contest was a great success, and the schools planned to repeat the event the next year.

The shadows of war in Saigon, Vietnam, 1970, Family photo

SAIGON, EASTER 1970

The U.S. Embassy gave me permission to visit Howard in Saigon for ten days at Easter 1970. The situation in the city was considered safe enough for relatives to visit their family members.

The flight from Manila to Saigon took about two hours. I had arranged for the children to stay at home with Remi and Leyte. A friend from the embassy would check on them every day. I knew they were well taken care of, but I still felt bad about leaving them for such a long time. However, the view from the window over the endless tropical forests below soon made my thoughts turn to other things. I could not see any villages below now, only once in a while a single tin roof shone up in the middle of the green rainforest.

After two hours we touched down on the runway of the U.S. airbase in Saigon. I could see the rows of huge "Galaxies," the transport planes of the American military. Rows of fighter planes and helicopters were ready to leave at any time.

As I walked down the gangway, a military band played. This official greeting was, however, not meant for me. Three planes, one carrying a general from New Zealand, was being received with all the honors.

I looked around and in the middle of all the military personnel I finally discovered Howard's happy face. We sank into each other arms, and Howard quickly pulled me into a large black car with the license plate CD. The chauffeur closed the door and the noise started to abate. While in Saigon, Howard had a car with a chauffeur at his disposal, who now tried his best to find his way through the clogged streets of the city.

I admired the stately old homes in the French colonial style, with columns and large verandas. Hundreds of scooters and motorcycles steered their way in a zigzag course between heavy South Vietnamese military vehicles full of young soldiers. A few yards further on, American army tanks blocked the way. Amid all this jumble of soldiers, scooters, and stinking transport trucks, a helpless policeman tried to control the traffic chaos.

Big American jeeps, army transports, sacks full of sand and barbed-wire rolls, and everywhere Vietnamese control posts—despite this massive military contingent, the city seemed to me relatively safe. Maybe it was the memory of my childhood in Vachendorf that gave me this feeling of security. As a child I had met the Americans as protectors after all the chaos at the end of World War II.

Howard lived in a small apartment on the fifth floor of a large, modern apartment house in the nicest part of the city. From there it was not far to the university. Beautiful, exotic, old green trees lined the streets. From the balcony that surrounded his apartment he had a fine view of the city and of the large river, the Cuu Long, a sidearm of the Mekong.

For the elites of Saigon, the war did not seem to be close. We played tennis with French friends at the French Club, and with American friends we played golf, while not far away heavy artillery fire was heard. Completely at ease, we hit our balls to the next green. No one showed any sign of fear, at least not on the outside.

For the first time Howard talked to me extensively about his work as Education Advisor to the South Vietnamese government. It differed very much from his earlier activity as dean in a college. As a dean, he had always liked to work together with young students. As advisor for higher educational institutions, he now had to cooperate mainly with adults who were politicians and only rarely with committed teachers. If he wanted to be successful in his new position, he had to learn to think and act politically. This meant that he had to try to understand the behavior of his colleagues, who, while concerned about doing their job well, predominantly were eager to advance their own political careers. Howard told me that he did understand this, but that this was not his way of working. Every day he became more and more aware of this fact. He missed me very much and wanted to live as a family, and he had made up his mind to look for a different kind of job, away from the war in Vietnam.

We spent the evening in one of the best restaurants in Saigon, on a roof terrace on one of the fine old houses from colonial times. A pleasant, cool breeze rose from the river; the air was mild and the food excellent. Actually, it is the Chinese style of cooking that prevails in Saigon, but this chef had been able to find a wonderful symbiosis of Chinese products and French cuisine, delicate and served with love; it was very pleasant to my European taste.

In Saigon two languages were spoken. Not only in international hotels but also in stores and schools and on the street, people spoke

Vietnamese and French. Even the names of the streets were in both languages, despite the fact that the French had left the country officially in 1954. Many Vietnamese also spoke, of course, English by now. But the French influence was very obvious everywhere. French colonial architecture prevailed, and French beds, bidets in every bathroom, and French elevators in the older houses that still functioned very well were all over Saigon.

Vietnam countryside, 1970, Family photo

On the streets the air was dense with exhaust fumes from heavy military vehicles and the dust stirred up by myriad scooters and motorcycles. Suddenly, amid this stinking gray fog, an apparition: Graceful young girls on scooters and motorcycles appeared out of nowhere. They floated like colorful butterflies in their yellow, blue, or white "ao dais," the traditional women's dress, through the streets. Most of them wore a tight, long dress over black or white silk pants. It was a bizarre picture to see these petite, graceful figures as they wove their way, through the traffic, their long black hair flowing behind them, with elegant white gloves and the two parts of their dress flapping behind them like wings. They seemed to me like a personified protest against the chaos that surrounded them.

Howard in his office in Saigon, 1970, Family photo

Occasionally the usual noise of the traffic was interrupted by the explosion of distant rockets or the rattle of machine gun fire. Nobody seemed to pay any attention, except when the sound was very close.

One dramatic incident took place directly in front of our eyes: Howard and I were having lunch on the terrace of one of the most elegant hotels in the center square of town. Suddenly shots rang out through the street not far from us. A young boy was being dragged across the street by some policemen. Behind him was a young girl who clasped his arm and pleaded in tears for the police to set him free. But they took him away.

The expression of sheer horror on the faces of these two young people made a great impression on me.

It happens all the time that as soon as someone has been accused of something, even if he is only an innocent bystander, he is arrested without asking whether he is guilty or not.

The government was becoming more and more concerned, and the reason for this rising nervousness was also the daily increase in refugees that flooded into the city.

Howard in his office, Saigon, Vietnam, 1969, News clipping

Thousands of farmers arrived with their last belongings from the countryside, fearing the Vietcong. Among them, cloaked by poverty, when friend and foe can no longer be distinguished, a number of enemy Vietcong infiltrated the capital of the South.

At one of the dinner parties that Howard and I attended, I met a prominent Vietnamese woman who had fled from the North to the city.

I was finally able to ask her a question that had already disquieted me in Manila. What would happen if the Americans left the country? She gave me an honest answer. She was convinced that that would mean the end of the country of South Vietnam;

On the streets of Saigon, 1970, Family photo

the Communist North Vietnamese would control the whole country within a short time.

On the following evening I experienced a sample of the conflict that was coming closer and closer. Howard and I spent a peaceful evening in a famous restaurant on a boat on the river Cuu Long. We were enjoying the wonderful dishes with seafood that were served with much good taste. The moon stood like a lantern above the dark forests on the other side of the river, and a blue haze tinted the romantic scene.

Eva in an "Ao Dai" the national dress, Saigon, 1970, Family photo

A whistling sound suddenly passed above our heads. Then there was a loud explosion on our side of the river. The impact was far enough away so that no one was hurt, but the guests scattered apart in shock. We had also looked for cover under the table. In the long silence that followed, we started on our way home as fast as we could. Howard tried to calm me. Every night Saigon was being attacked by rocket fire now. This was no big deal, and so far there had never been any extensive damage. I thought his explanation was anything but convincing.

Life in South Vietnam was threatening for everyone. Every day we heard how many people had been shot again, only because they had closer contact with Americans. Especially dangerous, it seemed, was the areas of schooling and education. Howard and his colleagues had strict orders not to compromise their Vietnamese

On the Mekong river in Vietnam, 1970, Family photo

friends. They were to stay away from official functions as well, because the Vietcong had put them on their black list. It was said that three million people were on this list to be eliminated.

The Vietcong always operated in small terror groups and not with military actions. The threat was always there. The enemy remained undetected.

Hue after the Tet Offensive

Howard had to travel to Hue on the border with North Vietnam, and I was allowed to accompany him. We flew in a small, six-seat military plane. The little plane was very shaky and passed close over the jungle. Below us was a terrifying scene: destroyed villages as far as the eye could see. This was the war! Here I could see and smell it. Billows of smoke hung above destroyed huts and deserted fields.

We passed many large defoliated forests. The "Agent Orange" bombers had not left anything alive. But they had not succeeded in hitting the true enemy. He was hiding in his mile-long tunnels underground. The iron will of these small soldiers was impressive. I asked myself how strong their conviction had to be in order to defy this superior enemy.

Once we saw a white cloud of paper scraps that slowly descended over the ground. It consisted of leaflets that the Americans distributed all over the country. They were part of the so-called "PSY-warfare" and were written in the Vietnamese language. They were supposed to educate the population about the benefits to them offered by the South Vietnamese government and their American friends.

*Our Christmas cards
1970, Family photo*

Howard described them vaguely to me. The village elders and the members of the Vietcong were promised amnesty. Nothing would happen to them if they would give up their support for the Vietcong and return to the South Vietnamese state; they would be well taken care of.

As I looked out the window, I realized that the layout of the city of Hue was already different from that of the other towns I had seen in Southeast Asia. Easily recognizable, the city had been planned around an extensive palace in the center, the royal palace. It was built as a square with a huge wall around it, fronted by a water ditch that was fed by a nearby river. Inside the wall I could make out the gardens and several smaller palaces and other buildings for the royal family. All the bridges had been destroyed by the Vietcong. Now auxiliary bridges and pontoons connected the streets. The university had also been damaged heavily during the Tet offensive in February. In the meantime, the buildings had been partly reconstructed and were to open for lectures soon.

We stayed in the apartment of a professor who had left or fled. We had invited the president of the university, a friend of Howard, for a small cocktail party. His wife was one of those charming Vietnamese women, beautiful, intelligent, and successful. She was dean of the Law School.

Our conversation touched on the six German medical doctors from the Medical Faculty that had been killed in February, a case that had caused foreign policy complications with Germany. Nobody knew what had really happened. Some claimed that the doctors had provoked enmities among the students by their authoritarian behavior and that personal animosities had triggered the killings. Others believed that they had just been part of the 2,000 victims among the population that the Vietcong had caused every day.

There was also mention of the fact that there seemed to be a number of sympathizers of the Vietcong among the student body who might have been involved in the gruesome killing of the Germans.

When we visited the city that afternoon, there still seemed to be a breath of death and decay hovering over the town. There was no traffic, few people hurried through the streets, and there were fresh graves on the roadsides. The mayor of the city invited me to witness the opening of a mass grave that had only recently been detected. I politely declined this macabre invitation.

Later they found many more mass graves in that area. It is estimated that 2,000 soldiers and just as many civilians had lost their lives during the Tet attack of the North Vietnamese.

The larger businesses had all been moved to Saigon. Therefore, I was surprised and very impressed by the sumptuous formal banquet that took place the next evening to celebrate the reopening of the university. Another surprise for me was my conversation with the president: He offered me a position as the dean of the Department of Foreign Languages. I was flattered and thanked him, but since I had two children, I did not think that Hue was a very safe place for us, and I declined.

Shortly before midnight, two young men of the "PSY-Corps" appeared. Dressed in the black uniform of the Corps they looked like mysterious shadows. It was their job to organize young people into a type of "boy scout" organization. They all wore these uniforms, boys and girls alike. They met to hear music, organize cookouts, and listen to speeches. Then they were taught to handle weapons and how to spy out Vietcong infiltrators. As soon as one of them showed up in a village, they had to report them. That was a task that many of these youngsters would have to pay for with their life, because then they themselves became victims of the Vietcong's revenge.

The young trainer we had met the evening before seemed to have been very successful in his work. The next morning we were invited to see how he handed out twelve medals to members of his group. They had killed twelve enemies without any loss in their own group. That was certainly worth a prize!

Disturbing memories of my own childhood and the recruiting ceremonies of the "Hitlerjugend" crossed my mind.

Howard and I also had the opportunity to attend a discussion with students of the university. The topic was, "What kind of democracy is right for Vietnam?" The discussion took place in the American Center. There were about ten students, but only three of them wanted to speak up. Two of them had been exchange students in the United States and spoke English quite well. The students stated that it was completely senseless to speak about "democracy" in the village. The farmers in the countryside had absolutely no idea who controlled the government in Saigon. That might as well be Nasser or the king of China; that was of no interest to them. For them there was only one person relevant and that was the chef of their province. He was the representative of the government. They felt loyalty toward him. But even he was not personally known to many of them. For most of these people, it was only the village elder who stood for law and order. It was complete nonsense to have elections in these villages with candidates from the province, let alone from Saigon that nobody knew. These people would only go to an election anyway to please their village elder.

We did not speak much as we returned to our quarters because our heads were full of conflicting thoughts. I climbed into bed over a machine gun mounted beside it. Obviously, people counted on attacks during the night. During the night we were awakened by machine gun fire several times. The military guards opened fire onto everything that came swimming down the river.

The next day we visited a small school in the middle of the jungle. The children were very disciplined and listened to their teacher attentively. They sat for hours on small wooden benches without tables, closely packed together, and did not utter a peep. Their teachers proudly showed us a locked cabinet with projectors for slides that the American government had donated. They were waiting for there to be electricity in the village, sometime in the future, so that they could use this precious gift.

The Royal Palace in Hue, Vietnam, 1970, Family photo

I examined a schoolbook. It was for the first grade. The pictures showed a small boy who sat on the lap of a friendly looking American soldier. While he was reading a story, the boy secretly stuffed sand into the barrel of his gun. Thus the little boy became a "hero." The village elder explained our bewilderment: From twelve midnight to twelve noon, the school belonged to the South Vietnamese, but from noon to midnight it served as the headquarters of the Vietcong.

As the clock struck twelve o'clock noon, suddenly everyone had seemed to scatter in all directions. As if on a secret command, the children left the school and disappeared into the huts of their families.

At that moment it became clear to me that coming to Saigon did not mean I had arrived in Vietnam. The grim Hue had shown me the true face of war. But only here in the midst of the jungle did I feel the immediate threat; only here had I come close to the true life of the people and their daily struggle for survival. The frontline was invisible and constantly in motion.

With mixed emotions, I boarded my plane to Manila after the eventful ten days. Soon Howard's application for a transfer was successful. In May 1970 he received an offer by the State Department for a post in Addis Ababa, Ethiopia. He accepted. We would be able to leave Southeast Asia. But before that, I decided to take a trip to Cambodia and to Bali.

Dark Clouds over Angkor Wat— Blue Skies Over Bali

The girls had gone to Hawaii to meet their father, and Howard could not get off work, so I had to go on my journey alone. Only one week and then I would meet Howard in Singapore and we would proceed from there to Bali. I was a bit apprehensive but at the same time was looking forward to my new adventures on my own.

I flew from Manila to Hong Kong and from there to Bangkok. I had reserved a room in the "most beautiful hotel in the world," the Oriental Hotel. My room enveloped me immediately with the enchantment of the Orient, and the perfume of the colorful bouquet of flowers on the table welcomed me into a country full of beauty and delight. This lively and international capital was the right starting point for a journey through an exotic country that had friendly and beautiful people.

I visited the "Floating Markets," where vendors sold their colorful products from their boats the next day. I was enchanted by the gracefulness of the people, always smiling and friendly. Later I discovered a type of flea market with all kinds of goods, and among all the odd articles I found a small antique bronze Buddha. The vendor told me it was from a Buddhist temple in northern Thailand and was an original from the 12th century.

Since I did not believe the man, I took the statue to the Bangkok Museum. I was overjoyed to hear an expert assure me that the piece was indeed an original from that time and that I should be aware that it should not be taken out of the country.

Today my little Buddha stands on my desk, inspiring me to take life with composure.

After a short trip to the northern part of Thailand, my next goal was Angkor Wat in Cambodia. Upon landing in Phnom Penh, it felt as if I had entered a completely different world. The city seemed colorless, and the people disturbingly sad and with no smiles on their faces.

Then I changed into a small airplane with only six seats. After a long flight over the endless jungle, we finally landed on the other side of the Mekong River, in Siem Reap. Again, I met with an oppressive atmosphere. There were hardly any tourists, and the people I met seemed to scrutinize me with a gloomy, impenetrable gaze. With an uneasy feeling in my stomach, I moved into the only little hotel that took in foreigners. There were only three other guests. Something intangibly threatening seemed to hover in the air during this summer of 1970.

All my dark thoughts disappeared, however, the next morning as I entered the mystifying jungle temples of Angkor Wat. I lost myself in the enchantment of the place, and immersed myself completely into its history. I had brought a little guidebook as my companion, since there was no one I could ask for information. I loved the stone reliefs on the walls of the temples of myriad beautiful, enticing young women, the "heavenly virgins," and the scenes of battles between the Cambodians and the Vietnamese people in the 15th century. It was all there—what the people of this area had experienced centuries ago: triumphant conquerors and subservient, vanquished victims, war and love.

When the sun was ready to set over the forest, I awoke from my dreams because it was time to leave.

I decided to return one more time to the mystic temples the next day. It was a mild evening, the sky painted with a golden light. I did not remember that in Southeast Asian countries darkness comes very suddenly, and I started on my way through the jungle to the ruins. I was walking along a narrow path when suddenly a group of men appeared out of the twilight of the forest. They wore only a loincloth and a gun strapped across their back, and in their hands they carried machetes. Close together, at a fast clip, they came toward me like a group of Stone Age hunters.

Curious as I was, I stopped and met this troop without fear. When they passed me eye to eye, however, I felt a chill running down my spine. I was looking into six completely expressionless faces. Their eyes were cold, completely empty and without any human feeling. At that moment I was convinced that these men could cut my head off while walking by without the least sentiment. Seconds later they had disappeared like dark ghosts behind the trees of the forest.

Never in my life before and never since have I experienced fear of another human being such as at that moment.

Cambodia had become a plaything for the international powers in their political struggle during the Vietnam War. In order to secure the areas for their own rearguard actions, President Nixon ordered the border areas of Cambodia bombed. From here the Vietcong brought their own supplies into the country. The Americans wanted to destroy the retreats of the Vietcong in the forests of Cambodia, but as always the attacks hit the wrong people, innocent women and children. Misery and hunger were the result. The ensuing poverty polarized the country: The Khmer Rouge were the winners, the Cambodian people the losers.

Singapore, 1970, Family photo

Eva and the snake in Singapore, 1970, Family photo

Angkor Wat, Cambodia, 1979, Family photo

The fuse had long been laid at the time when I met the warlike troop in the jungle of Angkor Wat. The faces of the men from the jungle were just a somber harbinger of a regime of terror that would cost the lives of two million people in the years that followed.

When I met Howard at the airport in Singapore, the world was in an equilibrium for me again. I had been sad, however, that he had to work and could not share these experiences with me. Now both of us were happy again. We spent one night in the traditional hotel in the colonial style, the famous Raffles Hotel. It was pure luxury.

Singapore, a thriving modern city, surprised us with its cleanliness and well-organized public conveniences. There was such a hustle and bustle on the streets, which were full of friendly people from all parts of Southeast Asia, China, India, the Philippines, Japan, and people from Europe and America. But most of all, it was full of the indigenous Malaysians! Singapore was and is a shopper's paradise, that is, if you like shopping.

Bali let me forget everything. We stayed in the only hotel that existed in 1970 on that island. Howard abducted me into a world of the truly blessed. This is how God must have planned paradise, before humans wreaked havoc in this world. We were surrounded by people who lived in perfect harmony with the plentiful, lavish nature around them. People in harmony with themselves and their gods, of whose good grace they seemed to be very well aware.

On every street corner and before every house we saw small boxes on a post, like birdhouses. In it were banana leaves, nicely arranged; a bit of rice; some small bits of chicken; and a flower. With these tokens of thanksgiving the people expressed their gratitude to their gods who had bestowed such riches on them.

The island seemed the epitome of tropical beauty. In a mild climate all year, the clear blue sky seemed to melt together with an emerald green sea. There were colorful wild orchids in the dark green jungle and the sounds of myriad colorful birds in the tropical rain forest that covered the center of the island. Because of that forest, Bali carries the name "the emerald island."

Angkor Wat, Cambodia, 1970, Family photo

Angkor Wat, Cambodia, 1970, Family photo

Along the coast and in the valleys, terraces of rice fields extend over the fertile land. Even on the steepest hills, the farmers wrench small lots from the fertile soil. For the Balinese, rice is the food of the gods. It shapes the landscape, the culture, and the life of the people. The fertile, volcanic soil blesses them with three harvests per year. Thanks to the gods!

We were surprised to hear that the way of cultivating rice has not changed since the time of the original ancestors of the present population. The work was hard. Even the smallest landslide could bring the intricate system of terraces out of balance. But the inhabitants are happy. Their faces seemed to reflect the beauty of nature around them. Wherever we went, people had a friendly smile on their faces and a flower in their hair, no matter what they were working on.

It seems that the gods had blessed these people with many different talents. Almost everyone here plays a musical instrument. Music is a part of life as well as the dance and the shadow play. The shadow play originated in Hindu literature and still has its place in Indonesia today. The player, called "Dalang," is a religious personage who can protect his listeners from bad ghosts for the time of the play. His flat puppets are carved from buffalo leather, and they tell stories from ancient times, which teach moral and ethical values and are accompanied by music and dance.

The impressive dances of the Balinese are also really dramas told by agile bodies and have a thousand year old tradition; they are still part of ritual ceremonies.

Hinduism has survived in Bali in its own separate form. With every step, one meets this mixture of Hinduism, Buddhism, nature religions, and the veneration of ancestors. Twenty thousand temples, pagodas, pavilions and shrines are witness to the presence of the celestial legions, accompanied by various spirits and demons.

Encounter in Bali, Indonesia, 1970, Family photo

Life on this "island of the gods," as it is respectfully called by its inhabitants, had in these few days transported us into a different world far from reality. Everything seemed so far away, the horrors of war in Vietnam, the sinister premonitions in Cambodia, and the hectic life in the big cities, Singapore, Bangkok, Hong Kong, and Manila.

The time had passed much too fast on the "island of the blessed." We had to return to reality. My twenty-second move was coming up.

Departure from Manila, Eva, Vivian, Ariane and Tuilan in the birdcage, 1970, Family photo

Chapter 13: My African Paradise

Poseidon had gone to the far off land of the Ethiopians,
The people furthest away at the end of the world,
Ethiopia, twofold divided
One part to where the sun rises,
The other to where the sun sets.
The hecatomb was sacrificed for him with sheep and oxen
There he sat down for the meal and took his pleasure.

(Homer, *The Odyssey*, Chapter I)

To Ethiopia Via Europe

In Manila the embassy had done a good job. Our complete household was packed up in boxes and stood ready to go. The girls had come back healthy and in good spirits from Hawaii and were looking forward to seeing their grandparents in Munich. Everything had been organized, and there was nothing else for us to do but to take our hand luggage and get on the plane to Europe.

We were looking forward to our summer vacation in *Quo Vadis* in June 1970. We had not been in Massa Lubrense and Munich for the last two years. Our first stopover was in Munich—Howard, the girls, and I, and in our hand luggage a bird cage, with Tuilan, our beautiful Siamese cat. At that time it was still possible to take along small animals in the cabin. The cat was a quiet and uncomplicated travel companion. She traveled in my bag, together with her own personal bathroom, a small shoe carton filled with sand.

In Hong Kong we had to change planes and spend the night. Suddenly, we had a problem: Tuilan was not allowed to enter the country. When we wanted to pass through customs with Tuilan in the bag, it turned out that we had forgotten to give her the required vaccination. This meant that Tuilan had to stay in quarantine and could not travel with us. The children immediately saw the problem. Tuilan would not be allowed to come with us to Europe. This was not acceptable! Ariane and Vivian sat down in the customs office and declared adamantly that they would not move one inch without their cat. Everyone was excited. After one hour on the bench in the office of the Chinese customs, the customs officer had reached the end of his rope and he angrily shouted at the girls, "Take your Miau and get out of here!" We had gotten our way and were very happy as we continued on our journey with Tuilan and the cat toilet.

My parents had come to the airport to pick us up. They were so happy to see us after such a long time. Munich had put on its spring dress. The trees in the park around the "Friedensengel" (The Angel of Peace) showed their light green leaves, and the air was mild. The linden trees were blooming and the sweet fragrance of their fine, white flowers drifted through the air.

We were happy to enter our small apartment in the Gruetznerstrasse. I opened the windows and listened to the jingle of the beer mugs and the happy laughter of the visitors in the Hofbraeukeller beer garden below, and the bells from the St. John's Church announced the hour of rest. I took a deep breath: A warm feeling of homecoming went through me. I was home, yes, this was our home. The shining eyes of the girls seemed to confirm my feelings. "Mama, now we go down and eat some Weisswurst, ja?"

After a wonderful week in Munich, during which we visited all our favorite places, such as the Marienplatz and the English Garden, we packed up again and drove South to our beloved villa *Quo Vadis*, together with my parents. The Gulf of Naples was our second home in the tides of our turbulent life. After some time there, I finally felt really well again. The time in Southeast Asia had taxed my physical and psychological strength more than I had liked to admit. In July and August, the temperature in southern Italy is also quite high, but the Mediterranean climate cannot be compared with the brooding, humid heat in Southeast Asia. We soon had recuperated and became curious about our new station in Addis Ababa.

The vacation time passed quickly. We met our old friends, Dorina D'Andrea, and Carmela and Angela Russo, and others in Massa Lubrense, and exchanged all the news of the past two years with the vendors and craftsmen. I saw to it that all the necessary repairs were taken care of. A house so close to the sea erodes rather quickly and requires lots of upkeep. I was glad to hear that not much had changed in this peaceful, friendly village, except that there was now a new post office.

At the end of August it was time to leave.

Again the well-known humming of the airplane motors. We were again on our way to a new country "furthest away at the end of the world." I looked out the window; below me I still saw "il mare nostrum," the Mediterranean Sea, but on the horizon already was the coast of an unknown continent, Africa.

I looked at my two girls. They were no longer children. Beside me I saw two young ladies, pretty like a picture and almost grown up. Two very remarkable personalities with very different characters. They had never complained about having to leave their friends behind. Since their birth they had been on this voyage with me. Always a new home, a new school, and new friends. Again and again we had to pack up our things, again have good-bye parties—just when they had become acclimated to their environment. I have never seen them cry, my brave girls. Without reproach they had accepted the situation. They had always given me the feeling that we were comrades and that to them, life was an exciting adventure full of challenges that one has to meet. Everything was all right the way it was.

Shortly before our departure for Addis Ababa, I had searched our globe for our new destination. I was awed: How small Europe seemed beside the continent of Africa! How far Manila was from Addis Ababa! Half of the globe lay between our last station and the place we would be staying for the next three years.

The State Department did not send their personnel for longer than three years to any foreign station. They believed that after a period of three years people "go native," that is, they become too rooted in the new culture. The State Department was convinced that one could only serve the interests of one's own country well as long as one had the necessary distance from the foreign country one was assigned to. From a national point of view, this may be true. I myself, however, considered it rather counterproductive that one had to leave a country when one had begun to understand its foreign social system and history.

It was exactly this issue that Howard had disputed in Vietnam: this lack of understanding for the social background of the guest country. He had met young graduates from America's elite universities, his colleagues at the American Office for Education, who ambitiously did their job without the least knowledge about the country they were working in. He had asked himself how they would be able to do a good job knowing neither the history nor the cultural background of the Vietnamese people they advised and with whom they had to cooperate.

Maybe Vietnam had been an exception. Full of optimism, Howard was looking forward to his new colleagues.

During the long hours of the flight I read a bit about the new, strange country where we would touch down within the next few hours. I had found a "Merian" journal from 1966 that served to get us into the right mood:

> Ethiopia is the oldest independent state in Africa, the only country that had never been under European colonial control, with the exception of a short period of occupation by the Italians from 1936-1941. From the standpoint of geography, culture and religion it is a continent by itself within Africa. The Ethiopians call it "a Christian island within a heathen sea." The name of the country used to be "Abyssinia." The word comes from the Arabic, meaning "abyss." This means great divides that cut up the countryside throughout; "Aithiopoi" the land of the people with the "sunburned faces," as the old Greek had called the people of Africa. For the old Egyptians it was the far away country where the incense came from, the mysterious land of "Punt." .

"Fasten your seatbelts, please!" Our lecture was abruptly interrupted. I closed the magazine, took out my camera, and managed to get a nice shot with the shadow of our airplane on the ground of the country we would soon set foot on. As always, I wanted to meet the new country with as little prejudice as possible and read up on the background later. We looked curiously out of the window as the plane slowly lost altitude.

One could not yet see very clearly, but then we saw for the first time rather bizarre, steep mountain ranges that suddenly changed from flat mountain tables to rugged valleys. Massive rock formations reached to the sky at an altitude of over 16,000 feet, as the captain let us know over the loudspeaker. The white, gleaming areas were salt lakes cut deep down in the valleys well below sea level.

The highland of Addis Ababa looked like a gigantic citadel built by nature whose many colored "tables," the so-called "ambas," projected into a blue sky.

Above the highlands of Ethiopia. old postcard

The road to the market between eucalyptus trees in Addis Abeba, Ethiopia, 1970, Family photo

I could see green tables that lost themselves in brown desert plains in the distance. The captain pointed out that in the south, one could make out the beginning of the Great African Rift Valley that stretches for about 4,000 miles from Syria through the Red Sea via Ethiopia and East Africa into Mozambique.

As we touched down, the air was clear, and we saw the green fields and some forests of the highlands. Every now and then we detected little round straw huts arranged in groups that seemed to be strewn on the landscape as if by chance. Red sandy roads appeared and disappeared again within the green of the fields.

It was the rainy season in Ethiopia when we landed. Not only did the countryside welcome us with a fertile green but the city also showed itself in lush colors. As we walked down the gangway, I breathed deeply; what a wonderful clear and fresh air!

The American Embassy had sent a car to pick us up, and now the Ethiopian driver was making his way through the streets that were partially covered with rainwater and mud. Beside the streets, barefooted women wrapped in long, white cloths were carrying huge bundles of firewood on their backs or had piled them on the backs of little donkeys, which they pulled behind them. The "people with the sun burnt faces," as Herodotus had called them, immediately attracted our attention. They were slim, tall, and dark-skinned, but not black. We noticed their finely chiseled faces, their delicate hands, and proud composure. They had small heads, and fine noses and lips. We admired especially the women, who had the most attractive, beautiful round eyes.

The road to the market in Addis Abeba, Ethiopia, Family photo

The road to the market in Addis Abeba, Ethiopia, 1970, Family photo

Woman carrying water, Addis Abeba, Ethiopia, 1970, Family photo

Ethiopian woman in her shamma, Addis Abeba, 1970, Family photo

We quickly left behind the uninteresting center of town with its modern buildings and areas of aluminum-covered huts that lined the streets, witnesses to the influx of thousands of farmers who had come to the city in search of work and a better life.

That the country was poor, we knew, but we had not expected how close to the minimum standards the people lived. I was impressed, because despite their destitute economic condition, the people in their beautiful long gowns expressed pride and dignity.

Even during our first ride the country emanated a special charm that all of us felt intensely. Tall, dark acacia trees pointed up to the sky, the soft green hills of the highlands reached into the far distance, and the fragrance of the eucalyptus forests were beautiful to us. Ernest Hemingway's great love for this continent came to my mind, as he had written in his book *Green Hills of Africa*:

> I could not believe that we had suddenly come into such a wonderful country. It was a country to wake from, happy to have had the dream ....

In the meantime, we had arrived at the outskirts of the city. The houses stood far apart, were built in the Western style, and looked very well taken care of. They were the homes of wealthy families and diplomats.

The city seemed to dissolve slowly into the wilderness, when we turned into the access road to a large property that ended in a circular driveway, an inviting entrance that had a garden and plants.

We had been expected. Our American "host family" and our servant team were standing as a reception committee in front of the doorway. We knew that we would have native servants, but I had not counted on such a large team. There they were, nicely dressed and with a dignified solemnity in their friendly faces as they greeted us, who would be their masters for the next three years: the cook, Gibrahnna, in his white uniform; the cook's helper; the housemaid Assada in a snow-white dress, turban, and apron; the two day and the two night watchmen, in washed out pieces of cloth, which they had wrapped artfully around themselves, leaning on their typical herdsmen's crooks; and the gardener. The way they were clothed in their mantels reminded me of ancient Romans in their togas, as they are depicted in the wall paintings of Pompeii.

Our home in Addis Abeba, fr. L. to R. the cook Gibrahanna, the maid Assada, Howard, Eva with dog, Ariane with dogs, Vivian, two stablehands Girma and Denny and our four horses, 1971, Family photo

The house was modern, and from the street it looked like a small bungalow. It had, however, twelve rooms distributed over several levels that led down to the garden. "Twelve rooms and eight servants—what luxury!" I thought. Shortly afterward I found the explanation.

Our "host family," a couple that the embassy assigns to every newcomer, introduced us to the most important habits of our guest country. First, they gave us a water-filtering machine, a gift from the embassy. Clean water was an important prerequisite for all newcomers in order to remain in good health.

Then they introduced each one of our servants to us, and told us where they had worked before. Gibrahanna, the cook, and his kitchen help, the maid for the housework and laundry, the gardener and the watchmen, two for the day and two for the night. They explained to us that a foreign household would need at least one watchman for the day to ensure safety from thieves and two for the night to guard against wild animals. You needed two guards, because one alone would fall asleep too easily. The two would make their rounds together during the night and keep each other company as they watched the fire all night long.

As we learned more and more about the former activities of our servants, and their family situation, it became clear to me why we had to employ so many servants.

The great droughts had driven the farmers from the countryside into the big city. There they hoped to be able to survive. But also in the city the people lived in bitter poverty and did not know how to feed themselves and their families. The blessings of the modern world were only accessible to a very small minority. The rest had to make a living on the outskirts of the city in shantytowns, makeshift houses with corrugated iron roofs that are so typical for the large cities in Third-World countries. A major contribution for these people that foreigners could make was to offer them employment, as much as possible. A job meant food, food for themselves and for their families. To do work with your own hands that a houseboy could do for you was not considered honorable by a servant. No, on the contrary, it was considered a sign of stinginess, a quality that is very despicable in such countries. Such a master would immediately get a reputation for not wanting the native people to earn anything.

Thus, we were able to feed eight families with our eight domestics.

To supervise so many servants was something one had to learn. The first thing I had to accept was that each of them would strictly refuse to do the work of one of the other co-workers. If one of them was missing, the job simply did not get done. At first, I thought they were too lazy to do additional work, but then I realized that it was simply the respect before the other co-worker whose space they did not want to intrude upon. Maybe they also wanted to demonstrate that neither of them was replaceable; a job was a very valuable good.

HAPPINESS ON THE EDGE OF THE WILDERNESS

We lived in a house with twelve rooms and were taken care of by seven dedicated servants. This was pure paradise! The climate was phenomenal; we felt like it was early summer all year. This is due to the altitude. Addis Ababa is situated on a high plateau 7,900 feet above sea level. It took us about six weeks to become adjusted to this altitude. In the beginning we could not sleep and were on edge all day. Then we really felt wonderful and fit, especially after the heat of Manila.

Soon we found out that you did not get very far with the car in Ethiopia. The countryside near us was only thinly populated. The people lived in their round huts, the "tukuls," on the plateau. There were very few villages and hardly any roads that connected them.

Most of the passable roads had been built during the short period of Italian occupation. The Italian occupiers were best suited to manage the construction on such a difficult topography. Some parts of their ingenious location routes are really technical masterpieces. Thus, it was the former occupiers that made an important contribution to the opening up of the country by building bridges, aqueducts, and tunnels. Later Haile Selassie had improved the air connections and thus improved the transport lines, but all these efforts did not have much impact on the inaccessibility of many parts of the big country.

Even in the surrounding areas of the capital there was little traffic on the roads in the Seventies. One of the main problems of the country was the resulting lack of infrastructure.

Nevertheless, we wanted to explore the countryside. We decided to buy horses and learn to ride them. Every family member had his own horse, and we bought two more for our guests. Now we had six horses in our stable, and we needed another servant who would take care of them. We employed Girma, an older man who had a lot of experience with horses.

The horses became a large part of our life. They were fast and of a nice size, not as tall as horses in Europe, but just the right size for the girls. A life with animals, this was what the girls had always dreamed of. We also found a friend, a Siamese tomcat that we named Rasputin, for Tuilan and guards for our large garden, two German shepherds.

 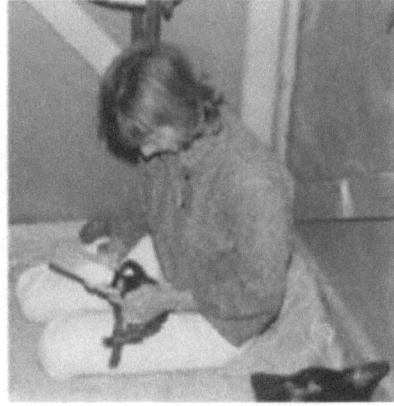

Our life amidst our animals in Addis Abeba, Ethiopia, 1970-1971, Family photo

Trip on horseback, Eva riding Tedj, Addis Abeba, 1970, Family photo

Now we had horses, and the necessary equipment, but none of us knew how to ride them. I searched for a suitable teacher and found a British lady who not only knew much about horses but also offered classes. This highly disciplined English woman was merciless. Every time we fell off the horse we had to immediately get back on because she believed that if you fell off a horse and did not remount, you would never get on a horse again. The first weeks were hard for me. I was covered with blue bruises, especially on my thighs. The girls did better than I.

The strict teacher was successful. Within only six weeks we were able to ride our horses, make them post or gallop, just as we wanted. Our teacher had also trained us to never get near a horse without a helmet.

We did, however, prefer the American cowboy-style saddle to the English saddle. We felt more secure in the "Western Saddle," because it had a pommel in the back and in front, where you could hold on if you needed to. Besides that, there were saddlebags on either side, where we could carry our picnic lunch supplies when we planned a longer outing.

My brave girls adjusted to the new life rather quickly. The school was no problem, because the International School in Addis Ababa did not differ very much from the International School in Manila. They did not have to work very hard, and homework was done quickly. So they had much time to get on their horses and explore the wild nature around them.

After the second semester, the girls changed to the Deutsche Schule to prepare for the German Gymnasium. Addis Ababa had in those days one of the best German schools abroad.

Eva on Sheik, 1971, Addis Abeba, Ethiopia, Family photo

THE BEAUTIFUL STRANGE COUNTRY

As often as we could, Howard and I took a ride on the horses with the children in the late afternoon.

As soon as we heard Howard's car turn into the driveway, Girma started to saddle the horses. On one mild afternoon we were ready to leave. We had planned a ride over the hill behind our house. Ariane's horse, Echo, was, as always, very impatient but did not like to be saddled.

I had put on my "camouflage" suit that I had tailored from army supplies at the market in Saigon. It was ideal for this climate, and I loved it. The material was light but did not allow the cold wind to pass through that usually blew on the hillside. At the same time it protected me from the burning African sun. Besides, it was absolutely impervious to sand and dirt.

My white horse, Scheich (sheikh) was a rather quiet horse. I put the bit in his mouth, lifted the saddle onto his back, and fastened the belt underneath his tummy. Scheich had his tricks. He inhaled during saddling to blow up his tummy, and then when I had mounted, he let go of the air and when he started to trot, the belt became so loose that the saddle started to slide down and I was in danger of falling off. Thus, I pulled the belt as tight as I could in order to outwit the joker. Then we put on our helmets and trotted out of the gate.

Howard usually took the lead, because these outings were his greatest joy. This meant that Ariane had to restrain Echo, because he did not like to allow anyone else take the lead and was anxious to take off.

We followed the footpath until the last tukul and then turned right over the hill and down into the valley, where we had to cross a small river to get to the waterhole. We encountered the women who were coming up from the valley with heavy, black jugs on their backs in which they carried the water for their daily use. They greeted us with a friendly smile.

The ground was red and corroded, and scarred by the wind. On the other side of the hill, the terrain rose up and then fell steeply down into the next ravine.

The slopes of the rugged valleys were densely covered with eucalyptus trees. There was no underbrush, and we could pass through in a light trot without the branches hitting us in the face. On the other side, there were cliffs and ridges densely grown over with shrubs. We scared up a group of black and white monkeys and now they were swinging from branch to branch over our heads, complaining with loud shrieks.

Eva and the girls, Addis Abeba, Ethiopia, 1970, Family photo

Picnic in the countryside, Addis Abeba, Ethiopia, Family photo

About one hour later we reached a clearing where the rain had washed away the earth. The rocky ground lay open under the hoofs of our horses. Suddenly I noticed a pile of stones, the shape of which looked strange to me.

I stopped my horse and jumped down, handed the reins to Howard, and began to poke in the ground.

The rain had actually washed up an ancient fireplace from the Stone Age. I saw two wonderful evenly carved stone axes and a number of sharp-edged, finely chiseled tools made from black, shiny obsidian. We were all excited. Imagine, in this place, a group of Stone Age hunters had actually cut up their prey and had chiseled their tools! What a discovery! We packed everything we'd found into our saddlebags and started home.

The horses immediately realized the change of direction and broke into a gallop to take the shortest way. We just let them go; we could never get lost, they always knew the direct way home to their stable.

When we reached our gate, the sun was setting behind the western hills.

The sparks of the fire of our night watchmen rose up into the darkness. In the distance we heard the sounds of the night, the characteristic hiccup whine of the hyenas. We had become accustomed to it, and it no longer scared us.

The hour of sunset in Africa has its particular charm. The colors and the expanse of the heavens seems much clearer and brighter than anywhere else in the world. Not even the sky above the Bay of Naples can compare to the endlessness of the deep blue and the glitter of these stars that make the universe seem so near.

Once the children were in bed, Howard and I would sit for hours on the terrace enjoying the closeness of the wilderness, its sounds and smells, the interplay between man and nature, and the strong forces of this beautiful and untamed country. We talked about our experiences of the day and our impressions of this country that fascinated both of us so much with its many treasures and stark contrasts.

Ethiopia combines all the climatic zones of the African continent on its territory. Accordingly, it shows the whole variety of geological formations.

The spectacular difference in altitude between the mountainous highland and the depth of the African Rift Valley is about 7,000 feet. Just as extreme are the differences between temperatures. The median temperature on the highland is about 18-20 degrees Celsius, while it can rise up to 60 degrees Celsius in the depression of the valleys.

The life of the people also reflects these extremes. On the one hand, there is the life of the farmers and nomads who eke out a bare existence as they have done for thousands of years; on the other hand, there is the feudal system of the emperor, Haile Selassie, who had tried for years to lead his country, ravished by draught and starvation, by means of the blessings of modern life to a better future.

Haile Selassie wanted to survive with the help of the Americans, while it was the American desire to lead the country step by step toward democracy.

It was Howard's special mission to help this process of democratization by means of education and information. He had to develop certain educational programs for teachers, professors, and other disseminators of political education and information that were to be passed down to the elementary schools and schools of higher education. One had to consider the fact that only a minimal fraction of the population was able to attend school at all. About 75% of the population consisted of analphabets.

Somehow time stood still in Ethiopia. The way people lived here, their culture and emotional setup, were so different from anything I had experienced. I never had met people who had to confront an uncontrollable nature in such an existential way.

Their daily life was controlled only by the course of the sun. Time was not divided up by a clock into twenty-four hours. Many of them still lived the archaic life of the nomads, following their herds from waterhole to waterhole, or as farmers they used primitive ploughs or their own hands to coax a meager harvest from the dry land. A large part of the Ethiopian people remained in the primeval form of human existence. Being exposed to the beginnings of mankind held a deep fascination for me.

In America I had experienced great cultural differences from Europe. In Asia I had met a completely different world, and it had been difficult for me to understand the Asian mentality. I had tried to dive into culture and religion. These people, despite their individual differences, they all moved within a common cultural heritage that had grown for thousands of years and had molded the people for generations.

But from the first moment I set foot in Ethiopia I felt the naturalness of this continent that combined the oldest cultures. In Africa I felt like living in a mythological past that was before the beginning of other cultures.

With Ethiopia we can look back on an ancient culture. I discovered it only later, when I was able to travel with Howard, the children, and my old school friend, Lilo, to the South of the country. The North of Ethiopia had a culture that present heirs can be proud to look back on, and which allows them to meet their present difficulties with pride and dignity. But Ethiopia was Africa, and it seemed to me that most of the country had remained in the period of the beginning of mankind.

The news about the latest, startling findings of paleontologists in the Rift Valley confirmed my feelings. They were able to prove that this area truly must have been the "cradle of mankind." Here man had ventured his first upright steps as *homo erectus* in the Danakil Valley. Only a few years later, in 1974, this theory was confirmed when Dr. Donald Johanson, who was digging in the desert of Afar near Hadar, found the skeleton of the oldest teenager. "Lucy" was 3.5 million years old and only about three-and-a-half feet tall. By the way, she owes her name to the Beatle song, "Lucy in the Sky with Diamonds," which the scientists were listening to on their transistor radio under the desert sky at that time.

For me, this was all so fascinating because I had wondered since childhood why man was the way he was. I asked myself, "What makes man tick?" I hoped to come closer to an answer in Africa. And I did.

The entrance gate to the Haile Selassie University,
Addis Abeba, 1970, Family photo

*Haile Selassie I, Emperor of Ethiopia 1930-1974,
visiting his university, 1970, Family photo*

HAILE SELASSIE UNIVERSITY

Shortly after our arrival, I had been offered a contract as a teacher of English by the administration of Haile Selassie University. I was overjoyed and accepted immediately. I hoped not only to get to know the people of this country better but also to be able to have an impact on the society by offering information and by training in communication skills.

The city of Addis Ababa was a modern city but did not really have any character. There was no old center but only a lot of nondescript high-rises. In the middle of these modern buildings was the palace of Haile Selassie.

Haile Selassie was a small man in a khaki uniform who was world-renowned, not only because he was the first one to give his country a constitution and had abolished slavery but because he was also a renovator of his country and had won great acclaim when he helped to found the Organization of African Union (OAU), which has its seat in Addis Ababa. In the Sixties, he traveled through the world in search of support for his country, which needed the help of foreign countries to battle hunger and poverty.

Haile Selassie lived in the middle of his town in a small oasis of peace and luxury within a stately mansion in a seemingly undamaged world. A friend of the Western world, he afforded himself his own private university, which was situated in one corner of his beautiful garden, the Haile Selassie University. It was a showpiece that seemed in stark opposition to the realities in the rest of the country and was eagerly supported by European countries and the United States. At that time we were still in the acute phase of the cold war and both sides were anxious to play a part in showing the youth of the continent the politically "right way."

Haile Selassie University became Howard's and my place of work. The beautiful gate at the entrance to the royal gardens was guarded by soldiers in white uniforms and decorative helmets. Right behind the gate began a broad road lined by magnificent old trees, where one could walk in the shade. In the center of this park, I had been assigned a lovely, summer pavilion as my classroom. I was overjoyed, but upon a second look I found it to be a rather rundown garden house. The place was unacceptable because in such a dilapidated place I could not teach my students. Therefore, classes would have to be postponed until I could solve that problem.

Since there was no way to organize professional help to have the house painted within a short time, I had to pick up the paintbrush myself. With the help of my cook and the gardener, I painted the whole classroom over the weekend. My students did not believe their eyes: their lecturer clad in an apron and with a paintbrush in her hand! They never had seen anything like that. A white lady who would perform such a menial labor by herself!

There was a lot that I had to learn about the local social structure and mentality.

One example: My gardener had been complaining about the fact that he was so poor. He had several sons whom he wanted to send to school, but he was too poor to do so. I remembered my large garden and the many heads of lettuce that grew there bountifully. Our family would not be able to eat all that salad. So I called the son of the gardener. I told him that he could take the lettuce and sell it on the market and keep the money.

One week later I discovered the lettuce was still there and was beginning to rot. I asked the boy why he had not taken the lettuce to the market. His answer was that his father was an honorable man who worked for a good family and earned the money for his family. He could not bring shame on him by going to the market and selling things like a peddler.

I decided to teach the boy a lesson. I had my girls cut the lettuce and put it into the saddlebags of their horses. Then they went to the houses of our neighbors and sold the lettuce. The boy was bewildered.

In Ethiopia only two social groups were considered honorable: the priests and the warriors. Merchants were looked down upon. This is why the commerce in the country was mostly in the hands of Italians and Indians. People who worked with their hands were considered lower class and the business in the market was done by women.

Another lesson for me was this: Every time when we parked our car, several boys appeared from somewhere and offered to guard it for a "little present."

In the beginning we declined the offer, because we did not see why we should have to "guard" the car on the side of the road on a street with almost no traffic. Shortly afterward on the way home our car began to sputter and stopped altogether. Suddenly the same boys appeared and offered to help us with our problem. Together with Howard they looked for the problem and found that the connection to the gas had been cut through. The boys fixed the engine trouble in a short time and were happy to receive some dollars for their help. We finally understood: Either we paid right away or later.

It was depressing to see the misery of the sick. Every morning on my way to the university I passed by the hospital of Addis Ababa. Every morning there were dead or dying people on the street, just a few yards away from the place where they might have been helped. They had walked for days until they arrived in the city, only to collapse shortly before reaching their goal.

The system of medical care was in a catastrophic condition. Medical education did not exist. Many women had bent spines due to the hard work in the fields and to carrying heavy loads. The distorted spine was the cause for serious problems during childbirth. I was told that when a very difficult birth took place the father would hang his trousers on a stick on top of the roof, hoping that God would see their plight and send help. What else could they do? The next doctor was at least a three-day walk away.

THE AMHARIC PEOPLE AND THE ORTHODOX CHURCH

While I researched the history of the country, I had to go back to the times of the Old Testament. I found Ethiopian and Arabic traditional writings that spoke about the mysterious Makeda von Saba, the "Negesta Asiab, the empress of the South (today called the "Queen of Sheba") who was said to have lived around 1000 B.C. She had undertaken a long journey to the court of King Solomon in order to profit from his wisdom and to establish economic ties with his country. The result of this journey, according to legend, was her son Ebna Hakim. The

Ethiopian history knows him by the name of "Menelik I." After the death of his mother, he reigned for another 35 years and is considered the ancestor of the Ethiopian dynasty. Emperor Haile Selassie was the last reigning descendent of this hierarchy of the Amharic people.

The Amharic people had been the ruling tribe of the country until the revolution in 1974. Over centuries they had defeated again and again many other tribes, such as the Gallas or the Danakils. Their descendents came from the Semitic peoples of South Arabia, and this heritage has defined the culture of the country up to modern times. Even today one can find their traces in the written sources as well as in archaeological excavations.

The Orthodox Church did not only determine the arts, painting, and architecture, but it had also influenced the content and form of the language. Up to the 20th century, only the priests had mastered the art of writing; the common people considered writing a dangerous work of the devil.

Ethiopian orthodox priests, Addis Abeba, 1970

In Ethiopia the church seemed omnipresent despite the fact that only 45% of the population was Orthodox Christian; another 45% were Sunni Moslems, and 10% believed in nature religions.

Many times I met these dark-skinned priests, dressed in white or colorful robes, as they led one of the numerous processions on a church holiday. Above their heads a colorful umbrella to shield them from the rays of the strong sun, they carried large, silver crosses. You could find these silver crosses everywhere on the market in all shapes and intricate designs, crosses for men, women, children, even crosses for soldiers to clean their ears, as I was told. At that time they were sold by the pound. Today they have become rare collector items.

I was also told that the devout Christians had to fast 150 days a year. This seemed almost cynical to me in a country where so many people had to fast due to their poverty. Religion, as a concept, did not seem to have meaning for most of the people. They needed a God they could call on to protect them from the destructive powers of nature or the revenge by other tribes. In the name of this God, the church organized festivals for the people that they celebrated with great joy and a lot of pomp.

It was Easter 1971. I remember this day with mixed feelings. The Mass on Good Friday in the church was impressive, but the celebration of Easter Sunday in the highlands was disturbing. Again these typical contrasts!

All of us had a few days of vacation and we had planned a longer outing into the highlands. Again we were under way on horseback, this time accompanied by our new stable boy as a guard. He carried our food supplies. As always, we enjoyed riding across the country through the wilderness, passing herds of peacefully grazing antelopes and Thompson gazelles.

Sometimes a small group of dik-diks, which looked like tiny toy antelopes, startled us as they appeared with enormously wide leaps and disappeared into the underbrush. On both sides of our trail, our old friends, the black and white monkeys, accompanied us as they clattered through the branches above.

Vivian looking at a weaverbird's nest, Addis Abeba, 1971, Family photo

As the sun was high we looked for a fit place to rest and have our picnic lunch. We passed a small village with several tukuls. I noticed some small rivulets that trickled through the dust of the main road. Vultures were circling in the air above, and a strange smell lay over the village. Then we saw a group of men on top of the hill who were slaughtering a cow according to the Easter ritual.

For us this was not exactly an inviting sight. Our boy explained that now the raw meat would be dealt out to the families and then the women would prepare the feast.

Meat was a very rare luxury. Everybody was in a festive mood. The women had already prepared the baskets with "injera," the Ethiopian sour bread. The village elder invited us to eat with them and celebrate the Easter feast, but we declined politely. We could not leave, however, without a token of friendship, and so we accepted a mug with "tedj," the sweet, homemade Ethiopian beer.

It was time to start our way back home. On the way, we stopped to have our picnic.

When we arrived home we were happy to come back into a modern, civilized household. The table was festively decorated with painted eggs and spring flowers, and a homey "Apfelstrudel."

We did, however, have to accept another invitation to an Ethiopian family celebration. One of Howard's employees had invited us for the baptism of his son. The family had put up tents and wooden benches. The servants passed the baskets with injera and spicy sauces, and jugs with tedj.

The highpoint of the festival arrived when we were asked to join the group around a big fire. There, a whole cow had been roasted over the fire and servants were cutting up the animal. They hung large pieces of beef over a wooden pole over their shoulders and walked along the benches. Little, sharp knives were handed out, and every guest was asked to cut a piece of meat for themselves. I had to think of the village feast in the highlands. The situation was the same, despite the fact that it was not such a bloody sight. Again, we were unable to eat a piece of this meat. We realized that it was very impolite toward our hosts to turn down their offer, because meat was indeed a precious, rare luxury, but our aversion was stronger. But, as it turned out, this had been our good luck, because on the next day, many of the guests were sick.

Only later were we informed that the cattle had carried dangerous worms that could cause serious intestinal problems in humans. The government was well aware of the problem and had tried several times to place veterinary doctors in the highlands in order to examine the cattle.

After some of these veterinarians had been killed, however, nobody could be found to do this job, and so everything remained as it had always been.

During discussions within the diplomatic corps we also heard about a new, unknown, and very dangerous sickness that was said to stem from monkeys and was passed on among humans by way of sexual intercourse. At that time there was no name for this sickness. Only later did we find out that in 1971 the first cases of AIDS had become known.

Ethiopian children, Addis Abeba, 1970, Family photo

Every Day Life in Addis Ababa

Our life in Ethiopia seemed like a constant change between different worlds, between poverty and misery on one side, and wealth and luxury on the other side.

The market was situated within the rich section of town and attracted everybody, the rich and the poor. Once a week I went there, accompanied by my cook, Gibrahanna, with a big basket.

We passed the "Lion Of Judah," the most eminent statue of the town; close by we passed Africa Hall, the most important building in town. As we walked down Churchill Street, I observed elegantly dressed Amharic ladies in their white "shammas" and looked with joy into their proud and self-confident faces.

The general market was a cosmos of its own, and despite the fact that the hygienic situation was unacceptable for us Western Europeans, I remained fascinated by it.

Wrapped up in my shamma, the ideal protection against dust and flies, I was soon familiar with all the stalls and moved like a native through the hustle and bustle of vendors and buyers. Asking advice from my expert cook, I examined vegetables and fruit and bargained about the price of spices. There was little meat, and if so, one could not buy it because of the unsanitary conditions. The whole milieu reminded me of the suq in Beirut. The vendors presented their goods in a picturesque and tempting way. Beans and other pulses, and spices, were offered in plain white enamel bowls or nice baskets on top of simple wooden tables. Behind them

At the market in Addis Abeba, Ethiopia, 1970, source unknown

were large natural burlap sacks filled with corn and millet. "Teff," a type of Ethiopian wheat, was stacked in the tents.

In the next lane, colorful, handmade rugs and fabrics were decorating the branches of the trees. Pure white cotton fabrics were presented in huge bales on top of makeshift, but artfully built, bamboo tables. Behind a curtain under the tent a handsome man was busy on his ancient Singer sewing machine to finish a client's order for a shirt or a shamma. His sewing table reminded me of my grandmother's old table. With incredibly fast fingers he sewed the traditional long garments. You ordered in the morning and everything was ready to be picked up by sunset time.

My favorite store was the "Salt Man's" stall. A vendor with beard and a white turban (a Moslem?) smashed the huge blocks of white, glittering salt into smaller pieces. These scattered like snow through the air. Stone salt is one of the most sought-after goods in Ethiopia. Camel caravans brought the large salt bars from the Danakil Valley by the Red Sea to the markets in the highlands and to Addis Ababa.

Elegant Ethiopian ladies, Addis Abeba, 1970, Family photo

What attracted me most about these markets was the beautiful look and the soft colors of all these natural goods. Everything was made of natural materials, linen, burlap, straw, wood, and bamboo. You saw no gaudy advertisements, no plastic or artificial materials—at least not yet! It was pure joy for my eyes.

As American citizens, we bought most of our food, especially the meat, from the PX store, which offers the same goods to Americans all over the world. There you could buy everything—clean, neat, and hygienically packed or deep-frozen. There you could get everything, and we lacked nothing.

Every day I found out more and more about the country. I began to love Ethiopia. My life was fulfilled, and I was happy in these roles as teacher, mother, and mistress of a large, warm and welcoming house. Most of all, I was a fulfilled and happy wife. Howard and I loved and respected one another and this love gave us wings the likes of which I should never experience again. The secret of our harmony was, I think, the fact that we loved and appreciated each other the way we were. There was no show. We felt in harmony with ourselves and with each other. We never lost any time or energy with senseless control games. We both had our personal area of responsibility. Important questions we discussed and decided in common. These were decisions that both of us could support, because they were based on the same set of values. Most of all, I was very happy to be able to bring up my two girls in such a wonderful, healthy, and stimulating environment. I hoped that certain values and perspectives on nature and people had become ingrained and would influence their lives as they grew up.

Bargaining/or crosses, Addis Abeba, 1970, Family photo

With a light hand we managed our immense workload. There were the children who demanded full attention, the work at the university, and our large household with seven, later eight servants, each of whom had their own personality. We had to manage these jobs with a quiet but firm hand in order to make everything function without friction.

And everything had to function, because above all, we had an enormous amount of social responsibilities. The cultivation of social contacts was a major part of our responsibility within the Foreign Service . It was not enough to do our professional work competently—our social competence was also required, expected, and noted by Howard's bosses. I later found a whole folder containing a confidential report with an assessment of Howard's and my social activities.

Despite the fact that I had never been very interested in the social events, I began to enjoy them. We met many interesting people at the numerous receptions of the embassy. These were the top people who represented their country, organization, or business entity abroad; scientists; professors; diplomats; and businessmen. They were all looking for the right contacts, because making the right contacts would determine the final success or failure of their respective missions.

The day usually had too few hours. I gave four three-hour lectures at the university. Then there were the voluntary English language lessons for nurses at the local hospital once a week. And then, there were all the social obligations in the evenings! Nine invitations per week was the rule. Most of them were in other homes or embassies, but we also held dinner parties in our home. On some evenings, there would be more than one invitation. These seemingly irrelevant chitchat parties turned out to be the pivotal point of our political effectiveness.

After a while I learned to make efficient use of these parties. Instead of wasting precious time with the superficial chitchat of people who were just trying to escape from their boredom, I tried to seek out those people that I needed to talk to. Then I unobtrusively joined the group they were engaged in. As soon as I could get a word in, I first asked about the well-being of their family and then quickly came to the point I wanted to make. That way I could see initial reactions to my ideas, for example, establishing a scholarship for needy students. I could find out whether there was interest in and money for the project, whether anyone else had the same idea in the past, or whether I did should not pursue the idea.

Especially interesting was my discussion with the Ethiopian health minister. She spoke openly and clearly about the problems in her country. After the usual exchange of polite social talk, she asked me how I liked it in Addis Ababa. I said that I had noticed that in the outskirts of town many women were openly practicing the trade of prostitution. I added that judging by the numerous beer cans openly displayed on top of a stick in front of a house, reflecting the motto "beer and service," there must be an immense number of prostitutes. I told her that I had been informed that 70,000 women were practicing prostitution and asked her if that was true.

The minister answered me with a question: "What would you suggest that we do? Chase these women and their children out of their houses so that they would go begging in the streets?"

It was not up to me to ask her, "What does your government do with the money given as aid by other countries?" so I remained quiet.

During another meeting, she gave me a similar answer. We were talking about the developing industrialization in Ethiopia, and I mentioned the increasing pollution of the air in the city.

She smiled at me with a blank look. "Please remember, my dear," she said, "that every smoking chimney is a proud sign of our progress."

I had to think of the many beggars that were crowding the streets, sick and covered with flies and without a home. "Preservation of the Environment" obviously was not an urgent topic for such a poor country as Ethiopia—such a concern was pure luxury.

I became acquainted with a young Russian lady at one of the parties. She was not only very beautiful and charming, but she had many other talents too. She spoke several languages and knew how to sew very well. She had opened a lovely boutique in the Hilton Hotel. Many wives of various diplomats were her clients. She was very intelligent and educated as well as widely read, and I went to visit her sometimes after teaching at the university, just to chat with her. So we became good friends, and I enjoyed her company.

Only much later did I learn that my Russian friend had been one of the best spies of her country. This is only one of the many interesting affairs that meant "business as usual" in the Foreign Service. You always had to expect everything. It was not always easy to assess people correctly.

The Towns of the North

In the fall of 1970 my school friend Lilo came for a visit. At that time she worked as a judge in Bavaria. For her, Ethiopia was an unknown country, and I was happy to discover together with her more of this fascinating world.

Our first trip was to the northern part of the country. We wanted to see Axum, the oldest town in Ethiopia.

After several hours in the car, we noticed a marketplace on the side of the road. The people were sitting on the red ground and were displaying their wares around them. Large black umbrellas gave them some protection from the scorching sun. We noticed a woman who was selling fresh injera. Beside her was a large, iron pot in which a delicious-smelling vegetable sauce was simmering. Despite the fact that we could not communicate in Amharic, we soon had a flat bread with a highly spiced vegetable sauce in our hands and enjoyed our picnic meal in the cool shade of a large acacia tree.

Contented and happy, we continued on our way. We passed women who were spinning wool while leaning on a shady tree. We also saw men who were working on small looms, producing the colorful fabrics that were offered in every market. Small boys were driving large Zebu oxen in a circle as they milled the grain under their hoofs. The grown ups would gather the grain and throw it up in the air with large baskets, until the wind had separated the grain from the chaff.

We watched women with heavy black jugs on their backs who were walking, alone or in groups, to the waterhole three to five miles away in some inaccessible valley.

A group of men that was sitting on the side of the street did actually annoy us very much. They seemed to be having a great time chatting with each other while following a very natural urge to relieve themselves. This was one way of socializing, which was a very old custom in Africa, and had been in ancient cities in Europe, as one can still see in the old baths in the ruins of the Roman city of Ephesus.

Axum, the center of the Orthodox Christian Church, also called the "Rome of Ethiopia," impressed us with its famous "grove of the steles." These monoliths rise up 30 to 40 meters into the sky and were constructed in the 4th or 5th century B.C. They reminded me very much of the obelisks of ancient Egypt. They represent buildings with many floors and are witness to the high craftsmanship of the ancient Axumite people.

The origin of this town is not known. Its founders had made the city the center of an important empire in prehistoric times.

During the zenith of their power, the Axumites reigned over northern Ethiopia, including today's Eritrea, as well as large parts of the Sudan and even Yemen on the Arabic Peninsula. Many findings of coins attest to the high culture of this empire. After the Christianization of Axum, the church "Marjam Tsion," St. Mary of Zion, the oldest church in southern Africa, was built. According to Ethiopian belief, St. Mary of Zion Church still houses the famous "Arc of the Covenant" from the times of Moses and therefore became the religious center of the Ethiopian Church for many centuries. After its destruction by the

Moslems, Emperor Fasilidas built a new church in honor of St. Mary. No woman has ever been allowed into this church up to today. This rule was strictly applied, even for Queen Elizabeth II of England, as she visited Axum together with Emperor Haile Selassie in 1964. A new Church of St. Mary of Zion next to the old one was completed in 1964. Unlike the original St. Mary of Zion, the new St. Mary of Zion allows entrance to women.

Our next goal was the world renowned rock churches of Lalibela.

At first we saw only a typical Ethiopian marketplace surrounding a small hotel and a gas station. There were only a few stone houses and numerous cottages. Then we discovered a small river that divided the town and led us to the famous rock churches on both sides of the river. They were part of the new "Jerusalem" that Emperor Lalibela had founded here in the 12th century. This small town became famous for these monolithic rock churches and is the center of religious life in Ethiopia even today.

UNESCO has nominated these churches as part of the World Heritage List because of their extraordinary monolithic architecture. All the churches have several aisles and are cut from red sandstone. They were built, so to speak, from above downward and from outside to inside from the surrounding red sandstone. On the outside, a small trench separates them from the rock of the surrounding highlands. The style of the façades and

Monolithic rock-cut churches in Lalibela, Ethiopia, 1970, Old postcard

the columns reminded me of the style of Roman classical antiquity. An old priest, impressively dressed in his white cloak, showed us ancient scriptures and books from the 14th and 15th centuries, written on parchment and bound into small leather cases to be carried by their owner during their journeys to the holy places. He also told us of the many miracle healings that had occurred in the well next to the church. We would have liked to stay and research more of these archeological jewels but is was time to leave.

Lilo and Eva in Lalibela, Ethiopia, 1970, Family photo

Our next goal was the ancient capital of Gondar. This was Emperor's Fasilidas's realm. Just like the European emperors during the Middle Ages, the Ethiopian rulers were forced to constantly be on the road through their empire. In 1640 Emperor Fasilidas had, however, begun to build a city around a large castle in the Southern European style, to establish a permanent seat of government. It was built in a strange mixture of Southern European and Indian style, which is probably due to the Portuguese influence of the founders and

Eva and Howard and a little lion in Gondar, Ethiopia, 1970, Family photo

their Indian builders. We visited the impressive ruins of the city and enjoyed the day and the wonderful mountain climate.

The origin of the Blue Nile river near the city of Bahir Dar, Ethiopia, 1970, Family photo

We were tired and full of many new impressions as we started our trip back to Addis Ababa. On the way we passed Lake Tana, the largest lake in Northern Africa, with the impressive waterfalls of the Blue Nile, which has its origin in this lake. "Tis Isat," "the Gushing Waters" is the most beautiful spectacle of nature that you can imagine.

The waters of the lake plunge over a sheer drop of 6,500 feet over the steep cliffs of the Rift Valley down into the lowlands. The colors of the rainbow become mixed with the contours of the landscape, with the leafy green of the trees, the dark red of the rocks and the intense blue of the African sky. I could feel the spirit from which these rock churches had been created. For me, this exciting confrontation with the nature of this continent was the final highlight of an eventful journey.

Awash National Park, Ethiopia, 1970, Family photo

Awash National Park, Ethiopia, 1970, Family photo

JOURNEY TO THE SOUTH OF ETHIOPIA

Our trip to the South became a program of contrasts. Howard and I started together with Lilo, the girls, and our American friends, Bill Losch and his wife, on a longer journey to Awash National Park and to the city of Harar in the deep south of the country, the center of the famous Ethiopian coffee production.

We started in the early morning hours in order to make good headway before the heat of the noonday sun. The temperature would change drastically once we made our way down into the Rift Valley. We went in two cars packed to the hilt and followed the road across the highlands and the savannas to the waterfalls of the Awash River.

At first we passed through fertile, black acres, where groups of farmers worked the ground together. They turned the black, gleaming soil with small shovels, singing rhythmic songs that synchronized their movements.

As we proceeded south, we met groups of women and young girls that scooped water out of a waterhole by means of animal skins. The pretty young girls seemed to be of a different race. Their dark skin was decorated with colorful beads, and they wore a short loincloth that covered their lower body. There we stopped to take a photo with our Polaroid camera. The girls, at first very shy, came closer as their curiosity got the upper hand, and when we showed them the photo they turned it at first upside down. But when they finally recognized first their friends and then themselves, they broke into a delighted giggle. We gave them the photo as a memento.

In the afternoon we met the first nomads. The men, tall, slim, and long-legged, dressed in only a loincloth, were standing on one leg and were leaning on their herdsman's crook. The other leg they had pulled up for rest. As they thus remained motionless by the wayside, they seemed like cranes at rest. Seemingly disinterested in the passing strangers, they held their heads up high and were obviously proud of their property, the herd they were watching.

The nomads in this dry and dusty region owned herds that consisted mainly of cattle but also goats, donkeys, and camels. These animals were used for meat only on very extraordinary occasions. The family clans lived mostly on the milk and the hides of these animals. The herds were really more of a status symbol for their owners. A nomad with two hundred animals, as measly as they might be, enjoyed a high rank within his tribe.

We fought our way forward on the unpaved road through clouds of dust and continued only very slowly. The washboard surface of the road did not permit us to drive faster than ten to twenty miles per hour. Three times we had to stop for a blown-out tire. Now we were on the road with the last one of our extra tires and hoped to get to Awash Park before sunset. We were lucky to have enough bottles with water in the trunk, because the heat was nearly unbearable.

We had already left the fertile highland with its grain and vegetable fields, at noontime, and were passing through the wide barren savannas, where we noticed the typical high termite cones. When we arrived in the green valley of the Awash River, luscious acacia trees lined the road. At the end of their branches dangled the neat nests of the weaverbirds that watchful bird mothers had woven intricately onto the tree. Among the trees, the flamboyant red of the "elephant trees made for a very exotic mood.

Awash Park compensated us for the long and tiring trip. We camped in a comfortable trailer owned by the company of Bill Losch and as the day quickly lost its light, enjoyed the sunset over the wilderness. Marabous storks were waiting with stoic calmness for their dinner, a hippopotamus was wallowing in the middle of the river, and a herd of antelopes came down to the water to drink.

In the early morning of the next day we continued our journey south. Harar lies about three hundred feet higher than Awash. The trip there was dusty and hot again. But we also passed wonderful sugar plantations, vineyards, and even met with a camel caravan. When we arrived in our little hotel in Harar, we were worn out and the first thing we needed was a shower to wash off the red dust that had covered everything and was sticking to our skin and hair.

We had a good cup of Ethiopian coffee and some refreshments and then went out to investigate this Arabic looking city. We started our tour at the old city wall that had been built during the time when the city was occupied by the Osmans and which encloses about a hundred mosques. When the call of the muezzin sounded above the roofs of the city, I remembered our time in Beirut. "Allahu Akbar!" Now I realized how closely the Islam connects the Arabic with the African peoples.

The pride of the nomads, Ethiopia, 1971, Family photo

Roadblock, South Ethiopia, 1971, Family photo

Nomads in the South, Ethiopia, 1971, Family photo

Harar is the capital of the province of the same name, and as the center of Ethiopian Islam since the 7th century, has influenced the culture of the southern part of the country.

Harar presented itself all in white: white cupolas, white façades, and white gates in the city wall. Even the population was mostly dressed in white, including the beggars on the streets. But then, in sharp contrast, the nomad women from the surrounding countryside wore colorful shawls and dresses.

Dignified old men with long beards, wrapped in stark white mantles and with a shepherd's crook in their hand, reminded me of Moses. A young mother

Nomads in the South, Ethiopia, 1971 Family photo

with her baby in her arms and dressed in pretty, colorful wraps reminded me of St. Mary.

In the market square we met young, full-bosomed, dark-skinned beauties wrapped in colorful clothes, wearing jewelry in gold or colored stones around their necks, arms, and ankles. Also mingling in the crowd were beggars and blind men and women, skinny and in rags. Among heaps of trash and wild dogs, the vendors offered fruit, vegetables, and aromatic spices in large baskets.

Eva building trust with the natives, in the South, Ethiopia, 1971, Family photo

We followed one street in the old part of town and passed a well-built old house; the beautifully carved door was half open. Curious as always, I pushed the door open and entered. The large court was filled with very young girls, children still, in very colorful dresses and wearing heavy lipstick and makeup and wearing lots of jewelry around their necks and arms. I was about to take a photograph, but then something seemed to hold me back. These girls seemed so grown up, self assured, and behaved so very differently than the other girls of that age that I had met in Harar.

Only then did I notice the old men who were standing there watching these girls and how some of the girls danced in front of the men in a very coquettish way. "What a strange orphanage!" I thought to myself, and returned to

Howard bartering with natives, South Ethiopia, 1971

the others. Only when I described to them the scene I had just witnessed did I suddenly realize that I had been in a children's brothel. Harar, what a colorful but strange world!

*Lilo and Eva in an abandoned nomad tukul,
South, Ethiopia, 1971, Family photo*

Camel herd south of Awash, Ethiopia, 1971, Family picture

Nomad girls at the market of Harar, Ethiopia, 1971, Family picture

On our way back to Addis Ababa we realized for the first time how inventive the people in Africa are with reusing modern waste. Old car wrecks, after being completely stripped off anything usable, still served as a play automobile for children, tires tied to the branches of tall trees functioned as swings, and metal containers for gasoline served as water containers for the women. The Ethiopians could use everything and knew how to improvise. Their creativity was without limits. With the increasing amount of garbage, the city's waste management, however, met their limits outside of the large city. Even the hyenas and vultures, the natural waste disposals, began to choke on the amount of plastic waste that began to accumulate in heaps beside the streets.

The city gate of Harar, Ethiopia L to R Lilo, Eva, Ariane, Vivian 1971, Family photo

In the streets of Harar, Ethiopia, 1971, Family photo

In the streets of Harar, Ethiopia. 1971, Family photo

The roses of Harar, Ethiopia, 1971, Family photo

The roses of Harar, Ethiopia, 1971, Family photo

THE DANCE AROUND THE FIRE

One day I had my most fascinating encounter with the spirit of Africa. Howard and I had taken a ride to the hills with a group of young moviemakers from Arizona. They were students of the University of Arizona and were guests in our house, and we had lent them our horses. The camera crew was looking for locations for a new movie about the beginnings of mankind they were making that featured the latest anthropological excavation sites in the Rift Valley.

In the evening, as we were returning home after our ride, our attention turned to a small tukul from which we heard the sound of a variety of drums. Curious, we stopped and dismounted. The tukul turned out to be a beer tavern. Several men were sitting on a bench and chatting. They were dressed in white clothes; their shepherd hooks they had left leaning outside the entrance where a large fire lit up the air. Its flames were flickering into the beginning sunset.

The vibrating, deep sounds came from a dark corner in the inside of the tukul. As I looked closer, I recognized three young men who were playing on their different sized drums with their agile, fast hands and produced several rhythms, sometimes soft and rhythmical and then forceful and turbulent. We slowly came closer and upon a sign by one of the men, obviously meant as an invitation, we entered the hut. I was the only female in the hut with the exception of the barmaid, who, wrapped up in her white shamma, moved silently between the tables. Obviously this was no place for women. We were curiously scrutinized but not in an unfriendly manner. Therefore, we decided to remain and sat down on one of the benches. I was wearing black pants and a black shirt and obviously was not immediately recognizable as a woman. The barmaid brought us glasses and filled them with brown tedj from a large black jug.

In the other corner an old man was playing on a little handmade violin. It had only one string and made monotonous, shrill, and melancholy lamenting sounds. Together with the dull, rhythmic sounds of the drums, the music began to have a hypnotic impact on the listeners.

Suddenly, outside the tukul, we could see through the open door a young, dark-skinned man emerge from the darkness. He had put down his white garment and began to move with the rhythm of the drums around the fire, at first slowly, and then at an ever-accelerating speed. His body was muscular, his black skin glistened, and the whites of his eyes and teeth flashed in the light of the fire.

The other guests watched him attentively. The dancer and the rhythmic sounds seemed to make for a kind of magical attraction. I was beginning to feel that I had a hard time keeping my feet still. Could I take part in this ritual, intimate, almost holy, event? Would I, a woman, a white foreigner, be considered a curious intruder and thus disturb those present who were watching in rapt attention?

I stood up and I began to slowly move in the rhythm of the drums. These seemed to adjust their speed to mine. Now the other men invited me with encouraging gestures to come forward and near the dancer in the center.

The family on an excavation trip with a camera team, Addis Abeba, 1971, Family photo

Picnic with our friends, Addis Abeba, Ethiopia, 1971, Family photo

Then we both stood there without looking at each other.

It seemed that our bodies adjusted automatically to the rhythm of the drums and the sounds of the violin and then joined together with the other body in the right movement. We never touched each other. Our bodies seemed in complete harmony with the drums, the magical sound of the violin and the other body. It was an "encounter of the other type," the encounter of two human souls in the primeval dance around the fire.

We danced for a long time until we became aware of our surroundings. The men watched us intently with a smile on their otherwise very serious faces. Again and again they motioned to us to continue dancing until they finally invited us to sit down at their table. They ordered a new round of tedj for us and let us understand that we were their guests. They spoke no English, and we did not speak the Amharic language. But communication had functioned on a different level and was perfect.

My Very Engaged Students

Communication with my students was indeed very complicated. I tried to introduce them to English literature, but after half an hour, every lesson took a turn to political issues. There were very intelligent and engaged students in my class. They were gifted, and all of them were interested in politics and really had a desire to learn. There was only one girl and she was extraordinarily talented.

My students were not able to deal with modern technology, but in discussions, they were highly involved, eloquent, and very informed opponents. On the outside they seemed quiet and level-headed, but in their hearts a fire was seething. I noticed this on the first day: Politics was their main topic of interest, and everything else they considered to be of secondary priority.

I could understand my students. They were the educated elite of a people that consisted of 80% analphabets, and they wanted to do something for their country—a country, in which the abyss between tradition and modern life was beginning to become more and more insurmountable.

In order to make their point clear to me, the students told me about the Borana tribe in the South of the country. Christianity had not yet reached this part of the country and the people still lived according to the their nature religion and the rules of ancestor worship. The Borana lived close to the border to Kenya and were semi-nomadic shepherds who wandered through the country with their herds of cattle. Within their tribe, the Borana live very peacefully, according to their ancient nature belief, and they lead a good social life. Men and women have equal rights Their behavior toward other tribes differs drastically, however, from the social norms of the Amharic people and from those of other neighbors who are Christians. Despite the efforts of the police and other government agencies, it has not been possible to prevent recurrent acts of violence during which the Borana mutilated the genitals of a male member of an enemy tribe and took them home to their village as a trophy. This custom was still being observed, because only by this act could a young man become a "hero" in his village and have the right to grow his hair in the typical style of the adult warrior. As he was accepted into adult male society, he was now allowed to woo a bride, marry, and raise his own family. These customs date back to prehistoric times, when the potency and the survival of their own tribe were at stake. Only the most numerous tribes could compete successfully and survive in the fight for the waterhole.

*My students from Haile Selassie University, Addis Abeba,
Ethiopia, 1971, Family photo*

In 1971 most Ethiopians were still living in bitter poverty, in the country as well as in the city. Despite this, the people were devoted and loyal to their emperor. The reason for this was not only the fact that he passed through the country in his state coach with large sacks full of bread to hand out to the population; the emperor was much more than a head of state to the Ethiopians—they believed in him as their king, sent by God.

Haile Selassie, from the beginning of his reign, had tried to develop his country by opening it to European education. He had laid the foundation of his university in 1949 with the following words:

> As we have said many times before, the well-being of our country depends above all on the education of its people. Just as Ethiopia is one country, all Ethiopians are one people and common education is the only way to guarantee this.

Despite all the efforts to modernize the country, however, Ethiopia remained a curious oddity within postcolonial Africa. Economically, it remained a rural, feudal system despite the fact that the emperor had set strict limits to the powers of the ruling noble families. But he was not able to carry out the necessary land reforms that would have negatively affected the interests of the powerful "elders" of the different tribes. Democratic structures were foreign to the country, because it had never been part of a colonial power structure.

Haile Selassie did succeed, however, in reforming his army. He also laid the cornerstone for a modern education system and advanced modern values in an environment that was basically traditional. Despite this, educated youth did not thank him for his efforts. The better educated the young elite became, the more they realized the contradictions between modern values and the ingrained, ancient feudal system, which was already destined for a final decline.

Addis Ababa was the largest city between Cairo and Johannesburg, but the countryside was unconnected to the rest of the country and had neither toilets nor clean drinking water. The students at the university were legally obligated, by virtue of their being students at the university, to work in the countryside during their vacation. They dug out latrines, an activity that actually was degrading in their eyes, with patience and great willingness. They worked without complaining because they were aware of the dangers and saw the needs. Clean water was a necessity for survival in Ethiopia. They wanted to do something for their people and for their country.

The students did surely not find knowledge about their country or learn about the need for change in the beautiful new Rose Kennedy Library, however. The building was usually empty. Maybe there was a good reason. In addition to observing the unused library, I had also seen the black blocks that occasionally appeared on text printed in many of the numerous newspapers that were available there. This told me that there was well-functioning official censorship. Instead of using the library, my politically very well-informed students queued up in front of a little hut covered by a cheap corrugated iron roof. When I asked them about their not using the library, they showed me copies of articles and books in English and propaganda material by Nyerere, the president of Tanzania, who propagated socialistic progress in Africa. Sometime later I learned that the hut was a distributor of Soviet propaganda. It seemed necessary to me to do something about this situation, and so I decided to add a unit about the language of propaganda to my lesson plan in order to sensitize my students to the dangers and possible effects of propaganda in general.

Inauguration of the John F. Kennedy Memorial Library, August 1969, Addis Abeba, Ethiopia, Family photo

I had always attempted to train my students in the typical Anglo-Saxon style of logical thinking and in the principles of classical rhetoric for use in oral and written communication. My teaching goal was to make the young people aware of the use of language, especially of the difference between denotative meaning and connotative meaning, between facts and fiction, especially in political propaganda.

Now I decided to teach a unit on connotation and denotation, and the meaning of words. During my studies I had worked on the differences in meaning in the English language. Semantics was always among the teaching subjects in British and American schools, as well as rhetoric and public speaking.

During my years as a language teacher, I had many times grappled with my experiences during the time of the National Socialists in Germany. I had made it a point to explain to young students how a whole people can be manipulated by the use of language.

I had prepared my lecture about "the use of emotional language in Nazi propaganda" very well. I used certain speeches from Nazi propaganda materials as examples and talked about the terrible consequences of those speeches in Germany during World War II. Among others, I used Hitler's inflammatory speeches against the Jewish population.

My students were so quiet during the whole lecture that you could have heard a pin drop. After class they came up to tell me that the lecture had been the most interesting of all my lectures and to ask if I would be willing to repeat it so that they could invite all their friends. In effect, they said to me, "Yes, it probably was not so very nice what Hitler had done to the Jews, but he had been very efficient and we would really like to learn how to make propaganda function, and we wonder how he could have been so successful."

At this moment, my eyes were opened. Despite my good intentions, I had just put a dangerous weapon into the hands of young people. They were not at all mature enough to properly handle such a weapon. My intention had been to make them aware of how they themselves were being manipulated for political purposes. And now I had achieved the opposite. These boys (there was one girl in the class) wanted to learn how to use language as an effective weapon.

The students had realized that their emperor had become dependent upon and at the mercy of the great world powers. As a friend of Western countries, he had received considerable financial support from them. With much acclaim by the media, they had sent help for hungry children and had supported several development projects. However, it seemed that the money never reached the people in Ethiopia. There were rumors that Haile Selassie had put aside a large part of the money in banks in Switzerland, a rumor that was being fomented by the Communists. But nobody knew exactly where the money had really gone.

A certain unrest seem to mount in the whole country and not only within the student population. The American Embassy had warned its employees to use increased vigilance. We were told about a "black list" that was supposed to have been found by members of the so-called Liberation Front. The names of some members of the Foreign Service appeared on this list, and these persons were thus destined for "free shooting." One of them was the Canadian ambassador, who was a friend of ours. His embassy took the threat seriously and assigned an armed bodyguard to accompany him, his family, and friends on their trips. We also were no longer allowed to take trips into the countryside on horseback without a guard.

We did not really take the political development very seriously until the following incident involving our friend Bill Losch, an American architect. He and his wife had accompanied us to Harar. He worked in Awash National Park for an American private investment firm. The plan was to build lodges, which were intended to attract tourists to the area, with the help of native workers under the supervision of American specialists. The project was going well, and we had not heard of any major problems.

One day his airplane was hijacked by a group of Ethiopian students. They forced the pilot at gunpoint to fly to Egypt. However, there they did not get permission to land, and when fuel was getting low they had to land in Libya. From there, Bill was finally able to call his wife and tell her that the American Embassy would fly him back to Addis Ababa within the next few days.

After his happy return, Bill recounted the dangerous incident as if it were an amusing adventure. He probably owed the happy end of the flight to the fact that the three students seemed to have been more scared than the passengers. In the general flurry of action, they had lost their facial masks and held their pistols pointed at the head of the pilot in their shaking hands.

By the hijacking they wanted to protest against the fact that strangers were taking over their country, and foreign influence was growing all the time.

Everything had ended well, but we still had not taken these signals seriously.

The terrible droughts had driven more and more people into the city. At first, the men came to town and tried to make a living somehow. Then the women followed with their children. The shantytowns at the outskirts of the cities continued to grow,, as did prostitution and infant mortality. The regime had opened up to Western values, and the people were flooded with the products of Western industries. The people were attracted to them but could not buy the goods, because they were too poor. Their old fashioned values no longer served the purpose of solving their everyday problems. Thus, they were pushed to the outskirts of society (the "'underprivileged"), and became part of a completely new social class that had never before appeared in the countryside.

The intellectual youth of the country realized the problematic consequences of the speed of technical advances and modern capitalistic values, and they knew about the insecurity of the people who could not follow the rapid developments and were without the ability to adjust to the changing conditions of life.

The students had tried to get the ear of the government but had no success, so they took to the streets. In the late Sixties, the students in America and other Western countries had set an example for the Ethiopian youth to follow.

In spring of 1971 the first incident happened. The university's students wanted to publish their own campus newspaper. When the administration refused permission, they decided to protest. They met peacefully on the campus square, carrying banners in their hands. The university administration called the army, which without any warning began to shoot at the defenseless youngsters. Five students died on that day, and many more were wounded.

On the next day, the administration closed down the university. The students were told to go home. They were warned that anyone who was caught on the street would go to jail. Only those who had a valid proof of work with them would be spared. Some of my students asked me whether I did not have work for them in our home so that they could stay in the city.

I discussed the question with Howard. He was of the opinion that we could not plausibly employ more than one more boy for the horses without getting into trouble with the state agencies or with our embassy. I employed my favorite student. I had noticed him before in class as being very intelligent and engaged.

Soon thereafter he would prove to be of great help to me.

Nomads at Lake Tana in the south of Ethiopia, 1971, Old postcard

The University had been closed in June. We were planning to go to Naples via Munich for our vacation in July. Since Howard had to work until the middle of July and the girls would also be in school until then, I decided to go ahead to Munich to be with my parents for a while and to prepare everything for our summer vacation.

Howard took me to the airport. It was a beautiful sunny spring morning.

As always, when we were alone together, we felt very close. The problems of everyday life were lost in the background. We philosophized about the future of Ethiopia and the political forces that were influencing Africa.

Howard accompanied me to the gangway and we lovingly embraced and said good-bye, adding, "Don't forget! Your husband loves you. In only two weeks we will be together again."

"Mourning Athena," marble relief, (460 B. C.E.) See Source Index

CHAPTER 14: EXPULSION FROM PARADISE

HOWARD'S DEATH

THERE WAS MUCH TO DO in Munich. The apartment in the Gruetznerstrasse had been rented for a year and it needed to be renovated.

Two days after my arrival, when I was just about to leave the house, I met a woman on the staircase. She was coming up the stairs in great haste, and her face showed obvious signs of distress.

"Who are you looking for?" I asked.

"I am looking for the apartment of Professor Holland."

"You have found it," I said. "I am Mrs. Holland. May I ask for the occasion of your visit?"

The lady hesitated. She seemed disconcerted and was searching for words. "I am working for the American Consulate in Munich. Here is an envelope with a plane ticket from Munich to Addis Ababa. You have to go back Ethiopia tomorrow. Your husband has had an accident, yesterday. He was dead when they brought him to the hospital. Don't worry about the children, they are well taken care of by your husband's boss, Mr. Sanders."

"Dear lady, this can only be a terrible misunderstanding! I am completely sure that this cannot be true," I heard myself say. She seemed to be surprised. I felt sorry for her to have to pass on such bad news, news that I could not accept as true at all.

I suppose that I was in shock, because I continued to react as though everything was completely normal. I did not even try to call Addis Ababa. This misunderstanding would be cleared up soon.

I continued to do all the things I had planned on that day.

When I went to see my parents, I only told them casually that I had to fly back to Addis tomorrow.

"I just have to clear up a misunderstanding. You don't need to worry!" I told them.

It had to be a big mistake that the embassy had made. I was still convinced of the impossibility of this message. Until the airplane touched down on Addis Ababa Airport, that is.,

I walked down the gangway and suddenly realized that there was a large group of people there to receive me. I saw many well-known faces, employees of the embassy, some Ethiopian friends, and among them, my two girls. Everyone was dressed in black.

So it was no mistake! It must be true. As if struck by lightning, I fell into a strange state of numbness. I seemed paralyzed, incapable of feeling anything. This was another me, who began to act like a robot. This robot consoled the weeping people, embraced the girls, and did what had to be done.

Howard's boss and his wife took the children and me to the embassy. There the ambassador expressed his condolences. I was also told that we would have to leave our house within three days because of safety concerns. "The embassy is not able to guarantee your security in the country any more," we were told. I would receive every possible support and help.

"Would it be possible for me to take my husband's body with me to Germany?" I asked.

"Yes, of course. But this will take two days to prepare the body," the ambassador said.

Somebody promised to take care of everything.

After that, I was being interrogated by the CIA. What exactly they asked me, I do not remember. Finally, they gave me a death certificate on which the following appeared: "Cause of death: Serious fracture of the skull and hemorrhage possibly due to a car accident."

Howard's little car, a Fiat Spider, had been found by the side of a road where there was usually very little traffic. The roof was open. The car was turned over; Howard's body lay in the trench beside the road.

How could this have happened? Everything seemed so strange. Howard had always been a very careful driver. He never drove too fast, and he never drank too much. Surely not on this evening, as all of his friends, who had seen him at this party, assured me. Furthermore, I could not understand the place where the accident had happened. This road was not his usual way home. Question after question came to me, to which I did not get any satisfactory answers.

I wanted to know more, but the embassy did not recommend any further investigation. There would be no autopsy.

There was nothing else I could do but to accept the thought that further inquiries into the cause of his death would not bring Howard back to me.

So I went along with what happened almost automatically. Within three days I would have to have packed up all our belongings in our house, a house that had been home to twelve people, six horses, eight dogs, and six cats.

I supervised the packing of the furniture as if in a trance, and I worked like a machine. At the same time I felt a great emptiness. Not even the children could overcome this emptiness. It was only the speed of the events with which everything was happening that saved me during those last three days in our "paradise."

The American pastor had planned a service in the chapel. I asked to have the coffin opened again. I put a red rose in Howard's hands and kissed his lips. They were cold and hard as stone.

Only now, when I saw Howard with my own eyes before me, could I believe what had happened. It was really so. His death was a reality.

The student, whom we had employed only a few weeks earlier, was able to take over many of the tasks that had to be taken care of. He distributed Howard's clothes among the employees, and paid the outstanding salaries.

The girls chose the people to whom we gave away our horses, and the dogs were given to our employees. The same happened to the four Siamese kittens. But Rasputin and Tuilan would accompany us to Germany.

The other events during those last three days in Addis Abba have been lost in my memory. I cannot remember at all our good-bye to Ethiopia. Only when we landed in Munich did I became aware of the people and things around me again. Dark clouds were hanging over the city and it rained heavily.

I felt like Ulysses, when he was washed ashore in the land of the Phaeacians, naked and desperate after he had clung to the mast of his sunken ship for three days and three nights.

Ariane had experienced Howard's death in a very personal way. Only years later she told me about her feelings and thoughts at that time. I want to report them here in her own words:

> On the evening of Howard's death I had taken a bath and then had wrapped myself into your big white bathrobe. Howard said good-bye to me before he had

to go to a party at Mr. Sander's house. He might be home late, he thought.

I gave him a bear hug around his waist and asked him to come back soon. It was a moment of great affection, like between father and daughter.

On this evening, however, I could not fall asleep right away as usual. It seemed to me that I lay in bed for hours, wide awake. Around midnight—it might have been later, I heard a car drive up our driveway. Something told me that it was not Howard—that it would never be Howard again. I cannot explain until today, why I had this feeling of certainty. I ran into the bedroom of my sister. She was asleep. "Vivi, wake up! Howard is dead!"

She looked at me in disbelief. Then both of us broke into completely inexplicable laughter.

At this moment, Mr. Sanders entered the room. He did not need to explain anything. We already knew.

"There has been a car accident. Howard had been thrust out of the car. He was dead immediately," Mr. Sanders said.

But I knew better. I knew that he had endured fear of death for a long time, because I had felt this myself, and it had kept me awake the whole evening. Some mysterious thing had happened.

Vivian and I spent the whole night together in my bed and never closed an eye, until it was time to get up and go to school.

In school, I could not concentrate on anything. I constantly had to cry.

Also, the lesson was not able to distract me. I missed Howard. I missed him painfully. I felt the feeling of love in me, with which he had said good-bye to me the evening before.

The other students made fun of me. Only later, after having been informed about what had happened, they came and apologized to me.

You arrived the next day. You looked very pale and nervous. You constantly walked around the house, giving orders. You seemed to have changed. But nobody had time to think in all the hectic activities. Everything had to be packed up, and maybe that was a good thing.

The nice student with the injured eye helped us, quietly and very conscientiously. He was very worried about everything. Without him we probably would not have been able to dismantle our big household. I often think of him. I wonder whether he was paid enough for all his hard work and how his life continued without your help.

We gave my beloved horse Echo to the neighbors, to Saba and her family. I was sure she would take good care of him, I thought. But when I finally got a letter with a picture, after I had written many times asking her to send me a photo, I was shocked. The photo was depressing: Echo seemed thin and scrawny and was standing all alone in a big field.

I do remember the last day in Addis Ababa very well. The weather was gray and rainy, like my heart. I did not think I would see any more smiles for a hundred years.

These were Ariane's words.

Gray and Rainy Like Our Hearts

When I returned after those three days to my homeland, Bavaria, it seemed as though everything had changed. The loveliness of the Bavarian hill country seemed quaint and unreal to me. The coziness of my Biedermeier Idyll seemed like the doll house I used to play with as a child. Now I had outgrown it, suddenly and with much pain. My beloved Bavarian "Gemuetlichkeit" in the beer garden of the Hofbraukeller, the humming sound of the happy people mixed with the jingle of the beer mugs, was no consolation to me. Just the opposite! Everything seemed to mock my pain.

I felt lost in an icy desert, surrounded by emptiness and an invisible threat. I had lost the ground under my feet.

I had looked into the face of death and had recognized it as the ultimate reality of human existence. I became painfully aware of the arbitrariness of our existence and the fateful consequences that a seemingly unimportant decision can have.

I had gone ahead to Munich to take care of banal preparations for our vacation.

Again and again I asked myself: "What would have happened, if I had been at this party together with Howard? Would he still be alive? Or would both of us be dead?"

How could a human being ever be happy in the face of this absurd last truth, death? What was the meaning of life if it had to end in nothingness?"

Those were the questions that turned around and around in my head.

For the first time, my lifelong companion had left me: my unlimited optimism, which had always given me the strength to face every problem. This time my own self had somehow gone astray.

And even Athena could not help me. She mourned.

Three days later, I was waiting for Howard's arrival at the Munich Airport by air freight. Dark and cloudy thoughts filled my head. After the sun had set, the last airplane from Athens landed, carrying a simple coffin with Howard's body. Together with other crates and boxes, he is being unloaded as "special luggage" and taken to a warehouse "Muenchen-Ostfriedhof."

A gray truck is already waiting. I sat down beside the driver and we went to the benediction hall of the local cemetery. I was still incapable of recognizing my surroundings. They were lost in the dark. Then the coffin was unloaded and disappeared into a special refrigerated room. I only wonder why the corpse has to be refrigerated when it has been embalmed for the long trip.

That is what remains of a human being, a person so full of joy of life and love. That thought did not leave my head. It was the only one that filled the inner emptiness. At that time I had no tears.

The tears only came later. I found them on my pillow every morning.

They came during those first morning hours filled with anxiety, when the shadows of the night are driven away by the clear light of the morning sun, and when the silhouette of a stark reality returned to my consciousness.

During those days, the people around me perceived me as a mournful, gloomy person, filled with grief, sorrow, and sadness, closed toward everyone.

My melancholy mood carried over to Ariane and Vivian. It was a heavy load that my teenage girls had to carry. They were just about twelve and fourteen years old. Both girls had built up a friendly and loving relationship with Howard. Now they also had to work through a painful loss. I felt that I could not help them much. At the same time, they had the feeling that they had to comfort their mother. They were definitely overstrained. But at least the three of us were together.

Vivian started to talk about her anxieties, even in a very general way. Life was not worth living in a time of atomic bombs and threatening disasters that were able to destroy all mankind. It was better to be dead than to have to wait for such a catastrophe, she mused.

Ariane had recurring nightmares. She dreamed that she somehow had to save me and tried unsuccessfully to carry me, because I was too heavy for her.

This was not a time when everybody talked about and knew about psychological shocks and their effects on children.

I realized, however, the preoccupations they both had, but I was too busy solving our everyday problems to worry about the question of how to react correctly.

Again, my parents came to the rescue. With loving care and support they helped the girls, and me, and grieved with us.

I was in a vicious cycle that was only interrupted by the urgent necessity to earn a living and to put our daily life onto an orderly track. My first decision was *not* to send the girls to a boarding school. Everyone advised me to do so. I believed that we should stay together during those difficult times as a family unit. We already had gone through so many changes together, and we would again master this situation together. Only together would we be strong enough to keep a feeling of family alive.

During those difficult days I realized how important the relationship between the two sisters would be for the future of my girls. I tried to support and strengthen this relationship whenever I could. Even when the two sometimes conspired against me, I still emphasized how important their love for each other was.

I knew, I would not always be around to give them the necessary support in difficult times. This conviction they have kept in their hearts until this day. Despite the normal situations of sibling rivalries, the two girls have always supported each other during problematic times with advice and assistance in a sisterly and loving way.

This is the only positive thing that remained in my memory of those terrible months after Howard's death.

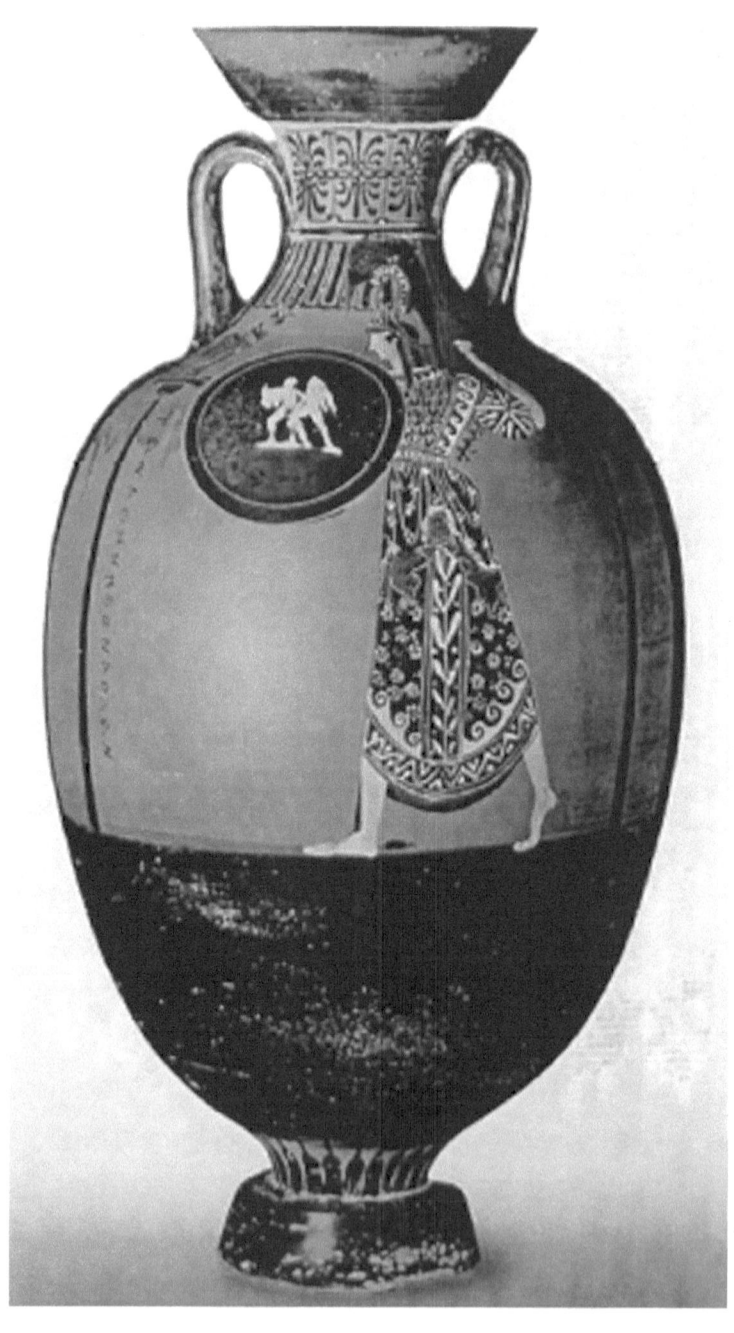

"Athena in Arms," Panatheanic black-figure amphora (5th century B.C.E.) See Source Index

Chapter 15: New Challenges in Munich

Dr. Kenneth Adler-the Regional Research Office

Life looked grim, but the first help came from the American Consulate. We did receive a pension, but it was too small to live on it in such an expensive city as Munich. The American Foreign Service had realized this fact and therefore had recommended me to the Consulate in Munich. In Munich a new office had been opened that was to work on opinion research for the USIS (United States Information Service). The purpose of the Munich office was to assist in conducting surveys of Western European public opinion about the United States and other Western countries. The office was also tasked with estimating the reach and effectiveness of U.S. government broadcasts to Eastern Europe, such as the Voice of America, Radio Free Europe, and Radio Liberty. (Radio Free Europe and Radio Liberty had their own research offices.)

With the help of local institutions, one did research concerning the effectiveness of the Radio stations as "Radio Free Europe," "Voice of America," and "Radio Liberty" in the countries of Eastern Europe.

The head of this new office was Dr. Kenneth P. Adler. He was of Jewish descent, spoke German fluently, and was a highly educated and sensitive man. He had escaped persecution in Germany because his parents had sent him to an English school at the age of thirteen.

At first he asked me to arrange the books in his library according to my ideas about the appropriate way of doing so, and only after I had finished did he consider me capable of being his assistant.

In the beginning I was really a terrible secretary. Until then I never had to type fluently and correctly from dictation. But Dr. Adler was the kindest and most patient person. He acted as though he did not see the many pieces of paper in the waste paper basket that contained papers with mistakes. And I tried to learn quickly. After six months I had learned enough to be able to type letters without a mistake. I had also begun to design questionnaires, and to evaluate them.

My work became more and more interesting, because I could accompany Dr. Adler on some of his trips abroad. For instance, I had the job of helping Dr. Adler evaluate the work of an opinion research office in Vienna. We wanted to know whether they really did effective work. At that time it was not possible to ask people in Poland, Hungary, or Czechoslovakia directly what their opinions were about the programs of foreign radio stations. So tourists from these countries who came by bus to Vienna were interviewed by means of questionnaires.

I had the interesting job of following the interviewers and observing them as they interviewed the tourists. This could happen at any time, even at two o'clock in the morning. It could happen that a whole bus was being "interviewed" at the same time under the watchful eyes of their "tourist guides." Obviously, the answers turned given were very general, and many people did not want to admit that they were listening to American radio programs. Of course these interviews were worthless, because they did not represent objective answers. Interviews were paid only if they had been individually carried out.

After two years, the interviews were canceled. Due to the research, U.S.I.S had come to the conclusion that all the interviews were not leading to satisfactory, objective results. The U.S.I.S. which also was responsible for the America Houses in the world, had to save money.

Dr. Adler was not only a patient boss but also a very understanding one. He was sympathetic to me in light of my personal problems after the death of Howard and my worries about the children. I was surprised to find that, despite the sad problems he and his family had experienced during Hitler's regime, he did not seem to feel any resentment against the German people. Just the opposite, he had saved his love for his German home in his heart.

He taught me a lot, and not only professionally. Mostly because of his humane point of view, he became a role model for me. We really understood each other and became true friends and remain friends today.

In the fall of 1971 we began to become adjusted to our new life in Germany—Ariane, Vivian, our two cats Rasputin and Tuilan, and me. Those two beautiful Siamese cats were the only companions that remained from our former life. One day Tuilan presented us with four blue-eyed, white-and-beige-marked kittens. In the evening when we sat down in our enclosed balcony while the sun set over the skyline of Munich and the kitties were purring in our lap, and we talked about the events of the day, the world seemed to be in order again for a short while.

Ariane and Vivian were fighting hard to adjust to the typical German way of life. For example: "What do you think you are doing?" or "Du spinnst wohl!" or "Are you crazy?" They were used to this way of disagreeing in a more polite and less antagonistic way, saying instead: "I can see your point, but I am sorry that I can't agree with you."

Wiener Platz in Munich, Germany, 1971, Family photo

Bridges over the Isar River in Munich, Germany, 1971, Family photo

Our life in all these countries and the international schools had had a strong influence on them. They had grown up while traveling the world, and now they felt closed in. They felt the life in our idyllic neighborhood as suffocating and limiting.

There were prohibitions everywhere. During noontime from one to three o'clock they were only allowed to tiptoe down the stairs. The neighbors were suspicious and wanted their peace and quiet. When they hear anyone coming down the stairs, they closed their doors. In the park, there were signs saying "Do not step on the grass!" They had exchanged the wide-open wilderness with a regulated city landscape.

On top of it all, Ariane and Vivian were in the middle of their teenage years and grappling with puberty. They refused everything that smacked of restriction of any sort or even parental authority. It was impossible "to put a square stick into a round hole." They simply were against everybody and everything, especially against the German school system, which at that time was still not very friendly toward children. I could sympathize with them, but unfortunately I could not change it.

Ariane began her German school year at the Gymnasium (high school) at St. Anna Square. When it was obvious that she would not pass that year, she changed to the Landschulheim on Lake Ammersee, where she stayed until her high school graduation.

She did not talk much about her problems and sorrows. She closed them up in herself.

Vivian attended the Edith Stein Gymnasium not far from our house. At that time it was still led by the Englische Fraulein, Catholic nuns who had dedicated their lives to the teaching of girls. She did not dislike the school but frequently felt that she was being observed with suspicion and misunderstood, despite the fact that she was considered to be a polite and friendly child. The religious education had a great influence on Vivian. Her faith helped her to find consolation in later years, when she was divorced. She also had her two girls baptized.

During this time I was not able to emotionally support my girls very much because I needed all my energy to get used to my new job. When I came home in the evening, I was so completely tuckered out and could not help with their homework, let alone fight with them about this.

Despite this, I tried to make life more enjoyable for them. Both loved the sport of horseback riding. Unfortunately, I could not fulfill their wish to take up this sport in Germany. Horseback riding is a very expensive sport here. Also, my idea to buy horses in Hungary and to ride them back to Bavaria with the girls remained a dream. We finally consoled ourselves with the idea that it probably would not have been very much fun to ride along prescribed paths through the Englische Garten. Wild cross-country riding as we had done Ethiopia had become a part of our past.

These problems that the girls felt confronted by were also for me a great problem. I was lucky, however, that my parents lived close to us and often helped out with advice and loving care.

A very important person in those days was my cousin Elisabeth. She was the Taufpatin (godmother) of both girls. Elisabeth had become a very engaged pedagogist and had founded in lower Bavaria a school for difficult children. She became a very important person in the local area until she returned to Vachendorf because her mother was getting old and needed her.

She had a wonderful way with children, and a marvelous way of getting their attention with humorous stories. Both my children and my grandchildren listened to her.

Our home in Munich, Germany, 1971, Family photo

My parents in 1974, Munich, Germany, Meinen Photo GmbH

THE XXTH OLYMPIC GAMES IN 1972 IN MUNICH

When we returned to Munich in June 1972 the whole city was had an air of ecstasy and happy expectations. In September the Olympic games were to be carried out in Munich.

Everywhere you went there were building sites. The well-known city silhouette had a new face. Behind the former "Schuttberg" (hill of debris from World War II bombing) a new television tower rose into the Bavarian sky. To the right, one could make out the new administration building of BMW, a modern high-rise in the shape of a four-leaf clover. In front of it was a new landscaped park with hills and a small lake, and in the middle of this extensive park, there it was! The great stadium, a true architectural masterpiece! The architect had covered part of the building by means of a tent-like roof whose structure was molded into the building as to fit into the landscape of the surrounding mountainous region of Bavaria. Since then it has gained worldwide fame.

The citizens of Munich, who lately had to battle with an angry crowd of protesting students and were worried about their Bavarian order, forgot all their anger and were looking forward with joy to host their international guests. The "World City with Heart" felt responsible for its name, and business people were hoping for good profits. The feeling of happy expectation seized everybody.

On August 26, when the games were opened with great festivities, everything was so right. The sunny sky showed the Bavarian colors of blue and white, the city seemed lit up, and the mountains scintillated in blue-gray hues in the distance. The opening festival was of breathtaking joyfulness. Athletes from 122 countries competed for gold, silver, and bronze in the most beautiful stadium in the world. Millions of spectators in the stadium and on television marveled at their feats.

The world seemed to be in order.

My father had bought some of the very desirable tickets, and the girls and I were in the stadium on the day that the young high-jumper Ulrike Meyfarth succeeded in winning with her sensational gold-medal jump for Germany, and when the German-born marathon runner, Frank Shorter, was the first to enter the stadium, and the spear thrower, Wolfermann, won another medal for his country. All of us, not only the people in the stadium, but also the guests in the streets of Munich, felt this rapture of this general elation.

And then the incredible happened.

In the early morning hours of September 5, eight Arab terrorists stormed into the housing area of the Israeli team, killed two of their athletes, and took five other athletes hostage. They wanted to free two hundred Palestinian prisoners who were in Israeli prisons. All of the hostages, together with five terrorists and one policeman, lost their lives.

Despite the shock and much discourse, it was decided to continue the games. The general joy, however, had disappeared. Munich, Germany, the whole world was in mourning.

I did not feel in the mood to attend the "military riding," for which my father had bought three tickets. All of us were so sad that we let these tickets expire, despite the fact that we had really been looking forward to that event.

Instead of going to that event, I walked across the Olympic field together with Ken Adler, hand in hand. We promised each other that in the future we would always do everything possible to help avoid the use of violence as a means of solving problems. What an illusion! Today we know that the assault in Munich was only the beginning. Our promise has not changed the world, but it has strengthened our friendship.

New Tasks at the University of the German Federal Armed Forces

In 1972 the new Universities of the German Federal Armed Forces were founded in Hamburg and in Munich. Chancellor Helmut Schmidt had established them in order to secure a technically perfect, speedy, and efficient education for the young officers of the Federal Armed Forces. He probably also intended to create an incentive for young men to join the military forces and serve another twelve years after the end of their education.

The Bundessprachenamt (BSA) near Bonn, the central agency for language training in the military and other federal services, was looking for a specialized language teacher who would build up a Language Center within the new University in Munich.

The American Consul had given me this information, and I immediately applied for the position.

For three days I was examined in the BSA concerning my professional qualifications. My master's degree in the teaching of English, the extensive training I had received in the Goethe Institute, my knowledge of modern methods of language teaching, and my teaching experiences in various foreign countries—all this was to my advantage. (Athena might have helped!) So I was successful and was offered the position in Munich rather than Hamburg, which had been an absolute requirement for me because of the children. We did not want to move again.

This time, I was really confronted with a very great and important challenge. I enjoyed this work very much, and it gave me great satisfaction until the day of my retirement, twenty years later. Athena, who was also the patron of the new university, had done a fine job.

Logo of the University of the German Federal Armed Forces, (Athena), Munich, 1972, Family photo

In the beginning, I started out as a teacher of English. The classes were taught in various buildings all over town until the construction of the university in Neubiberg was finished. In 1974, there existed no specialized agenda or curriculum for this new language center, nor any adequate reading materials or books.

A new system for examinations for language proficiency was being introduced that consisted of examinations on all four levels (1-4) in the four language skills (LSRW): Listening, Speaking, Reading, and Writing. The result was a number with four digits that made it easy to immediately know how good a student's language skills were.

Conference of the Foreign Language Experts, Munich, 1972, Family photo

At that time I worked together with only male colleagues who had been teaching English within the military for many years.

Soon it became apparent that for the establishment of a language center, an administrative head was needed who would create a program and control its implementation.

I applied for that job and, to my great joy, was hired soon after as the official director of the Language Center. Now I worked on the level of the civilian equivalent of the military rank of a colonel. Two secretaries and six full-time teachers were on my staff. This meant that at that time, I was the only woman in a management position in the University of the Federal Armed Forces.

I took my work very seriously. According to the opinion of the male teachers under me, I took it too seriously. I actually threw myself into my work. My task was not to develop a scientifically oriented teaching program but to adjust the existing teaching programs in the Federal Armed Forces to the needs of the new university. I did this by focusing on the development of an academic program on the university level. Furthermore, this program had to also include the special concerns of a military training program.

I had to find the right teachers, plan an efficient curriculum, plan the lessons, organize the many classes, organize written and oral examinations, plan the final examinations as well as the entrance examinations, and ensure speedy grading and correct classification of the results.

Every year we had about 500 new students. The required courses lasted one year, but could be taken in the first or the second year. We had 900 new students that had to be tested. They were assigned to classes in the first or the second year according to their level of competency. We did not have any beginners. All of these students were higher education (Gymnasium) graduates and had eight years of English.

It was my mission to assign each individual student to a class based on his previous knowledge so that he could achieve the next higher level of language facility within at least three years.

All of these tasks had to be carried out without computers!

My activities caught the attention of the professors. They opposed my plans to make language skills a part of the academic officer training. They argued that because of the already concentrated academic program into only three years, it was an unwarranted expectation to require the young officers to spend additional time on attending language classes.

This meant I had to fight. It was not easy to gain the respect of these professors, but I found allies among the commanding officers on the military side. So I continued to make language studies a requirement in the military officer training program. I found these officers to be always perfect gentlemen.

One of my problems was the fact that for the students it was not mandatory to attend classes. Without this requirement, however, it was not possible to teach our concentrated program effectively. Therefore, we could not guarantee that most of the students would pass their examinations. Mandatory attendance was not in agreement with the modern ideas of "academic freedom" of this new university, whose founders did, under no circumstances, want to gain the reputation of being another place for "military drill" in Germany.

I did not succeed in convincing the professors. So I had to meet the problem head-on. I actually spoke with Secretary of Defense Georg Leber, who was my supervisor. During an official reception for the secretary in honor of his first visit to the new university, I got his attention and explained my problem to him. Since Germany was a member of NATO, our officers surely had to know the English language. As director of the Language Center, I was responsible for the successful realization of our language program, but I had no means to implement my plans. Neither could I hope for the support from the academic side. The minister listened to me carefully, then he said "Das ist ja ein dicker Hund!" ("That is really a big problem!") and then he called his Inspector General and ordered him to do something about the problem.

I was informed two weeks later that a new ordinance had been issued by the Department of Defense announcing that the attendance of language classes was a "military duty" and therefore was mandatory. This was an order for both universities.

Hurrah! I had won!

As time went on, I succeeded in getting more money for our department in order to hire more teachers and an additional secretary. (These were the days before computers when everything had to be done by hand or with typewriters.)

My next project was this: expanding the number of languages that could be studied by a student who had passed the requirements for English.

Now the Language Center could also offer courses in other languages to students as well as interested members of the university staff: first French and later Italian, Spanish, and finally, Russian, Japanese, and Arabic. These courses became very popular, even among the professors. Today there is even a special position for a teacher whose only job is to organize these courses.

During all the years I had been working at the University of the Federal Armed Forces, I also learned some small tricks by which I could carry out my ideas even when they received initial opposition. I would first suggest my new idea in Munich, claiming that, at the university in Hamburg they practically already practiced mandatory attendance. Whereupon our President would respond: "Well, if they do this in Hamburg, we will have to join in."

Then I would go to Hamburg and tell the head of the Language Center there that we had plans for such-and-such innovations. Now my colleagues in the Language Center in Hamburg did not want to be left behind and decided that if these guys in Munich handle things in this way, we will have to go along. Back in Munich, I would report to the President on the situation and he seemed pleased.

I really enjoyed my work very much, especially because I was able to build something new, and my superiors were in far off Bonn and left me a lot of free room for the realization of my ideas. They had full confidence in me.

I not only had a lot of fun, but I was able to give our little family more financial security and the means to live an adequate lifestyle in expensive Munich.

The girls had begun to feel at home in the Gruetznerstrasse, and we enjoyed our common trips during vacation time very much. On the weekends we took biking or hiking trips to the lakes or the mountains south of Munich, and we spent our vacations in our beloved house *Quo Vadis* in Italy.

At noon on most days I had lunch at the university cafeteria and the girls went to my parents' house. Their household was still being directed by Maria, who had accompanied my parents to Munich when they moved from Bad Reichenhall. She cooked well and spoiled the girls a lot.

During the winter months I went with the girls to take skiing lessons in the mountains or sent them on tours with the Sport Scheck, a sports equipment store that organizes excursions for children and adults who want to learn how to ski. Vivian became an excellent skier, but Ariane suffered a lot in the cold weather, maybe because she was born in hot Arizona.

In the summer we took bike trips to the mountains or Lake Chiemsee, or we just sat in the beer garden and ate Weisswurst (Bavarian sausage) or radishes with black bread and cheese.

One summer Ariane spent in France to practice the language. I think she liked it, but I never heard her speak French.

Two years later both girls went to Starnberg. Vivian attended the International School in Percha. She liked the atmosphere there very much and studied with more engagement than she did at the German School. That was worth the additional money I paid for her to go to that private school.

Eva and the German-American Club at the University of the German Federal Armed Forces visiting the NATO School in Oberammergau, Germany, 1973, Family photo

My great wish was that the girls would take the German Abitur and enter a university, but I had to give up that desire.

Even as a child, Ariane had always been the artistic type. She could write with her left hand and upside down. Painting was her passion and her talent. She actually grew up to become a professional painter.

I am glad about this, because painting is another language, and in the language of art she can express many ideas that seem to be difficult to express in words.

Vivian had always been the more ambitious one of the two girls. The International High School in Starnberg and the following year in the Paris International College would prepare her for a college education in the United States. She also decided to go into art and then she studied graphic design.

Today she is working in this field and has become a professional. She still loves this work and is very successful in it.

Many Flowers, Few Roses

Three years had passed, and I still mourned for Howard. I was deeply aware that I would never find such a soulmate again.

Father began to worry about my state as a widow. He held the opinion that I was much too young for such a reclusive life as I was leading. He took me along to some of the parties in his fraternity, the Corps Suevia, for which he acted also as an accountant. But I did not like the gentlemen whom I met there and who courted me very politely. It was only when my girls also suggested that I should be looking for a nice man that I began to think in those terms. I wanted to avoid by all means to become dependent on the girls later in life or to give them the feeling that I was emotionally dependent on them. So I began to accompany Father more often to his Corps' reunions and parties.

I met several gentlemen who showed "honorable intentions." The first candidate was a well-known medical doctor in Munich. We got along quite well, but it soon became clear to me that he really was looking only for an assistant to help him in his medical office.

My next admirer was a gentleman who carried a title of nobility and was already in his advanced years. His daughter was of the opinion that her father should look for a nice well-educated lady who would take care of him in keeping with his position in his later years. But when I told him that I was planning to go to Hungary to ride back some horses with my girls, he frowned at me in doubt. This was no man for me either!

Then I met a good looking dentist with a Frankonian dialect. He seemed quite nice and fairly well educated. His wife had died some years before, and he lived with his two children in a very nice villa near Fuerth. Money was no issue; he had enough. There was a maid in the house. For vacation you went to Sylt, which was in vogue that year. He was looking for a nice woman who would be a good mother for his children and help him with the accounting in his dentist's office. We met several times in a restaurant and had dinner. Then he invited me to his home. I took my two girls along, because I wanted them to be part of such an important decision.

When we entered the house, the first thing I noticed were the spic-and-span waxed floors. The two children, a boy and a somewhat older girl, were sitting motionless on the sofa, dressed in their best Sunday clothes. They seemed like dressed up dolls, looked at us with wide eyes, and did not say a word. During the dinner they showed their best manners but never uttered a word. Politely they followed our halting conversation, while the cook, in a white uniform, served the several courses. Everything was perfect in this house. The curtains were not only white; they were "snow white" and starched. Everything was very German, so very orderly.

Ariane and Vivian constantly stepped on my foot under the table and frowned at me. We were of the same opinion: This was not our world.

The doctor had everything already planned in the event that we moved into his house. He showed me the plans for adding space to accommodate us. The girls would each have their own room. He was really very generous in his plans for the future. He also gave me a very expensive bracelet with matching earrings fashioned with valuable stones.

Ariane and Vivian in Quo Vadis, Italy, 1976

He really did everything to make a good impression on us. Everything was perfect—too perfect. There was nothing to complain about. Despite everything—every time we met I became more and more sure that this man was not a partner for our lifestyle. I felt sorry for him and wanted to do everything so as not to hurt his feelings. I requested some time to think about his proposition.

A short time later I flew to Italy, to *Quo Vadis*, in order to explore my feelings. My decision would affect not only me but would also affect the future of my children. For two weeks I pondered the question. Should I follow my head and be pragmatic, or should I let my feelings determine my decision? On the last day of my stay, I had finally made up my mind and wrote the decisive letter: I thanked him for his efforts and assured him that he had absolutely done nothing wrong, but unfortunately, I wrote, his perfect world was not my world, and that was truly my own fault.

My cousin Elisabeth still keeps a postcard that I had sent to her on that day. I had written her that I had finally definitely decided to live the rest of my life as a single woman.

But again things were to take a different turn.

"Satyr and Nymphe," from Red Figure Vases in Southern Italy. See Source Index

Chapter 16: A Life Between Two Worlds— My Life With Franz R. Huschka

Athena Meets Polypheme in the Gulf of Naples

It was a wonderful, cool morning. The sun had risen behind the hills of *Quo Vadis*.

I was in a hurry and hardly had the time to enjoy the shimmering glow on the waters of the Gulf. It was December 17, 1973. I had booked my flight from Naples to Munich and had to reach my plane, which was to leave at noon. Everything was packed up. The house had been closed up for the season. I was waiting for Guido D'Andrea. Guido had been our building supervisor during the construction of the house, and he had become a very good and caring friend over the years. Guido had promised to take me to the bus.

I was somewhat nervous. At the last moment I heard Guido drive up to the garage. It would be tight!

Indeed, as we were on the last part of the road up the hill, I heard the bus take off from the bus stop. What now?

I told Guido to follow the bus and then, at a suitable place, pass the bus and stop in front of him, in such a way that the driver had to stop. I simply had to reach this plane or my ticket would become invalid. Guido stepped on the gas and defying death, he chased after the bus. After a few minutes of a wild race on the road filled with fearsome curves, Guido managed to pass the bus on its next stop. I climbed on board the bus with all my luggage. Thanks be to God!

Relieved, I sank down on my seat and looked out the window. I loved this ride to Naples along the hilly coastline and through the old, narrow streets of the ancient cities. We passed Vesuvius, and I was surprised to see it glittering in white against the blue sky. It was covered with snow from the top down into the valley. This was a sight one can hardly ever see.

It was cold and drafty at the airport. I was glad that I had put on my fur coat. In the terminal there were no longer any tourists. Only local Italian people were still on their way so close to Christmas. When I arrived at the gate, the few passengers were being called up for boarding. I walked to the plane with my small handbag in my hand, followed closely by a gentleman, who was carrying a large branch of a lemon tree with several beautiful lemons on it. The plane was half empty and I sat down in a window seat. The gentleman with the lemons sat down beside me. I looked at him in surprise. He cut a fine figure. Not very tall but well built and dressed in the Italian style, open shirt collar with a fine silk scarf. He had snow-white hair and very vivid blue eyes. Most of all, I noticed his charming smile.

We immediately started up a conversation. He was an architect, and he was coming from the Isle of Ischia.

"Ah so, and I come from Massa Lubrense. I also have lemons in my garden at this time." As we talked we discovered very quickly our common love for Italy. He was born in Bohemia—the home of my mother! His wife had been killed in a tragic car accident. Yes, my husband also. My tears started flowing as I talked about Howard's death. He pulled out a fine handkerchief and dried my tears. I put my head on his shoulder. It all seemed so natural.

"Fasten your seatbelts and prepare for landing!"

"We cannot be in Munich already! It seems as if we had just started out from Naples!" I said.

When we got off the plane, it seemed as though we had known each other for years.

As we were waiting for the suitcases, Franz, the name of the gentleman with the lemons, told me that he had a villa on Ischia. I was enthusiastic. I could just see it before me. Without further ado we started toward the Airport Café and sat down for the longest cup of coffee I ever drank there. Franz went on talking about the tragic death of his wife three years earlier. Howard also had died three years previously. Was all this a coincidence?

It was then time to take a taxi home.

Three hours later the doorbell rang in the Gruetznerstrasse. I had just said hello to the girls and had unpacked my presents. There he was before my door: Franz Huschka.

He had entered my life like a lightning strike. We had been drawn toward each other like two magnets. From then on we seemed incapable of being apart from each other for more than two hours. We both always had a strange feeling of weak knees when the other one was close. Sitting hungry before a full plate of food, we were unable to swallow a bite. We were always lost in the trance of each other's presence. We were enough for ourselves. The world outside no longer existed.

(Athena had left!) Athena, my protectress, the goddess of wisdom and logical thinking had abandoned me. It was all about emotions now.

Whatever it was that had attracted me so magically is still a mystery to me.

Maybe it was his life-loving, optimistic mien, or the power of his imagination, his creativity—all this aroused in me a mixture of erotic passion and attraction, the likes of which I had never felt before. I had lost myself to him.

I had never had this type of encounter.

My love for Philip had been innocent. We did love each other, but neither of us had any experience, nor the time to let our love mature.

My love for Howard had certainly been the most mature type of love and mutual understanding between a man and a woman. But this type of passion that I felt now was completely new for me. This love was heaven and hell at the same time. It was what the French call a typical "amour fou" ("crazy love").

But we are still in the year 1973. We had not known each other for more than two weeks, but we were already in the country of our dreams. We celebrated Christmas together with the girls in the Casa Carina, the villa of the great magician. I called Franz a magician because of the houses he built and in reference to the episode in *The Odyssey* when Ulysses meets the enchantress Circe, who transforms his comrades into pigs, but cannot succeed in transforming him. I am intimating that he was a male Circe. The next description is also a reference to this episode how different people react to the house (Circe's palace).

Eva and Franz R. Huschka in Venice, Italy, 1975, Family photo

This time I enjoyed Italy as never before. There were moments when I was frightened about the vehemence of my feelings. The primordial wildness of his character held an intense fascination for me. He seemed to have characteristics my mother had that I seemed to have also. But I had always repressed them.

Franz was like a primeval force—his charisma, in his ability to persuade. I did not meet anybody who did not submit to his power of persuasion, even if that person had argued before for a completely different opinion. Franz did not allow anybody or anything to influence him when he was convinced of something. Logical reasoning was not his way. His enthusiasm and his optimism were infectious.

Franz's talent as an architect was admirable. When he set out to design a plan for a house for a client, he saw the completed building already in his imagination, even before he picked up a pencil. He loved every detail—his design encompassed the smallest flower in the garden and the knobs on the doors!

In this way he always convinced his clients of the rightness of his plans. The finished house would cost twice as much as the estimate, but in the end the clients were so happy with the result that they actually never changed anything, not even the color of the curtains.

The clients were very often women. They were easily convinced by his enthusiasm.

It was also they who called him "King Ludwig II," the eccentric Bavarian king known for his influence on art and architecture. Franz was well known in the whole city for his luxurious and sensuous architecture.

Of course, I soon came to learn that Franz also had bad qualities. This was the other side of the coin. He was egocentric to the point of hubris. Added to that was moodiness, extravagance, and vehemence. Blind with love, I simply went into denial. For all the signals that should have warned me, I found a fitting excuse in his having good qualities that balanced out the bad. Nothing could affect my feelings.

Wedding of Eva and Franz Huschka in Ischia, Italy, 1975, Family photo

I had moved into the new apartment that Franz had found in the best part of town, and Franz had made a decision. He had decided that we should marry. We married at first officially in the Munich marriage registry office and then on March 31, 1975, in the church on the Isle of Ischia.

Wedding on the island of Ischia, Italy, 1975, Family photo

Wedding on the island of Ischia, Italy, 1975, Family photo

My father and Franz' parents at the wedding, island of Ischia, 1975, Family photo

Wedding in the Casa Carina, Ischia, Italy, 1975, Family photo L to R Peter Bulva, Eva, Franz, Ariane, Vivian, Doris Kindersberger, 1975, Family photo

There was no problem with the Church, since I had not been married in the Catholic Church before. For me, it was important to seal our love also with the Church's blessing. I wanted to be a good example to the girls and not continue in "living in sin." I hoped also to seal our truthfulness and ask for the blessing of God for my new relationship. I could not believe that the wildness in him, which I loved so much, could not be domesticated. Warning signals!

It was a wedding, completely in the style of Franz Huschka, opulent, pompous, and beyond all bounds. The lovely church in Ischia had been decked out with flowers. A young girl, probably no older than twelve, stood near the organ and sang beautifully. She had this special rough voice that one knows from the Neapolitan folk songs. It seemed that the whole island was joyfully celebrating with us. Everybody had brought something. And the way they celebrated with us made Franz look like a typical Italian "Godfather" to me.

My father gave a moving speech, warmhearted and wise. He comforted me, because my mother had refused to come to the wedding. She had been against the marriage, and as consequence she had actually stayed home.

In the evening we continued to celebrate in the harbor of Ischia, Porto. Franz had rented half of the harbor. A well-known trio of musicians played Italian folk songs until early morning.

This wonderful night unfortunately ended with a spat between us. In the evening I became thoughtful and thought about my two girls. I was happy. But would this also mean happiness for my daughters? I think I wanted an assurance from Franz that all would be well. I don't remember. Anyway, I made the mistake of asking him that question. Franz became furious, accused me of being a hysterical mother, took his pillow, and spent our wedding night in the bar in the basement of the house. On the next day everything seemed forgotten.

After our wedding we lived life fast and furiously. We spent weekends in Paris in the Ritz Hotel, together with the girls in the Excelsior Vittorio in Rome, and later in the Waldorf Astoria in New York. Nothing seemed too far or too expensive. Franz was always generous, particularly with the girls, with whom he had established a warmhearted relationship.

Money was never a problem. My worrying questions, whether we could afford all this and how the economic situation really was, were always met with an impatient opposition. Franz did not allow any involvement by me in his business affairs because he said that I was "dangerously naïve."

In the meantime, we were living in a grand villa in Maria Theresia Strasse 19 in Munich that had about 3,230 square feet and 9-foot-high walls. Originally, I had presupposed that the girls would live with us. There was room for all of us, but Franz had decided differently shortly before the wedding. I had tried to contradict him, but of course Franz succeeded in convincing me that the

'L'apres midi d'unfaune,' Franz in Quo Vadis, 1976, Family photo

girls at this age would be overjoyed to be allowed to live by themselves. And also the girls, when asked, agreed with his opinion, especially since the villa was only a few minutes on foot from our home in the Gruetznerstrasse. And so I allowed myself to be convinced.

We led a pretty wild life in the Maria Theresia Strasse. The nights were long. I had fixed working hours at the university and thus had no time for Franz during the day.

Many times we partied until the wee hours of the morning. When we had guests, a lot of alcohol was consumed, and some glasses were broken. To throw one's glass behind oneself was a gesture of much joy in life, according to the Bohemian custom. Therefore, it did seem better that the girls had their own home.

The girls, however, were very happy with this solution. We saw each other almost every day and telephoned each other. The girls ate either with us or with my parents. I tried to exercise about as much supervision girls in their teenage years allowed.

Sometimes they even resented this supervision, such as when I came over for a visit in the evening to see if everything was all right.

They accepted Franz well as a new stepfather. He gave them nice presents and invited them often together with their friends to go skiing in the mountains and to Italy: Rome, Venice, and to Verona to go to the opera. Even today, Franz and the girls have a good friendly relationship.

THE *CASA CARINA*

The *Casa Carina* was not a simple vacation home in sunny Italy. The *Casa Carina* was like a dream that had become real set on a rocky hill above the waters of the Gulf of Naples .A stately mansion—a fairy-tale castle.

It was the incarnation of Franz's talent as an architect and artist, and it had the obvious signs of his character. But this I should only discover later.

After the death of his wife, Franz had received a large amount of money from her life insurance policy. With this money he wanted to create for her a memorial and at the same time fulfill a wish of his own: build a villa in the Gulf of Naples that would carry her name, Karin.

He started to search for a suitable place. He had looked at a piece of property on the Isle of Capri. After some exploration, he felt somehow cramped on that small island, and finally somebody offered him a piece of land on Ischia. It was in a breathtaking location, directly above the romantic harbor on the hillside with a gorgeous view of the Gulf of Naples. He bought it immediately. Then the building process was set in motion, which the people of Ischia remember even today.

His vision of the *Casa Carina* was already complete in his head. For the first time, he was his own builder-owner. He tried to save money when he built houses for his clients, but he was not willing to accept any compromises on *Casa Carina*. The result was thus a palace from the story of *1001 Nights* surrounded by a magical garden with palm trees, tropical plants, and a large swimming pool built into the hillside.

The villa had two stories, a large parlor, a large dining room with a dining terrace with a view of the harbor, and several storage rooms around a spacious, very modern kitchen. In the basement a large bar, a wine cellar, and a sauna made for a cozy retreat on cool days. The center of attention on the second floor was the splendid bedroom with its extensive, 800- sq.-ft. terrace overlooking the harbor and the Gulf. Besides that, there were another five guest apartments, each one with its own bath and sitting room. Each apartment was decorated in a different color. The tiles had been especially made in Tuscany and partly painted by hand. The material for the curtains and the matching wall covers had been colored according to order.

The whole house was filled with elegant furniture—the large seating area, the sofa and chairs were covered in white leather. Every room had beautifully fashioned chandeliers from Venice.

Franz searched everywhere for the most highly skilled craftsmen for this enormous project. He had them come from Czechoslovakia or from Germany. They came in a special trailer. Many came from Naples.

The glass for the 16-ft. window in the sitting room had to be transported from Germany in an adventurous journey by truck and boat and finally up the hill. Just before the entrance to the small street leading to the villa, a piece of the neighbor's wall had to be torn down in order to turn the curve.

The whole island was talking about the project. Even today, when I get into a taxi the driver asks me: "You are the signora from the Villa Carina, aren't you?"

The result as it presented itself to me was inspiring and threatening at the same time—it was an ode to the beauty of the landscape, to the joy of life, and to the love of pure luxury. But there was also a touch of immoderateness, and excessiveness.

The price for this white elephant was an architect business in Munich that was going bankrupt.

No wonder! But Franz did not seem to be concerned with money matters. And I did not dare to ask.

He engaged a couple from the island as driver and as cook and housekeeper. Franz did not want them to live in the house, because he liked to be there alone and undisturbed—but of course, always in pleasant female company.

Casa Carina was an enticing but also dangerous place. It seemed like the house of the sorceress Circe. Soon I noticed that everyone who entered the house was immediately polarized. Some people were so impressed by the opulence of the house that when they entered they only dared to tiptoe over the expensive floors. Others thought that in this "playground of the gods" all rules were suspended. We made the experience so that the house actually enticed people to excesses and even to physical violence. A "playground for the gods?"

Franz at least has always seen himself as a protégé of the gods, I often heard him say: "During my whole life I have always lived in the most gorgeous places and had the most beautiful women." If I think about it today, he may even be right. Franz is a person who either rides on top of the wave of joy or he raves in the deepest agony. There was little room in between.

In the first phase of our relationship, both of us lived with this feeling of intoxication. My work and even the children receded into the background for a while. I felt sucked into a whirlpool of emotions. Sometimes I was up high and then I was again down low in desperation, depending on the mood of my husband, which changed like the weather.

I could never see ahead or make plans. All events hit me unexpectedly, and I always was surprised by the happenings, which I could never explain.

Athena had said good-bye. Now Mars and Venus ruled.

There were times when we drove every weekend all night from Munich to Naples in nine hours. At 125 miles per hour we flew over the then-empty Autobahn. Our Jaguar rode so quietly and smoothly that I could sit and knit a sweater for Franz. In the morning, "the rose-fingered aurora" greeted us in Napoli.

There were three days of high life and endless nights when Franz could not end the day and would not come to bed. In the morning at five o'clock, I finally poured the final bottle of champagne into the swimming pool, hoping I could get him to go to bed. But no. He called for his Italian aide-de camp and ordered him to bring another bottle from the wine cellar. The day usually began in the early morning hours with a terrible fight about nothing. The reason was completely irrational. Franz would not accept any logical argument. He just wanted to fight, even if I agreed with him, he went on.

Casa Carina on Ischia, Italy, 1975, Family photo

This repeated itself again and again, and slowly I began to hate the *Casa Carina*.

I would have liked to blow the whole house into the air. I was convinced it was the cause for his inexplicable explosions of anger.

The first clouds showed on the horizon.

I was aware that the *Casa Carina* meant an immense financial burden for Franz. But it might be wrong to hold that as the sole cause of his frequent mood swings and explosions. Again and again my happiness with Franz was disrupted by his unprovoked, senseless, and violent temper tantrums. In these moments it seemed as if a demon was taking possession of him. He seemed to enjoy incensing me to the point where I would lose my temper as well. His eyes rolled, and he looked like one of those masks of demons from Thailand. He finally aggravated himself to such a degree that his rage would explode into physical violence such as smashing something or hitting me. When his tensions had been released, he calmed down and in the morning he did not want to be reminded of what had happened the night before. He would refuse to give me an explanation, let alone an excuse.

Nymphs in the bath, Quo Vadis, Italy, 1976, Family photo

I remember another aspect of Franz's character. One night in Ischia, I had already gone to bed and was asleep. Suddenly I woke up with a strange feeling. It was two o'clock in the morning. The bed beside me was empty, and Franz was not in the room. I got up in order to look for him. After a short while I found him downstairs in the bar. The light was turned down low and there was Franz, in close embrace with the seventeen-year-old daughter of the carpenter. The carpenter and his wife and daughter had been asked to stay in *Casa Carina* while he worked in the house. The situation was clear. I was furious. I knocked on the door of the girl's parents, and asked them to take a look at what their daughter was doing in our house. They were very decent people and were just as shocked as I was. The next morning they packed up their suitcases and left the house in a hurry together with their precocious daughter.

I confronted Franz with the situation. He only shrugged his shoulders and remarked that he just was lucky with women and that it was nice to be able to help such a nice young girl develop properly. This should have been a warning to me, but blinded with Amor's eye bandage, I saw the fault only with the girl.

At the end of the Seventies, the financial problems could no longer be denied. The money from the insurance had been spent, and the account with the Thurn and Taxis Bank, which had given Franz every kind of credit, probably not without good reason, had been emptied. Even Franz realized his situation. Every time we stood along the railing of the steamship, which took us to Ischia, I could feel how his body temperature rose because of his excitement. It seemed as if he had a fever. I could feel the heat all the way through his jacket. Franz knew that tomorrow morning the workmen would stand in front of the door in order to demand payment for their work, and the salaries they had not received for months. This went on for a while.

One evening Prince Johannes of Thurn and Taxis came to visit us personally. The prince was a very attractive man, with a golden cross dangling on his sunburnt chest and with unbelievable charm. I was surprised at how well educated and skillful an entertainer this latest offspring of the well-known principality was. We were all standing together on the terrace, the Prince in the middle, and admiring the colors of the sunset reflection on the sea. At this moment the prince put his arms around both of us and with a deep sigh said: "Ach, Mr. Huschka, now I should buy this castle from you too. But I already own so many castles!"

At least by now Franz realized that he would not be able to keep this dream castle any longer.

Shortly before that incident we had started an initiative to use the house commercially, but this endeavor also ended with a further loss.

Together with our Italian friend Enzo, I had succeeded in convincing Franz to host paying guests in the *Casa Carina*. The idea was to offer a fine place for rest and peace in a luxurious environment for rich businessmen and their families.

Franz accepted this idea with reluctance. Since we were not able to take care of our paying guests ourselves, Franz employed a lady from Garmisch-Partenkirchen, a resort town, the daughter of a well-known hotelier, who was experienced and had good contacts with a rich clientele. We were convinced we had found the right person for this job, and sought to find ways that we could make the stay of our guests even more pleasant.

When the lady from Garmisch arrived with seven suitcases full of fancy clothes and shoes, some movement came into the quiet house. At first, she ordered two extra deep-freeze boxes for the kitchen, and then she ordered unbelievable amounts of champagne, wine, and fancy food. There was a bill for 17,000 DM to be paid and further bills were still coming in, as we found out only later.

Then the first guests arrived, a family with teenage children from the Rhineland.

Franz and I and Ariane lived in the big bedroom to supervise our first undertaking.

Everything started out well. The lady from Garmisch had planned and organized everything exactly: a couple for the household as cook and driver for the guests, opulent dinners, and a lot of good wine and champagne. She also arranged for drinks on a bar set up beside the pool, new white bathrobes and towels for the sauna, and a car with a driver for trips to the Poseidon Gardens with its hot fountains and to the beaches of the island. Everything was planned for the well-being of our guests.

In the evening, a rich dinner was served. The ladies appeared in their most beautiful evening gowns. Ariane had even offered to serve drinks. She had been told to ask 18 DM for a drink. This seemed to her very immoderate, but everything seemed to run smoothly.

No wish remained unfulfilled, and our guests enjoyed their stay very much.

On the day of departure, the family said good-bye to us and was full of praise for everything. Franz thanked them and mentioned, by the way, that the bill was still to be paid. Our guests looked at us in surprise: "How can that be? We have paid your housekeeper yesterday!"

We had not seen her since the previous day and nobody knew where she was.

The lady had left—gone, together with all her suitcases and the guests' payment.

But Franz did not bring charges against her. I could not understand why.

This was not a one-time event. Several years before Franz had fulfilled himself another wish. He had furnished Lord's Pub, an opulent English style bar in Garmisch. Everything was the best, a la Huschka. The pub had a specially made couch covered in dark red leather, mirrors on the ceiling and walls, and chandeliers from Venetian workshops.

Since neither of us wanted to run the restaurant-bar, Franz leased it out to a Greek cook. After a short while, the elegant restaurant and the perfect kitchen were completely run down. Everything was so dirty that the guests did not want to eat there anymore.

One morning there was a telephone call from Garmisch. A neighbor of the restaurant said, "Mr. Huschka, you have to check on your restaurant, something there is not in order!"

When we arrived two hours later, we were shocked to see that the Greek had completely emptied out the restaurant. Furniture, rugs, lamps, and mirrors. Everything was already on a truck heading for Greece.

Also in this case, Franz did not bring charges against the thief. "You cannot put your hand into the pocket of a naked man," was his only comment and one of his favorite sayings.

A few years later, we had gone on a trip through Greece and spent some days in Athens. We had had dinner, watched a show, and were walking around in the Plaka, the old part of town. It was after midnight, and we suddenly had this idea: What if we could find our old "friend" from Lord's Pub? This guy surely had opened another bar, and if so, it could only be in the Plaka. We walked from bar to bar until we passed a small cellar restaurant that seemed strangely familiar to us. We entered and thought that we had been here once before. And what do you know? All the furnishings from Lord's Pub were there. The rug, the dark red sofas, the lamps, and the mirrors.

Suddenly shouts of joy! It was the cook, the old Greek rascal. He flung his arms around Franz's neck. The two men embraced and spent the rest of the night drinking one ouzo after the other and telling stories about the good old days in Garmisch. When the morning dawned, they parted like old friends, as though nothing had ever happened.

In 1976 Franz had to sell *Casa Carina*. What remained was only a beautiful dream that he had dreamed and realized. He no longer owned what had been the site of many fascinating memories. For Franz, the loss of the house seemed less sad than I had expected. Franz really was a nomad. He did not necessarily need to own a house. He needed to build. Building meant for him *life*. It was not his way of life to live from tilling one's fields, the laborious and patient sowing and harvesting. He wanted to use the property of others, build on it, and then move on. He had a good sense for good-natured women, women who were liable to be sympathetic to him, his goals, and his behavior. He took their treasure and their love with the distinct instinct of a predatory wild animal. Because money did not mean very much to him, he earned a lot of money and spent it generously. Money served him only for the satisfaction of his momentary desires.

One evening he did not have enough money in his pocket to fuel up the Jaguar. He went to the pawnshop and pawned his wedding ring, had his car filled up, and after that invited me for a dinner with oysters in a fabulous restaurant. I bought him a new wedding ring, but he lost it shortly afterward. I gave up and didn't replace it for him.

I tried to get the expenses for *Casa Carina* under control. I suggested that we make a budget for the house and its upkeep, but my efforts came to naught. I ran up against a wall—Franz himself and his manager. When I told him about my idea, he and his Italian "manager" Enzo reacted as if I had insulted them and let me know in loud voices, that they did not appreciate my interference in their affairs.

Franz's relationship to money only became dangerous for me after he had sold *Casa Carina* and began to concentrate on my house, *Quo Vadis*, in Massa Lubrense.

It was only logical that *Quo Vadis* became our common center of life after the sale of *Casa Carina*, because we both loved Italy and the Gulf of Naples.

The house in Massa Lubrense had technically not been very well built in the Fifties. It urgently needed renovation to make it more livable during the winter months. We agreed that something had to be done, and Franz threw himself immediately into the new project. At first, he gave away my old furniture to the gardener without asking me. He also did not consult with me in any of the other things he did. I did not have any say in these matters. He would say, "You don't know anything about architecture," and with that he stifled any further discussion. If I did not want to constantly fight with him, I had to give him free rein.

Franz did keep the basic structure of the house. The largest change was caused when floor heating was installed. The Romans had these comforts in their homes two thousand years ago. All of the floors had to be raised some ten inches, which meant that all the doors and windows also had to be raised. In the back of the house, where I had tried to grow potatoes, Franz placed a very romantic swimming pool. Both sides of the first floor were flanked with corridors, dug into the mountain, to insulate the house against the constant humidity. Franz built a glassed in veranda on the roof, and a sauna with a shower. It is probably the only sauna in the world that has a window with a view of the Isle of Capri.

My simple summer house had tuned into *House Huschka*. Like *Casa Carina*, it seemed sumptuous. Of course, I was happy about the technical renovations of the house, and I was happy about the beautification of my house, but I worried about the mounting expense of the project. The house was a construction site for three years. But then my *Quo Vadis* had been turned into a beautiful home with all the comforts one could imagine.

The Dance on the Rope

My life at the side of Franz Huschka was becoming more and more complicated.

I was not only a wife and lover but I also had two teenage daughters and a place of work that certainly also needed my attention. On some days the contrast between the home and work environments made me feel as if I were in a trance. At home, there was the glittering happiness and a luxurious lifestyle at the side of a wild and charming faun. At work, there was my profession, director of the Language Center at the University of the Federal Armed Forces of Germany. With Franz, I had to be the understanding wife—feminine, loving, and charming. At the university, I had to keep discipline as a person of authority, and I had to stand up like a man among men. At home, Franz accused me of behaving like a sergeant, and at the university the teasing of my colleagues about my too-feminine appearance. On some days I felt like a dancer on a rope without a net.

Despite all these contradictions in my everyday life, I considered us to be a happy family. The girls were growing up into women. I remember when Vivian drove very fast along the curved street to Positano, as if it were an act of provocative freedom. She was always with her boyfriend Carlo, with whom she was very much in love, but whom she did not want to marry. Later, this relationship did turn into a nice friendship for life.

Ariane was also together for a short time with a young Italian man. After graduation from the International School in Berg, she lived for a year in Florence in order to learn Italian and study art. She felt very good there and fell in love with a young dentist. We would have liked to see him as a son-in-law, but Ariane refused his marriage proposal.

During this time Franz furnished in Munich the well-known noble restaurant, La Piazzetta. It was planned to become a counterpiece to the Platzl near the Hofbrauhaus in Munich's center. It had its name from the world-renowned Piazzetta in Capri. The idea to establish a restaurant of this order had been born already during the time of the *Casa Carina*.

Franz's friends had planned an Italian restaurant according to their own ideas. Now the idea had matured and had become an order for Franz. It was a commission that exactly fit Franz's style—he was made for the part. He was able to play out his love for Italy. Money was no issue. Again, the result was a perfect fit. La Piazzetta was to become the most beautiful restaurant in the center of Munich. Ariane also played her part. Together they designed a splendid glass roof a la Tiffany, which had no equal in Munich.

Franz found the wooden wall coverings and some of the furniture in an old convent in Florence. The whole building would cost more than two million DM.

Ariane and Franz enjoyed their work together. It probably had a profound influence on Ariane's later major in college as an interior designer.

Tiffany glass ceiling in the restaurant La Piazzetta, Munich, Germany 1977, source unknown

La Piazzetta opened on May 5, 1982. It soon became the favorite restaurant of Franz Joseph Strauss, the Governor of Bavaria, and also a gathering place for many other Munich celebrities. It soon became "the" place for the Munich jet set. After a few successful years, unfortunately, it had to close because of bankruptcy. It was a sad loss for the Munich scene.

Change of scenery: A gray autumn day in Munich. Franz and I had just returned from Italy. We wanted to unpack our suitcases. A humid cold crept into our clothes. We looked at each other, then without word we put the suitcases back into the car and drove south to Venice. Wonderful days on the sunny Lido!

Another day we were on top of the Zugspitze, the highest mountain in Germany—Franz, Ariane, and Vivian, her friend David, and I. The new snow was glittering. The young people had already skied down the hill. Franz stood beside me: "Come on, let's shoot down, it is very simple!" And he was gone. I found myself before the dangerously steep hill, and my tears came. I had not ever skied very much and was also completely out of practice. I was scared to death.

But then my two girls came back and guided me slowly down the steep hill.

In the meantime, Franz had a great time in the ski hut. He was not interested in how I had managed to get down the hill.

We had a new hobby: Hiking with the International People Sports Club.

We were criss-crossing Bavaria, and Franz was always ten paces ahead of me.

In one summer alone we received a dozen prizes and three years later we received the Golden Pin for 800 miles on foot. That was the distance from Munich to Naples. We were proud of this achievement.

Ariane and Vivian were already studying in the United States and somehow the feeling rose in me that they might stay there. It seemed to be the time to build new bridges to that country. Franz had never been in the States, and I wanted to show him the country that had marked my life so profoundly. I also was convinced that the mentality there would attract him a lot.

"Runners", red.figured Amphora (4th century B.C.E.) See Source Index

The New York Marathon of 1981 was the right occasion for our trip to America. Franz was enthusiastic; he absolutely wanted to take part in this sporting event.

After three years of hiking, he felt well prepared. For me it was a good opportunity to see the girls again. Ariane came from Indiana, where she was studying at Ball State University in Muncie. Vivian came from Fort Worth in Texas, where she studied in the Texan Christian College.

We met on the evening before in the Waldorf Astoria Hotel. It became a long party. We were partying half of the night—until two o'clock—and I began to worry about Franz and his condition for the next day.

The next day came, as it had to come. We were barely ready to get out of the bed on the next morning. After a fast breakfast we hurried through the elegant reception hall of the Waldorf, Franz in short pants and tennis shoes. Outside an icy wind blew us in the face.

When we got out of the taxi on the Verrazano-Narrows Bridge, which connected Staten Island and Brooklyn, there were already 17,000 runners preparing themselves for the marathon. They lay in tents and had themselves massaged, prayed over, or meditated with, and tried to warm up with exercises.

Franz the hiker did not even have a jacket over his T-shirt, and there was no time for any warm-up exercises. The starting shot thundered, and the 17,000 runners pushed from three accesses onto the beautiful bridge in the direction of Brooklyn. It was an overwhelming sight. Everything had been organized perfectly.

I was convinced that Franz would at best only be able to run half of the marathon, 13 miles, and I had insisted that we would pick him up with a taxi at a certain street. The girls and I had found out on a street map of New York where the street was where we would meet Franz. I had told the taxi driver where he should take us, but after a few minutes he stopped and asked us to get off. The place was in the most dangerous part of the Bronx, where a small part of the marathon route went. He would not be responsible. If we wanted to go to that street, we would have to go on by foot. He would wait for us where we were.

We took off our rings and earrings and walked to the arranged street corner and looked out for Franz. I knew his speed and had figured out the time he would have to show up.

After a few minutes we saw him approaching in the middle of some runners. He was running as if in a trance and did not see us at all. We waved at him and called his name loudly, but he did not show any reaction. When he wanted to pass us by, I threw myself at him and pulled him against his will onto the side of the street. If I didn't catch him now, he would end up somewhere in New York, in his wet T-shirt and without a penny to take a subway.

"Why is this woman pulling him out? Let him run!" The black spectators on the street did not like this at all. I did not pay any attention, and I pulled him in the direction of the taxi and gave him something to drink. He was still pretty out of it and only slowly woke up from his trance. Back in the Waldorf we celebrated our "hero" at great length.

From that moment on, Franz was in love with America and would have wanted to stay there forever. But it was not so easy to emigrate. So he started to convince my girls that as a creative person one could only live in America. When I expressed my worries about that, he only responded, "They will come back."

The trip to New York was an emotional rest for me. Franz was the way I had always loved him, charming, enthusiastic, full of life, and generous. But after we had returned to Munich things went the same as ever, sudden mood changes, choleric outbreaks, and aggression.

At about that time I discovered the Arabian poet Khalil Gibran. His little book *The Prophet* became a wonderful companion for me. It is difficult to live according to his wise words, but they comforted me and put the troubles of our turbulent days into the right perspective:

> …Love one another, but make not a bond of love:
>
> Let it rather be a moving sea between the shores of your souls.
>
> Fill each other's cup but drink not from one cup.

Give one another of your bread but eat not from the same loaf

Sing and dance together and be joyous, but let each one of you be alone,

Even as the strings of a lute are alone though they quiver with the same music.

Give your hearts, but not into each other's keeping.

For only the hand of Life can contain your hearts.

And stand together yet not too near together:

For the pillars of the temple stand apart,

And the oak tree and the cypress grow not in each other's shadow.

"With these words Khalil Gibran seemed to have described my marriage with Howard. But how true was this for my marriage with Franz? And what was the deeper trouble? Some of this had probably already become clear to me, but I still was not capable to act accordingly. I was still a prisoner in the cave of my emotions. Somehow there was a huge rock guarding the opening. There was no escape!

Sartre describes this situation so well in his play *No Exit*. His protagonists find themselves in hell after a violent death. Now their punishment is the presence of the other ones. "I understand, here one is the other one's torture," one character says.

In those days, my feelings were constantly up and down. Was I happy or unhappy in this marriage? I cannot say. I looked for a method to judge myself more objectively to figure out my life. I designed a scale with three points on the plus side and three points on the minus side. Every day I observed my own feelings and marked the points in my calendar. When the points were connected, this system showed a curve that showed my feelings exactly.

After two months I had the truth in black and white. It was a curve that went from one extreme of three points up to the extreme point down, exactly according the moods my husband was in. When his bad moods turned into a threatening gruff, unjust scoldings, and extremely insulting words until he finally exploded like a kettle with boiling water, I felt terrible. I was not capable of handling this side of his character. In all the years of our marriage I could neither predict nor explain his moods. So I was not able to meet his aggression effectively or do anything about them.

I tried many times to get off of the emotional roller coaster. My many attempts to break out were always thwarted. We either were in a place that I could not leave, in a hotel, a driving car, or it was night. When I finally succeeded and left, Franz came after me until he had found me and brought me back.

It was also very difficult to come to an agreement with Franz. When we had finally found a common position about an issue, he was of a different opinion shortly afterward. When confronted with this change of mind, he would say, "What do I care about my stupid talk of yesterday?" In those moments I had the feeling of being confronted with one of those demonic mixed beings of the Babylonian gods and demons, with one of those beings that never spoke the truth and always changed their appearance.

Franz enjoyed the world of the economic elite of the Munich social class, mostly for business reasons. Small one-time flings or having a young mistress on the side was considered a peccadillo in those circles, if not trendy. Money was no issue in the rich Eighties, whether or not you had any. Politicians, the rich, and the beautiful romped around on the stage of Munich high society. The scene of "high cuisine" and gastronomes determined the stage. Bavarian brewery owners and top cooks determined the flair.

My Franz was full of self-confidence. Any kind of reproaches or accusations he denied with all his glibness. He won every dispute. Even when I had succeeded in showing him the evidence of his lies—quite plain, concrete evidence—I began to doubt my own knowledge.

Once I believed that I had clear evidence that Franz had affairs with other women. He eloquently denied this and called me a jealous wife. Exasperated, I finally hired a private detective to find out the truth. And sure enough, he presented me with clear evidence that my premonitions were correct. Franz even denied these pieces of evidence for several affairs ongoing at the time.

My teaching profession was to him only a stupid employee's job, whereas he was free to do what he wanted and was not dependent on anybody. Of course, one could not compare this with my "civil servant mentality." His goal seemed to put me down and make me lose my self-esteem.

But he did not succeed.

Despite all these problems, I did not think of divorce. Does it not say in the Bible, "Love is long-suffering and endures everything"? But where was the limit between loving understanding and self-destructive masochism? The answer to this question would take its time.

Ariane and Vivian, New Albany, IN, 1980, Family photo

THE CHILDREN LEAVE THE NEST

Your children are not your children.

They are sons and daughters of life's longing for itself . And though they are with you, they do belong not to you.

You may give them your love, but not your thoughts, for they have their own thoughts.

You may house their bodies but not their souls, for their souls live in the house of tomorrow, which you cannot visit, not even in your dreams.

You may strive to be liked by them, but seek not to make them like you.

For life goes not backward nor tarries with yesterday.

Khalil Gibran

The girls' decision to go to America was very painful for me.

It was the first time that the children were really separated from me. During recent years we had not lived together in one house, but we were really only a few steps apart from each other. We could get together whenever we wanted to. Now this was no longer possible.

I missed the girls terribly.

Ariane, after her final year in Berg and her year in Florence, had decided to go to high school in Evansville, Indiana, in order to prepare for college. Her father, Philip, lived there with his new family and also Grandpa Cox, whom she loved very much.

I had always been careful not to destroy the picture they had of their father. Just the opposite. After all, there was no feeling of enmity between Philip and me. Over the years, the girls had learned that he and I were very different from each other, which should, however, not influence their love for their father or for me.

After Vivian had decided for America, she finished her high school degree in the International School. For the following year, I arranged for her to spend her first year in college in the International College in Paris. After all, she was born in France and should improve her French in this country.

Franz and I drove with her to Paris to find a nice little apartment in the center of town, which she shared with her long-time friend Sabine. Vivian profited a lot from this stay in France. She discovered her love for the arts and, like her sister, wanted to go to college in America. She applied to the Texan Christian College in Fort Worth and was accepted. There she graduated in Graphic Arts.

In America she also met her former friend David McCasker again, whom she had already known in the International School in Berg.

Vivian's Wedding in Australia

One evening in May 1982 the telephone rang in Munich. It was already after midnight.

The call came from Melbourne, Australia. It was David. He asked me for the hand of my daughter.

Vivian? To Australia? I was very surprised and somewhat sleepy.

Whatever the reason, at this moment I made a decisive mistake. My first reaction to this question was to ask whether they intended to move permanently to Australia to spend their whole life there. I must have sounded somewhat worried. In any case, David must have interpreted my question as an affront against his person. It was too late to change this impression, and even if I uttered the expected "how wonderful!" later in the following conversation, from that moment on, we had started off on the wrong foot. Unfortunately, this event had devastating results in the relationship between my beloved granddaughters and me for the years that followed. This is a fact which makes me very unhappy.

The only wedding present Vivian wanted from me was that we should come to her wedding on August 4 in Melbourne. So Franz and I set out to fly to the other side of the world. And since it made no difference which route we picked, going east or west, we booked the return flight around the whole globe, with stops in Tahiti and Los Angeles.

The wedding was very nice for Vivian. She was a beautiful bride in her white dress, so slim and fragile with the old white lace veil of my mother. The dinner with many Australian relatives in the best hotel in town was impressive.

I worried very much about my girl. I could not imagine how she would be happy in this wild country on the other side of the world, so far away from the protective care of her family. She seemed much too delicate and sensitive for this rough country.

I myself felt the country to be oppressive, unbounded, and wild, and the people archaic and violent. Everything seemed so threatening and strange. I felt like the goddess Demeter, who, after the rape of her daughter Proserpina by the god Hades, wandered around the earth to find her. When she finally finds her in Hades's underworld, the gods show some consideration for her grief and decree that Hades had to allow his wife to come up to the earth again for half of the year to be with her mother.

Unfortunately in my case, no gods could be found who would send out such a decree.

With the exception of some sparse letters, communication was not very advanced in those days, and I tried to forget my worries about her.

However, Vivian returned with her family to our hemisphere in 1991. She moved to Houston, Texas, a state in the United States that may share some qualities with Australia as far as the landscape is concerned as well as the mentality of the inhabitants.

Our return trip around the other side of the world was most interesting but no consolation for me. Despite dreamlike beaches, South Sea romantic and smiling islanders in Bora Bora, I always had to think of the dismal history of these islands. In the 18th century the Europeans with their, at that time, usual contempt for human beings had almost completely wiped out the gentle original population. They introduced firearms, alcohol, and syphilis, and so destroyed their culture.

The girls did not give me much time to recuperate from this farewell. Just one year later Ariane had decided to get married.

Ariane Marries an American

During her last year in high school in Evansville, Indiana, Ariane had met a young boy, John Edmundson. Since Ariane already had her home with her father in Indiana, she applied to college in Muncie to get in-state tuition.

I had made it a condition for the girls that they should finish their college education and earn their own living for one year before getting married.

Ariane chose as her major art and interior design. John had finished high school and then joined the U.S. Marines. He had to go to Korea for one year. After his return, he wanted to use the GI Bill to also attend Muncie College, where he chose to study architecture.

Soon after John's return, Ariane and John informed me that they had serious plans to get married.

Franz and I immediately flew to Muncie in order to get to know John. The young man made a good impression. But I did not like the idea of also losing Ariane to America.

Wedding of Ariane to John Edmundson, July 1981, Munich, Germany, Family photo

I cautiously tried to raise the question that Ariane would probably always yearn for Europe and its culture. But John would not be put of. He loved Ariane and wanted a family.

A short time after this, Ariane and John got married at the registry of Evansville, Indiana. Without us. We were only informed later.

However, I was finally able to convince John to get married in the Catholic Church in Munich, for my and the grandparents' sake.

Their wedding should be an especially beautiful "Bavarian" wedding!

In July 1984 Ariane and John found themselves in front of the enchanting altar of St. George in the little church of Bogenhausen in Munich. I was happy about the young couple and prayed to God for his blessing. Ariane was a very modest, somewhat introspective bride. She looked lovely in the wedding gown in which I had married her father.

After the ceremony we got into a stately horse-drawn carriage and took the route through the English Garden to the La Piazzetta restaurant. On the way we passed the Chinese Tower, which is in the center of the English Garden. The proprietor of the restaurant at the base of the tower offered us a glass of champagne. We stopped the coach and drank with him and the people in the crowd. We did not know any of the people, but they were just happy to see us, because meeting a wedding company means good luck. And by happenstance, there was a band of Bavarian musicians playing at the tower, who played some special songs for the young couple when they saw that they were just married.

Of course, the celebration took place in La Piazzetta, which had been decked out with lovely flowers for the feast. The table had been set for about thirty people. Everyone had already arrived when the carriage with the wedding couple arrived—my parents, Franz's parents, and our closest friends. Ariane's school friend Angelika and her brothers were also there.

La Piazzetta was truly an appropriate setting for this feast. Ariane loved Italy and John has gotten to know Europe a little bit.

We were all very happy and had all sorts of plans for the future. Franz, Ariane, and John would open an architectural business in the United States. Everything seemed too good to be true.

My Tasks at the Federal Armed Forces University

Besides my very strenuous private life, I also had a profession that was very demanding but also provided many opportunities for interesting activities.

I had founded three clubs at the university: The German-American Club, the German-French Club and later, in 1991, the German-Russian Friendship Club. It was my intention to offer the opportunity to young military officers to go beyond borders and to arouse their interest in international affairs.

The German American Club is now almost thirty years old and found much acclaim among the young people.

Our officers, who had entered the military to make it their career, did not have any problem with the question of authority or discipline, in contrast to their colleagues of the same age at Ludwig-Maximilian University in Munich. It was fairly easy for us teachers to teach these disciplined, well-trained and clear-thinking young officers. There was no need for heated debates like in Hampton or Ethiopia. I did, however, regret that the additional lectures offered on political, philosophical, or current topics were not very well attended. The reason probably was the high demands put upon the students in the intensive program that was only three years. It was much more important that they became active in the clubs, where they could combine having fun and learning.

The structure of the German military command was significantly different from that of the American military command structure. That was new to me, because I had only known the American system because of Phil's work. In the German training plan, there is a subject called

Innere Fuehrung, which means "inner leadership." The purpose of that course was to train the self-confidence of the young man and at the same time help him develop his feeling of responsibility toward his subordinates. Very important was the so-called "Auftrags Taktik." This meant that the officer would get a certain order to reach a certain goal, but it was left to him to decide how to reach this goal.

Military parade at the University of the German Federal Armed Forces, Munich, 1984, Family photo

In the U.S. military, in contrast, the so-called "Befehls Taktik," which means "order tactics," was used. This meant that the order was given to reach a certain goal, but at the same time it included the exact steps that were to be taken. From these orders, there was absolutely no deviation permitted, even if the situation had changed.

In Germany we had a general military draft system until 2010. At that time the military was not a professional army. The aim was to train "the citizen in uniform," according to the ideas of Wolff Graf von Baudissin.

In America, a military man has "to get a job done." Drill, obedience, and unquestioning fulfillment of an order are the most important laws in the U.S. Army. Most of all, an absolute patriotism is the rule. This was definitely the most obvious sign of difference between the German and the American military. Since World War II, we Germans had severe problems with the concept of "patriotism." But it must be the utmost duty of the American soldier.

Compared to the training in the American military, our officers were being treated with kid gloves. At our university it was even possible to file a lawsuit against the superior officer of the university. Two young officers had to share a one-room apartment for six weeks due to a space shortage. They claimed that they could not study under such cramped conditions. In the U.S. Army an unimaginable occurrence would be to sue the university!

There was even an attempt to sue me for giving a bad grade once. The attempt was without success, but alone the request seemed unbelievable to me.

The university's administration wanted by all means to avoid the typical old Prussian drill. One did not want to be associated with any of the methods of the National Socialists' system. The model was a modern, open-minded Federal Armed Forces.

On the occasion of the trip of our German-American Club to the United States, our young officers became acquainted with a U.S. Officer Training School. The drill and the manners of the officers with their subordinates was a real shock. If an officer was not saluted exactly, if the tone of voice was not correct, or the angle of the hand on the cap was wrong, a punishment was given. At first our boys laughed about this. But after a while they became more and more pensive. They returned to Munich chastened and thoughtful.

One of the high points of my work at the university was a trip to Teheran in Iran.

There the Shah of Iran still reigned over the country, when the Bundessprachenamt (the central agency for language training in the military and other federal services) sent me there on an official trip. It must have been before 1978.

Together with two other colleagues, I had been instructed to choose from a group of sixty young officers those who would be suited for further education at the Federal Armed Forces University in Munich or Hamburg. To be exact, we had to test whether their knowledge of German was good enough to allow them to understand the lectures there.

So we flew to Teheran. From the outside, the city was like any other modern city, but I experienced again a very different world.

We met the group that was to be tested on the next day.

All of them were nice, good-looking, enterprising young men. For them a failing grade would mean a professional catastrophe. "The Shah will have us beheaded," they said half-jokingly. Despite that, we could only choose about one-third of them.

We wanted the tests to be absolutely fair and impartial. We had to test adequate oral skills as well as good reading comprehension of a medium-difficult text. We used a well-tried method: The student had to read a medium-difficult text of one-and-a-half pages within 20 minutes without the use of a dictionary. Then he had to answer questions and discuss within a conversation with the teacher that proved his comprehension of the most important points of the text.

To our surprise, we noticed right away that the candidates started to talk immediately about the text without listening to our questions. They waited for a key word in our question and then they began to repeat the text exactly from this point on. In only twenty minutes, they had learned the whole text by heart!

When we gave them questions of understanding, like why the man in the story had acted in such-and-such a manner, or what the main point of the story was, or even which conclusion one could draw from this text, they reacted surprised and could not answer.

It became clear that in their school system, as in their religion, to learn by heart had played the most important part. Their teachers in Germany later confirmed our impression later on.

It was not easy for me to tell those who had not passed the examination that they were not fit to study in Germany. They had all been working hard and had given their best.

With a strong feeling of uneasiness we had to leave many of them behind.

The islands of Sanibel and Captiva, Florida, 1989, postcard

Sanibel Island, Florida, 1989, Family photo

SANIBEL ISLAND

Ariane and John had moved to Florida in 1982. Their two children, Anton and Sophia, were born there. They had found a small house in Matlache, one of the islands that lie on the Gulf coast near Ft. Myers. Ariane established herself as a painter in a well-known gallery in Ft. Myers and greatly enjoyed working in her new tropical garden by the canal.

I still nurtured my dream: Franz and John should open an architectural firm in Florida, with Ariane as interior decorator—a "family business," if you like.

I suggested to Franz that he fly with me to Florida. He had so much enjoyed his trip to New York. Manhattan really fit his mentality: limitless skyscrapers, the realized dream of the "unlimited possibilities." So I hoped to be able to enthuse him also for my new dream.

453

Eva and Ariane on Sanibel Island, Florida, 1989, Family photo

Franz was easily convinced.

The international airport of Ft. Myers was small and pleasant. The warm, humid air smelled a little bit like salt, iodine, and kerosene. We rented a car and took off in the direction of the Gulf. On long, straight streets, we passed well-kept golf resorts and spacious apartment buildings.

Our goal was Sanibel Island, an island that was situated off the coast of Ft. Myers in the Gulf of Mexico and was still very natural. Ariane had told me about this enchanting island. After about thirty minutes, we reached the bridge that connects the mainland with the island. Above our car the first pelicans accompanied us all the way to the island.

Sanibel is a long, narrow island that is connected on its northern end by a small bridge to another small island, Captiva. In the North of Captiva, there are no roads. The houses of the nature lovers who build there can only be reached by boat. For people who love the simple life, this is pure paradise.

We drove along the main street of Sanibel and were immediately captivated by the charm of this island. The street, was an endless dome of Australian Pines. Between them were small but comfortable houses on stilts. A building regulation requiring stilts had been passed in 1910, when the whole island with all its orange and grapefruit plantations had been flooded and devastated by a hurricane. On the right and the left side of the street are the idyllic old schoolhouse, which had been turned into the island theater, the old book shop, and Bailey's General Store, the island's only grocery and hardware store. Since 1899 the Bailey family has run the store, initially called Sanibel Packing Company.

Sanibel is the island of educated Americans who shy away from glamour and whose money has made sure that no cheap and loud commercial interests have entered the island. The inhabitants prefer instead to have a huge parcel of land dedicated to the conservation of nature: the J. N. "Ding" Darling National Wildlife Refuge.

Again, I am entering another new world: tropical vegetation and white sandy beaches, light-colored, friendly houses with gray-brown shingle roofs, well-kept gardens that extend into nature, no big hotel tracts, no high-rises. On this island the beauty of nature dominates everything.

Franz liked the island so well that he bought himself a house on Umbrella Pool Road.

His elegant furniture from the *Casa Carina* was shipped over the Atlantic to Sanibel. Among the items was a very beautiful antique mosaic table and a splendid crystal chandelier from Venice.

Some time later, the chandelier almost fell on our heads during a Christmas dinner. No one was hurt, because we had just gotten up from our chairs and left the table, but the event seemed like a "mene tekel" and made me wonder.

We had planned to move to Sanibel permanently. Franz bought a huge piece of land from an old lady who immediately had fallen in love with him. She disliked the people in Sanibel and was happy to sell to an outsider.

Now we were owners of an enormously large piece of land that reached from the western side of the island to the eastern side and included a large piece of marshland.

Franz planned to divide the land into parcels, build beautiful houses that were adequate to the nature of the island, and sell them. Franz planned at first forty and later just twenty-five houses. In the end it was only eight.

During the economic boom of the Eighties, it had become trendy in Germany to have a house in Florida in order to flee from the cold winter. There were enough people with money. It actually was a very sensible business idea.

However, the local council thwarted our plans. For eight years they made us participate every so often in yet another council meeting to discuss our plans. They kept asking for yet another expert's certificate. The certificate had to prove that on the property there were no sea turtle holes, or water holes, or some other creatures, because the environment had to be protected. We basically agreed with these ideas, but finally it seemed that a group of people had put it into their mind to keep us from building on our land Why? We never found out. This was the disadvantage of this beautiful, natural, protected island!

Franz had borrowed money from the bank for the purchase of the property and the building project. It was quickly used up for all the certificates and lawyers, and the high interest. Added to the expenses were the many plane fares. I myself had invested $30,000 in the project. I never saw that money again. We had to sell the house on Umbrella Pool Road, including all the furniture.

That was the time when prices in Florida had again gone down, so we sold at a loss and were then sitting on a huge piece of land without a building permit and no money.

One bit of bad news came after another. I was tied to Munich, for there I had my job. It was our only sure income. But Franz needed me again and again in Sanibel for translations in the council meetings.

I had to fly to Sanibel for another "last" discussion of the council. The first meeting was postponed. Everything took longer than expected, and I had to postpone my flight back. For the first time I had to extend my vacation for one day. I had called the personnel office, but despite my doing that, a "palace revolution" started in my office. Some of my dissatisfied colleagues saw their chance. They immediately called the personnel office. Their aim was to have me dismissed from my position and to vote for a successor from their own group. They were of the opinion that I had accepted too much work for them with these new projects. A new boss, so they hoped, would restore their old privileges and allow them to come and go as they pleased. From that day on, there began a process of "mobbing," which caused me a lot of trouble. The secretaries were stirred up against me, and their jealousy was incited. Every small mistake was blown out of proportion and reported to the personnel office. Luckily, my bosses saw what was going on and continued to support me.

I was really under an enormous pressure—the pressure in my office and in Sanibel as well as the pressure on our finances. I noticed how even my handwriting changed. It had become small and scribbling. The letters were leaning once to the left and another time to the right. Alarming signals started to add up. I caused three car accidents in a row. They were only small scratches, but it was my own lack of concentration that had caused them. My nerves were absolutely shot.

The real problem was of course Franz. He was faced again with bankruptcy and I was not willing to sacrifice my home in the

Gruetznerstasse, or the villa *Quo Vadis* for this venture in Florida. When I asked Franz about the real state of our business, of which I also was legally a partner, he threw the entire folders down at my feet. I did not know what to do with these papers, because I had no business experience. As Franz realized that I would not be able to support him business-wise or financially, his interest in my person waned.

I was no longer of use to him, so he began to look around for other women. He even said this blatantly and openly, "Why don't you look for another man? Then I can do what I like."

In the meantime, Franz and John had also stopped talking because of business quarrels. Both of them were absolute control freaks. Of course, finances played a part. There was no longer any hope for a common architectural firm. The family venture had collapsed, and we faced bankruptcy. My marriage was in a similar condition.

The Victory of Athena

When Franz was in Munich, we had many fights. Many times I even went to my office to spend the night there in order to avoid another dispute. In the morning, when my secretary found me there, I felt very awkward. Many times I also fled to my parents. There I went into hiding until Franz had calmed down again. Or I called up my father to come to my rescue. My parents did not like what they saw and watched my situation with great concern, but they did not want to interfere in my marriage.

Things could not go on as they were. That had become clear to me already, but I was never capable of acting accordingly. Until one fateful morning.

I was in my office when I received a call from our maid. "Frau Huschka," she said. "I hate to get involved in this, but you should check sometime on what goes on in your apartment when you are not there."

I felt as if I was just struck by lightning. I told my secretary that I felt very sick and had to go home.

I opened the entrance door carefully so as to not make any noise. And there I saw Franz in the living room in an unmistakable position with a young woman. I knew her. She worked as a nurse for the old owner of the house who lived downstairs.

Both of them stared at me in surprise. "Aren't you ashamed of yourself?" I asked Franz. "No, why?" was his answer.

Any other word was unnecessary. I was not angry or sad, nor disappointed. I suddenly only felt a very strong feeling of determination.

I walked into the bedroom, threw some important things into a suitcase, went through the corridor past the living room, and closed the front door—forever!

The huge rock in front of the opening of my cave was suddenly blown away. The sunlight fell into my cave and I could see clearly again. Athena stood behind me. "Courage does not help you here; to flee is the only salvation!" she seemed to whisper.

I took a little detour via the Isar bridge on the way to the Gruetznerstrasse. I passed the statue of the golden Angel of Peace. and the Bavarian Government, and walked down to the bridge where the statue of Athena stands, right to the place where I had thrown my hat into the river when a child. And I enjoyed the same feeling of freedom. An enormous load had fallen off my shoulders. Finally, I had succeeded to free myself from my own hell.

Polyphem, Munich, 1990, Composite made of family photos

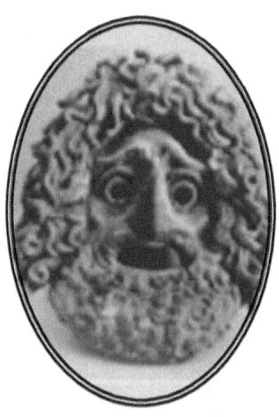

Chapter 17: Farewells and New Beginnings

The Divorce

I WAS LIVING AGAIN IN THE Gruetznerstrasse. I was not surprised. The decision to leave the marriage had long been looming on the horizon. It needed only that last push, to catch Franz "in flagranti," that last drop that made the barrel overflow. I had had to endure and forgive many hurts, and much verbal abuse, but infidelity I considered a basic betrayal of our love, and I saw no reason to continue our common life.

Besides that, this was not the first event of this sort, despite the fact that Franz always denied having affairs, and so it was clear that Franz would not change his behavior.

I entered my newly renovated apartment with only a small suitcase in my hand. With wise foresight I had kept my apartment in the Gruetznerstrasse and had renovated it after the girls had left Germany. Something in me had said, "You may need this apartment one day." It was a strange feeling to be there again. On the one hand, I felt very relieved, but on the other hand, I was very sad. I had hoped to grow old together with Franz after a fulfilled life. What an illusion!

Under the Maximilian's bridge on the river Isar, Munich, 1990, Family photo

Three years later, Franz and I found ourselves in front of the divorce judge. Both of us were very tense and avoided being alone together in one room.

I had silently hoped during those three years that Franz would come to his senses, because we basically had so much in common. When the judge asked me whether I agreed to go through with the divorce, I answered: "Under the condition that Franz does give up his present girlfriend, yes!"

So we were divorced, and despite the fact that we had already lived apart for three years, I felt very lost.

Franz had gone to the Czech Republic to his relatives who lived in a small village. There he had searched and found a nineteen-year-old girl, "a young girl one could bring up and train correctly." (*My Fair Lady* sends greetings!).

Shortly thereafter he found and bought a stately old manor house with extensive gardens and fields on top of a hill and renovated the house splendidly in his style. He married the young village beauty. Only with her help was he able to buy the property in the Czech Republic, because German citizens could not own property there.

This young girl would be a good nurse later when he was old.

Since the separation from Franz, I was well on my way to myself, a long way full of farewells and of letting go.

I had really started out on this way twenty years ago with the loss of Howard. Seven years later there was the long farewell of my beloved father, who had been for my whole life a good friend and protector. Father had suffered a stroke in 1978 and had to stay in a nursing home in the Tegernsee Valley during his last years. Maria stayed close by and took care of him. Mother came to see him as often as she could. Due to the caring help of Maria, it had been possible for my mother to keep her apartment in Munich.

After a second stroke, my father was moved to a clinic in Bogenhausen in Munich. Vivian, who had always loved my father very much, came from the United States to Munich in order to say good-bye to him. Her presence was very comforting for me. Only in the difficult hours of his death did I become fully aware of how much I had loved and respected him. Father had carried his difficult lot with impressive greatness. Stoical and disciplined, I had never heard him complain. Father died on April 20, 1979. He remains a model for the whole family.

The Man in the Shadow

During the time of the divorce and in the following years, my profession was of great support to me. The current projects and the reputation I had won over the years comforted me during the disappointment with Franz. I began to get used to the life of a single woman. In fact, I felt it as relief to be able to live without pressure, according to my own needs and that of my profession.

Several years earlier I had become acquainted with a professor of geodesy at the university. He had often watched me from afar during our lunch hours in the Mensa restaurant, when I had picked at my food without an appetite and with red, swollen eyes. Sometimes I had told him about the escapades of my unfaithful husband. He was a very caring and warm-hearted bachelor who had decided that he had to save me. However, in all the years of a comfortable friendship, I could not respond to the feelings he held for me. He would, however, not be put off and remained a good and patient friend with whom I could discuss all my problems and who would remain a faithful helper for me and my daughters at all times.

Prof. Gustav Neugebauer, the "man in the shadow", El Gouna Gouda in Egypt

We undertook several wonderful trips together to Florida, Turkey, and Italy, but I could not respond with the hoped-for closeness and warmth.

Once I even invited him to my beloved *Quo Vadis* in Italy. But this was nothing for Gustl. He did not react as I had expected. He remarked that in Italy there was too much garbage on the streets and that my house was too open and windy, and too cold. No word about the beauty of the place! He felt so uncomfortable that he moved to a hotel.

The reason was probably his bad health from his time in the war as a POW of the Russians. In addition, he did not like Franz, who had renovated the house with much too much "splendor."

Gustl had grown up in the Sudetenland. Patriotic and idealistic, he had been very young when he went to war. In Russia, he was wounded very seriously. Finally, at the end of the war, he had to witness the terrible fate of the expulsion of his people by the Czechs. He probably had never quite gotten over these severe physical and psychological wounds.

Despite the fact that I loved my profession, I had decided to retire at the age of sixty. My daughters were afraid that I would not know what to do with the amount of free time I would have. But in fact I was looking forward to the time when I could do all the things I was really interested in. I had so many interests. In all my life I have never ever felt bored.

The Grandchildren

On November 1, 1989, Vivian's first child was born in Australia, little Antonia. She named the girl in memory of my father, Anton Rasso Schrankl. Originally, she should have been named Aloisia, after my mother, but David did not like this name. Antonia was born one day before my mother's ninetieth birthday. What a nice birthday present!

In order to honor my mother accordingly, I had invited the whole family Schrankl to a celebration on the Fraueninsel (the women's island, where there is a 1,200-year-old convent) in Lake Chiemsee. Uncles, aunts, and friends—the whole Schrankl family—they all came by boat to the island. Despite the fact that my mother, modest and solitary as she was, had not wanted a celebration, the event turned out to be an evocative and memorable feast, which she did enjoy very much after all.

I had rented a NICE room.

Ariane and grandmother Lulu enjoying a "Mass", Maria, Lulu, Antonia and Amelia, Munich Germany, 1990, Family photo

I had rented a nicely room in the Hotel Linde under the linden trees on the island. Accompanied by the sounds of a local harp player, we enjoyed the traditional Bavarian specialties and exchanged the latest family news.

What a picturesque view! Most of the women were dressed in the traditional Bavarian dresses, and the men in leather knickerbockers. It was wonderful to see the large Schrankl family gathered together in the nicely paneled room with its original "Kachelofen" (tiled oven). The scene reminded me of the quaint pictures of the 19th-century painter Wilhelm Leibl.

I gave a short speech and then announced the great birthday surprise: the news about the birth of Mother's first great-grandchild, my first grandchild, in Australia. We raised our glasses to the health of the little Antonia in the far off country. Now we had three "scorpions" (the zodiac sign of Scorpio) in the immediate family!

Nine months later I set out for Australia to see my granddaughter.

Eva and little Antonia in Sidney, Australia, 1990, Family photo

David had found a job as manager of gas stations with Shell Oil Company and was making a good living. Thus Vivian, who had been working as a photographer, could now stay home with her little darling.

Little Toni seemed to be an above-average intelligent little person. She watched everything with interest. She missed nothing. When an object had caught her attention, she could occupy herself with it thoroughly and for a long time.

One thing I noticed already in the first days: this baby never smiled. When I told Toni later when she was a teenager about my first impression of her as a baby, she said: "Smiling is so boring!"

Vivi and David showed me Sydney, an impressive, international metropolitan city by the sea. It was influenced by the spirit and tradition of its white Anglo-Saxon immigrants and the first conquerors who came to this vast country, many of them against their own will.

We took a trip to the Gold Coast in Queensland, and visited parts of the outback, far away from civilization. I was amazed at the enormous distances in this continent and also about the strength of the relentless sun. The light-skinned people can only stay on the beach with long-sleeved shirts, sun hats, sunglasses, and sunscreen. The sea is wild and dangerous. The sea breaks on the rocky coastline in huge waves. On many beaches swimming is not possible because one has to watch out for sharks. But also in the interior lakes it is not safe to simply go swimming, because there the crocodiles live.

After my trip through this harsh country, I was no longer surprised that the population also showed a certain "rough charm."

David was a sports fanatic. He loved motocross racing, a sport I had seen in Europe. Vivian had no interest in the sport. But here in this rough land it requires great skill from its drivers and is accordingly very dangerous. This challenge was, however, not enough for David. He also trained for the "Iron Man" competition, an international triathlon competition in Hawaii that demands an extremely high degree of endurance and strength from the competitors. The participants have to swim 2.4 miles in the ocean, ride a bicycle for 112 miles across the uneven lava field, and finally continue to run 2.2 miles. And all this while the heat rises to over ninety degrees in the shade.

The newest hobby of David was "bungee jumping," which is more of a test for courage than a sport. In Germany, this type of entertainment has long been forbidden, because it is too dangerous.

Vivian must have felt my reservations about the country in which she now lived, because she assured me several times that she felt very well in Australia and liked living there.

She especially liked the wildness of the country and its naturalness. I found Vivian quite changed. She seemed to have given up a lot of her likes and dislikes and was adhering to her husband's value system. For example, her attitude towards the aborigines was now negative, and she considered the idea of the "survival of the fittest" (the stronger wins) perfectly okay.

The young father had his own educational methods. He did not tolerate it when Vivian cuddled or spoiled the baby. He considered it most important to toughen up his little daughter.

Vivian dared not contradict him, and my good advice was not wanted.

I had gained the impression that in David's family every showing of emotion or empathy was considered a sign of weakness. Was it that the people were influenced by their harsh country and tough history, when only the strongest and fittest had managed to survive? Was this really the right atmosphere for my Vivian?

When I had returned to Munich and some time had passed, I tried to put myself into David's world. His parents had worked for an Australian cement factory and had been sent by this firm to South America, Israel, and Germany. David's mother was an excellent housewife and cooked very well. She had devoted her whole life to her family. But she only was able to submit to the men in the family. She could not stand up for herself. For generations there had never been any professional opportunity for the women of the McCasker family. I tried to understand, but my emancipated way of thinking was out of place.

In 1992 Shell Oil Company sent David to Houston, Texas. In April 1991, Vivian's second daughter was born, little Amelia. Now Antonia had a little sister. I was somewhat relieved to know the family would live in America, which is at least a part of the Western hemisphere. Now Houston seemed much closer than "Down Under," as Australia is often called.

On July 7, 1990, my grandson Anton was born in Ft. Myers, Florida. His mother Ariane was well and the proud father was happy to hold the little boy in his arms.

Again, I took some time out and flew to Florida. There I heard the good news that Ariane and John intended to come live in Germany in the near future. I returned to Munich happy and satisfied.

Anton and little sister Sophia, Matlacha, FL 1993, Family photo

On July 1, 1993, Anton's little sister was born in Florida. Sophia became the sunshine of the family. One year later, the young family arrived in Munich.

My happy state as a grandmother was only of short duration. Ariane could not get along with the German weather and the mentality of the people. She also found it difficult to live in a small house with little space around her. My very lively grandchildren were not received very well in many places. They simply had too much energy. Whenever they stormed down the stairs or would not sit still in a restaurant, there was trouble. This meant constant worry for Ariane. She wanted to raise her children in complete freedom and was always in conflict with her surroundings.

John actually liked it in Germany, and especially he liked Bavaria. His practice position in the architectural office had been for only three years, and his contract was not renewed. The family returned to the United States in 1996. They moved to Houston, as Vivian had suggested. She had always wanted to have her sister close by.

I was happy with this decision, because Vivian was in need of her sister's presence, because she had had hard times behind her.

The change from Australia to Houston had started a serious marriage crisis. The problems escalated. After a violent quarrel, including physical abuse, the situation had become so unbearable for Vivian that the only possibility she saw was leaving the house together with her children.

When I heard about this development, I took the next plane to Houston in order to assist her.

Vivian had already found support in a house with a group of companions in distress and a very fine psychologist. She left and went to the house, and she received the best of care.

Four weeks later she had a job. She looked a lot better than she had on the day I had come to see her and had found the courage to take her life into her own hands. She worked for an advertising agency as a graphic designer. She did not earn very much there, but the job was decisive for her self-confidence. I noticed that Vivian had also found consolation and strength in the Catholic Church.

When Vivian moved into her own apartment with the children, David was, of course, not at all in agreement. He wanted her to return and live again within his family, where everyone stood under his command. But Vivian would have none of that idea. He asked me to intercede in his interest. But I rejected the idea. This was Vivian's decision alone, and I would not get involved, nor did I want Vivian to doubt her own decision. From then on David considered me his enemy.

Vivian and David were divorced. The children would live with her, but she had to share the custody with David. She could also not move out of the city.

Two years later, Achille came into Vivian's life. He was a good-looking Italian from Sicily. He was somewhat older than Vivian, but had a big heart for children. Achille had been Honorary Consul of Italy in Houston and had four grown sons and many grandchildren. Most of them lived in Houston. Now Vivian had become part of a typical large Sicilian-style family. The two fell in love immediately and are very happy together.

For her two girls, the divorce of their parents caused many problems. Most of them were caused by their father not respecting their mother and her decisions. Both girls had developed a very close relationship with their father. After the divorce, they started to idolize him. They were rebellious toward their mother, which is typical for adolescents, and they even insisted on moving in to their father's house in Oregon (David had gone to court to ask the legal system to allow the girls to live with him if they so chose).

That fact caused their mother great heartache.

I hoped that as they grew up, the girls would develop a more objective and independent judgment of their own about the reasons for their parents' divorce.

Eva and the grandchildren, Houston, TX, 1997, Photo by Barfield Photography L to R Amelia, Anton, Sophia, Eva, Antonia

"The big sister," Antonia & Amelia, Houston, TX, 1995 Photo by Barfield Photography

Happy days in Quo Vadis, Italy, 1997, Family photo

*Three angels in paradise, Vachendorf, Germany, 1992,
L to R Amelia, Antonia, Anton Family photo*

*Four actors on stage on the roof terrace of Quo Vadis, Italy 1997,
Family photo From L to R Sophia, Anton, Antonia, Amelia*

Three generations, Munich, Germany, L to R Ariane, John, Eva, Vivian, Sophia, Amelia, Great grandmother (Uromi), Antonia, Anton, Munich, Germany, 1997 Meinen Photograpie GmbH

Wedding of Achille Arcidiacono and Vivian, Houston, TX, 1999, Family photo

Chapter 18: A Russian Adventure

The German-Russian Friendship Club

On October 31, 1992, I retired. Again this meant another farewell. I had decided on this date, had prepared myself for it, and was looking forward to it. Despite this, the farewell was not as easy for me as I had expected. I did not mind turning over the job that I had had for almost twenty years to my successor, but it was not so easy to leave behind such an important period of my life.

Only three years had passed since the Berlin Wall had fallen on November 9, 1989. Gorbachev had torn down the "Iron Curtain" and Germany received the reunion between East and West Germany with great joy. There was a sense of a new era about to dawn, and we all shared this feeling. In this sense, I had started to establish connections, to get to know people, and to become friend with people in Russia. Encouraged by the good experiences with the German-American Club and the German-French Club, I had founded the Friendship Club. My curiosity was raised. I had seen a lot of the world, but I had never had any connection to the world behind the "Iron Curtain," Russia and China.

The endless countryside of Russia, painting by Isaac Leviton, Moscow, Russia (see Source of Illustrations)

My great-great-grandfather had fought for Napoleon in Russia. Now I wanted to get to know the country and the people to whom he owed his life so long ago.

A connection was made quickly. The community of Neubiberg, the seat of our university, was "Partner City" with Chernogolovka, a small town north of Moscow, and had developed an aid program for that town in Russia. Within the scope of that program, the first Russian visitors were beginning to come to Neubiberg.

Then a delegation from Neubiberg went to Chernogolovka. The mayor of Neubiberg had hoped to help build up democratic structures in the newly developed local municipality. The community of Neubiberg collected over a million euros for their Russian friends. That money was to serve not only for building up of community administration but also for establishing city-sponsored places for the education of young people. Part of the plan was to build a City Hall that was modeled after the city hall in Neubiberg. The idea was to help people to help themselves.

Chernogolovka is situated about 40 miles north of Moscow. It is a small town, like Neubiberg, and like so many of pre-planned cities that had been established during the time of Stalin. Most of these towns served one particular purpose: scientific and technical research for either the military armament industry or other government projects.

Their residents lived as an elite scientific community cut off from the rest of the country in order to keep the state of the research conducted there a secret.

On the road to Moscow, Russia, 1993, Family photo

Chernogolovka, Russia, 1993, Family photo

Chernogolovka was also a city with military secrets. It was also the one of the seats of the Russian Academy of Sciences. These circumstances were enough cause for the inhabitants to live a very secluded life.

Perestroika had loosened the fetters of the Russian people and was beginning to change the society, but the old structures were everywhere intact and the Academy of Science determined life in Chernogolovka. The Academy absolutely rejected the newly elected mayor and his local council.

They looked down with haughtiness on these "Western democratic toy games."

After some soul-searching it became clear to me that I would not be able to do much alone on my own. Therefore, I founded a club. Its members were some interested professors and students along with some rich business people as sponsors. It was called the German-Russian Association. Its purpose was, first of all, to promote communication between our two countries and then getting to know each other's cultures. As a constructive contribution on my part, I wanted to contribute what I could do best: I planned the establishment of a language center. Our Language Center at the university would serve as a model.

My first step was to take a few trips together with some interested professors to get to know the country and the people, and to establish some ties of personal friendship.

THE PEOPLE OF CHERNOGOLOVKA

My first trip to Russia changed many of my previous views about Russia. I had never before encountered such heartwarming friendship and hospitality as the people of Chernogolovka showed toward me. My contact person was Alexeji Ovchinnikov, a doctor of physics and a member of the Russian Academy of Sciences. I had met him during a formal dinner in Neubiberg given by the mayor of Neubiberg and the president of the university. He spoke English quite well, and we immediately took a liking to each other. During this dinner we talked about the present political situation in Russia and about Glasnost, and we decided that I would go to visit the Russian Academy of Sciences, which had a regional center in his hometown, Chernogolovka.

My Russian friends, Chernogolovka, Russia, 1993

In Chernogolovka he had prepared everything for my visit, and had made the critical contacts that permitted me to get a visa. One could not enter the country without such an invitation signed by some official organization. When I arrived, he hosted me in the well-known Russian manner, that is, hospitality 24 hours a day. Everything was perfectly organized; it was not considered right for me to go anywhere alone.

The result of that first trip was this decision: During my next six weeks of vacation, at spring break, I would teach the course "Rhetoric and Public Speaking" to interested professors at the Academy. That way I would be able to meet people and conduct a feasibility study for the Language Center.

I would be able to see the conditions firsthand. There were a lot of questions, such as whether there was a market for such a center, what the language proficiency of the future students was, how much would they be able to pay, whether there were good teachers available, what they would have to be paid, and who would work together with me.

Other questions I had were about the trustworthiness of the people and whether we could find space for the center, whether interference by the Russian government was to be expected, and other questions.

I spent my whole vacation that summer in Chernogolovka perfectly taken care of by two cheerful language teachers, Vera and Marina, and of course, by Alexeji.

During my stay he had organized my language course, had found a large lecture hall at the Academy, and had invited his favorite professors.

The Academy had made one of its guest apartments available, and a lady was found who cooked lunch for me and supplied me with the very best that was to be found in Russia at that time—milk, honey, good bread, and of course vodka. Every morning when I left my apartment, Vera and Marina were already waiting for me at the end of the staircase and accompanied me to the grounds of the Academy.

Russian women pay a lot of attention to their outer appearance. First of all, Vera and Marina taught me how I had to dress according to my role as a teacher at the Academy. I had not thought it fitting the situation in Russia to bring elegant clothes from Munich. On the contrary, I made a point of dressing rather plainly. But Vera and Marina were not pleased about that at all.

"How can the students get a good impression of you and your teaching, if you look like a woman from the working class?" So they decked me out as best they could. They lent me a nice shawl and some precious earrings, and started to give me the appropriate makeup. Only after I suited their picture of what they thought I should look like did they introduce me with great pride to the academic community.

People in Russia have enormous pride. Despite the poorest living conditions, the women always looked well dressed and nicely made up. Many times that meant sharing a nice winter coat among friends. Most of the clothes could only be obtained by means of exchange for other services. Many women tailor their clothes themselves and show great talent.

I soon found out that in Russia it was the women who kept the community together. It was they who kept up living standards for themselves, their children, and their husbands. A good education was of prime importance. Most of the children played a musical instrument, and the girls went to ballet classes. Every family owned a whole library of good books and a collection of interesting records with classical music, and often the latest jazz from the United States. Even if there was little room in a small apartment, bookshelves lined every wall.

I was impressed and tried to remember that I certainly did not see a representative sample of the whole population.

The men, however, seemed to be in crisis. Either they had lost their position as well-known professors, or they earned such a small salary for their work as to be insulting. And this circumstance was in spite of the fact that they were excellent scientists. Many times vodka had to comfort them, because everything depended upon money at that time, and individual achievement no longer mattered.

The wives went to the market to sell hand-painted Easter eggs or little pictures to the tourists. That way they earned some small additional money to pay for the rising costs of food and other goods for their households. Many things were acquired by barter. Ten hours of English instruction for the child and the mother would be exchanged for a new dress for the teacher.

Without their "dachas" ("country houses") my friends would not have been able to make ends meet. There they raised fresh vegetable and fruits in tiny gardens. The small plants, raised from seeds, were placed on a window sill in February to catch every ray of sun. After the middle of May everybody moved to his or her "dacha" and all other activities came to a rest. In the fall, the families gathered mushrooms in the surrounding forests, and dried them for a tasty dish in the cold season. Vegetable and fruit in glasses ensured the necessary vitamins for the wintertime.

Let me return to my English classes. The president of the Academy had given permission to me to use the large assembly hall for my classes.

On my first day, my heart beat violently. When I entered the hall, I found that fourteen highly motivated "students" were already waiting for me. I could see in their curious faces that they had high expectations. They were well-educated men and women, scientists all of them, who were waiting eagerly to improve their speaking skills in English

They already had a remarkable knowledge of reading and writing English. They were enthusiastic and involved, and wanted to know everything about Western countries, democracy, and the "good life," which, they believed, contrary to themselves, the West had been enjoying without doubt for many years. The people hoped that together with "democracy," the "good life" would also come to their lives quickly.

What an illusion! I for my part wanted to know everything about Russia from my intelligent students: the history, country, people—everything was interesting to me.

I learned rather quickly how life functioned in this country; the key word was "connections." Without the right connections nothing was possible in Russia. To have connections meant to be able to survive in daily life as well as to enjoy professional advancement. Connections were also the only guarantee for personal safety. For this reason, one depended only on the contacts within one's own social group. Contacts with people of other groups were always viewed with suspicion. Within their own group the people were enormously open. But everyone had to learn to act correctly within the group. As soon as one moved beyond the group, he or she was suspected by that group of being a "traitor."

Teaching English at the Russian Academy of Science, Chernogolovka, Russia, 1994, Family photo

Since "Perestroika" ("openness"), life had already changed radically for the professors at the Academy. The Russian government supported the Academy only to a small extent. That meant that professors who had received around 300 DM per month before now had to find someone who would pay them even that meager sum. The main job of the president of the Academy consisted of supplying his professors with fuel for heating and with food. Finally, he had an idea of starting a vodka brewery. That meant that the proud Russian Academy of Sciences had to sell vodka in order to feed its staff!

At any rate, that method turned out to be very successful. The "Academy Vodka," sold in the most attractive bottles, became known as the best vodka in Moscow.

It was obvious that the disinfecting effect of vodka kept the Russians pretty healthy. Hygienic conditions in the country were beyond description.

I well remember my first and last visit to the local marketplace. I looked around. The range of goods to sell was rather meager. However, there was good bread and lots of crates with potatoes.

Suddenly an old rattling car arrived and stopped in front of the empty butcher shop. The driver got out and opened the trunk. I could make out half of a recently butchered cow in a large puddle of blood. The women rushed to the cadaver and everyone tried to cut off the best piece. I doubted that the animal had been inspected and thought: "I have seen this scene during the Easter ceremony

Behind the Kremlin walls with Alexeji, Moscow, Russia, 1994, Family photo

in the Ethiopian village!" At this sight, I suddenly felt an urgent need for a glass of vodka. I steered toward the next stand in the market. There were plenty of these bottles to be found. "I swear that I will now become a vegetarian," I thought.

The Red Square in Moscow, Russia 1994, Family photo

This promise proved hard to keep. My friends really did everything to make my stay a pleasant one. Where they had found all these tasty specialties with which they spoiled me remained their secret. They took turns to set up a joyful party every evening with lots of vodka, champagne, and the typical humorous and profound toasts that are customary for parties in Russia.

When I got the chance to call my mother, I told her that never before had I eaten and laughed as much as during my stay with my Russian friends.

A short history of the country:

In the 13th century, warlike hoards of horsemen under Batu Khan, a grandson of Genghis Khan, invaded the areas of the Russians, a Caucasian people. In 1206 Genghis Khan had consolidated all of the

Eva in Suzdal, Russia, 1994, Family photo

Mongolian tribes and was threatening Europe. In the course of this siege, the population of Russia was reduced by two-thirds and many inhabitants were reduced to serfdom. After the defeat of the empire of Kiev (the Christian "Third Roman Empire') in 1240, the country was ruled by "the Golden Hordes" for the next 200 years and had to pay tribute to the Mongolian conquerors. These did not depose of the local rulers, but imposed overwhelming tributes on them, which these, in turn, extorted from their serfs often by cruel methods.

Only at the end of the 15th century Iwan II succeeded after cruel internal struggles, to free Russia from the "Golden Horde," the Islamic khanate that was the "scourge of Russia."

In 1472 Batu Khan married the daughter of the last Byzantine ruler, Constantine, and considered himself his heir, and Russia and its Christian Orthodox church as "the third Rome."

Russia thus missed the important developments in the rest of Europe during the Middle Ages that made for the establishment of a middle class of guilds of artisans and business owners. Full of self-confidence and pride, these people built those wealthy and beautiful medieval towns that are typical of urban life in Europe during the 13th and 14th century.

Several times Alexeji organized trips by car to Moscow and to places in the vicinity of the capital to show me the ancient cities of the "Golden Ring," Sagorsk, Vladimir, and Suzdal.

The medieval city of Sagorsk (originally called "Sergey Posad") greeted us from afar behind the old city wall with the golden-roofed domes of its glorious churches. It was and is today the seat of the Russian Orthodox Church. Here is its main shrine and spiritual center, the Cathedral of the Holy Trinity and the Monastery of St. Sergius. As soon as we entered through the ancient city gate, I could feel how this town has been able to preserve the original atmosphere and charm of times gone by. Even during Soviet times, the town was allowed to continue practicing the religious rituals of this faith. Its many churches had been recently repaired and the streets were full of young, good-looking Russian monks. Marina told me that in order to become a monk one not only had to excel in learning and dedication but one also had to be tall, good-looking, and have a beautiful voice.

I was surprised to see so many young men who had dedicated their lives to their faith.

The city I liked best was Suzdal. It was a charming small town on the unspoiled banks of a scenic little river, where I immediately felt the breath of medieval times. Like all the other religious centers, this little town had also been plundered and burned down by the Mongolian invaders. For two hundred years it lay in ashes until it was rebuilt. The typical old Russian wooden churches lend this town its distinctive contemplative and timeless atmosphere. After the fall of Kiev in 1240, Suzdal became the seat of the Russian Orthodox Church. During this time the five monasteries were built as well as the many, charming small churches. It is told that many wives of tsars who had fallen out of favor with their husband the tsar had spent the rest of their unhappy lives behind these walls. I imagined, however, that they might have preferred this pleasant, quiet place to the court in Moscow full of murderous intrigues.

Today the "new Russian businessmen" from Moscow book weeks of religious contemplation with the nuns in some of the monasteries. There is no better place than Suzdal for this kind of reflection.

At the end of my stay I decided to take a trip to St. Petersburg. The trip by night train from Moscow was not altogether without its dangers. After all the passengers were aboard, the doors were locked and the whole train was closely guarded. Men in dark uniforms and a gun in their holster patrolled every compartment. My compartment was quite comfortable and the bed was clean. I was lucky, because there was no other passenger and the guard took advantage of this and he took his shorts naps in the lower cot below mine. Tea was served, but I did not take advantage of it, because I was afraid to enter the toilets.

I was glad to arrive in St. Petersburg early the next morning. The wonderful old city with its golden cupolas made up for the long trip. I started my tour around the city at the Neva with its powerful type of magic. It is surprising how well the old palaces have been kept up during the Soviet times. It was obvious that the government had stage-managed very well the enormous difference between the unbelievable, extravagant splendor of the tsar's court and the dismal poverty of the simple population. I could just feel a revolution brewing in the air. Even while in Moscow, I still felt this difference. The carefully guarded sumptuous palaces of the Kremlin, and the museums like the Tretjekov Gallery on the one hand, and the poverty of most of the population on the other. "Real Potemkin villages, if you compare the living conditions of most of the population," I thought.

When I returned to Chernogolovka, my friends continued to take care of me with great dedication. However, this care not only served my personal well-being but also was part of a complete surveillance. The Russian secret service, the KGB, did not leave any foreigner out of sight. After all, Chernogolovka was one of the secret cities, in former times completely closed to foreigners. What did this lady, a member the University of the German Federal Armed Forces really want? Did she really come here for no other reason than to teach the professors of the Russian Academy of Sciences English? How strange! Why would anybody want to do this? This was very suspicious.

That thought, however, did not diminish my thirst for adventure in the least, and for my friends, providing for my needs was not an easy task. This was true, in particular, when I insisted on taking the bus to Moscow one day. They were not allowed to let me out of their sight. They were beginning to groan. But they accepted it with their typical

Russian joyousness and were secretly looking forward to an invitation to Munich.

The German class in a Russian school in Chernogolovka, Russia, 1994, Family photo

Most of all I was impressed by the children. I was invited many times to school classes. I noticed every time the heartfelt relationship between the teachers and their pupils. Despite strict discipline in the classroom, I felt this atmosphere of devotion on the side of the teachers and the loving respect of the children.

These teachers, most of them women, really took care of all the problems of their charges, even beyond the classroom, and at every time of the day or night. Many spent their free time together with the children of their class.

The children, in turn, showed their gratefulness by almost effusive signs of love and respect. Girls, as well as boys, showed their best manners. They were interested in learning as much as they could and even read advanced books about chemistry and physics, foreign languages, or history beyond their homework, which they showed to me with great pride when I was invited to their homes. The greatest compliment one could make about these children was: "He/she has a thirst for knowledge."

The girls struck me as being extraordinarily pretty and graceful. They either played some musical instrument or took ballet lessons, or both. The parents were very proud of their offspring, of their education and their good manners. When the adults sat down at the dinner table with their guests, the children politely withdrew to their rooms to read books.

My course in rhetoric was coming to an end. As a final exercise, I had planned a debate, where the class members could choose their own topic. They were to argue against each other in two groups. Afterward, each group would defend the opposite position. My students chose this topic: "Do Russian scientists have to leave their country in order to continue to serve science?" The only answer seemed to be: "Yes." The only argument they could find for remaining in Russia was the love for one's country.

My course was a great success and ended with the usual good-bye party.

The members of the class organized a picnic in the woods. They made a big fire over which they roasted spicy schaschlik, which we washed down with enormous amounts of vodka. There were no soft drinks or water and instead many heartrending, melancholy songs and guitar music. Thanks to God, I can hold my liquor quite well, because it is simply a part of good behavior to be able to drink vodka at any time of the day.

Picnic in the woods with my students from The Academy of Science, Chernogolovka, 1994, Family photo

THE LANGUAGE CENTER IN CHERNOGOLOVKA

When I arrived back in Munich I knew what I wanted: a Language Center at the Russian Academy of Sciences in Chernogolovka. It would be a language center that met the same criteria for excellence as the Language Center in Munich. In Chernogolovka I could make a contribution to the quality of life of the people, because this work was what I knew most about. I wanted to show modern methods of foreign language teaching and criteria for testing language skills using certificates that would clearly document a person's familiarity with a foreign language in all four skills: listening, reading, speaking, and writing.

I wanted to build an organization that would finance itself and have its own legal basis in order to offer certificates for language proficiency.

That way all children could be taught and not only those of rich parents who could afford private lessons. Later the teachers could take over the Language Center themselves. I could offer help to the teachers to help themselves. According to the proverb: "If you give a man a fish, you feed him for one day. But if you give him a fishing pole, he can feed himself for the rest of his life."

The two teachers, Marina and Vera, seemed well fit for this project. We soon found appropriate space, the "House of the Scientists," which was run by the Academy and was situated in the center of the little town. I succeeded in negotiating a good financial agreement, and we could rent some very nice rooms.

Back in Munich I was able to find appropriate equipment for the classrooms and office as well as language training material and books. Thanks to the generous contributions of the members of our German-Russian Association, I was able to buy a suitable copying machine. I was afraid that it might "get lost" during the shipping to Russia, so I took the machine as hand luggage on board the Aeroflot on my next trip. The stewardess was extremely nice and helpful, and even removed the whole seat next to me to make enough space for my package. I had decided to keep a watchful eye on my precious freight.

I was received with great joy and a huge bunch of flowers by my two ladies and Alexeji upon arrival at the Moscow airport. Personally taking items into Russia rather than shipping them was always the most secure method of getting things there. I had sent many children's books and a television set to Chernogolovka by the usual aid shipment method from Neubiberg, but none of them ever arrived at our address, even though I was present when all the other items of the aid package were unloaded. The books and the TV had simply been "lost." I did have a good idea where they had gone to, but insisting on that would have meant starting a fight with the municipal employees.

Despite my good intentions, every one of my steps was being watched with suspicion and envy. I was not in the correct social group and did not have the "right friends," as I was told later.

A famous proverb says: "You cannot understand Russia with your logical mind, you can only understand it with your heart." In Russia I met again the "Slavic" soul: emotional, irrational, and wild. I met all those qualities that I knew from my mother and Franz. I was most of all impressed, however, by the unbelievable patience and the endurance of these people. Most of the situations that I met in Chernogolovka would have raised protest and uproar in Germany—endless queues in front of stores or public establishments, lack of medicines and nursing care in the hospitals, dirty staircases in the houses that were never cleaned or repaired, areas where there was absolutely no lighting, and salaries that were not paid out for months. I was filled with great pity for these friendly and hardworking people every time they told me about their difficult life. I somehow was attracted to them, but at the same time I was filled with a certain trepidation, because I could not figure them out with my logical left-sided brain. I simply could not understand how these people could be so warmhearted and empathetic on the one side and on the other side so cruel and inhuman, as their history shows. Maybe there are still a lot of Mongolian genes forming part of the character.

The Language Center I was creating was intended to finance itself. The idea was this: Instead of making one student pay $12 for one English lesson, we could teach 12 students together in one class. In the beginning, the Center was financed by the contributions of the German-Russian Friendship Club, and the plan was that it would later generate enough income to meet its expenses, such as teacher salaries and rent.

We would offer English and German on different levels. Vera and Marina, however, reacted with a complete lack of understanding of this idea. It was only because I was their friend and because they liked me that they agreed to my plan. They thought: "Why should I teach a whole class with 12 kids in the classroom instead of one rich kid in my home for the same amount of money?" They did not think that if they worked together as a team they would be able to build an organization that had an advantage for everyone.

In Munich I organized a two-week practice teaching course for Vera and Marina in my Language Center at the University of Munich. At the Center I could introduce them to the organization, teaching methods, examination and testing methods, and curriculum planning. I particularly wanted to introduce them to the methods for examination and the assessment of the results.

Vera and Marina arrived in Neubiberg and were overjoyed about their first invitation to Germany. They assisted me during examinations in the four skills: LSRW—Listening, Speaking, Reading, and Writing on all levels, one to four. On completion, students received a certificate that showed the student's achievements.

Then we drew up a suitable certificate for our Language Center. It looked very professional. After finishing a course in English or German (Vera also taught German) the students would receive a certificate that showed their competency in the language in the four skills (LSRW) on levels 1 to 4.

I put a lot of effort into drawing up by-laws for the Language Center. I even had it checked for legal mistakes by the head of our university.

Back in Chernogolovka, I handed the statutes over to the president of the Academy with some pride. He seemed surprised. He ran over the text with a friendly smile, put the document into his drawer, and locked it with a thoughtful expression on his face. That document I gave him probably amused him; written rules on paper probably had no meaning.

The beautiful accounting book that I brought from Munich met with a similar fate. Income and expenses of the Center were supposed to be correctly documented—on one page, the income from the course fees, and on the another page, expenses for rent, teacher salaries, and so forth. I even had brought a file folder for receipts, because I wanted to know what happened to the money I brought from Germany. But the idea of a written receipt for anything seemed to be absolutely new to them.

When I asked Vera and Marina to sign a receipt for the copying machine and the material I had brought, they signed everything blindly. Once I drew Vera's attention to the fact that she had signed a receipt for DM 100 but had only received DM 50. She responded: "If you say so, you will probably be right." Trust in a person was of more value than accurate accounting. Keeping accounts in numbers was of absolutely no importance to my two Russian friends. After thinking about it, it seemed that somehow that made sense: Signing something for your boss was okay if he was your friend. If he was not, refusing to confirm something would not change anything anyway.

Another problem was the raising of tuition fees. Vera and Marina did not find it possible to charge the same amount for the courses from everybody. "We cannot ask the same amount from our friends as from a strange person," was their argument. They would have rather paid the missing fees from their own pocket than to ask the fixed price from their friends and acquaintances.

With our paramilitary guards and my teachers from the Language Center, Chernogolovka, 1994, Family photo,

Finally, I could not prevent the fees from finding their way immediately into the pockets of Vera and Marina. I also could not convince them to keep account of incoming and outgoing money. They remained of the opinion that bookkeeping was not worth the trouble. The Center would either have to pay too high taxes (52%) or the mafia would become interested in our business and would probably also want their share of the already low profit of the Center. It turned out that this was also the reason why—or so I was told—we could not do any advertising for our Language Center.

The Center is still in existence today, but it is not run in the same way as I had envisioned it. Teaching methods and the type of certification (competency in LSRW) have been well established. However, one cannot speak of an independent and correct keeping of financial accounts. Everything depends on the particular teacher in charge. I did reach my goal of introducing a modern system of teaching and testing foreign languages, and fair methods of examination. But I did not succeed in introducing a system whereby every adult, child, or young adult, regardless of ability to pay, had the chance to be taught equally, and the establishment of an institution independent from its personal management, one that has its own operating rules and its own legal basis.

I had probably imagined my challenge in Russia to be less complicated than it was, but I returned to Munich with many new experiences, and I had made a new good friend.

Alexeji is twenty-two years younger than I, but this does not have any influence on our friendship. We are connected by a spiritual bond that is difficult to describe. I would call it a type of "soul bonding." It means an almost telepathic connection that we were able to keep up over all these years.

I had met Alexeji right at the beginning of my Russian engagement. At that time, as a professor of physics at the university and a member of the Russian Academy of Sciences, he was caught up in the waves of rapid political and economic change. The "ideal world" in which he had grown up was breaking apart, and he took the political upheaval in his country very seriously.

I cannot say that it was love at first sight, but it was a strong feeling of liking right from the beginning. We were on the same wavelength in a most striking way. He would start a sentence, and I would continue it in his words and vice versa. His extensive classical education astounded me. He knew not only the Russian writers and composers, but he was also acquainted with those of the Western cultures. When I cited a line from the protagonist in Herman Hesse's *Siddhartha*, he could continue it. His knowledge of Western music and jazz was way beyond my own. Many times he presented me with some classical music CDs that were new to me.

Whether we met in Munich or in Chernogolovka, or talked on the telephone, we always thought about the same things and shared the same opinion, or were concerned about the same problem.

Both of us were aware of the limits of our relationship and were very concerned not to destroy our special friendship by overstepping its boundaries. Alexeji put our relationship into apt words. In Capri we once visited the chapel of St. George in the Villa San Michele. I said: "Let's pray that St. George will protect our friendship."

"Yes," he answered. "Let's pray that he will protect us from ourselves."

One cannot actually understand or analyze this relationship. It is astounding that two human beings, so different in background and living conditions, can find an understanding on the same wavelength such as this. What we both have in common is that we both love freedom and that, like two independent birds, we look at the problems of our world from a distance. Too much closeness would certainly not be conducive to our friendship.

Several years ago Alexeji finished his degree in constitutional law. Today he is advisor to the Duma and teaches as professor in the School for International Law in Moscow.

We have remained "soul mates" and are today still in contact.

The Russian delegation at the Oktoberfest in Munich, Germany, 1996, Family photo
L to R Prof. Wolfgang Tiller; UniBwM, Prof. Baturin, Director of the Institute of Chemical Physics at the Russian Academy of Science, Prof. Aldoshin; Dr. Alexeji Ovchninnikov; Center: Eva Maria Huschka, Director of Language Department at the University of the Federal Armed Forces of Germany

Chapter 19: Panta Rei—My Life Today

Globalization and Change

Today I live alone. But I am not lonely. Neither am I ever bored. I feel content in my world. Europe is my homeland—Bavaria, the Chiemgau, Italy, and my lovely apartment at the Wiener Platz in the center of Munich.

To me it is truly the ideal place to live my lifestyle.

The Wiener Platz is really a village square surrounded by the park of the River Isar right in the center of a big town.

It has, like villages in the countryside, a church with a tall gothic tower from which the bells toll at noontime and the beginning of the weekend.

The square is situated in the old part of Munich, and there are many small houses still there that date back into the 16th century.

Then there is the Gasthaus with its spacious beer garden, shadowed by tall, 100-year-old and older chestnut trees. If you like, you can bring your own picnic basket with food and your tablecloth. As soon as the sun comes out of the clouds, this garden, which is right below my balcony, is humming with the laughter of happy people, the clear voices of children, and the soft tinkling of the beer mugs.

I can eat my dinner on the balcony and enjoy the crowd of happy people below me. Munich seems to be celebrating all the time—celebrating life.

Several small cafés and an Italian ice cream place have put out tables and chairs, with sun umbrellas that always attract people.

At the market I can buy everything I need in the little huts that sell vegetables and fruit, some local meat and a stand with wonderful fresh fish. Everything else, like a bank, pharmacy, drugstore is close by.

From here I can take the tram to town, or the subway or the bus to other places. I can walk to downtown Munich in twenty minutes and reach the opera house by foot. On the way, I pass the most expensive shopping street in town, with its Gucci and Armani stores, but I seldom allow myself to enter a shop there.

I hardly ever need my car; it remains parked most of the time in front of my house.

The Wiener Platz is a meeting place for many different people. Since a park with tall trees and many sandboxes surrounds the square for children, many young mothers and fathers come here with their small children. The children ride their little bikes across the square while their parents take some time out in one of the surrounding cafés from which they can watch them.

You can find many immigrants here also. Some Turkish women in colorful scarves, many Italians, people from the Balkan countries, and even tourists find their way here.

Senior citizens find the place charming because they can sit here on a bench and watch the world pass by.

It is not a coincidence that the Wiener Platz is not far from the place where the statue of Athena is watching over the Isar River.

I spend most of the year in Munich. During the early summer months, I live in Italy, and once a year I fly to the United States, to Houston, Texas, for a "live meeting" instead of "SKYPE," with my daughters and grandchildren. I live in three very different cultures, and my life has remained full of variety and change. Despite difficult problems with my back, I feel healthy and happy.

It has always been my dream to create a lifestyle where I could combine the advantageous characteristics of the countries I had the good luck to visit. I sought to incorporate the spiritual heritage of Europe with the pragmatic optimism of Americans and their courage to confront life, to adopt the empathic concern for others as taught by Asian religions, and to exhibit the strength and uncomplicated love of life of the African people. .

During recent years, however, the differences between cultures seem to slowly blend with one another. It seems to me that the Western way of life is sweeping over the peoples like a tsunami, even in the furthest corners of the world.

Much has been written about the terrific speed of change in the 20th century, be it in the fields of politics, society, science, culture, arts, or ethics.

And now I am asking myself how this change has affected my own life.

I know today that I have met the limits of my adaptability.

The changes during the life of my mother had already been enormous.

Despite the fact that our opinions had collided many times, at least we were able to communicate with each other, because we had a common system of values. We spoke the same emotional language.

My grandchildren, however, live in a different world ands even speak a different language. I find it difficult to follow their language;

everything is concerned with the world of video games and the Internet, concepts and vocabulary that I am not familiar with.

Since I have started to write this book, activities in the world have been influenced by the possibilities of the Internet to an extent that was unimaginable when I grew up.

The amount of information—facts, messages, and news—that surrounds me, enticing me to surf the World Wide Web, seems to hover above me up in the air like a flock of birds. Sometimes I flee from my living room, which is crowded with telephone, television, heaps of newspapers, and my laptop, and I try to hide in the bedroom. But my head keeps spinning with hundreds of facts and opinions, and worries: the euro crisis, the war in Syria and Afghanistan, the atomic catastrophe in Hiroshima, Japan, and the problem of unemployment for so many young people in the world.

The speed with which things are done today also dismays me. The so-called multitasking, by which my daughters handle everyday chores, seems very strange to me. I do not believe that a human being can really concentrate well on different things at the same time. The results are too many mistakes, and most of all, the loss of the ability to pursue in depth any important issue. You will only have a superficial knowledge of what you think you know.

I share the dislike for the aggressive nature, hectic pace, and the constant acceleration of modern life with many people in this world. Like them, I often feel overpowered and perplexed by the constantly accelerated rate of progress, and I am searching for methods to resist it. The new vogue of "Entschleunigung"(slowing down), such as the "Slow Food" movement, is one of these methods.

I try to convince my daughters that one does not always have to go along with every new development. The classical idea of moderation and the golden rule does not only serve one's health but is also a good guide to enjoying the many little joys in everyday life.

Since the demise of Soviet communism, I believe that capitalism, with its materialistic view of life based primarily on the values of success and money, can no longer serve as a basis for a satisfying way of life. I hope it will be possible in the future to combine the values of individual freedom, hard work and success, and free enterprise with a feeling of responsibility for our neighbors who may not have had the good luck to be winners in the game of "survival of the fittest." At least this is what Christianity teaches us. I think we have the closest to this state now in Germany, a "Christian social democracy."

The instrumentalization of man and the exploitation of nature seem to only serve the purpose of keeping the present economic system alive.

The individual will feel more and more suppressed and helpless by the momentum of this system. In the end, we feel helpless, at a loss, and no longer in charge of controlling the course of our own life.

Once people have reached the limits of their adaptability, they tend to cling to conservative values, which, in turn, do not agree with the changing conditions of life. I think that the increasing religious fanaticism that we can see in all parts of the world is a direct result of this general state of uncertainty.

In the meantime, the wave of modernization has long reached Europe. The commercialization of all parts of life and the resulting "Konsumrausch" (compulsion to consume) can probably not be stopped, not even in faraway China and "on the roof of the world"—Tibet.

When I ask myself how the political and social trends of the 20th century have influenced my life, I can see that my life has been completely steered by the goals of American foreign policy. After World War II, it was the U.S. foreign policy to carry the political system of democracy to all the countries in the world in the hopes of keeping peace and avoiding another world war.

One of these programs was the famous Fulbright scholarship, the idea of exchanging students across the whole world and providing the possibility to study in the United States. This program has definitely steered my life in a completely new and different direction.

American friendship and support for the country of Israel and the resulting tensions in the Middle East resulted directly in Howard's and my expulsion from Beirut, Lebanon, in 1967.

Again, the U.S. intention to establish democracy in Southeast Asian and African countries had brought Howard to Vietnam and later to Ethiopia, where he subsequently lost his life. Both of these attempts to establish American influence abroad have failed and in the process have changed my life radically.

Are we on the right track?

Today I ask myself if our Western value of seeking personal happiness for every individual really is the best for all the peoples of this diverse world. Shouldn't it be possible for diverse cultures to reflect diverse values?

The question remains: What can each one of us do to make sure that the waters of the fountains of alternative ways of life continue to flow?

Attempts to develop a new way of thinking do already exist. I have found them in the "World Ethics,", an attempt to combine the different ethical values of various great religions and to pass these on to the next generation.

Perhaps we will thus be able to save some of the proven ethical values from the mega-market of different ways of life and carry them into the insecure future.

These are the questions that concern me today, because the future of my children and grandchildren are of great concern to me.

Like every grandmother, I love my grandchildren, but I am not really a "model grandmother." I am not content with reading fairy tales to them, uttering words of wisdom, sending nice birthday presents, or keeping up a summer home where they can always come and relax.

I want to get involved. It seems that from childhood on I have felt responsible to remedy something that I considered to be wrong. I am forced to take up problems and try to find solutions. "To make the world a better place to live in," was and still is my motto, especially when the people I love are concerned.

As a grandmother, I have to realize that most of the time "good advice" is not welcome, not even when based on my experience I can easily see ahead the consequences that will result from certain actions or mindsets.

Nobody loves Cassandra! Was it not this twofold gift she received from the gods: She could see into the future, but nobody ever wanted to believe her?

It is an old piece of wisdom that everyone has to have his own experiences and then has to suffer the painful consequences. This is especially true for my two daughters, who come from a family in which it is traditional to live an inner-directed life, to disregard what others say, and to be determined to getting one's way. Our maternal heritage—and for generations! My mother was this way, I am the same, and of course my two daughters are as well. Only the type of education has changed over the generations according to the corresponding "Zeitgeist."

I still remember when I had my first experiences as a young mother in the late Fifties with Ariane on my arm and in my hand the then-famous book *Baby and Childcare* by Dr. Benjamin Spock.

I learned everything from that book, from the correct use of diapers to feeding the baby and healthy food and the only "correct education," which was to Dr. Spock absolutely antiauthoritarian!

Dr. Spock, the father of antiauthoritarian education, was of the opinion that children would best develop when they were left completely free of any kind of outer constraint. The word "no" was an absolute taboo word in the education of children. The denial of spontaneous wishes would block the creativity and personal power of a child. Somehow the child would find his or her own way, a way was best suited for his or her individual nature.

At that time, I could not have foreseen that forty years later my grandchildren would reject vehemently this type of education. Today they feel that their mother does not give them enough limits and that she gives them too few rules for their life.

This is a topic that does not only concern my grandchildren. Some time ago I read in a German newspaper:

> The grandchildren of the wave of antiauthoritarianism are generally not up to the education of their own children. The "68-generation" has toppled old ideals and destroyed the social norms, but nobody has put anything new in their place since then.

It is very interesting for me to see how the way of raising children has changed over the generations and to see that the logical counteraction to every such wave continues. For example, my mother has always overprotected me and therefore has created a counteraction in me—a strong drive for freedom. I cannot say that my parents had brought me up in a very authoritarian way. However, the times and the society were very much formed by authoritarian structures. It would have been difficult to withdraw because the individual was not really aware of them. You simply did not contradict your father, or your teacher, let alone, the "Fuehrer" of the country.

Without giving it much thought, I wanted to give to my children the freedom that I myself had to fight for. On the other hand, the idea of an "antiauthoritarian education" was not really a concern in our mobile world, where we were in a different place every few months. The girls and I were happy to be a good team and really supported each other.

Ariane and Vivian had to stand on their own feet very early in life. This was the result of our living conditions. They seemed to have enjoyed their freedom, which, on the other hand, might have overtaxed them. However, both of them have become strong women who know how to get their own way.

Today my relationship to both of my girls is still very loving, even if some different ideas may cause some problems. The basis is our love for each other. We are connected both by family bonds and the memories we share and by our common values and ideas. The love for the arts are a source of happiness also in times of crisis to both girls.

We all love our house in Italy and above all, we all have love for the fine arts.

It is probably no coincidence that both daughters have found their profession in the field of art, which is for them a source of strength and joy. Thanks to God, the two sisters are always a comfort and support for each other.

Unfortunately, I have not succeeded to counteract the appeal of "Go West" with my children. Ariane and Vivian have decided for a life in the United States. They and their children consider themselves American. Their feeling for Germany is one of a romantic nostalgia. Today they live in a world that I am acquainted with but that has never become a part of me, and I am filled with melancholy and sadness that I can pass on only fragments of my beloved European heritage.

I often ask myself whether the human being has basically changed during his evolving phases. I have the suspicion that our modern life actually does cause a new step in human evolution and a new and different awareness of self in these new generations. Usually we can live quite well with the resulting differences in our opinions, as long as it does not concern questions of education. However, when the passing on of values and certain manners of behavior are concerned, our worlds often clash.

"Panta Rei"- everything flows—as Ovid stated two thousand years ago. This is true not only for my own life but also for my relationship to the United States. The two events I describe now serve as good examples.

First, It is spring 1991.

Iraq had occupied Kuwait and had bombed Israel with rockets. After weeks of discussions, the United States Senate decided with only a two-vote majority to attack Iraq. In Germany this decision met with general disapproval. However, I was of the opinion that the United States had done the right thing, and I decided to organize a march of protest in the center of Munich together with my friends from the German-American Club.

(See the picture)

Second, twelve years later, in March 2003.

Same place, same picture. However, the other way around.

Again, there was war in Iraq. This time it was George W. Bush, the son of the U.S. president who had started the first war. Europe was against it.

So was I. The story is well known and so is the outcome.

In March 2003 I joined a demonstration against the foreign policy of the United States, against its administration, and its unilateralism. Most of all, I opposed the propagandistic division of the world into "good" and "bad." You could not make it so simple, especially not the government of the only great power left in the world. Just the opposite: Power also means responsibility. It was this that the people on the Odeonsplatz wanted to tell the world amid the cold and snowy storm.

Eva leading a pro American demonstration, Munich 1991, Family photo

These two demonstrations, which I took a part in with great engagement and passion, show that a strong bond connects me with the United States.

The moral dilemma that the United States was so deeply involved in depresses me every day anew.

Ariane and Vivian have asked me many times to move to Houston. They want to take care of me in my old age when I would need help.

However, I cannot decide on this step. Every year when I visit the United States I feel more and more estranged—for many reasons.

I do not want to leave Europe.

There are my Bavarian roots that keep me here in Munich. These roots include our ancient Judeo-Christian cultural heritage, whose spiritual treasures I have not yet exhausted, and also my love for this charming "World City with Heart."

There is the Bavarian "Kulturlandschaft" (land cultivated by man), which finds its expression in the harmony between lovely landscape with mountains, hills and lakes and the baroque architecture of the churches, monasteries, villages, and quaint ancient towns.

There is also the natural, open, native character of the people, the so-called "Liberalitas Bavariae" and their love for the local dialect and the native costumes.

All of these attributes make me happy, and my heart feels empty when I am in another place.

Years ago I had felt the urge to follow my interest in archaeology, anthropology, and the early development of man. I hoped to thus be able to explain the nature of man better. Now I have enrolled at the Munich Ludwig Maximilian University as a guest listener in these classes. It gives me great joy to follow the traces of Europe together with other interested and interesting young and old people.

I am also attending lectures on the subject of "Intercultural Communication." Having lived in so many different countries, I am practically predestined for this field. Language plays a major part in this field, and therefore my interest lies there, as a language teacher. The study of intercultural communication as a science originated in the United States when it became generally recognized how ineffective the work of large companies abroad can be, when the employees do not understand the mentality of the guest country.

"We must understand the world with more respect for the differences between their peoples!" was the opinion of Wolfgang Schaeuble. I agree with the German Minister of Finance.

One field of interest leads to another. So these lectures have directed me to a very interesting voluntary activity. When I have time I help Turkish children with their homework in the Center for Turkish Women and Children.

Unfortunately, I can thus only make a very limited contribution to the solution of the most urgent problems of our time: the "clash of cultures" between the Western world and Islam. But this voluntary work is very important to me.

These young girls who are growing up between two worlds and have serious problems because of the conflict between the world of their home and family (with many restricting laws) and the world of the liberal social environment in Germany. These circumstances give me the opportunity to build a small bridge of understanding and trust.

My experiences when was teaching at the Beirut College for Women are very helpful.

Presently, I am reading the *Koran* with great interest and realize with dismay how much this wise book can be misused for political purposes. Explanatory publications like the one by the modern Christian theologian, Hans Kung, are however absolutely imperative for a good comprehension.

Beside these activities, I am an active member of the Studiengesellschaft fuer Friedensforschung (Organization for the Study of Peace). There I also met some compatible people. We are convinced that we must do everything we can to avoid international conflicts with peaceful means. This is the only way to break up the spiral of force that is developing in our world.

We find some answers, for instance, in the "World Ethics" project, where a consensus is sought

Eva in the traditional Bavarian dress. Munich, Germany, 2004, photo by Meinen Fotografie GmbH

concerning basic common morals. The theologian Hans Kung initiated this project.

My newest project may be called "examining my own traces."

I have bough a new camera and attended a class in photography at the community college.

It was my deep love for nature that led me to take up this hobby.

Then I ventured on my first project: The "Isar River and the Changes of the Seasons," a story in pictures of the river from the source to its mouth, the river that has accompanied my life for many years.

In spring I traced the source of the bubbling brook in the South of Bavaria and found it in the steep Karwendel Mountains.

In the summer I followed the river as it wound its way through the lovely valleys toward the bustling city of Munich in the north.

In the fall, the Isar has quieted down to become an imposing river that flows peacefully through the now colorful mystic lowland forest. In its waters are reflected the church towers of the ancient city of Landshut.

In the delta where the Isar flows into the Danube, I succeeded in catching the ghostly fogs of winter that surround the river at this time.

How has the river changed its character? How have I changed in the flow of my lifetime?

Is it like the waters of the Isar river? Do I remain true to my own nature? How have I changed by influences from other sources? Do I remain the same by changing myself?

Just like the human being, the river always flows in one direction toward its destiny.

Once a year I travel to the United States to experience my daughters, their families, and activities live, as opposed to via computer. The following "on the spot report" reflects how I see their life today.

The Day the Tornado Came

"Dinnertime," my son-in-law Achille is calling from the kitchen, "I have made for you the best carbonara from Sicily—the best in the world!"

An enticing odor of garlic and bacon wafts through the house and attracts all of us from our different hiding places.

Toni is sitting in front of her computer. She has still to finish her homework for tomorrow, a report. She types in "documentary," and various documentaries appear on the screen. She chooses a topic: "Predators of the Sea."

Quickly she condenses the content of the report and types like crazy. Then she runs to her mother in the office in the back of the house: "Mom, can you quickly design a cover for the report that looks much better?" As an A-student, she feels responsible to present her work optically perfect.

Is my granddaughter actually stealing content from the Web? I do not feel it is my place to admonish her. I simply observe. Perhaps someday soon I will be able to bring up the subject with her mother.

Vivian has beautifully decorated her office for her work as designer. The newest acquisition is on the desks, a large-screen computer. On the walls I see her tasteful sketches and designs, unconventional pictures—a bit Mexican.

At the moment, Vivian is involved in a videoconference with her colleagues in San Antonio. In this way she does not have to spend four hours to drive there, and she is relieved.

Houston Texas skyline, Copyright Texaswatersolutions.com

"Hey y'all, the carbonara is getting cold…" Achille's voice sounds louder.

Ami is still chatting with her friend, while petting the Siamese cat Beou, that is purring on her lap.

"Ami, listen, you just have to go to the movie with me tomorrow evening!" her friend says.

"No, I can't—our soccer team has to practice before the game."

From the television some strange sounds reach my ear, like a woman sighing heavily and shedding tears. There must be some soap opera on.

There are several telephones in the house and they seem to be ringing constantly. Now a few neighbors are stopping by to say hello and chat about the latest news in the neighborhood.

I am also sitting in front of my computer in my "mother-in-law apartment" above the garage. I am trying desperately to find some news about what is happening in the world.

What is going on in this crazy war in Iraq? Who will win the next election? I give up and walk through the garden to the back entrance of the main house. On the door there is an old sign: "ENTRÉE DES ARTISTES."

I walk up the old, creaking wooden stairs. Under each step I read in colorful writing: "Welcome to our home,

> Make your dreams
> Come true,
> One step,
> At a time.

Earlier this afternoon Vivian had taken me along on a drive downtown. There had been a tornado warning on the news.

Suddenly an enormous thunderbolt nearly threw us out of our seats.

The tornado had arrived.

It seemed as if Zeus, the father of the gods, called the "cloud gatherer," was hurling his flashes of lightning at the city. He was ordering everybody to stop the hectic hustle and bustle and pause. The dark clouds opened in one place and the rain came drumming down in torrents into the streets. These were flooded immediately, and the water began to seep into the cars that had come to a halt. At the last moment, Vivian steered her jeep to the median strip, and then we were stuck.

Achille called from his mobile phone and wanted to know where we were and whether we were okay.

I was happy about this unexpected interruption and hoped to finally have some time to talk to my daughter in peace. However, Vivian pulled out her mobile phone and began to continue her business calls as cool as a cucumber. She and the person she called discussed the cheapest offer for the Christmas T-shirts for the holiday festivities at the Texas Children's Hospital.

The other people around us did the same; they waited, made telephone calls or pulled out their laptops to continue their work.

After an hour, two friendly young men pushed us onto the road. They got completely covered with mud, but they waved at us and said, "Good-bye! Have a good day!" and disappeared.

Vivian started up the jeep. This time we made our way, while the other exits and streets were still under water.

On a bridge, the driver of a truck was being pulled from his vehicle by a helicopter. He had saved himself by climbing onto the roof when the truck got stuck in a tunnel that had quickly filled up with water.

Many people left their cars on the road, climbed over the four-foot sidewall, and went into a nearby pancake shop to eat.

'We were glad to have gotten back without any troubles, and we had taken a short nap.

Later that evening I hear Achille call, "Hey, people, the carbonara is getting cold...!"

A telephone rings; Vivian says, "No, I am sorry. I simply did not get around to finishing it." Her voice sounds tired. She had promised to make a design for an invitation to a benefit concert for "Old Music" in the opera house of Houston—a contribution to a good cause. She always gets asked to do these jobs because her husband is a member of the board. These people don't realize that she has a full-time job and a family.

Finally, we are all sitting around the antique table in the dining room.

"First we say grace," says Achille, and all of us join hands.

"Thank you, Lord, for this day—thank you, that none of us got hurt by the tornado," he says,

"And our cars weren't hurt." adds Ami.

"What was the best thing that happened to you today, Toni?" I ask.

"We had a lot of fun today when we walked home barefoot. In some places the water reached up to our shoulders and we could swim. It was lots of fun!"

I am really tired. At home in Munich it was three o'clock in the morning. This jetlag is killing me. Munich seems so far away, and so does Naples. They both seem slightly unreal to me.

On the wall hangs an old map of the world.

I search for the small image representing Europe. Somewhere between the 40th and the 42nd parallel, I believe. At least that's where it was when I left Europe.

Back to nature, the grandchildren in Quo Vadis, 1997, Family photo R to L: Sophia, Amelia, Antonia. Anton

THANKSGIVING IN THE COUNTRY

I had planned to spend Thanksgiving together with the whole family outside the city in the country. But plans were changed again, as they usually were.

Vivian felt that she and her family should spend this important holiday that combines American tradition, religion, and patriotism, together with her father Philip and his new family in Indiana. Tradition had suddenly become very important in this family, since an uncle has found out that the family Cox actually is descended from the first settlers who came to America on the *Mayflower*.

Vivian did not get a day of vacation. This meant they had to leave at noon on Wednesday. Four people in the Jeep Cherokee, packed full, to drive the 800 miles! It would take about twenty hours to reach Indiana and then, again twenty hours to drive back home. There would be 33 million cars on the road during the weekend. They were expecting snow for the states in the Middle West, Indiana, and Illinois. Thus Vivian would be only one day with the Cox family. On Sunday evening they would have to be back home.

I am sitting beside my son-in-law John Edmundson, whom I will call Hercules in this story, in his pickup truck. He had stopped by on his way home from work to get me. His architectural office is in downtown Houston. The trip to his house in the country would take at least two hours with all the holiday traffic.

We pass the "Spaghetti Bowl," where six highway bridges cross one another, and then we enter the "fast lane" for trucks and vehicles with at least two passengers. The traffic moves smoothly.

Then we leave the highway and turn into a small country road.

In November, darkness comes early and descends slowly over the wide fields and dark woods. I can still make out the open meadows with herds of the typical Texas Longhorn cattle. In between the meadows are fenced-in paddocks with horses. Sudden shadows chase across the road: deer that pass through the open spaces between the solitary houses.

In many of the houses, the American flag is laid down on the roof; many people also fly the state flag of Texas. Texas, this state of the multinational oil companies, was a separate country in the 19th century for a time, and therefore the pride of the Texans is just as big as everything else in Texas.

No doubt these are God-fearing, patriotic people.

I have been told that some people had a shield on their door saying, "We don't call the police. We shoot by ourselves!"

A shudder of dismay is creeping up my spine; it would be dangerous to put a foot down on their lawn and knock on their door.

"We live out here, because we hate life in the city," John explains. "The children should not have to breathe polluted air. They should grow up healthy and most of all, strong."

After a long while, we finally turn into a lane that leads onto a large, three acre piece of property. The attractive, New England-style house is hidden behind large trees. There is also a romantic-looking small lake behind the house that supplies water to the house.

The dogs recognize us immediately. Wagging their tails, they came running toward us. Following them, Sophia races across the lawn. Her blonde hair flying behind her, she shouts: "OmiNonna, OmiNonna, I am glad you came!"

The large, two-story living room receives us with the homely smell of the crackling fire in the open fireplace and the aroma of the smoked turkey.

Holiday feeling meets me in this friendly, wide-open house, nicely furnished and decorated in the country style by Ariane. Then I stumble over a gun leaning ready to hand in the corner. Again, a faint touch of dismay was creeping up my spine.

"Hey, Anton, how are you, my dear boy?" I hear myself asking, as I stand in the entryway to the house.

"Fine!" he said.

As Anton notices my worried look, he says: "Don't worry, OmiNonna, that's only my BB gun. You can't really shoot with it. But maybe Santa Claus will … ," he suddenly falls silent, as he notices the stern expression on his father's face.

"And what do your neighbors say, when there is shooting in this house?" I ask.

"We don't take no crap from nobody! Right, Anton?" thunders Hercules, and Hercules Junior, dressed in the same overalls as his father, proudly nods his head and disappears outside into the bushes.

"Hello, Mama, come in and make yourself comfortable. Would you like a bottle of German beer?" Ariane's soft and friendly voice comes from the kitchen where she is busy preparing dinner and some different dishes for the feast the next day.

On my first night in the country I cannot sleep. As I am looking out of the window, the moon lights up several deer, which are peacefully grazing on the lawn near the chicken coop.

Only last week raccoons had carried off three of the cute black and white chickens before Anton had chased them away with his BB gun.

On the next morning, Anton (his name is really John Anton, but I like to call him Anton after my father) is taking me on a tour around the house and garden. He has sacrificed an hour from his video game-playing just to show me everything.

On the small path we find a small dead snake.

"This one is not dangerous," Anton reassures me. "But I'll show you the most dangerous one of all, the coral snake. That one is more dangerous than the rattlesnake, the moccasin, or the copperhead. We have them all in the garden. Their bite is absolutely deadly," .

"How nice!" I think, smiling at him.

The nature around the house is definitely more unfriendly than the lovely forest in Bavaria, I think, looking around more closely.

As we return to the house, Anton takes a small, orange snake out of the freezer. I am impressed. But this sight does not reassure me.

When we arrive back in the house, I hear Sophia admonishing me: "Before you change your shoes when you come in from outside, you have to watch that there is no small scorpion hiding in one of them."

My worry about the children must be showing on my face, and Hercules, arms akimbo, tries to calm me: "The kids just have to learn to watch out for themselves. Three hundred years ago it was no different. Otherwise our ancestors would not have survived."

However, this statement also does not comfort me.

Early next morning Hercules's droning voice awakens me.

"Come on, everybody get up! We have a lot of work to do!" he calls.

We will have eighteen guests for Thanksgiving dinner.

The two turkeys weigh about ten pounds each, and they will take five hours at least to get smoked.

I still have to bake the bread. In my family, everything is homemade.

We will take the furniture out of the living room and set up the big picnic table in there.

"Anton, don't sleep, get busy!" Hercules says.

I think, "This man will never stop sounding like a Marine sergeant!" and I stumble sleepily into the bathroom.

"Goodness, it is only seven thirty in the morning!" I say to no one in particular.

The large picnic table from outside has to be taken inside. Hercules braces himself against the home-made picnic table with bench in order to move the bulky piece of furniture into the living room.

"Anton, watch out, you are too weak—everybody help out," Hercules says.

Hercules Junior (Anton), with knitted brows, pushes with all his might, murmuring something.

The expression on his face seems to say: "Just wait until I am strong enough so that I will not have to accept these insults anymore!"

After the table is placed before the open fireplace, I begin to decorate the tables with baskets filled with vegetables, fruit, and colorful autumn flowers.

About four o'clock when the sun is about to set, friends with their families start to arrive. The many presents they brought they deposit on the kitchen counter: wine, salads, h'ors d'oeuvres, and sweet desserts.

Two hours later the first turkey is ready!

Cutting turkey, roasts, and steaks is of course a male's preserve. With great pride Hercules heaves the crisply baked turkey from the oven onto a large serving plate.

"Ahhh, delicious!" he says. "Take your plates and come and get it!"

"Stop! We need a prayer and a toast," I interrupt.

"In this place, there is too much yakking about religion already," Hercules growls, but then he lowers his head in agreement. Family and guests do likewise.

"Thank you, Lord, for all your gifts and for this chance to be together today!" I say.

I add a toast from Bavaria: "Wohl bekomms, esst und trinkt, so jung kimma ma nimmer z'sam." (To your health, eat and drink; we won't meet again as young as we are today.)

Then young and old fall silent.

How lucky we are these days, compared to the life of the Pilgrims!

In the meantime, it is now dark outside. The conversation centers on the meal. I can see that everybody had been hungry and enjoyed the wonderful smoked turkey and all the other traditional side dishes, like sweet potatoes, corn, and other vegetables.

After the guests have dessert and some glasses of wine or a mug of beer they become more talkative again. The conversation centered mostly about local affairs. Most of the guests soon leave, and peace is beginning to fill the house. Only the fire is still bristling in the fireplace.

Suddenly, black shadows are whisking down the stairs and from room to room.

This is the time of the cats.

One of them is sitting on the mantelpiece. Another one is sneaking soundlessly over the kitchen counter. A third one is purring around Sophia's feet.

"How many cats do you have now?" I ask in surprise.

"The five that we always had, plus the two little black ones. We decided to keep them after all. We did not want to give them away," says Ariane.

"I don't feel as secure as I did in former times," Aubrey, a painter who was a neighbor and friend, says with a worried expression on his face. He had been voted onto the City Council the previous week.

"Since September 11, 2001, there are too many people here that scare me," he says. "For them, everything is black or white. They believe that George W. Bush and the United States are right and the others are wrong, and that we have to fight these ungodly terrorists, because God is on our side, no two ways about it! To stand up for a different opinion is very dangerous."

He continues, "I myself want to save the beavers in this region. Isn't there a party in Germany who wants to save nature, the Green Party?"

"You would be surprised what these arch-conservatives say," remarks Hercules. "For example: 'We have to defend ourselves against these godless terrorists, over there and also here. But Jesus is on our side!' The worst ones are these nerds, who think they know everything, these eggheads who write books and tell lies about Jesus."

"The Bible tells us that God has created man in seven days, and that Adam and Eve were the first human beings. And what do these people tell the children? That our ancestors were apes! These books should be forbidden and the teachers should be fired!" Hercules roars.

"I better think twice about what I say," grins Aubrey.

"Don't worry," says Hercules. "The most important thing is that we are strong, and these guys will be scared of us."

Trying to change the subject, I ask Sophia: "What do you have to swear in school every morning?"

Sophia puts her right hand over her heart and recites: "I pledge allegiance to the flag and to the republic for which it stands! One nation under God indivisible, with liberty and justice for all. I pledge allegiance to the Texas flag...."

Anton interrupts her: "And this is the pledge in my school: 'I am a Nichol Sawmill Bulldog. I take pride in myself. I am responsible for my actions. I don't blame someone else. I choose to be happy to show that I care, to love and be honest, to be kind and to share. Today I will work hard and do always do my best. For all of these choices put us above the rest, because N.S.E. is a great place to be.'"

Ariane had told me that she had tried to go to church with the children.

She had chosen a "non-denominational church" where she had hoped to find more openness and less bigotry.

Then the minister started to preach to the crowd, especially to the children: "Always remember, there are we, who stand for Jesus, and there are the others. Who do not. These people are our enemies. You have to watch out for them. When you hear that somebody talks and says something against Jesus or what is in the Bible, you have to immediately close your ears—like this—(the speaker covers his ears) and pull down your visor (he pulls an imaginary visor over his eyes). Now children, look, you all pull down your visor like this."

Ariane continues: "At that point I got up, took the children and left the church, went outside, and took a deep breath of fresh air."

The next day Hercules and Junior disappear into the woods. Together with some of their neighbors, they cut some trees and prepared the logs for the winter.

"Anton really worked hard," says Hercules, as they came back home, tired and all sweaty in their overalls.

Sophia is driving the small tractor around the garden and transports the logs behind the chicken coop.

In the meantime, Ariane has retired into her studio. It is a small, quaint old wooden house about three miles down the road by the old railroad tracks. The house is about eighty years old and dates from the time when Magnolia (the nearest town) still had a railroad station.

It has always been a dream of hers to have her own art gallery. Several times a week she goes there, because she finds the peace to paint. She also frames her own pictures. The walls are filled with pictures, many portraits that rich Texan families have ordered to be painted from a photograph. There are also colorful paintings of flowers and different interpretations of her own. The many beautiful pictures she had painted in Italy have not found a buyer yet.

Ariane has to earn some extra money to fill up the household money. The large house and the family were expensive. Therefore, not much time remains for housework. Her interest lies more in the decoration of the beautiful house. The walls are covered by colorful, handwoven blankets in the Mexican style.

The Mexican influence is seen everywhere, in the happy colors of pictures and houses and of course in the food:

"Tex Mex" is everywhere.

I am studying the walls and floors.

"In the morning I hit the ground running and then I continue to run all day. I simply have no time to clean everything up all the time!" Ariane says as she looked at me with her disarming sweet smile.

Yes, that is my Ariane.

On Sunday I prepare a German-style dinner in the garden. I am putting a huge iron kettle with goulash onto the open fire. This will have to cook for one hour at least. When I come to visit, the children always ask me to cook my famous goulash. I cook a lot of goulash so that Ariane can put some in the freezer. But Anton usually finishes it off quickly.

Hercules smiles contentedly and raises his beer bottle: "Cheers!"

On the next morning, the sun rises above the trees, it will be another hot day.

"It is strange," I think, "Here in Texas I am always combing my hair straight, but somehow it always stands on end."

Winged Siren, black-figured amphora (5'h century B.C.E.) found in a necropole near Sorrento, Italy, in 1956, (see Source of Illustrations)

CHAPTER 20: REFLECTIONS

THE SONG OF THE SIRENS—CANTO III

IT IS JUNE, THE MOST beautiful time in *Quo Vadis*. Time of the Siesta, "Ein weisser Glanz liegt ueber Land und Meer und duftend schwebt der Aether ohne Wolken" (a white sparkle lies over land and sea, and fragrant ether floats above without a cloud), the famous German poet Johann Wolfgang von Goethe writes in his *Italian Journey*. This describes so beautifully the brilliance of the light in the Gulf of Naples.

I am sitting in the shade of the old fig tree. A refreshing breeze from the sea below is blowing up the slope, passes through the house, and invites the silver leaves of the olive trees behind the house to dance in the sun.

For a short time I feel like a part of eternity, right here and now, between the sea and heaven above.

My eyes are lost amid the blue of the hydrangeas and the purple of the bougainvilleas that climb up the old garden wall.

From the beach, the soft murmur of the waves as they rush against the rocks, interrupted by the clear happy voices of the children, rises and mingles with the gentle splashing of the pool behind me.

In the neighbor's lemon grove, the common everyday noises remind me that siesta time is over and that people have returned to their work. There is the humming of the neighbor's saw and at regular intervals the tooting of the bus horn as it is turning a sharp curve on the road to Sorrento.

The birds in the olive trees are keeping up a lively conversation. The small one, on a branch right above me, warbles in various cadences. Then he falls silent, listening respectfully to the answer of his friend in the adjacent territory, which sounds like his own echo.

I am looking out to the sea. The Isle of Ischia has disappeared amid the haze as usual at this time of the day. I cannot make out the horizon where the sky disappears into the sea. Only one large ship seems to hover in the air. Every day at the same time it sails from Naples down south to Sicily. Three times the muffled sound of the ship's siren flows across the coast as the ship passes the Punta della Campanella. The passing ships 2,000 years ago hailed their protectress Athena, who had her temple at the tip of the peninsula across from Capri. In Roman times, it was Minerva, and today it is Mother Mary who protects all men out at sea.

Here in Massa Lubrense time seems to have come to a halt.

Massa Lubrense in the Gulf of Naples, Italy, 1994, Family photo

The inhabitants of this small community have been able to defend themselves from the waves of mass tourism by practicing a "soft tourism" in this area. No new high-rises or hotels scar the lovely landscape. Official building permits have not been issued for forty years. Exceptions excluded!

Instead of building more hotels, peasants practice "agritourism" on their farms. They invite guests to share their life. This system is subsidized by the Italian state and has proven very successful.

The wide piazza, with its old baroque church on one side and a terrace that looks toward Capri on the other, has been preserved the way it looked during the Middle Ages. The piazza is wide open and adorned with shady trees and two small fountains that are surrounded by rose gardens. Large advertising posters do not destroy the idyllic picture, except twice a year when the lemon festival or the canoe marathon along the coast is announced.

The street that leads down to the harbor is lined with small shops that sell vegetables, bread, or fish. It passes by the convent church, where archeologists suspect the foundations of the ancient temple of the Sirens are. The old priest there had succeeded in saving some beautiful mosaics from Roman times, just in time before the harbor was reconstructed, when the mosaics were in danger of being lost forever.

Buses filled with tourists are not well accepted here. Only those tourists who like to hike over the mountains or along the ancient Via Minerva to the tip of the peninsula to the Punta della Campanella find their way into this village.

And then there is Monte San Constanzo, for me the most beautiful place in the world. When I climb up the ancient narrow stone road and sit down at the side of the little chapel, I forget all my worries. They say it stands on the foundation of a small Greek temple. I am sure it does, because the Greek always built temples on mountaintops like these.

To my right the houses of Naples are barely visible in the mist of the morning. Beside the city, the proud outline of the volcano Vesuvio reaches into the sky. Right in front of me, as a prolongation of the peninsula, the Island of Capri seems to float in the waters. To my left extend the shimmering blues of the Gulf of Salerno.

For forty years I have climbed up to this hill every year to enjoy the beauty of the place. I bring only my very good friends up here, and the place has not lost its fascination for me in all these years.

"Only a moment between two eternities," I wonder who has written this on the wall of the little chapel.

Since my retirement I have started to attend lectures in archaeology at the University of Munich. I have always been interested in this field and now it has attained concrete meaning here in the Gulf of Naples. Wherever you dig into the ground you can find some of "that old stuff" as the peasants disparagingly call it.

I find many figures on the Sorrentine Peninsula that show me the way back into antique times, to Greek myths and my special objects of interest, the bird demons of the Sirens.

Behind the tip of the peninsula, in the waters of the Gulf of Salerno, are three small islands called "I Galli," or "Isole delle Sirene." According to legend, they are the fossilized bodies of the three Sirens, who had, after Odysseus had spurned them, thrown themselves with grief into the sea where their bodies had turned to stone.

The body of one of them, Parthenope, had washed ashore where Naples is today. There the people built a temple for her and called the ancient town "Parthenope." Later the Greeks built a new city nearby and called it "Neapolis," the new city.

Her name is still omnipresent. The University of Naples carries her name; the address of my villa *Quo Vadis* is Via Parthenope 19.

Sunset over the Sirenuse Islands and Capri, Italy, 2005, Family photo

Who are these mysterious creatures?

The picture of the mythological seductresses with the body of a bird and the head of a woman has changed very much in the course of centuries. Originally, the idea of the Siren stems from the ancient Egyptians. I think that part of their heritage goes back to the world of the mixed demons of the ancient Sumerians in Mesopotamia, today's Iraq. In Egypt, even male Sirens were found. They are creatures from the world of death, similar to the ba-bird, who protects the dead. They accompany the warriors as they go to war. We can find relatives of these winged creatures in the Cretan culture and even in the Old and New Testaments. They are sisters to the Christian guardian angels.

In Greek mythology, Sirens are active in the border sphere between life and death. As transcendental creatures, half-bird and half-human, they assist man as friendly and comforting spirits helping humans pass from one sphere to the other. This creature also accompanies the goddess Athena, who helped Hercules in his fight against Hydra. The archaeologist Ernst Buschor calls them "muses of the hereafter" connected with the rites of death.

In Homer's *The Odyssey* the Sirens are also connected with death. He places them near Hades, the entrance to the world of the dead in Lake Averno, a dark lake on the other side of the Gulf of Naples. The poet Sophocles calls them "Phorcys's daughters that sing the songs of Hades." They live on the rocks in the sea and with their soft and lovely chants bring the curious sailor to his death.

It is here, on the southern tip of the Sorrentine Peninsula, where Odysseus is said to have defied the temptation of the seductresses.

> The Sirens who enchant all who come near them. If any one unwarily draws in too close and hears the singing of the Sirens, his wife and children will never welcome him home again, for they sit in a green field and warble him to death with the sweetness of their song. There is a great heap of dead men's bones lying all around, with the flesh still rotting off them.
>
> (Homer, *The Odyssey*, Chapter XII)

Here the Sirens show their other face, similar to the harpies, who remind us of the forces of nature who can destroy life. These forces have shaped the face of this restless volcanic coastline for centuries.

As we know, despite Circe's warning, Odysseus cannot be kept from satisfying his curiosity. He closes the ears of his oarsmen with beeswax and has himself tied to the mast of his ship so he can listen to the song of the Sirens while his companions safely pass this place of seduction and bring the ship to the harbor. By this ruse he is able to avoid the deadly temptation and can continue his journey home.

According to legend he returned to this place and built a temple to Athena in gratitude for his save return home.

It is believed that not far from this place another temple for the Sirens was constructed, where rites of death were performed. Today all remnants of this temple have disappeared. Perhaps it has been swept into the sea long ago

by the constant movements of the earth like so many other buildings.

I personally am convinced that this temple was nearby, because some years ago a beautiful vase was found in an ancient grave with the picture of a winged Siren, which must have served as an urn. I saw this vase five years ago in the Sorrento museum.

Since then it has disappeared, so I decided to make a vase just like it in my pottery class. I did, and it turned out fine, not quite as finely crafted as the original, but anyway. Now I have my own Siren vase!

My question is: What was it that the Sirens sang to tempt Odysseus?

> "Come here," they sang, "renowned Ulysses, honour to the Achaean name, and listen to our voices. No one ever sailed past us without staying to hear the enchanting sweetness of our song, and he who listens, will go on his way not only charmed, but wiser, for we know all the ills that the gods laid upon the Argives and Trojans

before Troy, and can tell you everything that is going to happen over the whole world."

(Homer, *The Odyssey*, Chapter XII)

This offer is nothing else but the one that the snake made to Adam and Eve in Paradise: to eat the forbidden apple of knowledge and to become as wise as God.

The Sirens offered joy and omniscience. This certainly was a good offer for Ulysses.

But according to the Greek understanding, Odysseus allowed his reason and self-control to control his "hot desire." These virtues saved his life.

While sitting in my garden paradise I wonder what the Sirens had promised me. And did they keep their promises?

Joy of life, as well as the search for wisdom, has always been the purpose of life as well as a temptation. Was this what the Sirens promised me?

I certainly have found much joy in these blessed coasts—the charm of nature with its forever changing pictures, the mild climate, and the friendly people, with whom I was allowed to spend many days in this house.

Whenever I was unhappy I just had to come here, because no sorrow could withstand the power of this place. Here in the Gulf of Naples I never feel lonesome—on the contrary, I feel integrated into the myriad generations that have lived here before me.

There is hardly anyplace where the changes on the surface of our planet as well as the course of history are as evident as here.

Many of the peoples that have shaped the history of Europe have passed through here! The inhabitants of the caves in the Stone Age, the early Etruscans, the seafaring Phoenicians, the Greek of the Magna

Graecia, Romans, Visigoths, Carthagens, Normans, Spanish, French, and the many others whose names have been lost—all of them came here and disappeared again, but they left traces and they carried the charm of these coastlines with them to another world.

Even in times when I thought I had lost my courage to live, this place has replenished me with comfort and confidence. Again and again I found the strength to take my life again into my own hands and start anew.

The times of crisis also give the chance to mature as an individual and become wiser.

Maybe it was this chance that the Sirens have promised me.

Insights

Which insights have I been able to collect like jewels for my treasure box?

One of the books that had influenced my thinking early in life is *The Plague* by Albert Camus. The North African city of Oran is suddenly cut off from the world because of the outbreak of the plague. Inside the city, the medical doctor Bernhard Rieux is fighting courageously against the deadly disease. Camus has him say: "The Plague, that is life and that concerns all of us." And at the end of the book he concludes: "The only thing that man can win in this game with the plague, are insights and memories."

The most important insight one can win in the course of life is the knowledge about oneself. This is what is written above the Oracle of Delphi: "Know Thyself!" I also have learned many things about myself.

From childhood on I have chosen the road to freedom. Later in life, fate has opened this road many times for me. If the road was closed, I fought for it to open. But I know that personal freedom ends where the rights of others begin. This commandment can be found in all religions, even in ancient Egyptian thought and also in Confucius's idea of "social harmony." Without it, peaceful human coexistence is not possible. "Do unto others as you would have them do unto you!" The "Golden Rule."

Freedom does not mean to do what one likes, but to be in the position to set one's own rules.

"Freedom and happiness you will find in those things that lie within your own self. If, however, you imagine to be free where others command, you will not succeed and will be at odds with yourself and the people around you," writes the Greek philosopher Epictetus in the year 500 before Christ.

And Marcus Aurelius, philosopher and Roman Emperor, believes: "Freedom gives you happiness. It means independence from outer constraints and inner compulsions, which hinder a person to achieve the goal that he has chosen for himself." This sentence I can accept 100% for myself.

"Who am I?" This question we will ask ourselves at some point—at the latest toward or even at the end of our life.

The modern French philosopher Jean Paul Sartre answers this way: "You are what you do." This means you are not the result of your intentions but the sum of all your actions.

"Freedom is not only the insight or the mere will to do something, but it is the action you have taken," says also the philosopher Karl Jaspers.

The Americans have shortened this wisdom into the wonderful formula: "Just do it." This short sentence hangs on the wall of my kitchen, and has been an incentive for me to actually tackle the things that I am convinced of.

INNER FREEDOM

In order to reach inner freedom, you first of all have to let go! To free oneself from the dependency on the opinion of others! He who is unable to do this places himself in a hell of one's own free will.

This also means that the picture one has of oneself should not be what is in the eyes of others.

Sartre's play *No Exit* deals with this thought.

Three people find themselves in hell. There they are confronted with themselves only, and there are no mirrors.

"When I cannot see myself in the mirror, I ask myself whether I do exist," says Estelle, one of the women. Hell consists of being confronted with oneself without the help of a mirror.

However, to be really independent from others, to be really free, also means a lot of loneliness.

I have never been afraid of loneliness.

Consequently, my freedom is my happiness.

Happiness

To me "happiness" is a feeling of the moment. It reminds me of the display of fireworks. It is exhilarating, awe-inspiring, and of short duration.

It is much more than contentedness.

I have often met this feeling in my life. One cannot force happiness to happen now and immediately and under certain conditions. Like love, it is a free bird that comes unexpectedly and goes. It has its own agenda.

One can, however, discover under which conditions a person may feel happiness.

Here are some of the conditions that contribute to my personal happiness:
- The feeling of living in harmony with myself and my environment, here and now, even if this feeling should later turn out to have been an illusion;
- To find myself as part of the Creation while being out in nature, in the forest, up in the mountains, and out at sea;

- To experience the beauty of a landscape with all my senses;
- To enjoy the beauty of a piece of art;
- To be involved in an important project and to do "a good job;"
- To work with dedication and passion on a project for its own sake;
- To travel in distant countries and to understand the deeper meaning of the culture and the people;
- To experience the joy of "Eureka," the sudden understanding of a question and its answer and the correlation of things;
- To feel part of an old and rich culture in my homeland or in Italy;
- To partake in the company of people who accept each other and have a real interest in each other;
- To experience empathy with one another among true friends;
- To give and receive true love;
- And finally: To feel the love and company of the members of my family.

All of these situations are sources of my strength and my well-being, my security, and my happiness.

My friends are an important part of my life. Having lived such a mobile life, it is not easy to make and keep true friends. I was lucky to have found true friends who are dear, self-aware, educated, and profound persons. There are not many, but I am connected with them across the borders of my home and country by heartfelt affection.

All of the above-described situations offer many moments of happiness. They are not always dependent on the presence of others.

Pompeii "Casa del Amore punito" or House of Vettius, excavated 1844, see Sources Index

LOVE

On the wall of my bedroom in *Quo Vadis* there is a copy of a Pompeian wall painting that shows an apparently playful scene. An elegant lady in a blue gown in Pompeian style, in a thoughtful pose, touches the shoulder of a small winged boy who is crying to comfort him.

In specialized literature, this picture has the title *Venus and Cupid Punished*.

I have often asked myself why Venus, the goddess of love, should be punishing her small son, Amor, the symbol of erotic attraction. What did he do? Has he treaded on her toes, mixed up her plans, or not acted according to her orders? Did he again shoot his arrows blindly without thinking?

I myself had to learn that erotic attraction does not have very much to do with true love. Those who mix these feelings up will end up in misfortune. Long ago the Greek and Romans knew this, and they have distinguished between "Amor" and "Psyche,' spiritual love. They considered their marriage as the highest happiness man can achieve.

There have been three important relationships in my life. Each one was dominated by one of these types of love, and they were right for the particular phase of my life in which they occurred. Each one showed the different facets of my character.

The Absence of Love

Unfortunately, I had to live through periods of the absence of love.

There was, for one, the difference in the culture and education between Philip and me and the resulting estrangement.

Then there was the inner and outer chaos after our divorce.

The shock and sorrow about the loss of Howard lasted a long time. The dark shadows this tragedy cast over my life, and the life of my daughters, are still present.

The pain of not being understood and the lack of a feeling of security within a very close relationship, and the feeling of loneliness due to lies and betrayal, were followed by an increasing lack of self-confidence.

I had to suffer through all these phases, and I accept them today without complaint, because only by passing through them can I reappraise my actions and find the way to myself.

I would judge differently today some of the things I did and some of the things I didn't do. On the whole, I regret more the failure to take action. Idleness and the wrong ideas about leaving others to do their own thing have kept me all too often from taking appropriate action during the upbringing of my children or in other relationships. Always being on the go, I often neglected to consider the needs of others.

I am grateful to my parents, because their love and respect have given me the courage to take risks and confront problems. Despite the fact that my mother was a melancholic person who did not love life, I was able to keep my optimism and basic trust that in the end, I would be able to solve all problems positively.

The Purpose of Life

I believe the purpose of life is life itself and the continuation of life. I also believe that the human being and his development is one part of a continuous creation.

Therefore, man must make his positive contribution to the existence and preservation of nature and its creatures. That is his purpose.

Man has also the responsibility to contribute to make the world a better place to live in.

To be "human" means to develop the positive creative potential that God has given us.

The task of a government is to ensure an environment where this process is possible for every one of its citizens.

It is also my responsibility to contribute to build such a government. I consider my contribution to have chosen my profession as a teacher. To educate comes from the Latin word "e-ducare," which means to bring out the inherent faculties of a person.

Human beings are manifold, and every one has many layers and is complex. One should beware of making quick judgments. The "truth" has as many faces as the beholder. I remember the story of the three blind men who were asked to describe an elephant. Each of them, touching only a part of the animal, describes the elephant completely differently. I have learned not to believe by hearsay or by what others report. Go and look for yourself and make sure that you have enough background knowledge to see the whole picture and come to an objective conclusion!

People: I have met many people from different cultures or social backgrounds.

These encounters have taught me this: If you approach a person with interest and respect for his dignity, one can usually trust in his goodwill.

I think it is our task to avoid being on the side of the negative spirits, even if it seems more lucrative or if these seem to be overwhelming at times. Instead, one should put one's weight into the scale of the positive spirits, even if sometimes one can do very little. "It is better to light a candle than to curse the darkness!"

I have talked about the search for knowledge. It is good, it is right, and it is fun to search for knowledge, but I believe one thing to be even more important: "One cannot search for knowledge and at the same time heal, so let us go and heal as fast as we can. This is the most important thing," says the Dr. Rieux in *The Plague*. According to Camus, this goes for all people who try to fight against evil, who cannot be saints but who try to be a healer.

The intellect alone will not succeed in life without empathy and compassion toward others.

The love of life is the most wonderful gift God has given us. Very often this force finds its expression in works of art, in paintings, architecture, music, and most of all in dance.

I love life, and I thank God that he has permitted me to live in places on this earth where it is possible to live a full life.

Unfortunately, this cannot be said about many places on this earth.

SPIRITUAL LIFE

Even during the time of my youth, when I was in the Convent of St. Zeno in Bad Reichenhall, I enjoyed turning my thoughts inward. I was looking for God not so much at the church altar but rather in myself, when I could speak with Him quietly in the cloister of the convent.

I was convinced that God's eye sees everything, that He was inside of me every day as I went to school, went for dinner, and at play. I have always thanked Him for the world full of wonders that He has created.

"Your God is kind and compassionate. It is He who sends the water from the sky to let you drink and also the trees where your herds are grazing. The seed, the olive trees, the palm trees and the vine grow by His mercy. All this is a clear sign for people who think," says Mohammed in the *Koran*.

I believe that God approves of the fact that I lived my curiosity and tried to develop the talents He had given me.

(I never took the opposite opinion of the Mother Superior in the convent of St. Zeno seriously.)

Another encounter with God happened during the construction of my villa *Quo Vadis* in the Gulf of Naples. Since I consider religion to be "lived life" and a house to be the "outer skin" of me, I inquired into the relation between God and me. I knew that I needed a protected space around myself, but this space should at the same time be permeable for the world around me, for God's beauty and His creatures. This would also be the place where I had the time to research the many truths that the great religions of this world offer us. I think I have succeeded in creating such a space in *Quo Vadis*. This is why I feel in union with God there more than in any other place.

It makes sense to me that the *Koran* forbids one to make a picture of God and to pray in front of it. Who can understand the whole grandeur of God?

My relationship to Jesus Christ is less abstract. I have often asked Him for advice when I did not know what to do. Then I sensed

The origin of the Isar river in the Karwendel mountains, Germany, 2008, c kruen.de

Him standing in front of me, looking at me with kind and thoughtful eyes. Then He let me know without compromise what I should do. I think I have read enough in the Bible to understand which message He has sent us. Most of the time I followed His advice, but sometimes, unfortunately, I did not.

In the Gulf of Naples, where the constantly changing formations of the volcanic underground move the face of the earth, one can clearly realize that God's work is never static and that His Universe is in a constant state of change.

Munich's "Volksbad" on the Isar, 18x24 cm, oil on canvas, c 201 I, Julie Galante

When in Africa, Howard and I discussed the same ideas, because we often spoke of God and the topic of death. Both of us agreed that the basic principle of God is the constant change in the cosmos and that death was a part of this process.

During the time that I was allowed to share with Howard, he had been truly "human." He did not want to amass wealth; he just wanted to develop the potential that God had given him to be human and to give love. I believe that when he died he only changed his form of existence into another sphere.

The next intensive encounter with death I had when my mother died in April 1999 at the age of almost 100 years. It was a slow farewell. In the last year of her life, we had many good conversations during her daily walks in the park along the Isar River.

Mother tried to encounter death with composure.

"One has to die of something," she said, "and we have to make room for others." She did not really feel comfortable any more on this planet. She did not get along anymore with the faith of her childhood, so she asked the Catholic priest of our St. Johann's Church for a conversation. He came with a candle and told her to pray. But he could not answer her questions according to her satisfaction. Mother was caught in the faith of the God of her childhood, who would receive her with mercy but would also punish her severely for her misdeeds. In order to free her from this fear, I had to clear up my own ideas first.

She finally died in peace and with curiosity about the future. Man is much more than what he believes to know about himself. She was convinced that God would allow her to continue to watch as guardian angel over the life of her family. And I have the feeling that she is still guarding all of us.

On the whole, I think I have lived a full and authentic life. The price for this, however, is losses, farewells, pains, and insecurities.

I am glad I did not miss any one of my experiences. I only regret the things I have refrained from doing. Sometimes to do nothing is just as wrong as doing the wrong thing.

I believe that one must not fear death, especially if one considers it just a transition from one form of existence into another.

Isarmuendung, The river Isar enters the Danube near Deggendorf, Southern Germany, Found on Wikimdia.de

The ancients called it "Panta Rei," everything flows.

No one has found better words than the Greek poet Ovid, as he so beautifully described the basic principle of life in his *Metamorphosis*:

> There is no thing that keeps its shape, for nature, the innovator, would forever draw forms out of other forms. In all this world—you can believe me—no thing ever dies. By birth we mean beginning to re-form a thing's becoming other than it was; and death is but the end of the old state; one thing shifts here, another there; and yet the total of all things is permanent.

"The game is over" and many questions remain unanswered.

Siren, terracotta figure, 5th century B.C.E. southern Italy, postcard, (see Source of Illustrations Nr. 22)

Acknowledgements

I WANT TO THANK THE PEOPLE who have assisted me with their professional know-how to present this book in its present form.

This is my translation from the German original book 'Quo Vadis, die Odyssee einer Frau im XX. Jahrhundert".

First of all I want to thank the journalist, Nicola Bude, my 'ghost writer'. In the original book she succeeded with her language competency and her empathy to select the most important parts of my oral accounts, put order into the stories of my life and to find the right tone befitting my personality.

My American editor, Bonnie Granat, has given my translation the final touch. With her great professional know-how, insights and her patience, she succeeded in finding the right tone to make American readers visualize the scenes that took place in such different cultures.

My thanks also go to my daughter Vivian Louise Arcidiacono. As a graphic artist, she has put many hours into the layout of this beautiful book.

Index of Illustrations

Number	Date		Source
001	1906	My Grandmother Theresia Ilmberger	family photo
002	1906	Family Ilmberger, Lulu, Theresia, Eduard, Alois	"
003	1906	Lulu und Eduard	"
004	1900	Downtown Munich City	old postcard
005	1918	Lulu playing the piano	family photo
006	1917	Lulu and her two cousins	"
007	1929	Lulu the young teacher	"
008	1911	The village of Vachendorf	old postcard
009	1915	The Schrankl Family. On the left upper side Anton Rasso	family photo
010	1903	Grandparents Schrankl, Eliesabeth und Michael	"
011	1900	The 'Schrankl House' in Vachendorf	"
012	1923	The young University Fraternity student	"
013	1929	Lulu and Anton	"
014	1931	Lulu and Anton	"
015	1931	Landsberg/Lech. City Square	old postcard

016	1932	Grandmother Schrankl	family photo
017	1935	Statue of Athena on the Isar river	"
018 + 019	1935	Munich, Eva and her Mother	"
020	1936	Munich, Eva	"
021	1935	Munich, Odeonsplatz. Eva	"
022	1970	Vachendorf today	"
023	1936	Vachendorf, Grandfather Schrankl and Eva	"
024	1936	Vachendorf, Eva and her two friends	"
025	1937	Berlin, my parents	"
026	1938	Christmas in Berlin, with our housemaid Maria	"
027	1942	My father, Colonel Anton R.Schrankl	"
028	1942	Grandfather Schrankl with cousins Bernhard, Eliesabeth and Eva (fr.l.to.r.)	"
029 + 030	1943	Vachendorf, summer and winter	"
031	1943	My father and I in Vachendorf	"
032	1944	The children of Vachendorf	"
033	1945	75% of the City of Munich has been devastated in 1945	old postcard
034	1945	The American Protestnt Church in Traunstein	family photo
035	1945	The High-School student	"
036 + 037	1947	Eva and Maria (teenager)	"

038	1947	Eva and my best friend Lilo	private photo
039	1949	The 'Carl's Gymnasium' (Highschool) in Bad Reichenhall	"
040	1949	The Convent of St.Zeno in Bad Reichenhall	"
041	1949	The Cloister of St. Zeno in Bad Reichenhall	"
042	1952	Celebrating the Abitur (German highschool diploma)	"
043	1952	Our class of 1952 at the diploma festivities. Eva in the middle between our director and the Class teacher.	"
044		Blackfigured vase, Ulyssees and the sirens (4th century b.C.)	see p.
045	1952	New York	old postcard
046	1952	Foreign students in Evansville College	private photo
047 + 048	1953	'Carmen (Eva) is awaiting her blind date	"
049	1953	Philip and Eva in 'Turmoil', Evansville	"
050	1953	Lt.Philip D.Cox and Eva, a happy mariage	"
051	1953	Honeymoon trip, California coast	"
052	1953	Philip on his way to Korea	"

053		The Abduction of Europe by Zeus Attic red-figured crater, 490 b.C.	see p.
054	1954	Eva in Hawaii	private photo
055	1954	With our beagle 'Sinbad' on the road	"
056	1954	Eva is building furniture in Sacramento, Cal.	"
057	1955	The Rio Grande in Texas	"
058	1956	Small ranch in Texas	"
059	Aug. 1957	Baby Ariane in Phoenix, Arizona	"
060	1957	Indian Pueblo Village in Arizona see p.	"
061	1956	Endless highways in the West	private photo
062	1957	Ariane and Henry in Turmoil	"
063	1957	Family Cox, l.to r. 1st row: Dr.Warren M.Cox jr., Eva Maria, David Cox, Barbara Cox, 2nd row: Ruby (Ting) Cox,	"
064		Ulyssees and the siren Redfigured stamnos (5th century B.C.)	see p.
065	1958	Ariane and our dog Arco at the entrance gate to the 'Ferme de Bel Air' in Pont-a-Mousson, France	private photo
066	Christmas 1958	The family under the Christmas tree	"

067	1959	Christmas Grandmother Omi and Arco, France	"
068	1959	Christmas Ariane and Vivian under the Christmas tree	"
069	1959	Ariane and Vivian	"
070	1959	Philip and Ariane and Vivian	"
071	1963	"Little sister, come and dance with me!" (German nursery rhyme}	"
072	1959	In the Villa of Axel Munthe on Capri	"
073	1959	The sphinx in the villa of Axel Munthe	"
074	1959	On the newly bought piece of property	"
075	1959	The harbour Marina Lobra	"
076	1960	Philip and Eva. The house Quo Vadis is being built.	"
077	1962	The entrance to villa Quo Vadis	"
078	1984	A modern 'villa sul mare'	"
079	1986	-----	"
080	1962	The young family	"
081	1962	Hermine, Ariane and Vivian are greeting their dad, passing over the house	"
082	1964	Vivian, Angela and Ariane	"
083	1963	Ariane, the young painter	"
084	1963	Eva on the rock, where she saved a youg man's life	"

085		The battle of the Giants (Pergamon Frieze, 180 b.C.)	see p.
086	1962	Vivian, Ariane and Hermine in front of the entrance to the College of William and Mary, Williamsburg, Va.	private Photo
087	Nov. 22. 1963	Eva, John Jay McCloy, president of Student Council, and President Dwight D. Eisenhower	"
088	1963	Jazz session in the Bronx	"
089	1964	Master's Degree from Columbia University Eva and her daughters	"
090	1964	The family on the campus of Columbia University in New York	"
091	Aug. 28, 1963	Martin Luther King in the March on Washington	newspap
092	1963	The Fight for Equal Rights	"
093	1963	Martin Luther King	"
094	1963	Vivian and 'Sinbad the Sailor'	private Photo
095	1963	Ariane and Sinbad	"
096	1963	Ariane and Vivian in Hampton, Va.	"
097	1963	Learning to ride a bike on Ward Dr.	"
098	1963	Vivian's 4th birthday	"
099	1966	Eva Maria Holland	"
100		Phoinix and Briseis, redfigured plate (480 b.C.)	see p.

101	July 26, 1966	Wedding of Prof. Dr. Howard K. Holland and Eva Maria Cox, Mandelstrasse, Munich, Germany	private picture
102	1966	Howard in the alps of Austria \	"
103	1966	Honeymoon in Athens, Greece	"
104	1966	Ariane and Vivian on the ship to Beirut, Lebanon	"
105	1966	Happy days in Beirut, Lebanon	"
106	1966	"	"
107	1966	Eva and Howard in Beirut	"
108	1967	In the streets of Aleppo, Syria	"
109 + 110+111	1966	In the streets of Beirut, Lebanon	"
112 + 113	1966	In the suq of Beirut	"
114	1966	A courtyard in Beirut, Lebanon	"
115	1966	"	"
116		Illustration in "1001 Nights. This is the way my students imagined their future	See p.
117	1967	Roman ruins in Baalbek, Syria	"
118	1967	Traditional beehive houses in Syria	"
119	1967	The inside of a beehive house	"
120	1967	Women in the traditional embroidered dresses in Syria	

121	1967	Eva in Damaskus, Syria	"
122	1967	The ancient fortified castle of Aleppo, Syria	"
123	1967	Taking a rest on top of a pile of canon balls, Aleppo, Syria	"
124	1967	Veiled girl soldiers in Aleppo, Syria	"
125 + 125 =126	1967	Scenes in a Palestinian refugee camp, Beirut	"
127		Athena and Nausicaa, redfigured amphora (470 b.C.)	see p.
128+129	1967	Trips through the countryside in Bavaria, Germany	private ph.
130	1967	The Fraueninsel in Lake Chiemsee, Ariane and Vivian	"
131	1968	Teaching German at the Goethe Institut in Bavaria	"
132	1968	Eva and the girls with the rickshaw through Hong Kong, China	"
133	1968	A happy reunion, Eva and Howard	"
134	1968	Eva, Vivian and Tuilan the cat in Manila, Philippines	"
135	1968	Siesta in the patio, Manila, Phil.	"
136	1968	Vivian and our cook, Manila, Phil.	"
137	1968	Eva is planning the meals for the week week with Leite	"

138	1968	Eva with the cat Tuilan	"
139+140	1968	Manila, Philippines	"
141 + 142 + 143 + 144	1969	In the countryside of Manila, Phil.	"
145+146	1969	Doing the Hula Hula at Christmas in Manila	"
147+148	1969	The family at the Pagsanjan Waterfalls, Philip.	"
149	1970	The American Women's Club in Manila	newspaper
150	1970	The folksong festival in Manila, Phil.	newspaper
151	1970	The shadows of war in Saigon, Vietnam	private photo
152 + 153 + 154	1970	Vietnam contryside	"
155	1970	Howard in his office	"
156	1970	On the streets of Saigon	"
157	1970	Eva in an 'Ao Dais', the national dress	"
158	1970	On the Mekong River	"
159	1970	Our Christmas card	"
160	1970	The Royal Palace of Hue, Vietnam Eva and the wife of the University President "	"
161	1970	Singapur	"
162	1970	Eva and the snake, Singapur	"
163	1970	Angkor Wat, Cambodia	"
164	1970	Angkor Wat, Cambodia	"
165+166	1970	Angkor Wat, Cambodia	"

167	1970	Eva, Vivian, Ariane and Tuilan in the bird cage Departure from Manila	"
168	1970	Above the highlands of Ethiopia	"
169	1970	Landing in Addis Abeba, Ethiopia	"
170	1970	Tukuls in the highlands of Ethiopia	"
171	1970	The road to the market between eucalyptus trees	"
172	1970	The road to the market, Ethiopia	"
173	1970	Woman carrying water, Ethiopia	"
174	1970	Ethiopian woman in her 'shamma'	"
175	1970	In the countryside, Ethiopia	"
176	1970	Our house in Addis Abeba, frm l.to r. Gibrahanna, the cook; Assada, the maid; Howard; Eva with the dog; Ariane with the cat; Vivian; Girma, the horse groom; second horse groom and our four horses	"
177 + 178 + 179 180 + 181 + 182	1970	Our life amidst of our animals	"
183	1971	Trips on horseback, Howard and the girls	"

184	1971	Eva on 'Sheik'	"
185	1971	Eva and the girls	"
186	1971	Pick nick in the countryside	"
187	1971	The entrance gate to Haile Selassi University	"
188	1971	King Haile Selassi visiting his University	"
189+190	1971	Ethiopian Orthodox priests	"
191	1971	Vivian is admiring the nests of the weaver birds	"
192+ 193	1971	Ethiopian children	"
194	1971	At the market in Addis Abeba	"
195+196	1971	Elegant Ethiopian ladies	"
197	1971	Bargaining for crosses	"
198	1971	The monolithic rock-cut churches in Lalibela, Ethiopia	"
199	1971	Lilo and Eva in Lalibela	"
200	1971	Eva, Howard and a little lion in Gondar, Ethiopia	"
201	1971	The sources of the Blue Nile in Ethiopia	"
202	1971	Awash National Parc, Ethiopia	"
203	1971	Awash river	"
204	1971	The pride of the nomads, near Gondar	"
205	1971	Road bloc	"
206	1971	Nomads on the road south	"
207+208	1971	Eva and Vivian building trust with the natives	"

209	1971	Abandoned nomad tukul, Lilo and Eva		"
210	1971	Camel herd south of Awash		"
211	1971	Nomad girls at market of Harrar, Ethiopia		"
212	1971	The city gate of Harrar; from l.to.r. Lilo, Eva, Ariane, Vivian		"
213+214	1971	In the streets of Harrar, Ethiopia		"
215 + 216 + 217	1971	'The Roses of Harrar'		"
218+219	1971	The family on an excavation trip with a camera team from the University of Arizona		"
220	1971	Pick nick with our friends		"
221	1971	My students at the Haile Selassi University Lilo and Eva (far right)		"
222	1971	Nomads at Lake Tana in the South of Ethiopia		"
223		'Athena mourning', (Acropolis 460 b.C.)	see p.	
224	1971	Athena in Arms, panathenaic amphora (5th century b.C.)	see p.	
225	1971	'Wiener Platz', Munich, Germany	private photo	
226+227 1971		Bridges over the Isar River; Munich Germany		"
228	1972	Logo of the University of the Federal Armed Forces		"

229	1972	Conference of the Foreign Language Experts	"
230	1973	Eva and the German-American Club at the Unniversity visiting the NATO school in Oberammergau	"
231	1974	Ariane and Vivian in Quo Vadis, Italy	"
232		'Satire and Nymphe', redfigured amphora (4th cent.b.C.)	see p.
233	1975	With Franz Huschka in Venice, Italy	private photo
234	1975	Wedding with Franz Huschka in Ischia, Italy	"
235+236	1975	Wedding with Franz Huschka My father and Franz' parents	"
237	1975	Wedding in the 'Casa Carina', l.to r. Peter Huschka, Eva, Franz, Ariane Vivian, Doris Kindermann	"
238	1976	'L'apres midi d'un faune'	"
239 + 240 + 241 + 242	1976	The 'Casa Carina' in Ischia, Italy	"
243	1976	'Nymphs in the bath' in 'Quo Vadis'	"
244	1977	Tiffany glass ceiling in the restaurant 'La Piazzetta'	"
245		Runners, red figured amphora (4th cent.b.C.)	see p.

246	1977	The two sisters	private photo
247	July 1984	Wedding of Ariane and John in 'La Piazzetta' Munich, Germany	"
248	1984	Military parade at the University of the German Federal Armed Forces in Munich, Germany	"
249	1989	Sanibel Island, Florida	"
250	1989	Eva and Ariane in Sanibel Island	"
251	1990	Polyphem	"
252	1990	Below the Maximiliansbridge on the river Isar	"
253	1991	Together with Prof. G. Neugebauer (the 'man in the shadow') in El Gouna in Egypt	"
254	1990	Ariane and Grandmother Lulu	"
255	1991	With little Antonia in Sidney, Australia	"
256	1993	Anton and little Sophia	"
257	2001	Eva and the grandchildren	"
258	1993	Antonia and Amelia	"
259	1993	Happy days in Quo Vadis, Italy fr.l.to.r. Anton, Antonia, OmiNonna (Eva), Amelia and Sophia in the middle	"

260	1992	Three angels in paradise: Ami, Toni, Anton in aunt Eliesabeth's magic garden	"
261	1993	Four actors on stage on the roofterrace of Quo Vadis fr.l.to.r.: Sophia, Anton, Antonia, Amelia	"
262	1997	Four generations: from l.to.r.: Ariane, John, Eva, Vivian Sophia, Amelia, grandmother Schrankl, Antonia, Anton	"
263	1993	The endless countryside of Russia, painting by Isac Levitan	see page
264	1993	On the street to Moscow	private photograp
265	1993	The buildings of Chernogolovka, Russia	"
266	1993	My Russian friends	"
267	1994	Teaching English at the Russian Academy of Science	"
268	1994	Behind the Kremel walls with Alexeji	"
269	1994	The Red Square in Moscow	"
270	1994	Eva in Suzdal, Russia	"
271	1994	The German class in a Russian school	"
272	1994	Pick nick in the woods with my students	"
273	1994	Teachers of my 'Language Center' with paramilitary protection	"

274	1996	The Russian delegtion at the Munich Oktoberfest Director of the Institute of Chemical Physics, Russian Academy of Science, Prof Aldoshin, Dr. Alexej Ovchinikov In center: Eva M. Huschka, director of the Language Center of the University of the German Federal Armed Forces, Munich	"
275	2003	Pro American demonstration on the Maximilianstreet in Munich led by Eva M. Huschka	"
276	2004	Eva in the 'Dirndl', the Bavarian traditional dress	"
277	2006	View of Houston, Texas	"
278	2007	'Back to nature', The grandchildren in the tree.	"
279		'The Sirens', red-figured amphora (5th century b.C.) f found in an ancient necropolis near Massa Lubrense, in 1956	see p.
280	1994	Marina della Lobra, the harbour of Massa Lubrense	private
281	2004	Sunset over the 'Sirenuse Islands' and Capri	
282		Casa del Amore punito, Pompeji	see p.

283	2008	The source of the Isar River in the mountains of the Karwendel	private photo
284	2008	The river Isar	"
285	2008	The river Isar enters the Danube near Deggendorf	"
286		Siren (terra cotta figure, southern Italy,(5th cent. B.C.)	see p

www.ingramcontent.com/pod-product-compliance
Lightning Source LLC
Chambersburg PA
CBHW030143100526
44592CB00009B/98